Lorna Belcourt

The Home Canning and Preserving Book

BOOKS BY ANN SERANNE

The Art of Egg Cookery

Your Home Freezer

The Complete Book of Freezer Cookery

The Complete Book of Home Baking

Delectable Desserts

The Complete Book of Desserts

The Epicure's Companion (WITH JOHN TEBBEL)

Happy Living (WITH EVELYN ENRIGHT)

The Complete Book of Home Preserving

With Eileen Gaden:

The Blender Cookbook

The Best of Near Eastern Cookery

The Church and Club Woman's Companion

The Sandwich Book

The Home Canning and Preserving Book

By ANN SERANNE

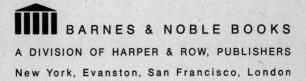

BARNES & NOBLE BOOKS
A DIVISION OF HARPER & ROW, PUBLISHERS
New York, Evanston, San Francisco, London

First BARNES & NOBLE BOOKS edition published 1975.

STANDARD BOOK NUMBER: 06–463424–8

81 10 9 8 7 6 5 4

Little does the American housewife realize or recognize the profound debt she owes to those unheralded pioneers in the research and development of food chemistry. It is to those tireless workers in food research today, both in private industry and in government agencies, that this book is dedicated.

Contents

JELLY MAKING WITH JUICES CONTAINING

FRUIT	PREPARATION	CUPS OF WATER NEEDED FOR EACH 4 CUPS FRUIT
Apples, tart	Remove blossom and stem ends and slice	2
Blackberries	Wash, stem, and crush	none
Crab apples	Same as apples	2
Cranberries	Wash and stem	2½
Currants, red	Wash, stem, and crush	¼
Gooseberries	Wash and stem	to cover
Grapes (underripe)	Wash, stem, and crush	¼ to 1
Guavas, sour	Same as apples	4
Loganberries	Wash, stem, and crush	¼
May haws	Wash and stem	2
Oranges, sour	Wash, peel, seed, and chop	4
Plums, tart	Wash and stem	1
Quinces	Wash. core, and slice	3
Raspberries	Wash, hull, and crush	¼
Scuppernongs	Wash, stem, and crush	¼ to 1

THE RIGHT AMOUNT OF ACID AND PECTIN

COOKING TIME	CUPS OF SUGAR NEEDED FOR EACH 4 CUPS JUICE
Boil slowly until soft	3
Cook slowly for 10 minutes	3
Boil slowly until soft	3½
Boil slowly 5 to 10 minutes	3
Boil slowly until soft	3 to 4
Boil slowly until soft	3 to 4
Boil slowly 15 minutes	3 to 3½
Boil slowly 30 minutes	4
Boil slowly until soft	3
Boil slowly until soft	3 to 4
Boil slowly until pulp falls apart	4
Boil slowly until soft	3
Boil slowly 45 minutes	3
Boil slowly 10 minutes	3 to 4
Boil slowly until soft	3

Introduction

Our earliest ancestors, who felled the saber-toothed tiger, the great mammoth, the cave bear, and the woolly-haired rhinoceros with clubs of rough stone, speared fish with bone harpoons, clothed themselves in the skins of wild animals, and lived in caves and shelters of rock, knew nothing of preserving food. Not having yet discovered fire, they lived on raw flesh and marrow and such roots, berries, and fruit as came their way. Like the animals in Walt Disney's *Vanishing Prairie*, primitive man killed to survive. He sated his appetite on the still warm flesh of his kill, and made as many meals as he could from the slain animal before the flesh became putrid. As winter approached he stored his kill deep within his cave in the coldest spot or hung it in a sheltered place outdoors to freeze. He learned from the animals to store a supply of seeds, nuts, and grain in dark holes among the rocks of his dwelling. But many times he went without food and his offspring died of hunger. Only the hardiest survived, for man did not know how to preserve his food for times of want.

Once early man discovered fire, some two hundred and fifty thousand years ago, life became a little easier. He learned to warm his cave and heat his food. By chance, perhaps, he dragged home a slain bear and hung the carcass at the entrance of his cave over the fire that smoked and smoldered on the damp floor of rocks. The smoke permeated the flesh, gave it a new and interesting flavor, and improved its staying power. And so man in his stumbling infancy discovered the preservative qualities of smoke.

It was not long, in the prehistoric span of the ages, before salting provided another method of keeping raw meat for weeks or months instead of days. Probably the aborigines observed the deer and the buffalo gathered at a salt spring and lapping the surface of the dry soil. They, too, tasted the salt deposits and found salt to their liking. They added it to their food and discovered that when the salt was sprinkled liberally on meat or fish the flesh remained in an edible condition for a considerable time.

With smoked and salted meats to guarantee a food supply, primitive men could now band together, and entire tribes could follow the herds of wild animals to assure a constant supply of fresh meat. But one day man tired of his nomadic life. He and his family and friends settled in a favorable spot beside a lake or stream. They domesticated the wild animals, built homes, and learned to plant seeds and cultivate crops.

Ancient lake dwellers were advanced agriculturists. This we know from deposits of calcined grains found in the mud beneath the lakes, where they have been preserved for thousands of years. Here were found the distinguishable remains of wheat, barley, millet, and peas, fruit, berries, and nuts. We know little of how they planted their seed, cultivated the soil, and harvested their crops. Probably they used pointed sticks to till the soil and crushed their corn with the same type of stone mills found among the remains of the men of the Neolithic, or Stone, Age.

We do know, however, that the rough instruments were of the crudest kind; that it was hard work to till and harvest the soil. But at last man was assured of a daily supply of food. He now had quite a surprising variety of food within his limited means—fresh meat from his domesticated flocks, meat, fruit, and root vegetables stored in cool caves and cellars, dried grain and nuts, sun-dried fruit, and smoked and salted meat and fish. Still there was much waste as well as a great deal of flavor change in the preserved foods. Man was well aware of the putrefactive changes in perishable foods, but he was not cognizant of the microscopic plants and bacteria that caused the mold and spoilage. Although he learned to make cheese and wine some two thousand years before the birth of Christ, and maintained a yeast culture to raise his daily bread, the phenomena of fermentation remained a mystery for many years.

Though not understood, fermentation was responsible for the preservation of foods in vinegar. Though the pleasing acidity of limes, lemons, and wood berries was familiar not only to the cave man and the tree dweller but to citizens of the ancient world, it was not until the alcohol in neglected wine changed to acetic acid that vinegar was discovered. The very name is derived from *vin aigre*, or sour wine, and, like salt, vinegar proved to be a most successful preservative. In Egypt and Greece flowers, herbs, roots, and vegetables were preserved in vinegar. Figs, apples, plums, cherries, and pears were selected with great care and preserved in a mixture of vinegar and honey. Meat and fish were preserved in salt and vinegar. Apicius taught the ancients to cover pieces of pork with a paste of salt, vinegar, and honey. Pickled foods were agreeable additions to daily meals and helped to satisfy the increasing craving in civilized nations for a more varied diet.

Honey, though an expensive commodity, proved to be an effective preservative, used alone or in combination with vinegar. The Romans selected the finest fruit with the utmost care, and leaving it attached to the stem, suspended it in honey. It was not, however, until the culture of sugar cane began in the West Indies in 1550 that sugar was considered as a substitute for honey in conserving fruit.

In the Middle Ages sugar was eaten and used in various ways in cooking, but it was quite a luxury. Even in the seventeenth century sugar was used sparingly. It was not until the nineteenth century that it became a staple ingredient in every household, and our great-great-grandmothers were able to occupy a considerable part of their warm-weather days gathering fruit and berries and making them into jams, jellies, and preserves for the winter months.

The nineteenth century proved to be historic in the development of modern methods of preservation. The pioneer work in the field of food canning by Nicolas Appert was the basis for the canning industry of today. Pasteur's studies in bacteriology led to a fuller understanding of this new technique and, eventually, to the perfection of the canning not only of fruits and vegetables but of protein foods as well.

Of equal importance was the nineteenth-century development of artificial refrigeration—the precursor of quick freezing. Although natural ice had been used to preserve food for some time, the method of making artificial ice was invented by the Frenchman Ferdinand Carré, in the decade between 1850 and 1860. In 1860 he patented his ice-making machine, putting to practical application the experiments made by Lavoisier and Faraday on the liquefaction of gases. And once again scientific research contributed to the comfort and luxury of our modern life.

In this book I have presented the latest scientific methods of food preservation, beginning with canning and working back through the ages to the oldest method of preservation—older than man himself—drying, the method that nature uses to preserve seeds from one season to another. The last chapter is a digest of my book, *Your Home Freezer* (Doubleday & Company, 1953).

CHAPTER ONE

Home Canning

Until the beginning of the nineteenth century foods were preserved only by the ancient methods of smoking, drying, pickling, or preserving in sugar. The Napoleonic wars were directly responsible for the development of a method of subjecting food to high temperatures and sealing it tightly in hot clean jars.

When Napoleon's soldiers were dying in vast quantities from scurvy, owing to the lack of fresh fruits and vegetables in their diet, Napoleon persuaded the French government to offer twelve thousand francs to anyone who discovered a practical way to preserve food. A Frenchman by the name of Nicolas Appert had been experimenting with pickling, brewing, and distillation for fifty years, and the government offer intrigued him. He worked methodically and prodigiously for almost fourteen years before he submitted his discoveries, and in 1809 he was awarded the prize for originating the vital process that today is known as the life line of America. No other single discovery has contributed so much to the general well-being of mankind.

15

But much had to be learned before canning was perfected. Appert had found that eliminating air from cooked foods prevented spoilage, but he never knew the reason why. He never knew that the bacteria in the air, rather than the air itself, were the destroying elements. With primitive equipment, his method worked, though his premise has been proved wrong. His principle was put to commercial use in 1830, and on his principle is based one of the largest industries in the world today. Little wonder that Monsieur Appert is regarded as the father of canning.

But it is Louis Pasteur whom we honor for his discovery of the fundamental causes of putrefaction. Pasteur determined what we all take more or less for granted today: that the exclusion of air from foods is important to food preservation because air is the carrier of living organisms—the molds, yeasts, and bacteria—which cause fermentation.

Once the results of Pasteur's experiments were announced, the growth of the canning industry in America was rapid. Canneries mushroomed all over the country and competition was keen. Ignorance caused failure and tragedy, but little by little modern scientists educated the canner in an understanding of bacteriology and impressed on him the necessity of scrupulous cleanliness.

In the early days of canning the open-kettle method was used. The 212° F. temperature—the highest temperature possible by this method—was effective in the preservation of tomatoes, red and green peppers, and other acid fruits. The fruit acid, in addition to the boiling temperature, was sufficient to inhibit the growth of harmful organisms. But the canning of meat and most vegetables was still a treacherous business at best in either home or factory. The addition of chemicals such as salt or calcium chloride raised the temperature of the boiling juices to as high as 240° F. and eliminated some of the inevitable spoilage at the expense of flavor and texture.

It was not until the advent of the pressure canner that alkaline vegetables and meat were canned to the satisfaction and prosperity of the canner, and to the non-hazardous advantage of the consumer. Today in home canning, as well as in commercial factories, the open-kettle method of canning has been supplanted by the pressure-cooker method for all vegetables, poultry, fish, and meat.

In less than a hundred and fifty years the preservation of food by heat has been developed from a risky venture to an industry that extends the seasons from one spring to another and augments our bountiful supplies of indigenous foods with delicacies from almost every country in the world.

The housewife has applied modern scientific principles to home canning with the result that thousands of jars and cans of food are successfully preserved each year in homes throughout America with an awareness, but little knowledge, of the micro-organisms that cause spoilage. Perhaps some understanding of the minute forms of life that are present in the water we drink and in the air we breathe will make the home canning of food more interesting.

WHY FOODS SPOIL

Molds Most people are familiar with the molds that grow in dark, damp places where there is little breeze to dry the minute threads that spread with startling rapidity. Though generally harmless, they can sometimes render food unfit for consumption.

Molds can grow in the light as well as the dark if they have sufficient moisture and, since they have the ability to flourish in an acid medium, they readily attack acid fruit and tomatoes. Molds confine their growth to the surface of a food, but as they grow they give off a peculiar odor, which frequently penetrates and flavors the food, making it decidedly unattractive to the palate.

In the beginning, mold plants are white, soft, and fluffy. As they multiply and develop they become blue, green, brown, or yellow. Small branches extend upward, bearing colored spores, while the tiny roots of the plants are firmly imbedded in the food upon which they are growing. The spores drop and are carried by air currents to other foods, where a new plant begins to grow if the spores find the right conditions for their development.

There are countless mold spores in the air waiting for a fertile resting place, and no food can remain exposed without the spores falling on it. Molds, however, are easily killed at a temperature as low as 180° F., so that if fruit, vegetables, or meat are properly processed and carefully sealed for protection, molds cannot develop as long as the container remains airtight.

Yeast Like molds, yeast plants are fairly simple to control in canning. But while molds have only recently been utilized for the welfare of mankind in the manufacture of various miracle drugs such as penicillin, yeast has always been our friend. Without yeast there would be no wine, no fine cheese, no leavened bread.

Yeast is a minute fungus that grows by sending off buds or spores to form new plants. These spores are abundant in the air and multiply rapidly when given food, moisture, and warmth. The properties of yeast that make it so vital to some foods can also start fermentation and inevitable souring in canned fruits and vegetables if the

17

yeast plants are not destroyed. This presents no serious problem, for yeast spores and plants are killed at temperatures from 160° to 190° F.

Bacteria   Molds and yeasts are generally grouped under the term "fungi." Bacteria, the unicellular micro-organisms that are the greatest enemies of canning, are classed as schizomycetes. They are present everywhere and reproduce with fantastic speed. One bacterium can produce millions of bacteria in the space of a few hours.

Bacteria are not destroyed as easily as molds and yeasts, for they are much more resistant to high temperatures. In the growing stage bacteria can be killed by subjecting them to boiling temperature for various lengths of time. But certain bacteria produce spores that are highly heat-resistant. These spores have the ability to remain dormant for a long time, resisting destruction when they find themselves in unfavorable circumstances, and resuming rapid reproduction when conditions become more favorable. As a result some bacteria can withstand boiling temperatures for as long as sixteen hours.

There are many different kinds of bacteria: some are meritorious, such as the bacteria that form the viscous, colorless mass called "mother of vinegar" that turns fruit juices into vinegar; some cause only mild digestive disturbances; and others are deadly.

Bacteria include parasites (organisms that feed on live plants and animals) and saprophytes (organisms that live on dead plants and animals). The deadly *Bacillus botulinus,* familiar to most of us through knowledge, fortunately, rather than experience, belongs to the saprophyte group. This treacherous villain of the canning world finds itself at home in non-acid vegetables and in fish and meat. It has been the cause of much alarm and frequent death.

Few bacteria grow in the presence of a large quantity of sugar (such as is used in the making of jams and jellies) or in acid fruits or tomatoes. If the food being canned is sufficiently acid, even *botulinus* bacteria are easily destroyed at boiling temperature. Also, *Bacillus botulinus* will not develop in a salt solution, if the brine contains about 10 per cent salt, or about 1½ cups to 1 gallon of water.

But many bacteria spores, and especially *botulinus,* will thrive in non-acid foods such as meat, fish, and starchy vegetables—corn, beans, and peas—even though processed at boiling temperature. Today we know that no housewife should attempt to can any protein food or non-acid vegetable without a pressure cooker.

Equipment for Home Canning

Most of the equipment needed for home canning is in the average American kitchen. You will need, of course, large spoons and ladles, sharp knives and peelers, jar and bottle funnels, a colander or a large wire strainer, cup, pint, and quart measures, and you should have an inexpensive kitchen scale. The weight of most food products can be estimated in cups and pints, but a scale insures greater accuracy. In addition, you will need a pressure cooker for canning meats and non-acid vegetables, a large preserving kettle, deep enough to have an inch or two of water over the tops of the jars, and a rack to keep the jars from touching the bottom. And you will need either glass jars or regulation tin cans.

GLASS JARS

The standard Mason jar is the glass jar most familiar to all of us. There are, however, several other types, and more are being designed every year. Chances are that you already have a supply of jars that need only a thorough washing and new rubber rings to be ready for the newly canned foods, but even the standard Mason jar has several different types of closures, and unless you are aware of this, you may get an inefficient seal that would result in spoilage. The following pictures represent four of the leading types of jars and closures available today.

Before starting to can with glass jars Check your jars and lids. Be sure that the lids fit the jars perfectly, for screw bands and metal lids are not interchangeable. Wash the jars in hot, soapy water and rinse them thoroughly. Discard any jars that have cracks or chips, for defects in the jars can prevent an airtight seal. Also wash the lids, except those with self-sealing compound. For these special lids, follow the manufacturer's instructions; some need boiling and others need only a dip in hot water.

Check your supply of new rubber rings. Don't try to wash and use old ones, for the elasticity of the rings will have been exhausted. Scrub new rubber rings with a brush in hot, soapy water and rinse. Dissolve 1 tablespoon baking soda in 1 quart cold water. Put the rings in this solution, bring the liquid to a boil, and boil for 10 minutes. Again rinse the rings well.

19

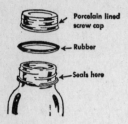

JAR NO. 1. Standard Mason jar with porcelain-lined zinc cap and shoulder rubber ring. Wet the rubber ring and fit it down onto the shoulder of the jar. Don't stretch the ring more than necessary. Fill the jar and wipe the rubber ring and the jar rim clean. Screw the cap down firmly and then turn it back ¼ inch. Process and, as soon as you take the jar from the canner, screw the cap down as tightly as possible to complete the seal.

JAR NO. 2. Standard Mason jar with top-seal rubber ring, glass lid, and metal screw band. Fill the jar and wipe the rim clean. Wet the rubber ring and fit it on the glass lid. Put the lid on the jar, rubber side down. Screw on the band until it is tight but not overly tight or the jar may break. Then turn back almost ¼ inch, but be sure the jar and the band are meshed. Process and, as soon as you take the jar from the canner, screw down the band firmly to complete the seal.

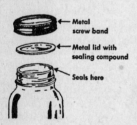

JAR NO. 3. Standard Mason jar with flat metal lid with sealing compound, and metal screw band. Fill the jar and wipe the rim clean. Put on the lid with the sealing compound next to the glass. Screw the metal band down tightly. This is a self-sealing type of closure: even when the band is screwed firmly in place, the lid has enough give to let the air escape during processing. After processing, take the jar from the canner, but don't tighten the lid again or you may break the seal.

JAR NO. 4. Wire-bail-type jar with rubber ring and glass lid. Wet the rubber ring and fit it down on the ledge on top of the empty jar. Fill the jar and wipe the ring and jar rim clean. Put on the glass lid and push the long wire over the top of the lid so that it fits into the groove. Leave the short wire up. Process, and as soon as you take the jar from the canner, push the short wire down to complete the seal.

To sterilize jars All jars should be sterilized by boiling them or by heating them in the oven before they are filled with food.

Cover clean jars in a large container with hot water, bring the water to a boil, and boil for 10 to 15 minutes. Let the jars stand in the hot water until ready to fill them. Or stand washed and dried jars upright on a cooky sheet in a cool oven. Set the oven to 250° F. and heat the jars for 30 minutes after the oven reaches the set temperature. Turn off the heat, open the oven door, and let the jars stand in the warm oven until ready to be used.

TIN CANS

The use of tin cans in home canning is coming back into vogue. Certainly tin cans stack better than glass jars, and many people accustomed to using tin cans swear that foods keep longer and better in can than in glass. This is probably true, for cans keep out light as well as air.

Tin cans in lots of 100, as well as an inexpensive hand sealer, are available at better hardware stores throughout the country or may be ordered from large mail-order houses.

The types of tin cans used in home canning are:

Plain tin—for apples, apricots, asparagus, green beans, white cherries, okra, peaches, pears, peas, spinach, and tomatoes; meat, fish, and poultry.

C-enamel—for lima beans, corn, and carrots.

R-enamel—for beets, berries, red cherries, fruit juices, plums, pumpkin, rhubarb, sauerkraut, squash, strawberries, and sweet potatoes.

The best sizes for home canning are:

No. 2 can—which holds 20 ounces, or about 2½ cups.

No. 2½ can—which holds 28 ounces, or about 3½ cups.

Before starting to can with tin Sort cans, lids, and gaskets. Use only cans that are in good condition. Discard any cans or lids that are rusted, dented, or badly bent, as well as scratched or torn gaskets.

Wash the cans in hot, clear water and drain them upside down. Don't wash the lids, for washing may damage the gasket. If the lids are dusty, wipe them with a damp cloth.

Check your sealing machine to make sure that it is in perfect working condition. It is best to test it by putting a little water into a can and sealing the can. Then submerge the can in boiling water for a few seconds. If air bubbles rise from the can, you will know that the seam is not tight and that the sealer must be adjusted according to the manufacturer's directions.

Processing

The term "processing" means the heating of filled and sealed jars or cans of food for a specific length of time at the specific temperature necessary to destroy all bacteria in the food.

As previously explained, tomatoes and most fruits do not need pressure processing, nor do pickled vegetables or sauerkraut. As a matter of fact, fruits and juicy vegetables that contain acid retain better color, flavor, and texture if they are processed or sterilized at or near 212° F., or the boiling point of water at sea level. However, the boiling point of water falls 1° F. for each 500 feet of elevation, so it is necessary to process even fruits and tomatoes at a pressure of around 5 pounds at altitudes of 1500 feet or more.

WATER-BATH PROCESSING

In the canning of fruits, tomatoes, and pickled vegetables at low altitudes, the water-bath canner comes into full swing. Any large, deep kettle with a tight-fitting cover may be used. A rack or false bottom on which to stand the jars should be placed in the bottom to raise the jars above the bottom of the kettle and to permit the circulation of boiling water. The kettle must be deep enough to allow for an inch or two of water over the tops of the jars plus a little extra space for boiling. Clothes boilers have often been converted into water-bath canners. A pressure canner may also be used, but the cover should be left open to allow for the escape of steam and to avoid building up pressure.

Fill the kettle with water deep enough to cover the jars or cans completely, and heat the water almost to boiling. With a jar lifter, carefully lower the hot, filled, and sealed jars or cans into the hot water, placing them so that they do not touch each other. If cold, raw fruits are packed in glass the water should be hot but not boiling. Add more boiling water if necessary to bring the water at least an inch over the tops of the jars or cans. Cover the kettle and bring the water to a rolling boil. Turn down the heat and boil gently but steadily for the amount of processing time given in specific directions for each product being canned. As the water evaporates in the kettle, add more to keep the jars covered at all times.

At the end of the processing time, remove the jars or cans with a jar lifter. Complete the seal on the jars, unless self-sealing jars were used, and cool. Cool cans in cold water, changing the water often to cool them rapidly.

PRESSURE CANNING

Non-acid vegetables, meats, poultry, and fish all require processing in a pressure cooker. The small everyday pressure cookers are not satisfactory for processing jars or cans of food. If you cannot afford a large pressure canner, initiate a co-operative plan to share the cost of one with some of your friends. Follow the directions that accompany the cooker, for various makes differ slightly in details. But in general:

Put enough boiling water into the cooker to reach the rack. Place the filled and partially sealed jars or the sealed cans on the rack so that steam can flow all around each. Tin cans may be staggered without a rack between the layers. Secure the lid of the cooker and place it over the heat with the petcock or the weighted gauge open. **Do not close the petcock or gauge until a jet of live steam has been coming from the vent for 10 minutes.** This insures that all the air has been driven from the canner. Then close the petcock or put on the weighted gauge and let the pressure rise to 10 pounds (240° F.). The moment that 10 pounds pressure is reached, start counting the processing time, regulating the heat to keep the pressure exactly at that point. Fluctuation of pressure causes the liquid to boil out of the jars. Process for the amount of time given in the directions for the specific product you are canning.

If glass jars are used At the end of the processing period, remove the canner from the heat and let it stand until the pressure drops slowly to zero and remains at zero for several minutes. Never try to rush the cooling, for a sudden drop of pressure will cause a great deal of breakage and a loss of liquid from the jars. Allow 20 minutes' resting period. Then slowly open the petcock or take off the weighted gauge. Unfasten the cover and tilt the far side up so that the steam escapes away from you. Take the jars from the canner and complete the seals at once, if the jars are not the self-sealing type. If liquid boiled out in the processing, seal the jars just as they are. Do not open the jars and add more liquid. Place the hot jars top side up on a folded cloth out of a draft to cool. Give each jar enough room for the air to get around all sides.

If cans are used Release the pressure in the canner as soon as the processing time is finished by opening the petcock or removing the weighted gauge to let the steam escape. Then carefully remove the canner cover. Cool tin cans in cold water. Remove the cans from the water while they are still slightly warm so that they will dry quickly in the air. Stagger the cans so that the air can circulate around them.

CARE OF CANNED FOODS

When jars are cool test the seal by turning the jar partly over. If you find a leaky jar, use the food right away or turn the contents into another jar and process it again. Wipe jars with a damp cloth, then dry. Label jars or cans carefully with the date and contents.

Store canned foods in a cool, dark, dry place. If the storage spot is too warm, canned foods lose quality rapidly. If the place is damp, tin cans and the metal lids of glass jars will corrode, causing eventual leakage.

SPOILAGE

If immaculate cleanliness is observed and directions followed scrupulously, there is no reason why food should spoil. Occasional carelessness may result, however, in spoilage, and spoiled food should not be used. Examine each jar or can carefully before opening it. Bubbling or foaming in a jar, leakage around the lid, unpleasant or unnatural appearance or aroma, bulging can ends or jar lids are all warnings. Discard the contents immediately. Do not taste to see if the food is spoiled.

To be entirely safe, boil home-canned vegetables for at least 10 minutes before using them. Cook spinach and corn, meat, poultry, and fish for 20 minutes before using them.

Canning Fruits, Tomatoes, and Pickled Vegetables

GENERAL METHOD

1. Select the best quality fruit for canning. Choose fresh, firm fruit and can as quickly as possible. If you must hold it, store in a cool, well-ventilated spot.

2. Sort the fruit for size and ripeness. Fruit of approximately the same size and maturity will cook more evenly than a mixed batch.

3. Wash the fruit thoroughly, for dirt contains some of the bacteria that are the hardest to destroy. Wash small batches of fruit at a time under cold running water. Don't let the fruit soak in the water, and handle it gently to avoid bruising.

4. Prepare the fruit. Peel, pit or core, and cut as desired. Scalding is an effective way to remove the skins from peaches and tomatoes.

5. Pack. There are two methods of packing fruit, tomatoes, and pickled vegetables—the **hot pack** and the **cold pack.** Most fruit is improved by precooking in a light syrup and packing hot in sterilized jars or tins, though some fruit may be packed cold and then sterilized.

6. Process in boiling-water bath (**see Index**).

7. Cool jars or tins, label, and store in a cool, dry place.

Hot pack   In this method the fruit is heated before it is put into containers. It may be heated in a syrup of sugar and water, in water alone, or in extracted juice. Juicy fruits and tomatoes may be packed hot in the juice that cooks out when they are heated, without the addition of any water whatsoever.

The fruit should be near the boiling point when it is put into either glass jars or tin cans. It should be packed fairly loosely and covered with syrup or juice.

Cold pack   The cold, raw fruit is put into containers and covered with hot syrup, water, or extracted juice. With this method a more attractive pack results, for the fruit may be arranged in uniform layers in the jars. Raw foods may be packed tighter than hot foods, since they shrink during the processing. Tomatoes are pressed down tightly into the containers so that they are covered by their own juice, and no liquid need be added.

If packing in glass   After filling glass jars, work the blade of a knife down the sides of the jar to remove air bubbles, and add more liquid if needed to cover the fruit. Leave a little head space at the top of the jar according to instructions for specific products. Wipe the ring and jar rim clean and screw on the cap. Adjust the cap according to the type of jar you are using (**see Index**).

If packing in tin   The temperature of the fruit must be at least 170° F. when the cans are sealed. To insure this temperature and to drive out any air that has been trapped between the pieces of fruit it is necessary to heat the filled, open cans. This step in canning is known as **exhausting the cans.** In addition to driving out the trapped air, the process helps to prevent loss of flavor and discoloration, and prevents the cans from bulging at the ends or rupturing at the seams.

To exhaust tin cans   Place the open, filled cans in a large kettle containing boiling water to about 2 inches below the tops of the cans. Cover the kettle, bring the water to a boil, and boil steadily for 10 minutes.

This step in canning with tin may be avoided IF the temperature of the food is not allowed to drop below 170° F., but unless you take the precaution of testing the contents of each can with a thermometer, it is best to exhaust the cans.

After exhausting, remove the cans from the water one at a time. Add more boiling liquid if it is needed to cover the contents of the can, place a clean lid on the can, and seal at once.

If you don't exhaust the cans, work out air bubbles with the blade of a knife, add more boiling liquid if needed to cover the contents completely, and seal at once.

THE USE OF SUGAR IN CANNING FRUIT

Sugar helps canned fruit hold its color, flavor, and shape, but it is not essential to prevent spoilage. Fruit will keep without sugar, providing it is processed carefully.

To can without sugar   Pack prepared raw fruit in hot, sterilized jars and fill the jars to within ½ inch of the top with boiling fruit juice or water. Or preheat the fruit for about 3 minutes in a little water or its own juice and pack hot. Process in exactly the same way as for sweetened fruit.

To can with sugar syrup   Combine sugar with either water or extracted fruit juice, bring to a boil, and boil for 5 minutes. Remove the scum.

	SUGAR	WATER OR FRUIT JUICE
Thin Syrup	1 cup	3 cups
Medium Syrup	1 cup	2 cups
Heavy Syrup	1 cup	1 cup

Approximately ¾ to 1 cup syrup is needed for each quart jar or No. 2½ can of canned fruit.

Light corn syrup may be substituted by measure for half the sugar called for in making syrups. Or mild-flavored honey may replace from one third to half the sugar. When using honey, add it to the hot syrup just before pouring the syrup over the fruit in the jars. Boiling causes a flavor change in honey.

To extract fruit juice   Crush very ripe, juicy fruit, bring it to a boil over a gentle flame, and strain the juice through a jelly bag.

To can with sugar   If fruit or berries are very juicy and you are using the hot-pack method, dry sugar may be added to the fruit. Measure the fruit into a preserving kettle and add from ½ to 1 cup sugar for each quart of the raw fruit. Let the fruit and sugar stand for 2 or 3 hours to start the juice flowing or heat very slowly, shaking the kettle to prevent the fruit and sugar from burning, until enough juice is drawn out of the fruit to form a syrup. Bring the fruit to a boil, boil for 5 minutes, and pack fruit and juice in hot sterilized jars to within ½ inch of the top. Wipe tops carefully and seal.

APPLES

Hot pack   Wash, pare, and core the apples. Cut them in halves, quarters, or slices and drop the cut fruit into water containing 2 tablespoons each of salt and vinegar per gallon of water. Drain and precook the apples for 3 to 5 minutes in **thin syrup** or water.

IN GLASS: Pack the hot fruit and syrup in jars to within ½ inch of the top. Adjust jar lids and process in boiling water:
Pints or quarts: 15 minutes
IN TIN: Pack the hot fruit and syrup in cans to within ¼ inch of the top. Exhaust and seal the cans and process in boiling water:
No. 2 or 2½ cans: 10 minutes

APPLESAUCE

Hot pack   Make applesauce, unsweetened or sweetened and seasoned to taste.

IN GLASS: Pack hot applesauce in jars to within ¼ inch of the top. Adjust the lids and process in boiling water:
Pints or quarts: 10 minutes
IN TIN: Pack hot applesauce in cans to the top. Exhaust and seal the cans and process in boiling water:
No. 2 cans: 10 minutes
No. 2½ cans: 15 minutes

APRICOTS

Follow directions for **peaches.** It is not necessary to peel apricots unless you wish to do so.

BEETS, PICKLED

Hot pack Cut the tops off the beets, leaving about 1 inch of the stems. Wash the beets, cover them with boiling water, and simmer until they are tender. Cool slightly and remove the skins. Slice the beets or leave the small ones whole.

Dissolve 2 cups sugar in 1½ cups vinegar and ½ cup water and bring the liquid to a boil. Pack the beets in glass jars to within ½ inch of the top and cover with the boiling pickling syrup, leaving ½ inch head space. Add 1 teaspoon salt to quarts; ½ teaspoon salt to pints. Adjust the lids and process in boiling water:

> Pints or quarts: 30 minutes

BERRIES (except Strawberries)

Wash the berries in cold, running water, drain well, and hull or stem them.

Hot packing is best for firm berries Add from ½ to 1 cup sugar to each quart of berries. Cover the pan and heat the berries slowly to the boiling point, shaking the pan almost constantly to keep the berries from burning. Simmer for 3 minutes. To prevent berries from floating to the top of the jar, let them stand in the hot syrup, after they are cooked, overnight to plump. Reheat to the boiling point before packing.

> IN GLASS: Pack the berries and their juice in jars to within ½ inch of the top. Adjust the lids and process in boiling water:
> Pints or quarts: 15 minutes
> IN TIN: Pack the berries and their juice in cans to the top. Exhaust the cans and process in boiling water:
> No. 2 cans: 15 minutes
> No. 2½ cans: 20 minutes

Cold packing is especially good for red raspberries and other soft berries

> IN GLASS: Pack the raw berries in jars to within ½ inch of the top, shaking the jar occasionally for a full pack. Cover with boiling **syrup,** leaving ½ inch head space, adjust the lids, and process in boiling water:
> Pints or quarts: 20 minutes

IN TIN: Pack the raw berries in cans to within ¼ inch of the top, shaking the can while filling it for a full pack. Fill to the top with boiling **syrup.** Exhaust the cans, seal, and process in boiling water:

No. 2 cans: 15 minutes
No. 2½ cans: 20 minutes

CARROTS, PICKLED

Follow the recipe for **pickled beets.**

CAULIFLOWER, PICKLED

Select young white heads of cauliflower. Wash well and break the cauliflower into even-sized flowerets. Do not use a knife. Soak the cauliflower overnight in a brine made by dissolving ½ cup salt in 1 gallon water. In the morning drain and pack the cauliflower loosely in clean jars. Combine 3 cups vinegar, 1½ cups water, 1 to 2 cups sugar, 1 tablespoon salt, and 2 tablespoons mixed whole pickling spices, tied in a bag. Bring the mixture to a boil and simmer for 30 minutes. Fill the jars to the level of the rubber ring with the pickling solution, adjust the covers, and process in a boiling-water bath:

Pints: 60 minutes
Quarts: 70 minutes

CHERRIES

Wash, stem and, if desired, pit the cherries. Follow the directions for canning **berries,** but if the cherries are unpitted, a little water must be added in hot packing to keep the cherries from burning. In cold packing, use a **medium syrup** for sweet cherries and a **heavy syrup** for sour cherries.

CURRANTS

Follow the directions given for **berries.**

FIGS

Figs are the exception to the rule. They have little or no acid content and so they must be processed in a pressure cooker. Select tree-ripened but not overripe figs. Leave them on the stems. Wash the figs, cover with fresh boiling water, and let them scald in the boiling water for 3 to 4 minutes. Drain.

IN GLASS: Pack the hot figs in jars to within ½ inch of the top and cover with boiling **medium** or **heavy syrup,** leaving ½ inch head space. Adjust jar lids and process under 10 pounds pressure:

Pints: 35 minutes
Quarts: 60 minutes

IN TIN: Pack the hot figs in cans to within ½ inch of the top and fill to the top with boiling **syrup.** Exhaust the cans and seal. Process under 10 pounds pressure:

No. 2 or 2½ cans: 40 minutes

GOOSEBERRIES

Follow the directions given for **berries.**

GRAPES

Slightly underripe Thompson seedless grapes are excellent for canning; so, too, are ripe muscats or Concords. Follow the directions for **cold-packing berries.** Use a **light, medium,** or **heavy syrup** according to preference and eventual use of the fruit.

MUSHROOMS, PICKLED

Wash mushrooms thoroughly and pack them into pint jars. Set the jars on the rack of a steam kettle, cover the rack with hot water, cover the kettle, and steam for 15 minutes.

Prepare a spiced vinegar by adding 2 tablespoons mixed pickling spices, tied in a bag, to each quart of vinegar. Bring the vinegar to a boil, simmer for 30 minutes, and pour it over the mushrooms in the jars, leaving ¼ inch head space. Adjust the covers on the jars and process in a boiling-water bath for 30 minutes. Seal and store.

PEACHES

Wash the peaches. To loosen the skins, dip them in boiling water, then quickly in cold water. Remove the skins, halve and pit the peaches, and slice, if desired.

Hot pack Heat the peaches through in simmering **syrup.**
IN GLASS: Pack the hot fruit and juice to within ½ inch of the top. Adjust the lids and process in boiling water:
Pints or quarts: 20 minutes
IN TIN: Pack the hot fruit and juice in cans to within ½ inch of the top. Exhaust the cans and seal. Process in boiling water:
No. 2 cans: 25 minutes
No. 2½ cans: 35 minutes

Cold pack Prepare the peaches as above.
IN GLASS: Pack the raw peaches symmetrically in jars to within ½ inch of the top and cover them with boiling **syrup,** leaving ½ inch head space. Adjust the jar lids and process in boiling water:
Pints: 25 minutes
Quarts: 35 minutes
IN TIN: Pack the raw peaches in cans to within ¼ inch of the top. Fill the cans with boiling **syrup,** leaving ¼ inch head space. Exhaust the cans, seal, and process in boiling water:
No. 2 cans: 25 minutes
No. 2½ cans: 35 minutes

PEARS

Wash the pears, peel, halve, and core them. Follow the directions for **peaches,** using either the hot- or the cold-pack method.

PLUMS OR FRESH PRUNES

Wash the plums. To can them whole, prick the skin of each plum in several places with the tines of a fork. Freestone varieties may be halved and pitted.

Hot pack Heat the plums in **syrup** to the boiling point.
IN GLASS: Pack the hot fruit and syrup in jars to within ½ inch of the top. Adjust the jar lids and process in boiling water:
Pints or quarts: 15 minutes
IN TIN: Pack the hot fruit in cans to within ¼ inch of the top and fill the cans with boiling **syrup.** Exhaust and seal the cans and process in boiling water:
No. 2 cans: 15 minutes
No. 2½ cans: 20 minutes

Cold pack Prepare the plums as above.

IN GLASS: Pack raw plums in jars to within ½ inch of the top and cover them with boiling syrup, leaving ½ inch head space. Adjust the jar lids and process in boiling water:
Pints or quarts: 20 minutes
IN TIN: Pack raw plums in cans to within ¼ inch of the top and fill the can with boiling **syrup.** Exhaust the cans, seal, and process in boiling water:
No. 2 cans: 20 minutes
No. 2½ cans: 25 minutes

RHUBARB

Wash young, tender rhubarb and cut it into ½-inch lengths. Add ½ cup sugar to each quart of rhubarb and let it stand for several hours to start the juice flowing. Then bring fruit and sugar slowly to a boil.

IN GLASS: Pack the hot fruit and juice in jars to within ½ inch of the top. Adjust the jar lids and process in boiling water:
Pint or quarts: 10 minutes
IN TIN: Pack the hot fruit and juice in cans to the top. Exhaust the cans, seal, and process in boiling water:
No. 2 or 2½ cans: 10 minutes

STRAWBERRIES

Wash and stem perfect berries. Add ½ cup sugar to each quart of berries and bring slowly to a boil, shaking the pan almost constantly to keep the fruit from sticking. Remove the fruit from the stove, cover, and let stand overnight to plump. In the morning bring the strawberries quickly to a boil.

IN GLASS: Pack the hot fruit and syrup to within ½ inch of the top. Adjust the lids and process in boiling water:
Pints or quarts: 15 minutes
IN TIN: Pack the hot fruit and syrup in cans to the top. Exhaust the cans, seal, and process in boiling water:
No. 2 cans: 10 minutes
No. 2½ cans: 15 minutes

TOMATOES

Select perfect, ripe tomatoes. Sort and wash the tomatoes, discarding any spoiled or partially spoiled ones. To loosen the skins, dip a few tomatoes at a time into boiling water for ½ minute, then dip them quickly into cold water. Cut out the stem ends and any green or yellow portions and peel the tomatoes.

Hot pack Cut the tomatoes into halves or quarters and bring to a boil, stirring frequently to prevent them from burning.

IN GLASS: Pack the hot tomatoes and their juice in jars to within ½ inch of the top. Add 1 teaspoon salt to quarts; ½ teaspoon salt to pints. Adjust the lids and process in boiling water:
Pints or quarts: 10 minutes
IN TIN: Pack the hot tomatoes and their juice in cans to within ¼ inch of the top. Add 1 teaspoon salt to No. 2½ cans; ½ teaspoon salt to No. 2 cans. Exhaust and seal the cans and process in boiling water:
No. 2 or 2½ cans: 15 minutes

Cold pack The tomatoes may be left whole or they may be halved or quartered. Prepare them according to the directions above.

IN GLASS: Pack the raw tomatoes firmly in jars to within ½ inch of the top, pressing gently to fill all the spaces. Add 1 teaspoon salt to quart jars; ½ teaspoon salt to pints. Adjust the lids and process in boiling water:
Pints: 35 minutes
Quarts: 45 minutes
IN TIN: Pack the raw tomatoes firmly in cans to the top, pressing gently to fill all the spaces. Add 1 teaspoon salt to No. 2½ cans; ½ teaspoon salt to No. 2 cans. Exhaust the cans, seal, and process in boiling water:
No. 2 cans: 45 minutes
No. 2½ cans: 55 minutes

Canning Vegetables

GENERAL METHOD

1. Select young, tender vegetables at the peak of perfection and can them quickly while they are still garden-fresh. Not more than 2 hours from garden to can is ideal, but if you must hold them, keep them in a cool, airy place. When you buy vegetables for canning, try to get them from a nearby farm garden.

2. Use only perfect vegetables and sort them for size and ripeness. Sorted vegetables cook more evenly and result in a more uniform product.

3. Wash vegetables thoroughly in running water if possible to remove any soil. In soil are found some of the bacteria that are the hardest to destroy. Wash the vegetables in small lots, and don't let them soak in water or much of the food value will be lost. Handle them carefully, so as not to bruise them. Wash crisp greens in two baths of warm water first to remove the sand, then give them a final rinsing in cold water.

4. If desired, cut the vegetables into uniform sizes.

5. Whether canning in glass jars or in tin, all authorities now recommend blanching vegetables before canning them. This simply means that the vegetables should be precooked in just enough boiling water to cover them for a few minutes before they are packed into hot sterilized jars. The blanching shrinks the product, making it possible to pack more food into the containers, and it drives the air out of the cells of the vegetables, thereby reducing the destruction of vitamins by oxidation during the processing. It cuts down on processing time and assures that the vegetable will be thoroughly and evenly heated to the center of the container. The blanching water should be used to fill the containers instead of boiling water, for it contains any water-soluble vitamins and minerals that were leached out in the blanching.

6. Pack the hot vegetables loosely in hot sterilized glass jars to within ½ inch of the top. This applies to all vegetables except corn, peas, and limas: these need 1 inch of head space. Cans may be filled to within ¼ inch of the top for most vegetables. If glass jars are used, pack the vegetables as symmetrically as possible to make the jars look attractive. Long vegetables are interesting if kept whole and packed lengthwise. Kitchen tongs help to place the vegetables where you want them. Add salt—1 teaspoon per quart; ½ teaspoon per pint —and fill the containers with the boiling-hot blanching water to cover the vegetables. Glass jars need ½ inch head space, but cans may usually be filled to the top. If the blanching water runs short, add boiling water. If the blanching water from a vegetable such as asparagus tastes bitter, you may wish to discard it and use fresh boiling water instead.

7. Remove the air bubbles in jars or cans by working the blade of a knife up and down the sides of the container. Add more liquid if needed.

8. Seal jars or tins.

34

IF GLASS JARS ARE USED: Wipe the jar rim and rubber ring with a clean cloth wrung out of clear, hot water, so that no speck of food will keep the lid from making an airtight seal. Adjust the clean, hot lids according to directions for the particular type of jar used (**see Index**).

IF TIN CANS ARE USED: The food in the cans must be at least 170° F. before the cans can be sealed. The food in the can must be heated to drive out air and help preserve the color and flavor of the vegetable. Sealing while hot also prevents the can ends from bulging or the can from bursting at the seams. This heating is called **exhausting the cans.**

To exhaust tin cans   Place the open, filled cans in a large kettle with boiling water 2 inches below the top of the cans. Cover the kettle, bring the water to a boil, and boil for 10 minutes, or until the temperature in the center of the can reaches 170° F. Remove the cans from the water one at a time. Replace any liquid spilled from the cans by filling them to the top with boiling blanching water or fresh boiling water. Place clean lids on the cans and seal at once.

9. Process in a pressure canner at 10 pounds pressure (240° F.) for the specified time given for the particular vegetable being canned. Follow the manufacturer's directions for your own canner. For details of **pressure processing, see Index.**

ALTITUDE PROCESSING: Increase the pressure 1 pound for each 2000 feet above sea level. When 10 pounds (240° F.) is specified at sea level, use 11 pounds at 2000 feet; 12 pounds at 4000 feet. A weighted gauge may need to be corrected for high altitudes by the manufacturer.

10. Remove the containers from the pressure canner.

IF GLASS JARS ARE USED: Take them carefully from the canner so as not to disturb the closures. Grasp the jar at the shoulder rather than by the lid. Complete the closure unless self-sealing tops were used and cool the jars on a rack or thick cloth away from drafts.

IF TIN CANS ARE USED: Plunge the cans at once into cold, clean water. Change the water as necessary to cool the cans quickly, but remove them while still slightly warm so that they will dry quickly. Stagger the cans if you stack them so that air can circulate freely around them to aid cooling and drying.

11. When the containers are cool, label intelligently and store in a dry, cool spot.

Note   The legal weight of a bushel of a vegetable differs in various states. The weights given for the following vegetables are only average, and the yield of canned vegetables approximate.

35

ASPARAGUS

1 bushel (45 pounds) yields 11 quarts
4 pounds yield 1 quart

Wash the asparagus, trim off the tough ends and thick scales, and cut into 1-inch pieces. Cover with boiling water, bring the water back to a boil, and boil for 2 to 3 minutes.

IN GLASS: Pack the hot asparagus in hot sterilized jars to within ½ inch of the top and cover with either the hot blanching water or fresh boiling water, leaving ½ inch head space. Add 1 teaspoon salt to quarts; ½ teaspoon salt to pints. Adjust jar lids and process at 10 pounds pressure:
Pints: 25 minutes
Quarts: 55 minutes
IN TIN: Pack the hot asparagus to within ¼ inch of the top. Fill the cans to the top with the hot blanching water or fresh boiling water. Add 1 teaspoon salt to No. 2½ cans; ½ teaspoon salt to No. 2 cans. Exhaust and seal the cans and process at 10 pounds pressure:
No. 2 or 2½ cans: 20 minutes

BEANS, LIMA

1 bushel (32 pounds) yields 6 to 8 quarts
4 to 5 pounds in pods yield 1 quart

Select garden-fresh, young tender beans. Shell and wash the beans. Cover them with boiling water, bring the water back to a boil, and boil for 1 minute.

IN GLASS: Pack the hot beans to within 1 inch of the top and cover with boiling water, leaving 1 inch head space. Add 1 teaspoon salt to quarts; ½ teaspoon salt to pints. Adjust jar lids and process at 10 pounds pressure:
Pints: 35 minutes
Quarts: 60 minutes
IN TIN: Pack the hot beans to within ½ inch of the top and fill the cans with boiling water. Add 1 teaspoon salt to No. 2½ cans; ½ teaspoon salt to No. 2 cans. Exhaust and seal the cans, and process at 10 pounds pressure:
No. 2 or 2½ cans: 40 minutes

BEANS, SNAP

1 bushel (30 pounds) yields 15 to 20 quarts
1½ to 2 pounds yield 1 quart

Wash the beans thoroughly and trim the ends. Cut the beans into 1-inch pieces and cover with boiling water. Bring the water back to a boil and boil for 5 minutes.

IN GLASS: Pack the hot beans to within ½ inch of the top and cover with the hot blanching water, leaving ½ inch head space. Add 1 teaspoon salt to quarts; ½ teaspoon salt to pints. Adjust jar lids and process at 10 pounds pressure:

Pints: 20 minutes

Quarts: 25 minutes

IN TIN: Pack the hot beans to within ¼ inch of the top and fill the cans to the top with the hot blanching water. Add 1 teaspoon salt to No. 2½ cans; ½ teaspoon salt to No. 2 cans. Exhaust and seal the cans and process at 10 pounds pressure:

No. 2 cans: 25 minutes

No. 2½ cans: 30 minutes

BEETS

1 bushel without tops (52 pounds) yields 17 to 20 quarts

2½ to 3 pounds yield 1 quart

Sort the beets into small, medium, or large sizes. Cut off the beet tops, leaving 1 inch of the stems. Wash the beets thoroughly and cook them in boiling water until almost tender and the skins slip easily; approximately 15 minutes for small, 20 minutes for medium, 30 minutes for large. Skin and trim. Leave the baby beets whole and halve, quarter, or slice the medium and large beets.

IN GLASS: Pack the hot beets to within ½ inch of the top and cover with fresh boiling water, leaving ½ inch head space. Add 1 teaspoon salt to quarts; ½ teaspoon salt to pints. Adjust jar lids and process under 10 pounds pressure:

Pints: 25 minutes

Quarts: 55 minutes

IN TIN: Pack the hot beets to within ¼ inch of the top and fill the cans to the top with fresh boiling water. Add 1 teaspoon salt to No. 2½ cans; ½ teaspoon salt to No. 2 cans. Exhaust the cans and process under 10 pounds pressure:

No. 2 or 2½ cans: 30 minutes

CARROTS

1 bushel without tops (50 pounds) yields 16 to 20 quarts

2½ to 3 pounds yield 1 quart

Select garden-fresh, young carrots. Wash and scrape the carrots and slice or dice them. Tiny carrots may be left whole. Cover the carrots with boiling water and bring the water again to a rolling boil.

IN GLASS: Pack the hot carrots to within ½ inch of the top and cover with the boiling-hot blanching water, leaving ½ inch head space. Add 1 teaspoon salt to quart jars: ½ teaspoon salt to pints. Adjust the jar lids and process at 10 pounds pressure:
Pints: 20 minutes
Quarts: 25 minutes
IN TIN: Pack the hot carrots to within ¼ inch of the top and fill the cans with the hot blanching water. Add 1 teaspoon salt to No. 2½ cans; ½ teaspoon salt to No. 2 cans. Exhaust and seal the cans and process at 10 pounds pressure:
No. 2 cans: 20 minutes
No. 2½ cans: 25 minutes

CORN

1 bushel in the husks (35 pounds) yields 8 to 9 quarts
1 dozen medium ears yield 1 quart

Cut both ends from the ears to facilitate husking. Husk the corn, remove the silk with a stiff vegetable brush, and wash the ears.

Cream-style   Cut the kernels from the ears at about the center of the kernels, then scrape the cobs with the back of a strong knife. Measure the corn into a kettle and add 2 cups boiling water to each 4 cups corn. Heat the mixture to the boiling point.

IN GLASS: **Use only pint jars.** Pack the hot corn to within 1 inch of the top. Add ½ teaspoon salt to each jar, adjust the lids, and process at 10 pounds pressure for 85 minutes.
IN TIN: **Use only No. 2 cans.** Pack the hot corn to the top and add ½ teaspoon salt to each can. Exhaust and seal the cans and process at 10 pounds pressure for 105 minutes.

Whole-kernel   Cut the kernels from the ears at about two thirds the depth of the kernels. Measure the corn into a kettle and add 2 cups boiling water to each 4 cups corn. Heat to the boiling point.

IN GLASS: Pack the hot corn to within 1 inch of the top and cover with the hot liquid, leaving 1 inch head space. Add 1 teaspoon salt to quart jars; ½ teaspoon salt to pints. Adjust the jar lids and process at 10 pounds pressure:

Pints: 55 minutes
Quarts: 85 minutes
IN TIN: Pack the hot corn to within ½ inch of the top and fill
to the top with the hot liquid. Add 1 teaspoon salt to No. 2½
cans; ½ teaspoon salt to No. 2 cans. Exhaust and seal the
cans and process at 10 pounds pressure.
No. 2 or 2½ cans: 60 minutes.

GREENS

To can greens such as Swiss chard or beet tops, follow the directions given for spinach.

OKRA

1 bushel (26 pounds) yields 17 quarts
1½ pounds yield 1 quart

Can only the tender pods. Wash and trim the pods, cover them
with boiling water, and boil for 1 minute.

IN GLASS: Pack the hot okra to within ½ inch of the top and
cover with boiling water, leaving ½ inch head space. Add 1
teaspoon salt to quarts; ½ teaspoon salt to pints. Adjust the
lids and process at 10 pounds pressure:
Pints: 25 minutes
Quarts: 40 minutes
IN TIN: Pack the hot okra to within ¼ inch of the top and fill
the cans with boiling water. Add 1 teaspoon salt to No. 2½
cans; ½ teaspoon salt to No. 2 cans. Exhaust and seal the
cans and process at 10 pounds pressure:
No. 2 cans: 25 minutes
No. 2½ cans: 35 minutes

PEAS, GREEN

1 bushel in pods (30 pounds) yields 12 to 15 pints
2 to 2½ pounds in pods yields 1 pint

Shell tender, garden-fresh peas and wash the peas in cold running
water. Cover them with boiling water and bring the water back to
a boil.

IN GLASS: Pack the hot peas to within 1 inch of the top and
cover with boiling water, leaving 1 inch head space. Add 1
teaspoon salt to quart; ½ teaspoon salt to pints. Adjust the
jar lids and process under 10 pounds pressure:
Pints or quarts: 40 minutes

IN TIN: Pack the hot peas to within ¼ inch of the top and fill the cans to the top with boiling water. Add 1 teaspoon salt to No. 2½ cans; ½ teaspoon salt to No. 2 cans. Exhaust the cans and seal and process at 10 pounds pressure:
No. 2 or 2½ cans: 30 minutes

PEPPERS, GREEN

Wash the peppers, cut out the stem ends, and remove the seeds and cores. The peppers may be left whole or they may be halved, quartered, or cut into long strips. Cover the peppers with boiling water and simmer for 5 minutes.

IN GLASS: Pack the peppers to within 1 inch of the top and cover with the boiling blanching water, leaving ½ inch head space. Add 1 teaspoon salt to quarts; ½ teaspoon salt to pints. Adjust the jar lids and process in a boiling-water bath for 45 minutes or under 10 pounds pressure:
Pints: 20 minutes
Quarts: 25 minutes
IN TIN: Pack the peppers to within ½ inch of the top and fill the cans with the boiling blanching water. Add 1 teaspoon salt to No. 2½ cans; ½ teaspoon salt to No. 2 cans. Exhaust the cans and seal. Process in a boiling-water bath for 45 minutes or under 10 pounds pressure:
No. 2 cans: 20 minutes
No. 2½ cans: 25 minutes

PIMENTOS

Wash the pimentos in cold water, then roast them in a hot oven (450° F.) for about 5 minutes, or until the skins blister. Drop the pimentos into cold water and peel. Cut out the stem ends and remove the seeds and cores.

IN GLASS: Pack the pimentos flat in pint jars. Add no liquid. Add ½ teaspoon salt and adjust the jar lids. Process in a boiling-water bath for 40 minutes or under 10 pounds pressure for 20 minutes.
IN TIN: Pack the pimentos flat in No. 2 cans. Add no liquid. Add ½ teaspoon salt. Exhaust the cans and seal and process in a boiling-water bath for 40 minutes or under 10 pounds pressure for 20 minutes.

PUMPKIN, CUBED OR PURÉED

>   50 pounds yield 15 quarts
>   3 pounds yield 1 quart

Wash the pumpkin, cut into sections, and remove the seeds and peel. Cut the flesh into 1-inch cubes.

Cubed   Add just enough water to cover the cubes and bring the water to a boil.

Purée   Steam the cubes for about 25 minutes, or until tender, and press through a food mill or fine sieve. Simmer the purée until it is heated through, stirring constantly.

> IN GLASS: Pack the hot pumpkin in jars to within ½ inch of the top. Add no liquid or salt to the purée. Cover the cubes with the hot blanching water and add 1 teaspoon salt to quarts; ½ teaspoon salt to pints. Adjust the lids and process at 10 pounds pressure:
> Pints: Cubed, 55 minutes
>   Puréed, 60 minutes
> Quarts: Cubed or puréed, 90 minutes
> IN TIN: Pack the hot pumpkin cubes to within ¼ inch of the top and fill the cans with the hot blanching water. Add 1 teaspoon salt to No. 2½ cans; ½ teaspoon salt to No. 2 cans. Pack hot pumpkin purée to within ⅛ inch of the top. Add no salt or liquid. Exhaust the cans and seal. Process at 10 pounds pressure:
> No. 2 cans: Cubed, 50 minutes
>   Puréed, 75 minutes
> No. 2½ cans: Cubed, 75 minutes
>   Puréed, 90 minutes

SPINACH AND OTHER GREENS

>   1 bushel (18 pounds) yields 6 to 9 quarts
>   2 to 3 pounds yield 1 quart

Can tender, young garden-fresh spinach leaves. Pick over the spinach, discard any yellow leaves, and wash thoroughly to remove sand and dirt. Cut off the stems and tough midribs. Steam about 2½ pounds of spinach at a time for about 10 minutes, or until the leaves are wilted.

> IN GLASS: Pack the hot wilted spinach loosely to within ½ inch of the top and cover with boiling water, leaving ½ inch

41

head space. Add ½ teaspoon salt to quarts; ¼ teaspoon salt to pints. Adjust the jar lids and process at 10 pounds pressure:
Pints: 45 minutes
Quarts: 70 minutes
IN TIN: Pack the hot wilted spinach loosely to within ¼ inch of the top and fill the cans to the top with boiling water. Add ½ teaspoon salt to No. 2½ cans; ¼ teaspoon salt to No. 2 cans. Exhaust the cans, seal, and process at 10 pounds pressure:
No. 2 cans: 60 minutes
No. 2½ cans: 75 minutes

SQUASH, SUMMER

1 bushel (40 pounds) yields 16 to 20 quarts
2 to 2½ pounds yield 1 quart

It is not necessary to peel summer squash. Scrub the skin thoroughly with a stiff vegetable brush, trim the ends, and slice ½ inch thick. The larger slices should be halved or quartered to make pieces of uniform size. Add just enough water to cover the squash and bring the water to a boil.

IN GLASS: Pack the hot squash to within ½ inch of the top and cover with the hot blanching water, leaving ½ inch head space. Add 1 teaspoon salt to quarts; ½ teaspoon salt to pints. Adjust the jar lids and process at 10 pounds pressure:
Pints: 30 minutes
Quarts: 40 minutes
IN TIN: Pack the hot squash to within ¼ inch of the top and fill the cans to the top with the hot blanching water. Add 1 teaspoon salt to No. 2½ cans; ½ teaspoon salt to No. 2 cans. Exhaust the cans, seal, and process at 10 pounds pressure:
No. 2 or 2½ cans: 20 minutes

SQUASH, WINTER

Prepare, pack, and process in the same way as **pumpkin,** either **cubed** or **puréed.**

SWEET POTATOES

Wash sweet potatoes or yams and cook them in boiling water or steam for 20 to 30 minutes, or until partially soft. Remove the skins

42

and cut the potatoes into uniform pieces. Sweet potatoes may be packed dry or wet.

IN GLASS: **Dry pack.** Pack the hot sweet potatoes tightly to within 1 inch of the top, pressing them down gently to fill all spaces. Add no salt or water.

Wet pack. Pack the hot sweet potatoes to within 1 inch of the top and cover with boiling water. Add 1 teaspoon salt to quarts; ½ teaspoon salt to pints.

Adjust jar lids and process at 10 pounds pressure:
Pints: Dry, 65 minutes
   Wet, 55 minutes
Quarts: Dry, 95 minutes
   Wet, 90 minutes

IN TIN: **Dry pack.** Pack the hot sweet potatoes tightly to the top of the can, pressing them down gently to fill all spaces. Add no salt or water.

Wet pack. Pack the hot sweet potatoes to within ¼ inch of the top and fill the cans with boiling water. Add 1 teaspoon salt to No. 2½ cans; ½ teaspoon salt to No. 2 cans.

Exhaust the cans, seal, and process at 10 pounds pressure:
No. 2 cans: Dry, 80 minutes
   Wet, 70 minutes
No. 2½ cans: Dry, 95 minutes
   Wet, 90 minutes

VEGETABLES, MIXED

Prepare the vegetables and cut them into desired uniform size. Mixed-vegetable combinations or vegetable-soup mixtures may be made from two or more of the following vegetables: tomato, corn, lima beans, peas, okra, carrots, turnips, celery, onions. For soup, the vegetables should be cut into small pieces. Cover the vegetables with boiling water, bring the water again to a boil, and boil for 10 minutes. Pack the boiling-hot vegetables in glass or tin to within ½ inch of the top and cover with the boiling-hot blanching water, leaving ½ inch head space in glass jars. Add 1 teaspoon salt to quart jars or No. 2½ cans; ½ teaspoon salt to pint jars or No. 2 cans. Adjust the lids of jars; exhaust and seal the cans. Process at 10 pounds pressure:
Pints or No. 2 cans: 60 minutes
Quarts or No. 2½ cans: 70 minutes

Canning Fish and Sea Foods

The general principles of **pressure canning** must be followed in canning fish and sea foods. The canning of these products is practical only for those living close to the source of supply of really fresh fish. Fish caught by the fisherman of the family or the surplus catch of non-commercial fishermen are of indisputable freshness, and inexpensive enough to warrant canning. Fish purchased at a retail market for home canning would cost more than the commercially canned product.

As soon as the fish is pulled from the water it should be killed and bled immediately. It should not be thrown into the bottom of the boat where it is exposed to the sun and where it will bruise itself as it flops helplessly against the side of the boat. After bleeding, the fish should either be packed in crushed ice or it should be cleaned, the cavity rubbed with fine pickling salt, and the fish then packed in a well-ventilated, shaded box.

Fish should be canned as soon as possible after they are taken from the water. A delay at any stage in the canning procedure allows for the deterioration of texture and flavor.

Preparing fish for canning Even if the fish were cleaned on the boat, they will require further cleaning in the kitchen. Scale the fish, cut off the heads and tails, and remove the fins. Remove any bits of membrane and blood clots from the cavity and wash the fish in cold fresh water. Most fish should then be soaked in a brine, made by dissolving ½ cup salt in 1 gallon water, to draw the blood from the flesh. The length of soaking time depends on the particular fish and will be found in specific instructions.

Before the fish are caught Check your supply of jars and lids or cans. In most cases fish products should not be packed in containers larger than 1 pint. It is difficult to pack fish in narrow-mouthed or tall-necked jars, so wide-mouthed jars with short necks should be used. The wire-bail Mason jar with a glass top that fits down on a rubber ring and is sealed with a wire clamp may be used, but better still is the wide-mouthed jar of the self- or vacuum-sealing type, fitted with an enameled metal top edged with a gasket. Jars sealed by porcelain-lined zinc screw caps are not recommended.

Discard any jars or lids that are cracked or chipped, for defects in either jar or lid can prevent a perfect airtight seal. Check wire clamps to make sure they are tight and are free from rust or dirt. Wash the jars in hot soapy water and rinse them well. Then place them in scalding water for 10 to 15 minutes. Wash and scald the lids too, unless the manufacturer directs you not to. Keep both jars and caps hot until used. Be sure you have enough *new* rubber rings. Scrub the rings in hot soapy water, then boil them for 10 minutes in 1 quart water to which has been added 1 tablespoon baking soda. Rinse well.

If using tin cans, use either plain tin cans or the special cans made for shellfish known as C-enamel, sea food formula cans. The regulation C-enamel and R-enamel used for canning fruits and vegetables are not suitable for fish. The fat may cause the enamel to peel off and, while this is not harmful, the appearance of the canned product is affected. Check the cans, lids, and gaskets to make certain they are in perfect condition. Discard any that are badly bent, dented, or rusty. Discard lids with scratched or torn gaskets. Wash the cans in clear, cool water, but don't wash the lids.

Check your can-sealing machine to see if it is working properly. Put a little water into a can, seal it, and then submerge it in hot water for a few minutes. If air bubbles rise from the can the seam is not tight and the sealer must be adjusted.

SIZE OF CANS SUITABLE FOR FISH OR SEA FOODS

CAN SIZE	CONTENTS IN CUPS	CONTENTS IN FLUID OUNCES	RECOMMENDED USE
No. ½	1	9	Minced clams and tuna-style packs
No. 1	1⅓	11	Wet-pack shrimp, clams, oysters, gumbos, and chowders
No. 1 tall	2	17	Salmon, shad, mackerel, and other solid-pack products
No. 2	2½	21	For other products not specified

Check your pressure cooker A reliable pressure cooker is absolutely necessary for the safe processing of fish and sea food. **Fish is generally processed at 10 pounds pressure, or 240° F., at sea level.** The cooker should be equipped with an "industrial" type thermometer as well as the pressure gauge, as a double check on the accuracy of the pressure in the canner.

ALTITUDE PROCESSING: Add 1 pound of pressure for each 2000 feet above sea level, and process for the length of time given in specific directions. At any altitude the reading on the thermometer must be 240° F. at 10 pounds pressure.

A processing period of not less than 90 minutes is recommended for the safe sterilization of No. 2 cans. Pint jars should be processed for 100 minutes.

When the lid is fastened on the canner the vent must be left open until a jet of steam has been escaping from the vent for at least 10 minutes. Then the vent can be closed and the pressure allowed to build.

When processing time is finished, the pressure in the cooker, especially when canning in glass, should be released slowly. Rapid reduction of pressure in the cooker will cause a great deal of breakage. Allow 20 minutes resting period for glass before opening the petcock.

GENERAL METHOD FOR CANNING FISH AND SEA FOODS

Salmon, shad, and other firm-fleshed fish are simply cut into container-length pieces and packed raw in the containers. Other varieties of fish are cooked for a short while before they are packed. Precooking produces a firmer product and makes filling easier.

Containers should be packed flush to the rim with raw fish, for sufficient shrinkage takes place during the processing to create a head space. Leave ¼ inch head space when packing precooked products.

Fish raw- or hot-packed in glass or hot-packed in tin do not need to be exhausted before the containers are sealed and processed. Only cold-filled, raw-packed, or precooked and cooled products in tin containers need to be exhausted (see Index) before the cans are sealed. If a partial vacuum is not created in cans before they are sealed, the ends may swell after the cans are processed and cooled.

Containers should be cooled as rapidly as possible after processing, to prevent further cooking of the contents in the can. Plunge cans into cold running water, but remove them while they are still slightly warm so they will dry quickly. Glass jars should be stacked so that air can circulate freely around them, but they must be protected from drafts.

When glass containers are cool they should be washed and dried.

All containers should be inspected carefully for any signs of leaks or defects before they are stored, and no attempt should be made to reprocess fish products from leaking containers.

Label containers and store in a dark, cool place. Most fish products improve in flavor if they are allowed to age in the can for 2 to 3 months before they are used.

Warning Certain fish, such as sea trout and grayfish, are unsuitable for canning. If you have any doubts, and if specific instructions are not found in this chapter, write to your State Experiment Station or to the United States Department of Agriculture for information.

SALMON, SHAD, AND OTHER FIRM-FLESHED FISH

25 pounds fish, uncleaned, yield 12 pint jars or No. 2 cans

Remove the scales, fins, and heads, clean the fish thoroughly, removing all traces of blood, and wash in cool water. Do not remove the backbone, for it contains valuable minerals and is made soft and edible during the processing period.

Cut the fish into container-length pieces and soak the pieces for 60 minutes in a brine made by dissolving 1 cup salt in 1 gallon water. The brine should be used only once, but 1 gallon is sufficient for 25 pounds of cleaned fish. Drain the fish and pack the pieces solidly in pint jars or No. 2 cans even with the rim, without crushing or bruising the flesh.

> IN GLASS: Adjust the jar lids and process at 10 pounds pressure (240° F.):
> Pints: 1 hour and 40 minutes
> IN TIN: Exhaust the cans, seal immediately, and process at 10 pounds pressure (240° F.):
> No. 2 cans: 90 minutes

MACKEREL, LAKE TROUT, WHITEFISH, MULLET, AND OTHER FRESH-WATER FISH

35 pounds fish, uncleaned, yield 12 pint jars or No. 2 cans

Remove the scales, fins, and heads and clean the fish thoroughly. Discard the thin belly section by cutting away a ½-inch strip on each side. Split the fish but leave the backbone intact, and cut the fish into container-length pieces. Soak the pieces for 60 minutes in a brine made by dissolving 1 cup salt in 1 gallon water. Drain the fish and pack the pieces solidly in glass jars or No. 2 cans even with the rim. Alternate head and tail sections for a solid pack and, if packing in glass, put the skin side next to the glass.

Submerge the open jars or cans in a kettle of brine made by dissolving ½ cup salt in 1 gallon water. Bring the brine to a boil and simmer the fish in the containers for 20 minutes. Invert the containers on a wire rack to drain for 2 to 3 minutes. Add 1 bay leaf and a slice or two of onion to each container. Adjust jar lids; seal cans. Process at 10 pounds pressure (240° F.):

> Pint jars: 100 minutes
> No. 2 cans: 90 minutes

MACKEREL, HERRING, OR MULLET IN TOMATO SAUCE

Follow the directions for canning **mackerel,** but instead of adding a bay leaf and sliced onion to each container, pour hot **tomato sauce** over the fish. Leave ½ inch head space in pint jars; fill No. 2 cans to the top. Adjust jar lids; seal cans immediately, and process at 10 pounds pressure (240° F.):

> Pint jars: 100 minutes
> No. 2 cans: 90 minutes

Tomato Sauce Peel and press through a fine sieve or food mill enough fresh tomatoes to make 4 quarts of tomato purée. Add 6 tablespoons cider vinegar, 2 tablespons minced onion, 2 tablespoons salt, 1 tablespoon grated horseradish, and 1 teaspoon pepper. Bring the purée to a boil and simmer for about 1½ hours, or until the purée is reduced to half its original volume, stirring frequently to prevent the sauce from burning.

SALT MACKEREL OR MULLET

> 28 to 30 pounds mackerel or mullet, uncleaned, yield 12 pint jars or No. 2 cans

Clean the fish, remove the fins, and cut off the heads and tails. Split the fish lengthwise, but do not remove the backbone. Discard the thin belly section by cutting away a ½-inch strip on each side. Cut the fish into container-length pieces and soak the pieces for 60 minutes in a brine made by dissolving 1 cup salt in 1 gallon water. Drain the fish for about 10 minutes, rub the pieces with fine pickling salt, and pack them in a stone or earthenware crock with as much dry salt as will cling to the flesh. After 3 hours rinse the salt from the fish in fresh water, and drain again.

Pack the fish into pint jars or No. 2 cans, alternating head and tail pieces to obtain a uniform pack. Arrange the containers in a pressure canner containing 2 to 3 inches of hot water, bring the pressure up to 3 pounds (220° F.), and cook the fish for 20 minutes. Let the pressure in the canner fall to zero before opening the canner.

Invert the containers on wire racks to drain for 3 minutes. Seal the cans immediately; adjust the jar lids. Process at 10 pounds pressure (240° F.):

> Pint jars: 100 minutes
> No. 2 cans: 90 minutes

SMOKED MACKEREL OR MULLET

> 60 pounds freshly caught mackerel or 30 pounds smoked mackerel yield 12 pint jars or No. 2 cans

Split the fish open along the back and clean the cavity thoroughly. Wash the fish and soak them for 1 to 2 hours in a saturated brine solution made by dissolving 4 pounds pickling salt in 6 quarts water.

Rinse the fish in fresh cold water, drain, then dry them on sticks in a current of air for about 2 hours, or until skin becomes dry and shiny. Smoke the fish in a light cool smoke for 2 hours (see **Chapter Seven**). Increase the density of the smoke and continue to smoke for about 2 hours longer, or until the surface of the fish is straw-yellow.

Remove the backbones and cut the smoked fish into strips about 2 inches wide and the length of the container. Pack the fish solidly in containers, using 16 ounces for a No. 1 tall can, and 20 ounces for a pint jar or a No. 2 can.

Arrange the containers in a pressure cooker containing from 2 to 3 inches of hot water, bring the pressure to 10 pounds, and cook the fish for 20 minutes. Let the pressure in the canner fall to zero before opening the canner. Invert the containers on a rack to drain for 3 minutes. Then right them and pour about 3 tablespoons hot olive oil into each can. Seal cans immediately; adjust the lids on jars. Process at 10 pounds pressure (240° F.):

> Pint jars: 100 minutes
> No. 1 tall or No. 2 can: 90 minutes

Whiting may also be smoked and canned as above, except that the fish are split or boned, and are brined for only 1 hour before they are smoked.

SPICED SALMON, SHAD, MACKEREL, TROUT, OR LAKE TROUT

27 to 30 pounds fish, uncleaned, yield 12 pint jars or No. 2 cans

Scale the fish. Remove the fins, cut off the tails and heads, and wash thoroughly. Leave the backbone intact.

Cut the fish into container-length pieces, and soak the pieces for 60 minutes in a brine made by dissolving ½ cup salt in 1 gallon water. Drain well.

Fill pint jars or No. 2 cans loosely with the fish, using about 20 ounces to each container. Fill the containers with a mixture of half water and half **spiced vinegar (see below)**.

Exhaust both glass and tin by putting the containers in a kettle with warm water to within 2 inches of the rims, bringing the water to a boil, covering the kettle, and simmering the fish for 20 minutes.

Invert the containers on a wire rack to drain for 3 minutes. Right the containers and fill them with enough spiced vinegar to cover the fish. Add 1 bay leaf, a slice or two of onion, and a few pickling spices. One tablespoon olive oil may be added before the can is filled with the spiced vinegar.

> IN GLASS: Adjust the jar lids and process pint jars at 10 pounds pressure (240° F.) for 90 minutes.
>
> IN TIN: The cans must once more be exhausted for about 10 minutes, or until the temperature in the center of the cans reaches 170° F. Seal the cans immediately and process No. 2 cans at 10 pounds pressure (240° F.) for 80 minutes.

Spiced Vinegar   Combine 2 quarts distilled vinegar and 1 quart water. Add 4 tablespoons sugar and the following spices tied in a bag: ½ tablespoon each of white peppercorns, mustard seed, and whole cloves, 1 teaspoon each of cracked cardamom seeds, cracked whole ginger, and crumbled bay leaves. Bring the liquid to a boil, simmer for 1 hour, and strain.

ALBACORE, TUNA, KING MACKEREL, OR LARGE MACKEREL

26 pounds fish, uncleaned, yield 12 ½-pint jars or No. ½ cans

Clean and bleed the fish thoroughly and wash well in cold water. Discard strips ½ inch wide from the belly section. Place the fish in pans with perforated bottoms and stack the pans in a pressure cooker containing 2 to 3 inches of hot water in the bottom. Cook the fish at 10 pounds pressure for 2 hours, then cool for 4 to 8 hours. When cool, scrape away the skin and discard the backbone and the streaks of dark flesh along the sides. Cut the meat into pieces about ½ inch shorter than the height of the container.

Put ½ teaspoon salt into each ½-pint jar or No. ½ can, and fill the containers solidly with the fish, using small flakes to fill in empty spaces. Fill the containers with hot vegetable oil. Olive oil is best, of course, but peanut or cottonseed oil may be used.

> IN GLASS: Adjust the jar lids and process at 15 pounds pressure (250° F.):
> ½ pints: 80 minutes
> IN TIN: Exhaust and seal the cans and process at 15 pounds pressure (250° F.):
> No. ½ cans: 70 minutes

CODFISH FLAKES

> 16 pounds fish, uncleaned, yield about 4 pint jars or No. 2 cans

Clean and wash the fish thoroughly, removing all traces of blood. Cut the fish into large chunks and soak the chunks for 60 minutes in a brine made by dissolving 1 cup salt in 1 gallon water. Rinse the fish and drain well. Place the fish in pans with perforated bottoms and stack the pans in a pressure cooker containing 2 to 3 inches of hot water in the bottom. Cook the fish at 10 pounds pressure (240° F.) for 30 minutes, and cool until the flesh can be handled. Separate the flesh from the skin and bones. Discard any dark or discolored pieces of flesh. Pack the fish flakes tightly in pint jars or No. 2 cans so that no air spaces are left.

> IN GLASS: Adjust the jar lids and process at 10 pounds pressure (240° F.):
> Pints: 100 minutes
> IN TIN: Exhaust and seal the cans and process at 10 pounds pressure (240° F.):
> No. 2 cans: 90 minutes

RIVER HERRING

> 25 pounds herring (uncleaned) yield 12 pint jars or No. 2 cans

Scale the fish, remove the fins, and wash the fish thoroughly. With a sharp knife cut through the backbone of the fish just behind the head. Continue to cut along one side of the fish just behind the gills to the belly and continue along the belly to the vent. Remove the head and viscera, wash the cavity, scrape it clean of blood clots, and rinse.

Prepare a brine strong enough to float an egg (about 4 cups salt to 1 gallon water), and in it soak the fish for about 6 hours. If the skin begins to wrinkle or change color during the soaking period, remove the fish immediately.

Cut the fish into lengths suitable to fit into pint jars or No. 2 cans. Pack the fish in the containers, alternating head and tail pieces for a uniform pack. Fill the containers to the top with a brine made by dissolving 1½ tablespoons salt in 1 quart water.

Both tin and glass containers should be exhausted for about 10 minutes in simmering water, or until the center of a container registers 170° F. Seal cans immediately; adjust the lids on glass jars. Process at 15 pounds pressure (250° F.):

> Pint jars: 70 minutes
> No. 2 cans: 60 minutes

RIVER HERRING ROE

> 10 pounds roe yield 12 pint jars or No. 2 cans

Wash the roe in fresh, cold water, and discard any bits of "black skin" or intestine. Spread the roe on a wire screen for 10 minutes to drain.

The roe swells a little in the processing, so fill the containers only three fourths full by volume. Better yet, weigh 14 ounces of roe for each pint jar or No. 2 can.

Fill the containers to the top with a brine made by dissolving 2 tablespoons salt in 1 quart water.

> IN GLASS: Adjust jar lids and process at 15 pounds pressure (250° F.):
> Pints: 70 minutes
> IN TIN: Exhaust the cans, seal, and process at 15 pounds pressure (250° F.):
> No. 2 cans: 60 minutes

WHITING

> 26 to 30 pounds whiting, uncleaned, yield 12 pint jars or No. 2 cans

Scale the fish, remove the fins, cut off the heads and tails and the narrow strips of thin belly flesh. Wash the fish thoroughly and cut them into container-length pieces. Soak the pieces for 90 minutes in a saturated brine made by dissolving 4 pounds pickling salt in 6 quarts water. Drain well.

Fill the containers compactly, alternating head and tail pieces. Put the containers into a pressure cooker containing from 2 to 3 inches of hot water, bring the pressure to 3 pounds (220° F.), and cook the fish for 30 minutes. Let the pressure fall to zero before taking the cover off the canner.

Invert the containers on a rack to drain for about 3 minutes. Right the containers and add to each 1 bay leaf, 6 peppercorns, and 3 tablespoons hot olive oil. Seal cans immediately; adjust jar lids. Process at 10 pounds pressure (240° F.):

> Pint jars: 100 minutes
> No. 2 cans: 90 minutes

FISH CHOWDER

Fish chowders—Manhattan, New England, or your own special formula—may be successfully canned. Follow the formula recommended by the United States Department of the Interior, adding or subtracting to suit your individual taste.

Simmer 4 pounds edible scraps of fish with fish bones and heads in 1 gallon water for 2 hours and strain, reserving the broth.

> ¾ pound salt pork, diced
> 1½ cups chopped onion
> ½ cup flour
> 2 quarts hot strained fish broth
> 2 teaspoons salt
> ½ teaspoon pepper
> 5 pounds potatoes, peeled and diced
> 5 pounds boned, cooked flaked fish

In a kettle cook the salt pork and onion until the onion is soft and golden. Stir in the flour and add gradually the hot fish broth. Cook, stirring constantly, until the soup is thickened. Add the salt and pepper and bring the soup to the boiling point.

Into each No. 2 can or pint jar put ¾ cup each of the diced potatoes and the flaked fish. Fill the containers with the hot soup. Seal cans immediately. Adjust the lids on glass jars. Process at 10 pounds pressure (240° F.):

> No. 2 cans: 80 minutes
> Pint jars: 90 minutes

To serve, dilute the chowder with an equal quantity of milk, bring to a boil, and correct the seasoning with salt and pepper.

53

WHOLE CLAMS

This method is recommended by the United States Department of the Interior as suitable only for:

> Atlantic Coast quahogs or hard clams
> Pacific Coast butter, littleneck, razor, and hard clams
> 3 gallons of shucked clams, including the clam liquor, yield 12 pint jars or No. 2 cans

Scrub the clams and put them in a tub of clean salt water. Rather than use ocean water, which may be contaminated, make a fresh 10 per cent brine by dissolving about 1½ cups salt in 1 gallon of fresh drinking water. Add a few handfuls of corn meal to the brine and let the clams remain in it for 12 to 24 hours.

Open the live clams over a pan and save the clam liquor. Open the body of the clam and scrape out the dark mass, which might result in discoloration of the canned product. If littleneck clams are used, snip off the neck.

Wash the clams in a brine made by dissolving ¼ cup salt in 1 gallon of water, and blanch the clams for 1 minute in boiling water containing 3 teaspoons lemon juice to 1 gallon water. Drain.

Pack 1¾ cups clam meats into a No. 2 can or a pint jar. Bring the clam liquor to a boil, boil until it is reduced to about two thirds its original volume, and strain. Fill the containers to within ¼ inch of the top with the hot clam juice. Adjust the lids on glass jars; seal cans immediately. Process at 10 pounds pressure (240° F.):

> Pint jars: 70 minutes
> No. 2 cans: 60 minutes

MINCED CLAMS

> 3 gallons of shucked clams yield 12 No. ½ or No. 1 cans or ½-pint jars

Follow the instructions given for canning **whole clams,** but before filling the cans, grind the blanched and drained clams through the fine blade of a meat grinder.

Pack the ground clam meats into containers as follows:

> No. ½ or No. 1 cans or ½-pint jars: 6 ounces, or ¾ cup
> No. 2 cans or pint jars: 12 ounces, or 1½ cups

Reduce the clam liquor over a hot flame to two thirds its original volume and fill the containers with the hot juice, stirring until meats and juice are well mixed. Seal cans immediately; adjust jar lids. Process at 8 pounds pressure (236° F.):

      No. ½ or No. 1 cans: 60 minutes
      No. 2 cans: 80 minutes
      ½-pint jars: 70 minutes
      Pint jars: 90 minutes

CLAM CHOWDER

Wash soft, hard, or butter clams thoroughly. Shuck the clams, reserving the clam liquor, snip off the siphons, open the bodies, and discard the dark body mass. Wash the clam meats and blanch them for 1 minute in boiling water containing 2 tablespoons salt and 1 tablespoon lemon juice to each quart. Drain the meats and chop enough to measure 9 cups. Strain and measure 2 quarts clam liquor.

In a large kettle cook 1½ cups diced salt pork and 1½ cups minced onion until the onion is soft and golden. Mix ½ cup flour with enough of the clam juice to make a smooth, thin paste. Add the rest of the clam liquor to the pork and onion mixture and bring to a boil. Stir in gradually the flour paste, and cook, stirring constantly, until the soup is thickened. Add 2 teaspoons salt, ½ teaspoon white pepper, and ½ teaspoon thyme. Peel and dice enough potatoes to measure 9 cups and cover them with cold water.

Into each No. 2 can or pint jar put ¾ cup of the diced potatoes and ¾ cup of the chopped clam meats. Fill the containers to the brim with the hot soup. Seal cans immediately. Adjust jar lids. Process at 10 pounds pressure (240° F.):

      No. 2 cans: 75 minutes
      Pint jars: 80 minutes

NOTE: To prepare for the table, add an equal volume of milk, water, or clam juice and bring the chowder to a boil. Correct the seasoning with salt and pepper.

OYSTERS

> 3 bushels of unshucked oysters yields about 12 pint jars or No. 2 cans, although the yield will vary with the locality and the time of year

Wash the oysters in a weak brine solution made by dissolving ¼ cup salt in 1 gallon water.

Place the oysters in a metal basket and steam them in an ordinary cooker at 212° F. for 10 to 15 minutes or under 10 pounds pressure (240° F.) for 5 minutes.

55

Shuck the oysters into a weak brine (¼ cup salt to 1 gallon water) solution to keep them from discoloring, then wash them thoroughly in a large quantity of weak brine to remove all the sand and grit.

Drain the washed oysters well and fill containers as follows:
- No. 1 picnic can or ½-pint jar: 8 ounces, or 1 cup
- No. 1 tall can: 12 ounces, or 1½ cups
- No. 2 can or pint jar: 16 ounces, or 2 cups

A small amount of weak brine should be added to each container.

IN GLASS: Adjust the lids and process at 10 pounds pressure (240° F.):
- ½ pints: 35 minutes
- Pints: 50 minutes

IN TIN: Exhaust the cans and seal. Process at 10 pounds pressure (240° F.):
- No. 1 picnic cans: 29 minutes
- No. 1 tall cans: 35 minutes
- No. 2 cans: 42 minutes

ATLANTIC AND GULF COAST CRABS

24 pounds average-size, live crabs yield 12 ½-pint jars or No. 1 cans

Can only live, good-sized crabs. Whole crabs cannot be cooked before they are shelled and cleaned, for the blood of the crab contains compounds that cause discoloration. So . . .

Dip the live crabs in ice water for several minutes to make them sluggish. Then grasp the body and break off the claws and legs. Discard the legs, but reserve the claws. To remove the back shell, insert the fingers in the leg holes and pull the shell apart. Discard the gills and other inedible parts and wash the bodies in fast-running cold water. Put the bodies and large claws in a perforated container, lower the container into a pressure canner containing 2 or 3 inches of water in the bottom, and cook the crabs at 8 pounds pressure (236° F.) for 10 minutes.

As soon as the crabs are cool enough to handle, pick the meat from the bodies and claws, keeping it separate. Wash the meat in a brine made by dissolving ½ cup salt in 2 quarts water. Drain the meat well, then dip it in a solution made of 2 quarts water and either ¼ cup lemon juice or ½ cup vinegar.

Press the crab meat with the hands to squeeze out excess moisture and pack about ⅝ cup or from 6 to 6½ ounces into No. 1 standard

(Eastern oyster) C-enamel cans lined with vegetable parchment paper or into ½-pint glass jars. Pack the body meat and the claw meat separately. Pour enough weak brine, made by dissolving 1½ tablespoons salt in 1 quart water, into each container just to cover the meat. Exhaust and seal tin cans; adjust lids on glass jars. Process at 5 pounds pressure (228° F.):

No. 1 Eastern oyster cans: 80 minutes
½-pint jars: 90 minutes

DUNGENESS OR PACIFIC CRABS

13 to 15 average-sized crabs yield 12 No. ½ cans or ½-pint jars

Dungeness crab meat is canned in very much the same manner as the **Atlantic** or **Gulf Coast crabs**. The legs are not discarded, for they contain some fine meat.

Before picking the meat from the legs and bodies, Dungeness crabs may either be cooked under 8 pounds pressure (236° F.) as described for Atlantic crabs or they may be cooked for 20 minutes in boiling water to which has been added 1 cup salt and ¼ cup vinegar for each gallon. Black peppercorns and bay leaves may also be added.

Pack the leg and claw meat on the top and bottom of the containers with the body meat in the center.

CRAB SOUP AND GUMBO

Your favorite recipe for crab soup or gumbo may be successfully canned, providing you do not overcook the vegetables. Bear in mind that the processing time needed to preserve the product is sufficient to cook most vegetables thoroughly.

Make the soup in the regular way and bring it just to a boil. Pack the boiling-hot soup in containers to the top. Seal cans immediately. Adjust lids on glass jars. Process at 10 pounds pressure (240° F.):

No. 1 cans: 45 minutes
No. 2 cans: 75 minutes
Pint jars: 80 minutes

The following recipes are recommended for canning by the United States Department of the Interior. The seasoning may be adjusted to taste:

Crab Soup

8 cups crab meat
1 cup butter
2 cups each diced green pepper, celery, and onion
4 cups cooked tomatoes
15 cups water
¼ cup uncooked rice
1½ tablespoons salt
1 teaspoon white pepper

Pick over the crab meat carefully, discarding bits of shell, then wash and drain. Melt half the butter in a kettle and in it cook the pepper, celery, and onion until soft. Add the tomatoes and heat. In another saucepan stew the crab meat in the remaining butter for 3 minutes and add to the soup. Add the water and bring the soup to a simmer. Add rice, salt, and pepper and stir vigorously. Can immediately.

Crab Gumbo

8 cups crab meat
1½ cups olive oil
1 cup flour
2 cups minced onion
1½ cups minced green pepper
8 cups cooked tomatoes
1½ tablespoons salt
1 teaspoon white pepper
¼ teaspoon ground mace
¼ teaspoon powdered thyme
8 cups cooked okra
4 cups hot water
1 clove garlic, minced

Pick over the crab meat carefully, discarding bits of shell, then wash and drain. In a large kettle heat the olive oil and very gradually stir in the flour to make a smooth paste. Add the onion and green pepper and cook, stirring, until the onion is soft. Add the tomatoes and spices, and bring the soup to a boil. Add the okra, hot water, crab meat, and garlic, and bring the soup almost to a boil. Can immediately.

SHRIMP

18½ pounds green headless shrimp yield 12 pint jars or No. 2 cans

The cans used should be C-enamel, sea food formula, or plain cans with parchment linings.

Can only freshly caught shrimp. As soon as the shrimp are taken from the water they should be beheaded. If the heads are removed at this time, the black vein that runs along the back of the shrimp will be pulled out as the head is removed. This cannot be done once the shrimp have been out of the water for half an hour. As soon as the shrimp are beheaded they must be packed in finely crushed ice until they reach their destination. Once ashore, canning should be done immediately.

Wash and peel the shrimp and rinse them in fresh, cool water. Cover the shrimp with a strong brine made by dissolving ½ cup salt in each quart water, and let them soak for 20 to 30 minutes, stirring occasionally, so that the brining will be uniform. Fill a wire basket half full of the shrimp, and dip them in a boiling brine made in the same proportion as the soaking brine. Bring the brine back to a boil, and simmer the shrimp for 6 to 8 minutes. Add salt to the brine after each batch in the proportion of 1 tablespoon salt to each quart water, and use a fresh brine after every 4 batches. Spread the cooked shrimp on a wire-mesh screen to cool and dry, using an electric fan to speed the process if possible, for the shrimp must show no surface moisture when put into containers. Fill the containers as follows:

> No. 1 can or ½-pint jar: 6 ounces, or ¾ cup
> No. 2 can or pint jar: 12 ounces or 1½ cups

Fill the containers with scalding brine made by dissolving 1½ tablespoons salt in 1 quart water. Seal cans immediately. Adjust the lids on glass jars and process immediately:

	AT 10 POUNDS PRESSURE (240° F.)	AT 15 POUNDS PRESSURE (250° F.)
No. 1 cans:	20 minutes	10 minutes
No. 2 cans	30 minutes	15 minutes
½-pint jars:	25 minutes	13 minutes
Pint jars:	35 minutes	20 minutes

LOBSTERS

Plunge live lobsters into boiling water containing 2 tablespoons salt to each gallon of water. Bring the liquid again to a boil, and cook the lobsters for 15 to 30 minutes, depending on their size.

Cool the lobsters immediately in cold water containing 1 tablespoon salt per gallon. Split the lobsters lengthwise, discard the black vein that runs down the tail and the small sac that lies just below the head, and remove the edible meat in as large pieces as possible. Crack the large claws and remove the meat. Wash the meat in running water and drain for 5 to 10 minutes.

Dip the meat in a solution made of 2 quarts water and either ¼ cup lemon juice or ½ cup vinegar. Press the meat gently to remove excess moisture and pack 6 ounces, or ¾ cup, in No. 1 standard Eastern oyster cans, C-enamel cans lined with parchment, or ½-pint glass jars. Place the tail meat on the bottom and the claw meat on top. Fill containers to the top with a hot brine made by dissolving 3 tablespoons salt in 1 gallon water. Exhaust and seal tin cans. Adjust the lids on glass jars. Process immediately:

	AT 5 POUNDS PRESSURE (228° F.)	AT 10 POUNDS PRESSURE (240° F.)
No. 1 cans:	80 minutes	60 minutes
½-pint jars:	90 minutes	70 minutes

Canning Poultry and Meats

Beef, veal, mutton, lamb, pork, venison, rabbit, and squirrel may all be canned successfully in the home. So, too, may all the various kinds of poultry and game birds; chicken, duck, goose, guinea hen, turkey, pheasant, and quail can all be preserved in either glass or tin for future use.

Commercial canners are going in for variety in these competitive days. Specialty grocery shelves are filled with unusual canned items such as duck in orange sauce, chicken in red wine, squabs in Madeira sauce. Guinea hens, squabs, and turkeys are being wrapped in parchment paper to prevent the flesh from coming into contact with the can, and they are preserved in their own stock.

The housewife can easily experiment along these lines in her own kitchen with fine results providing the rules for the safe processing or sterilization of these foods are rigidly followed. Scientific research has proved without a doubt that the pressure cooker is vital to the preservation of protein foods. Ordinary boiling temperatures are not sufficient to destroy the bacteria spores that could result in food spoilage and poisoning.

Before starting to can poultry or meats   Check your supply of jars and lids or cans. The wire-bail type Mason jar with a glass top that fits down on a rubber ring and is sealed with a wire clamp may be used, but better yet are jars of the self- or vacuum-sealing type, fitted with enameled metal tops edged with gaskets. Discard any jars or lids that are cracked or chipped, for defects in either jar or lid can prevent a perfect airtight seal. Wash the jars in hot soapy water and rinse them well. Wash the lids too, unless the manufacturer directs you not to. Be sure that you have enough *new* rubber rings. Scrub the rings in hot soapy water, then boil them for 10 minutes in 1 quart water in which 1 tablespoon baking soda has been dissolved. Rinse well. Be certain that you understand the closure of the particular type of jar you are using. For types of jars, **see Index.**

If using cans, use plain tin cans in good condition, preferably those with paper gaskets. C-enamel and R-enamel cans prevent some foods from discoloring, but this is not the case with meats and poultry. The fat may cause the enamel to peel off and, while this is not harmful in any way, it makes the canned product unattractive. Check the cans, lids, and gaskets to make certain they are in perfect condition. Discard any that are badly bent, dented, or rusty. Discard lids with scratched or torn gaskets. Wash the cans in clear cool water, but don't wash the lids.

Check your can-sealing machine to determine whether it is working properly. Put a little water into a can, seal it, and then submerge it in hot water for a few minutes. If air bubbles rise from the can, the seam is not tight and the sealer must be adjusted.

SIZE OF CANS SUITABLE FOR POULTRY OR MEATS

No. 2 can holds 2½ cups, or 20 ounces
No. 2½ can holds 3½ cups, or 28 ounces
No. 3 can holds about 4 cups, or 33 ounces

Check your pressure cooker If your pressure cooker has a weighted gauge, make certain it is thoroughly clean. A weighted gauge needs no adjustment, but a dial gauge should be checked every season before it is used, and oftener if you use it frequently. Ask your manufacturer or dealer about checking the dial. If the test shows your gauge reading is high or low, tie a tag on the canner stating how many pounds it is off. If the gauge is off more than 5 pounds, you'd better get a new one, otherwise correct it as follows:

Meat is processed at 10 pounds pressure, or 240° F., at sea level.

If the gauge reads high, add 1 pound for each pound the gauge is high.

If the gauge reads low, deduct 1 pound for each pound the gauge is low.

1 pound high—process at 11 pounds
1 pound low—process at 9 pounds
2 pounds high—process at 12 pounds
2 pounds low—process at 8 pounds

ALTITUDE PROCESSING: Add 1 pound of pressure for each 2000 feet above sea level, and process for the length of time given in specific directions.

When the lid is fastened on the canner the vent must be left open until a jet of steam has been escaping from the vent for at least 10 minutes. Then the vent can be closed and the pressure allowed to build.

When processing time is finished, the pressure in the cooker, especially when canning in glass, should be released slowly. Rapid reduction of pressure in the cooker will cause a great deal of breakage. Allow 20 minutes resting period for glass before opening the petcock.

What to can Can only meat that is in perfect condition, from healthy animals that have been slaughtered in a sanitary, professional way. The flesh of freshly killed animals should be well bled and chilled for at least 34 hours to remove the animal heat. For canning meat in large pieces, use the loin or other cuts suitable for roasting or for steaks or chops. For stew meat, use the less tender cuts of meat and the scraps from the better cuts.

Two methods of canning poultry and meats Poultry and meats may be packed hot and partially cooked or they may be packed raw. Both methods are given in the specific directions that follow, providing that both methods are equally desirable for the particular product.

POULTRY, RABBIT, AND OTHER SMALL GAME

4½ to 5½ pounds of chicken, dressed, undrawn, to be canned with the bone, yield 1 quart jar or 1 No. 3 can.
7 to 8 pounds of chicken, dressed, undrawn, to be boned and canned, yield 1 quart jar or 1 No. 3 can.

Hot pack, with bones Singe the bird and wash it well, but don't soak it in water. Wipe with a clean cloth, draw the bird, and cut the meat into serving pieces. For a quick way to cut up a bird without drawing it, **see Index.** Bone the breast, saw the drumsticks off short, but leave the bones in the other meaty pieces. Discard any large lumps of fat and sort the meat into meaty pieces and bony pieces. Set aside the giblets to can separately. The liquid used to hot-pack poultry is preferably the broth made from the bony pieces of meat.

BROTH: Cover the bony pieces with cold water, bring the water to a boil, and simmer the meat until it is tender. Drain the broth into a bowl and skim off the fat. Strip the meat remaining on the bones to can as little pieces.

Place the meaty pieces of chicken in a large kettle and add hot broth to cover the meat. Cover the kettle and simmer until the meat is medium done, or until almost no pink color shows at the center of the pieces. Stir occasionally so that the pieces will cook evenly.

Salt does not help to preserve canned meat, but it may be added for flavor if you wish. Put 1 teaspoon salt into a quart jar or a No. 3 can; ¾ teaspoon salt into a No. 2½ can; ½ teaspoon salt into a pint jar or a No. 2 can.

First pack the second joints and drumsticks around the container with the skin next to the glass or tin. Fit the breasts into the center and arrange the smaller pieces where needed to pack the can firmly, leaving about 1 inch head space in glass jars and ½ inch in tin cans. Cover the meat with the hot broth, leaving 1 inch head space in jars; fill cans to the top. Work out air bubbles by drawing the blade of a knife up and down the sides of the jar or can and add more broth if needed to cover the meat. Adjust the lids on glass jars. Exhaust cans and seal. Process at 10 pounds pressure:

> Pint jars: 65 minutes
> No. 2 cans: 55 minutes
> Quart jars, No. 2½ or No. 3 cans: 75 minutes

Hot pack, without bones Follow the directions for **hot pack, with bones,** but remove the bones from all the pieces of meat, either when it is raw or after it is precooked. Process boned poultry at 10 pounds pressure:

> Pint jars: 75 minutes
> No. 2 cans: 65 minutes
> Quart jars, No. 2½ or No. 3 cans: 90 minutes

Raw pack, with bones Bone the breast, saw the drumsticks off short, but leave the bones in the other meaty pieces. Set the giblets aside to can separately. Set the bony pieces aside for canned chicken broth.

If salt is desired put 1 teaspoon salt into a quart jar or a No. 3 can; ¾ teaspoon salt into a No. 2½ can; ½ teaspoon salt into a pint jar or a No. 2 can.

Pack second joints and drumsticks around the container, with the skin next to the glass or tin. Fit the breasts into the center, and arrange the smaller pieces where needed to pack the container firmly, leaving 1 inch head space in glass jars; pack cans to the top.

Set the open jars or cans in a large kettle containing hot water to within 2 inches of the top of the containers. Cover the kettle, bring the water slowly to a boil, and cook until the meat is steaming hot and medium done, or for about 50 minutes in cans; 75 minutes in glass jars. For complete accuracy, use a thermometer. When the center of the jar registers 170° F., the meat has been cooked enough. Adjust lids on glass jars; seal tin cans. Process at 10 pounds pressure:

Pint jars: 65 minutes
No. 2 cans: 55 minutes
Quart jars, No. 2½ or No. 3 cans: 75 minutes

Raw pack, without bones Remove the bones from all the meaty pieces of chicken and follow the directions for **raw pack, with bones.** Process at 10 pounds pressure:

Pint jars: 75 minutes
No. 2 cans: 65 minutes
Quart jars, No. 2½ or No. 3 cans: 90 minutes

CANNED QUAIL IN WHITE WINE

Clean, pluck, and singe 6 plump quail and cut off the head and feet. In a heavy kettle put ½ cup diced fat pork and ¼ cup each finely chopped carrots, onions, and celery. Arrange the birds on this bed and add a spray of celery tops and just enough dry white wine to cover. Add 6 peppercorns and ½ teaspoon salt and bring the wine to a boil. Cover the kettle tightly and bake it in a moderate oven (375° F.) for 35 minutes.

Remove the birds from the liquid and pack them in hot sterilized quart jars, 2 to a jar. Strain the cooking liquid and fill the jars with it, leaving 1 inch head space. Adjust the jar lids and process at 10 pounds pressure for 40 minutes.

The quail may be stuffed before they are cooked, if desired. In this case the processing time at 10 pounds pressure should be increased to 60 minutes.

Stuffing Chop the quail livers and cook them in an equal amount of hot butter for 1 minute, stirring constantly. Add ¼ pound fresh lean veal, ¼ pound fresh lean pork, and ⅛ pound fresh fat pork, all finely chopped. Add salt and pepper, 1 crushed juniper berry, and a pinch each of marjoram, thyme, and sweet basil, and cook over a moderate flame for 5 minutes, stirring constantly. Put the mixture through the finest blade of a food chopper, adding as you grind 1 teaspoon each of parsley, chives, and onion. Moisten with 2 tablespoons brandy and ½ teaspoon lemon juice. Stuff the quails, sew up the openings, and truss as you would a chicken.

GIBLETS

Can chicken livers alone. Gizzards and hearts may be canned together. Use only pint jars or No. 2 cans.

Hot pack Cover the giblets with broth made from the bony pieces of chicken or with hot water. Cover the pan and cook the giblets until almost done, stirring occasionally. If salt is desired, put ½ teaspoon into a pint jar or a No. 2 can.

Pack the hot giblets loosely in the jar or can, leaving about 1 inch head space in glass jars; ½ inch in cans. Cover the giblets with the hot cooking liquid, leaving 1 inch head space in glass jars; fill cans to the top. Work out the air bubbles with the blade of a knife, and add more liquid if needed to cover the meat. Adjust the lids on jars. Exhaust and seal the cans. Process at 10 pounds pressure:

Pint jars: 75 minutes
No. 2 cans: 65 minutes

CANNED HOMEMADE PÂTÉ

Cook until tender, in chicken stock to cover, the gizzards, livers, and hearts of the chickens to be canned. Strain, reserving the broth, and put the giblets through the finest blade of a meat grinder several times. Moisten to a paste consistency with a little melted butter, some of the broth, and sherry. Season to taste with salt and pepper if necessary, put the paste into a blender, and blend until the paste is smooth. Reheat, stirring, until the paste is very hot.

Pack the hot paste in ½-pint jars, leaving ½ inch head space. Adjust the jar lids and process at 10 pounds pressure for 60 minutes.

CANNED BEEF, VEAL, PORK, OR LAMB

The untrimmed weight needed to fill a quart jar or a No. 3 can is:
Pork loin—5 to 5½ pounds
Beef rump—5 to 5½ pounds
Beef round—3 to 3½ pounds

For canning large pieces of meat, use the loin or other finer cuts suitable for roasts, steaks, or chops. For stew meat, use the less tender cuts of meat and the smaller pieces trimmed from the better cuts.

The meat may be packed hot or raw. In either case, cut the meat from the bone, and reserve the bones to make stock or soup. Trim away most of the fat without slashing the flesh excessively. Cut the meat into chunks that will fit easily into the jars or cans, always cutting so that the grain will run lengthwise in the container.

Hot pack Put the meat into a large shallow kettle with just enough water to keep the meat from sticking. Cover the pan and cook the meat slowly until it is medium done, turning the pieces occasionally so they will cook evenly.

Salt does not help to preserve meat, but it may be added for flavor. Add 1 teaspoon salt to quart jars or No. 3 cans; ¾ teaspoon salt to No. 2½ cans; ½ teaspoon salt to pint jars or No. 2 cans.

Pack the hot meat in the jars, leaving about 1 inch head space in glass; ½ inch in cans. Cover the meat with the hot meat juice, adding hot broth or boiling water if needed, leaving 1 inch head space in glass jars; fill cans to the top. Work out air bubbles with the blade of a knife, and add more liquid if needed to cover the meat. Adjust the lids on glass jars; exhaust and seal tin cans. Process at 10 pounds pressure:

> Pint jars: 75 minutes
> No. 2 cans: 65 minutes
> Quart jars, No. 2½ or No. 3 cans: 90 minutes

Raw pack If salt is desired, measure it into clean, empty containers. Use 1 teaspoon salt in quart jars or No. 3 cans; ¾ teaspoon salt in No. 2½ cans; ½ teaspoon salt in No. 2 cans. Pack the raw, lean meat in the containers, leaving about 1 inch head space in glass; fill cans to the top.

Set the open containers in a large kettle containing warm water to within about 2 inches of the tops of the containers. Cover the kettle and bring the water to a simmer. Cook for about 50 minutes in cans; 75 minutes in glass jars; or until the meat is medium done. For complete accuracy, insert a thermometer in the center of the container, and when the thermometer registers 170° F., the meat has been cooked long enough.

Press the meat down into tin cans to ½ inch below the top, and add boiling water to fill the cans to the top, if needed. Also add boiling water to glass jars if needed to cover the meat, leaving 1 inch

head space. Adjust glass lids; seal cans. Process at 10 pounds pres
sure:

> Pint jars: 75 minutes
> No. 2 cans: 65 minutes
> Quart jars, No. 2½ or No. 3 cans: 90 minutes

GROUND MEAT

The smaller pieces of meat from the choice cuts, as well as the less
tender cuts of meat, may be ground and canned.

Use only fresh, cold meat, free of fat, and put it through a meat
grinder. Salt may be added if desired: 1 teaspoon to 1 pound of
ground meat. Mix well.

Hot pack   Gently press ground meat into thin cakes that can be
packed in glass jars or tin cans without breaking. Arrange the cakes
on an oiled shallow baking pan and cook them in a moderate oven
(350° F.) for about 30 minutes, or until there is almost no red color
at the center of the cakes. Pack the hot cakes in containers, leaving
1 inch head space in glass; ½ inch in tin. To facilitate the removal
of the cakes from the container, place a round of parchment paper
between cakes.

Skim the fat off the liquid in the baking pan, add hot water to the
pan, and cook, stirring, over a moderate flame until the liquid boils.
Cover the meat with the liquid, leaving 1 inch head space in glass;
fill cans to the top. Work out the air bubbles by running the blade
of a knife up and down the sides of the container, adding a little
more liquid if needed to cover the meat. Adjust lids on glass jars;
exhaust and seal tin cans. Process at 10 pounds pressure:

> Pint jars: 75 minutes
> No. 2 cans: 65 minutes
> Quarts, No. 2½ or No. 3 cans: 90 minutes

Raw pack   Use tin cans only.

Pack raw ground meat firmly into tin cans to the top. Put the open
cans in a large kettle containing hot water to about 2 inches below
the tops of the cans. Bring the water to a simmer, cover the kettle,
and cook for about 75 minutes, or until the meat is steaming hot. For
accuracy, insert a thermometer in the center of one of the cans.
When the thermometer registers 170° F., the meat is done. Press the
meat down to about ½ inch below the top. Exhaust and seal the cans
and process at 10 pounds pressure:

> No. 2 cans: 100 minutes
> No. 2½ or 3 cans: 135 minutes

SAUSAGE

Flavor freshly ground sausage meat lightly with onion, garlic, and spices. Herbs may be used, but it is best to omit sage, as this herb is likely to give a bitter flavor to canned sausage. Shape the meat into cakes and proceed as for **ground meat, hot pack** only.

CORNED BEEF

Wash the corned beef and cut it into suitable lengths for packing. Cover the meat with cold water and bring the water to a boil. If the broth tastes too salty, drain, cover with fresh cold water, and again bring the water to a boil.

Pack the hot meat in containers, leaving 1 inch head space in glass jars; ½ inch in tin cans. Cover the meat with the hot broth or with boiling water, leaving 1 inch head space in glass jars; fill cans to the top. Work out air bubbles with the blade of a knife and add more liquid if needed to cover the meat. Adjust lids on glass jars; exhaust and seal tin cans. Process at 10 pounds pressure:

> Pint jars: 75 minutes
> No. 2 cans: 65 minutes
> Quarts, No. 2½ or No. 3 cans: 90 minutes

MEAT-VEGETABLE MIX FOR STEW

The following proportion of meat and vegetables has been approved for home canning, but your own stew mix can also be successfully canned. Do not spice or season highly.

> 2 quarts stewing meat, cut into 1½-inch cubes
> 2 quarts potatoes, peeled and cut into ½-inch cubes
> 2 quarts carrots, peeled and cut into ½-inch cubes
> 3 cups celery, chopped
> 7 cups onions, 1 inch or less in diameter, peeled

Raw pack   Mix the stew ingredients. If salt is desired, put 1 teaspoon into quart jars or No. 2½ cans; ½ teaspoon salt into pint jars or No. 2 cans. Fill containers with the stew mix to the top.

> IN GLASS: Adjust lids, and process at 10 pounds pressure:
> Pints: 60 minutes
> Quarts: 75 minutes
> IN TIN: Set the open cans in a large kettle containing warm water to within about 2 inches of the tops of the cans. Cover the kettle, bring the water to a simmer, and cook the stew in the cans for about 50 minutes, or until a thermometer placed

in the center of one of the cans registers 170° F. Seal the cans and process at 10 pounds pressure:

No. 2 cans: 40 minutes

No. 2½ cans: 45 minutes

PORK AND BEANS WITH SAUCE

Sort and wash dry kidney or navy beans and soak them overnight in cold water to cover. In the morning, drain, cover with boiling water, and boil for 2 minutes. Set the beans aside and let them soak for 1 hour. Then heat the beans to boiling and drain, saving the liquid for making either a **tomato** or a **molasses sauce (see below)**. Fill containers three quarters full of the hot beans, add a small piece of salt pork, and add sauce, leaving ⅛ inch head space in glass jars; ¼ inch head space in tin cans.

IN GLASS: Adjust the lids on the jars and process at 10 pounds pressure:

Pints: 65 minutes

Quarts: 75 minutes

IN TIN: Set the open cans in a large kettle containing warm water to within 2 inches of the tops of the cans. Cover the kettle, bring the water to a simmer, and cook the beans for about 15 minutes, or until a thermometer inserted in the center of one of the cans registers 170° F. Seal the cans and process at 10 pounds pressure:

No. 2 cans: 65 minutes

No. 2½ cans: 75 minutes

Tomato Sauce

3 cups tomato juice

1 cup bean liquor

2 tablespoons sugar

2 teaspoons salt

1 tablepsoon minced onion

¼ teaspoon mixed cloves, allspice, mace, and cayenne

Combine the ingredients and heat to the boiling point.

Molasses Sauce

1 quart bean liquor

3 tablepsoons dark molasses

1 tablespoon vinegar

2 teaspoons salt

¾ teaspoon ground mustard

Combine the ingredients and heat to the boiling point.

CANNED BAKED BEANS

Sort and wash kidney or navy beans, and soak them overnight in water to cover. In the morning, drain, and cover with fresh cold water. Add 1 onion and 2 cloves garlic, both peeled, a large chunk of fat salt pork, and salt lightly to taste. Bring the water to a boil and simmer the beans for about 1 hour, or until barely tender.

Remove and slice the pork. Cover the bottom of a large ovenproof casserole or crock with the slices of pork, add the beans, and sprinkle with allspice. Dissolve 1 teaspoon mustard in 1 cup of the bean liquor and pour it over the beans. Add more bean liquor just to cover the beans, cover the casserole, and bake the beans in a moderate oven (350° F.) for about 4 hours, adding a little more bean liquor when necessary.

> IN GLASS: Fill jars to within ½ inch of the top with baked beans.
> Adjust jar lids and process at 10 pounds pressure:
> Pints: 80 minutes
> Quarts: 100 minutes
> IN TIN: Fill cans to within ½ inch of the top with the hot baked beans. Exhaust the cans by heating them in simmering water for about 15 minutes, or until a thermometer inserted in the center of one of the cans registers 170° F. Seal the cans and process at 10 pounds pressure:
> No. 2 cans: 95 minutes
> No. 2½ cans: 115 minutes

CANNED SOUP STOCK

Cover bones or chicken or meat with lightly salted water and simmer until the meat is tender and the stock is concentrated. Strain the stock into a bowl and skim off the fat. The shredded pieces of cooked meat may be added if desired. Pour the hot stock into containers, leaving ½ inch head space in glass jars; fill cans to the top. Adjust jar lids; seal cans. Process at once at 10 pounds pressure:

> Pint jars or No. 2 cans: 20 minutes
> Quart jars, No. 2½ or No. 3 cans: 25 minutes

CHAPTER TWO

Fruit Juices, Syrups, Purées, and Vinegars

When the harvest yields more fruits and berries than you can possibly jam, jelly, or freeze, and you can't resist filling the larder even fuller than it is with the lush, inexpensive seasonal crops, the juice of fruits may be simply extracted and bottled for future use. Later it may be made into jelly when your present supply is exhausted, or it may be used as the basis for innumerable fruit-flavored desserts, sherbets, ice creams, puddings, gelatin desserts, and sauces. Served as a carbonated beverage, it is a refreshing relief from the so-called "fruit drinks" made from artificially flavored and colored syrups.

EXTRACTING AND BOTTLING FRUIT JUICES

Select sound, ripe fruit with an agreeable flavor and aroma. Fruit that is insipid will not make good juice. Sort the fruit carefully and discard any that is imperfect.

71

Wash the fruit carefully in cold, running water to remove the dust and dirt found on all freshly picked fruit, especially those that grow close to the ground. The dirt contains bacteria that are hard to destroy.

There are two methods of extracting fruit juice—the cold process and the hot process.

The cold process consists of crushing the fruit by means of a potato masher or a food chopper, then pressing the fruit in a cloth or a fruit press to extract most of the juice. The simplest method of pressing the juice for the small quantities generally wanted for home use is to empty the fruit into a long flannel sac. Both ends of the sac are then twisted tighter and tighter, pressing the juice from the fruit in the center of the sac.

Sometimes, especially in pressing grapes, only the "free-run" juice is desirable. This is the juice found between the skin and the pulp, and only enough pressure is needed to burst the skin and let the "free-run" juice flow, producing a clearer, more fragrant, and delicately flavored juice.

Hot process Heating fruit and berries before pressing them increases the flow of juice, intensifies the color, and results in a more distinctive flavor than when juice is derived from the cold process. Hot pressing also releases and develops the fruit pectin so necessary for the natural jellying of fruit juice. If jelly is to be made later from the preserved juice, the hot-process method of extracting the juice must be used.

For berries and juicy fruits, put half the fruit in a preserving kettle and mash thoroughly with a potato masher. Add the rest of the fruit and heat slowly over a large pan containing hot water. The temperature of the fruit juice should not go above 190° F., and better flavor and color will result if the fruit is not allowed to come into direct contact with the heat. Fruit juices are injured if they are allowed to boil. Longer heating is required to extract the juice from the less juicy fruits, and to those that are quite dry a little water must be added.

Strain the juice through a heavy flannel cloth wrung out of cold water.

Bottles that can be sealed with corks or crown-type caps, or fruit jars with glass or self-sealing lids, may be used for bottling fruit juice. Zinc-topped jars should not be used. Wash and sterilize the containers and stand them in hot water until ready to fill.

Fill hot bottles just to the neck with the juice, leaving 1 inch head

72

space if the juice is hot; 1½ to 2 inches head space if the juice is cold. Fill hot jars to within 1 inch of the top.

If the juice is extremely tart, from 1 to 8 tablespoons sugar per quart of juice may be added according to taste.

Pasteurizing fruit juices To retain the fresh fruit flavor and to prevent the growth of yeasts, the bottled juice should be reheated or pasteurized. Pasteurization differs from sterilization in that below-boiling temperatures are used.

A large preserving kettle or an ordinary old-fashioned washboiler makes a suitable home pasteurizer. Put a rack in the bottom or cover the bottom with a heavy towel to prevent the bottles from coming in direct contact with the bottom of the boiler. Place the bottles on the rack or towel and add warm water to within 2 inches of the tops of the bottles. Heat the water very gradually to 175° F., and keep the water at this temperature for 30 minutes by reducing the flame or by adding cold water from time to time. Cork, cap, or seal the containers and put them in a place free of drafts to cool. Label, and store in a cool, dark place.

FRUIT SYRUPS

Some fruits—such as peaches, pineapple, and strawberries—retain more natural color and flavor if they are made into syrups. The sugar seems to bring out the flavor of these fruits. Fine-flavored syrups for use in carbonated beverages, desserts, or ice cream toppings can be made from these fruits as well as from apricots, blackberries, cherries, currants, raspberries, and pomegranates.

Wash the fruit and crush it in a preserving kettle. Heat the fruit over boiling water to 160° F. and strain the juice through a cloth or jelly bag. Add from 2 to 4 cups sugar for each quart of juice and stir until the sugar is thoroughly dissolved. Fill sterilized jars or bottles to within 1 inch of the top and **pasteurize** in a water bath at 180° F. for 20 minutes. Cap or seal, cool, and store.

FRUIT PURÉES

Use ripe but sound fruit. Wash the fruit and cut larger fruit into sections. Put the fruit in a preserving kettle and heat it very slowly, adding a little water if the fruit is dry to keep it from burning. Simmer until the fruit is soft and press fruit and juice through a sieve or food mill. Stir in sugar to taste and heat the sweetened purée to the boiling point, stirring constantly. Pack the hot purée in hot sterilized jars to within ½ inch of the top. Adjust the lids and process in boiling water for 20 minutes. Seal, cool, label, and store.

APPLE JUICE

One of the most popular fruit juices today is unfermented apple juice, or sweet cider. It is available in such quantities that it seems highly improbable that the average housewife would bother to make it in her kitchen.

Apple flesh is so firm that a small fruit press is essential if a high yield of juice is to be obtained. The apples used should be tart and fine-flavored. The Winesap, Yellow Newton Pippin, Roxbury, Spitzenberg, and Northern Spy all make good cider. The apples must be sound and free from decay or worms. They must be thoroughly washed before they are crushed, to remove the dust that would spoil the juice.

For a small quantity of apple juice, wash the apples and cut them into quarters. Put the apples in a fruit press and extract the juice. Heat the juice to 165° F., cool, and strain through filter paper or through a flannel cloth wrung out of cold water.

Bottle the juice and pasteurize it in hot water at a temperature of 170° F. for 30 minutes. Cork, cool, and store.

The length of time that cider may be kept unpasteurized or open before it ferments and becomes "hard" varies with the amount of fermenting agents present in the juice and the storage temperature.

BERRY JUICE

It is usually advisable to add a small amount of sugar to berry juices, for some—such as loganberry and blackberry juice—if unsweetened lose most of their color and flavor during storage.

Heat berries to 160° F., crush them thoroughly with a potato masher, and strain the juice through two layers of cheesecloth or through a jelly bag. Stir in ½ cup sugar to each quart juice. Bottle and pasteurize in hot water held at a temperature of 175° F. for 20 minutes. Seal, cool, and store.

GRAPE JUICE

Grapes should be crushed as soon as possible after they are harvested. Pick the grapes from the stems and discard any underripe or decayed fruit. Put 10 pounds grapes in a kettle with 1 cup water. Heat the fruit to 165° F., and maintain that temperature until the grapes are soft, or until they will crush easily with a potato masher.

Crush the grapes and strain the juice through a double layer of cheesecloth. Pour the juice into 1-gallon jugs and pasteurize them for 40 minutes in hot water held at a temperature of 165° F. Seal the jugs and let the juice stand for 3 months to allow the tartaric acid to crystallize. Rebottle in smaller containers and pasteurize for 20 minutes in hot water held at a temperature of 160° F. Seal, cool, and store.

TOMATO JUICE

Wash ripe, juicy tomatoes, remove the stem ends, and cut the tomatoes into sections. Simmer the tomatoes until soft, stirring frequently. Press through a strainer or food mill. Add 1 teaspoon salt to each quart of juice and reheat to the boiling point. Pour the boiling juice into hot glass jars to within ¼ inch of the top. Adjust the lids and process in boiling water:

Pints or quarts: 15 minutes

Or pour the boiling juice into tin cans to the top and seal the cans immediately. Process in boiling water:

No. 2 or 2½ cans: 15 minutes

TOMATO PULP OR PURÉE

Wash ripe, juicy tomatoes, remove the stem ends and any green or yellow portions of the tomatoes, and quarter, but do not peel. Simmer the tomatoes until soft, stirring frequently, then put them through a strainer or fine colander. The finer the strainer or colander, the finer the pulp. Separate the first thin juice that runs through the strainer from the thicker purée. Boil the thin portion of the juice in a shallow, open kettle until it is reduced to about half its original volume. Add this to the thicker juice and continue to boil until the desired thickness is reached, stirring frequently.

Fill hot, sterilized jars or cans to the top with the boiling-hot purée. Add ½ teaspoon salt per pint of purée. Adjust the lids of jars. Seal cans immediately. Process in a boiling-water bath:

Pint or quart jars, No. 2 or No. 2½ cans: 10 minutes

ITALIAN TOMATO PASTE

> 4 quarts ripe tomatoes, sliced
> 2 tablespoons chopped sweet basil leaves
> 2 teaspoons salt
> ½ cup chopped celery
> ½ cup chopped carrots
> 1 large onion, chopped
> ½ teaspoon pepper

Combine all the ingredients in a kettle, bring to a boil, and simmer until the vegetables are very soft. Press the mixture through a fine sieve into a heavy-bottomed saucepan and cook over an asbestos mat for about 3 hours, or until the paste is thick. Pour into small jars, adjust the lids, and process in a boiling-water bath for 5 minutes.

Fruit Vinegars

There are dozens of kinds of vinegars—exotic ones, robust ones, fruity ones, subtle ones—and the process of making any one of them is simple and natural.

We usually think only of apples or grapes as the bases of vinegar, but actually any food with a good amount of sugar content can be made into vinegar. Fine vinegars can be made from peaches and persimmons, from pears, oranges, berries, figs, and many other fruits. It may also be made from maple syrup, honey, or molasses.

The process of converting fruit juice into vinegar is both biological and chemical. The chemical changes are caused by living agents, and because these living agents or bacteria are sensitive to their environment, certain care must be taken and certain conditions maintained in the making of fruit vinegars.

Two very separate and distinct transformations take place. The first is familiar to all who know anything about wine. The sugar content of a fruit juice is first converted into alcohol through the fermentation action of yeast. The second is the transformation of the alcohol into acetic acid, or vinegar, by the action of vinegar-producing bacteria.

Both these phenomena are so natural that they will occur all by themselves if fruit juice or wine is allowed to stand open to the air, for there are enough yeast and acetic bacteria in the air to cause the changes. But by utilizing compressed yeast and acetic acid, both the processes may be accelerated and controlled.

TO MAKE FRUIT VINEGAR

First the fruit juice or fruit mash must be prepared. Only ripe fruit should be used, and any decayed or overripe parts of the fruit should be discarded. If spoiled fruit is allowed to go into the batch, the flavor of the vinegar will be injured and unfavorable bacteria will retard the process.

Apples or grapes should be crushed and pressed to extract as much juice as possible. A bushel of apples should yield from 2 to 3 gallons of juice. A bushel of grapes will yield from 2¼ to 4 gallons of juice, depending on the variety and maturity of the grapes.

Peaches and pears should be halved and crushed or mashed. A bushel of tree-ripened peaches or pears should fill a 4-gallon crock about two thirds full.

Persimmons, figs, and other fruit high in sugar and low in moisture must have water added to them. Usually an equal quantity of water by weight can be added and the mash will still retain enough sugar content to make good vinegar.

For home use, straight-sided stone jars holding from 4 to 6 gallons make excellent containers. These must be scoured and scalded each time they are used. Whisky or brandy barrels may be used. Vinegar barrels cannot be used, for the acetic acid remaining from the vinegar will prevent the growth of the yeast necessary for the first transformation of the fruit juice into alcohol. New barrels should be washed with scalding water.

With fruits like apples, grapes, and oranges, where the juice can easily be extracted, the expressed juice should stand for a day or two in containers covered with several layers of cheesecloth to allow the sediment to settle to the bottom. The clear juice is then drained off into other containers for the first step in the making of vinegar—the alcoholic fermentation. If the sediment is not removed at this time, it may interfere with the fermentation process.

The sugar content of some fruits, such as peaches or pears, is more completely utilized, however, if the juice is not separated at all from the pulp during the fermentation period.

Alcoholic fermentation   At ordinary room temperatures fruit sugar changes very slowly into alcohol, because the yeast fungi in

77

fruit juice are very small in number, and because other bacteria are present which slow down the fermentation. This is quite easily overcome by the simple expedient of adding a culture of active yeast. Through the addition of compressed yeast softened in fruit juice, the yeast fungi quickly gain control over other organisms, and the sugar in the juice is changed into alcohol before any other bacteria have an opportunity to attack it.

It is most important that all the sugar be used up before the acetic bacteria are given their chance, for even a very small amount of acetic acid interferes seriously with the growth of yeast. About 1 yeast cake is needed for every 4 gallons or less of mash or juice.

Fill a 4- to 6-gallon crock or barrel two thirds full of juice or crushed fruit. Mix 1 yeast cake thoroughly with a little of the fruit juice and stir the mixture into the fruit mash or juice. The crock or barrel should be stored in a place where it is exposed to a constant temperature of about 70° F. The best results are not obtained if the container is placed in a cold cellar. The opening of the container should be covered with cheesecloth to prevent insects from entering, but it must not be covered tightly. Within a few days a violent fermentation will begin. This is due to the production of carbon dioxide gas, and the mixture should be stirred every day to prevent a crust from forming on the surface. At the end of the fourth day, and each day from then on, the mixture should be tested by means of a sugar hydrometer. When the readings remain the same and do not decrease, it means that all the sugar in the fruit has been converted into alcohol and the fermentation is complete.

If vinegar is being made from fruit mash the juice should, at this time, be separated from the pulp. Strain the juice through cheesecloth into a clean crock.

Acetic fermentation Fill a clean crock or barrel three quarters full of the alcohol-fermented juice. In this case the container may be one that has previously contained good vinegar, for now is the time for the acetic-acid-forming bacteria to take over and convert the alcohol to vinegar. Again this process is a slow one unless it is helped along by the addition of a starter. What better starter could you find than a good vinegar? The vinegar should be unpasteurized. Any good strong vinegar will do, but one containing "mother" is best. Add about one part vinegar to four parts fermented fruit juice. Cover the crock with a double layer of cheesecloth to keep out the dust and, if the crock is kept in a light place, put a lid lightly on top to exclude the light but not the air. Store where the temperature is about 70° F., and in 3 to 6 months all the alcohol will be converted into acetic acid.

After a few days a thin film will appear on the surface of the fermented juice. This is the "mother of vinegar," and care should be taken not to disturb this film. Test the vinegar with a hydrometer and when the hydrometer registers zero in alcoholic content, the vinegar is ready to be used.

As soon as the vinegar is finished it should be filtered and bottled, and stored in a dark, cool, dry place to age. Pour the vinegar through a flannel cloth, wrung out of cold water, several times, or until the vinegar is clear and bright.

Bottling and pasteurizing vinegar While air is so important during the process of turning alcohol into acetic acid, it is only destructive to vinegar once the process is complete. If fine vinegar is exposed to the air it will soon become worthless and unflavorful. Vinegar also attains its greatest flavor if it is allowed to age in closely stoppered bottles from 6 months to 1 year before it is used.

If you have a large amount of vinegar, it is wise to pasteurize it, for this is the best method of preserving the flavor and strength of vinegar.

Submerge sealed bottles on a rack or folded towel in a warm-water bath. Heat the water to from 140° to 160° F. and maintain this temperature for 5 minutes for pint bottles and 10 minutes for quarts.

Small quantities of vinegar do not need pasteurizing. Simply bottle them in convenient-sized containers and cork tightly. Some "mother" may form, but this can be used advantageously when you begin to make another batch of vinegar.

WINE VINEGAR

Wine vinegar is the same product as a vinegar made from grape juice, except that the process is shortened. The sugar content of the grape juice is already turned to alcohol in the fermentation process that turned the juice to wine.

Some wine vinegars are superior to others and the answer to this is easy: the quality of the vinegar is in direct proportion to the quality of the wine used to make the vinegar. So don't feel too upset if some of those vintage wines you've been hoarding have started to sour. True, they are not fit to drink at table, but they will make some of the choicest vinegar you have ever enjoyed.

Wine vinegar can be made from white or red wine, from champagne or vin rosé, or from a combination of them all, but for a pure red or white wine vinegar, do not mix the reds and whites.

Most table wines contain from 12 to 14 per cent alcohol by volume. To make vinegar, the alcoholic content of the wine should be around 8 per cent, so it is necessary to dilute the wine with water.

Stir distilled water gradually into the wine, testing frequently with a hydrometer, until the hydrometer registers 8 per cent alcoholic content. Then pour the wine slowly into a large glass jar through a glass funnel lined with filter paper and filled with white cedar shavings. Repeat this filtering process for 10 to 14 consecutive days, using the same filter paper and shavings. By this time the wine will begin to smell a little sour.

Fill glass containers no more than three quarters full of the aerated wine, cover the tops of the containers with a double thickness of cheesecloth to keep out the dust, and let the wine stand at room temperature for about 8 months. The natural transformation of acetic acid from alcohol is a slow one, but during the time a thin film of organic mold will form on the surface of the liquid. Be very careful not to disturb this film until it grows to the thickness of half a dollar. Then shake the jar and the film will sink to the bottom of the container. This film is the "mother" of vinegar, and each time it develops to the right thickness it should be shaken to the bottom.

Test the vinegar occasionally with a hydrometer. When the hydrometer registers zero alcoholic content, the vinegar is finished. But, like wine, vinegar improves with age. Draw off three quarters of the vinegar and filter it several times through a glass funnel lined with filter paper until the vinegar is sparklingly clear. Bottle, cap, and store the vinegar. Add new wine to the vinegar and mother remaining in the jar for a new supply. This time the process of converting the alcohol to acid will not take so long, as the old vinegar left in the jar will act as a "starter."

QUICK WINE VINEGAR

In order to speed up the transposition of alcohol esters into acetic acid, the wine must be combined with cider vinegar and "mother" of vinegar. If you have a bottle of cider vinegar that has been opened for some time, the chances are that the "mother" has already formed in it. If not, you will have to buy some from a local vinegar plant. Put some of the "mother" of vinegar into a clean crock and add 1 quart each of wine and cider vinegar. Cover with several layers of cheesecloth and let the mixture stand at room temperature for several days. Then add enough wine to fill the container three quarters full and let it stand for 3 to 6 weeks. Test the alcoholic content with a hydrometer, and when the hydrometer registers zero the vinegar is ready to be used. Strain, bottle, and, for best results, let the vinegar age for a few months.

PERPETUAL VINEGAR

Strain a bottle of wine, white or red, into a large crock or jug. Add a little "mother" of vinegar and 1 pint cider vinegar. Cover the crock with several layers of cheesecloth to keep out the dust, and continue to add leftover table wine in small quantities. In about 8 months the vinegar may be bottled for future use and allowed to age, or it may be used directly from the crock. Continue to add leftover wine so that the supply of wine vinegar will be continuous.

VARIETY VINEGARS

Just as there are marked differences between one type of vinegar and another, endless variations of flavors can be developed from any one kind of vinegar. Vinegar may be flavored with herbs—tarragon, basil, sweet marjoram, or chives are the favorites. Cider vinegar gives fine results, but many prefer to use wine vinegar as a base for the herb flavors. Garlics and shallot-flavored vinegars are ideal for use in salads or for adding zest to a sauce or a marinade. Occasionally lovers of the unusual will flavor their vinegar with spices, with lemon, tomato, or pimento juice—sometimes they go so far as to inject a little raspberry or strawberry juice into their favorite brew.

SPICED VINEGAR

In a saucepan combine 1 quart vinegar, 1 teaspoon each of chopped chervil and parsley, ⅛ teaspoon salt, ½ teaspoon each of dry mustard, ground cinnamon, cloves, celery seed, paprika, and mace, 1 bay leaf, 1 clove garlic, mashed, and 2 whole cloves. Bring the vinegar to a boil and simmer for 2 minutes. Cool and filter into a bowl. Let stand for 4 days, strain, and bottle.

HERB VINEGAR

Put into a quart jar 1 tablespoon chopped mint leaves, 1 teaspoon chopped tarragon leaves, 6 tablespoons chopped chives or scallions, 1 tablespoon chopped chervil, 1 teaspoon dry marjoram, 1 small bay leaf, and 1 whole clove. Fill the jar with vinegar, let stand for a week, and then strain through flannel or filter through filter paper. Bottle, seal, and store.

PEPPERY VINEGAR

Put into a quart jar 4 dozen hot red peppers about 1 inch long. Fill the jar with vinegar and seal. Let the jar stand in a warm place for 2 weeks, shaking the jar every day. Strain, bottle, seal, and store.

SPICED RED WINE VINEGAR

To 1 quart red wine vinegar add ½ teaspoon each of grated lemon peel, mace, dry mustard, cinnamon, cloves, white mustard seed, black mustard seed, onion salt, thyme, black pepper, and paprika, and 1 teaspoon celery salt, 1 clove garlic, ½ teaspoon cayenne, and 2 bay leaves. Bring the vinegar to a boil, cool, and strain through filter paper or flannel into a china bowl. Cover the bowl with a clean cloth and let the vinegar stand for 3 days. Again filter or strain the vinegar, pour into sterilized bottles, and seal.

TARRAGON VINEGAR

Pack a quart Mason jar loosely with sprays of fresh tarragon and fill the jar with vinegar. Let stand in a dark place for 10 days. Strain or filter the vinegar, pour into sterilized bottles or jars, and cork or cap. Store in a cool, dark place.

FRESH BASIL VINEGAR

Put 1 cup fresh basil leaves into a heated quart Mason jar and fill the jar with hot vinegar. Seal the jar and let it stand for 2 weeks, shaking the jar each day. Strain the vinegar through flannel or filter it through filter paper and pour into sterilized bottles or jars. Cork or cap the containers and store in a dark, cool place.

MINT VINEGAR FOR SAUCES

Mix 2 cups young spearmint leaves, shredded, with 1 cup sugar and let stand for 5 minutes. Bring to a boil 1 quart fruit vinegar. Add the sugar and spearmint and stir, crushing the leaves against the side of the pan. Simmer for 3 minutes and strain the vinegar through flannel or filter it through filter paper. Bottle and let ripen for several weeks before using.

SWEET, SPICED VINEGAR FOR FRUIT SALADS

To 1 quart vinegar add 2 cups sugar, 1 tablespoon each of chopped cinnamon sticks and white mustard seeds, 1 teaspoon each of allspice, cloves, thyme leaves, and salt, and 4 bay leaves. Bring the vinegar to a boil and pour it over a lime or lemon, thinly sliced. Strain or filter the juice, bottle in sterilized bottles or jars, and cork or cap. Store in a dark, cool place.

GARLIC VINEGAR

Crush 3 large cloves garlic, add 1 quart vinegar, and mix well. Let stand, covered, in the refrigerator for 2 days, then filter or strain, pour into sterilized bottles, and store in a dark, dry place.

RAVIGOTE VINEGAR

Combine 1 teaspoon each of fresh tarragon leaves, chives, and shallots, all finely chopped, ⅛ teaspoon each of grated lemon rind and onion, and 1 clove garlic, mashed. Add 1 quart vinegar and 1 tablespoon brandy and let stand in a warm place for 2 weeks. Filter, bottle, seal or cork, and store in a cool, dark, dry place.

CHAPTER THREE

Preserves

Fruits, sparkling bright and translucent, surrounded by syrup as thick as honey should not be confused with canned fruits. In general, any fruit cooked with sugar—marmalade, jam, or conserve—can be considered a preserve, for the word "preserving" is used to cover the entire field of food preservation. Specifically, a preserved fruit is very different from jam or jelly. It is fruit that has been cooked in syrup until tender and transparent. Whether the fruit is whole or cut into pieces, it should keep its shape in the surrounding syrup. When a preserve is finished, the cells of the fruit are filled with flavorful syrup in place of the natural juice of the fruit.

In order to achieve a perfect preserve one must understand the principles of this particular method of preservation. The juice within the raw fruit and the hot syrup surrounding it are of different densities. As the fruit is cooked in the syrup, the juice is drawn out of the fruit cells into the syrup by a process known as osmosis, and syrup takes its place. This process of give-and-take continues until the syrup within the cells of the fruit and the syrup surrounding the fruit are both of the same density.

84

If the fruit is put into a syrup that is too heavy, the juice will be drawn out of the cells so fast that the syrup does not have a chance to replace it, and the fruit will shrivel and become tough. The outside of the fruit quickly becomes coated with the thick syrup, preventing the syrup from penetrating to the heart of the fruit.

Although scientists have discovered that each different fruit should be individually treated, there are certain fundamental rules that apply to all fruits to be preserved.

Firm-ripe rather than soft-ripe is the perfect maturity for the preserving kettle, and whether the fruit is left whole, halved, quartered, or cut into pieces, the size should be uniform. All the pieces will then cook in the same length of time and the finished preserve will be more attractive.

From ¾ to 1 pound of sugar for each pound of fruit is used in making preserves, and the sugar is added to the fruit in several different ways, depending on the type of fruit used. Juicy fruits and berries may be sprinkled with the sugar and let stand overnight. The sugar draws out the fruit juice, making enough liquid to form a syrup without the addition of any water.

Juicy fruits with a firm skin, such as plums, may be cooked directly in a medium syrup. As the juice cooks out, it thins the syrup to the right degree to let the syrup enter the cells of the fruit.

Firm fruits, such as the quince, require special handling. In the past this fruit was steamed or boiled before it was preserved, but in the precooking a great deal of the delicate flavor of the fruit was lost. Now we know that raw quince or hard apples may be put directly into a thin syrup so that they will have time to cook soft before the syrup becomes too concentrated.

On the other hand, sour or acid fruits may be put into a heavy syrup without danger of crystallization. The acid changes some of the sugar into a form which will not crystallize readily.

During the cooking of any fruit in the syrup it may be necessary to add a little boiling water from time to time. This is especially true if a small amount of fruit is being cooked in a large pan. If the syrup becomes too thick, boiling water should be added about ½ cup at a time.

When the fruit is tender and transparent, sugar syrup has replaced the fruit juice in the cells. At this point the syrup may be allowed to thicken as it boils with the fruit; the cooking evaporates the water in the syrup, concentrating it to a higher density. Or the syrup may be concentrated by alternate cooking and resting periods, for most preserves are improved by standing immersed in the syrup

85

for 12 to 24 hours. This gives the fruit a chance to plump and the syrup to thicken by evaporation of the water in it.

A candy thermometer is useful to determine when the syrup has concentrated to the right degree for packing the fruit in jars. The syrup must be thick, with a density of from 50° to 60° Balling on a saccharometer. When the thermometer registers from 222° to 224° F., this point has been reached for most fruit. For very sour fruits like currants or sour cherries the perfect finishing point is 226° F.

Preserving Fruits and Nuts

GENERAL METHOD

1. Select firm-ripe fruit in perfect condition.

2. Prepare the fruit as you would for the table, slicing large fruit if desired.

3. Drop the fruit into boiling syrup and cook rapidly over a hot fire until the fruit is clear and tender. Fast cooking will result in a product that is sparkling and bright. Slow cooking dulls the fruit and darkens the color. At all times the fruit must be well covered with syrup, and if the syrup gets too thick before the fruit is tender, boiling water should be added, ½ cup at a time.

REMEMBER, the sweeter the fruit, the thinner the starting syrup. The harder the fruit, the thinner the starting syrup.

To make the syrup, dissolve the sugar in the water, bring to a boil, and boil rapidly for 5 minutes.

TO MAKE SYRUPS OF VARIOUS DENSITIES

CHARACTER OF THE FRUIT	CHARACTER OF THE SYRUP TO USE	CUPS OF SUGAR PER 2 QUARTS OF WATER	DENSITY BALLING SCALE
Very Sweet or Very Hard	Very Thin	1	10°
Medium Sweet or Medium Hard	Thin	1¾	20°
Sweet or Slightly Soft	Medium Thin	3¼	30°
Slightly Sour and Soft	Medium Thick	5¼	40°
Sour and Soft	Thick	8	50°
Very Sour	Very Thick	12	60°

4. Continue to cook the fruit until the thermometer registers from 222° to 226° F. At this point the syrup has reached a density of from 50° to 60° Balling—the perfect density for packing preserves.

5. When preserves are packed hot or the fruit is covered with hot syrup, no further processing is necessary. In most cases, when preserves are packed cold it is a wise precaution to process the jars in a water bath. Since the sugar syrup is a preservative in itself, it is only necessary to guard against molds. Processing the jars for about 20 minutes in simmering water (180° to 190° F.) is all that is required to destroy molds. An easier method is simply to cover the surface of the preserves with melted paraffin before capping the jars.

Once the basic principles of preserving are understood, you can add your own touches to make each jar unique and individual. A few maraschino cherries, whole or chopped, or ½ cup seeded raisins add a special touch to pale preserves. Add them a couple of minutes before taking the preserve from the fire. Walnut meats, halved or chopped, hickory nut meats, or blanched almonds may also be added as you take the preserve from the stove.

Pineapple juice or orange juice substituting for part of the water adds additional flavor to bland fruits such as apples, pears, or peaches. Grated orange or lemon rind or a little freshly ground nutmeg points up the flavor of many preserves. Mixed spices tied in a bag—cinnamon or ginger, clove or allspice, or a mixture of them all —may be cooked with any preserve.

When the syrup has been concentrated to the right density, it may be flavored with cognac, rum, dry white wine, sherry, Madeira, or port. To preserve the flavor of the wine or spirit, add it to the syrup after the preserve has been taken from the fire.

Pickled preserves or pickled fruits are made by substituting vinegar for one fourth to one third of the water used to make the syrup. For **pickled fruits, see Index.**

APPLE PRESERVE

Use apples that will hold their shape while cooking. Peel and core 2 pounds apples. Cut large ones in halves or quarters. Leave small ones whole. Peel but do not core crab apples.

Combine 4 cups sugar and 2½ cups water and bring to a boil. Cool the syrup, then add the apples and cook gently until they are transparent. Pack the apples hot into jars. For spiced apple preserve, tie 1 tablespoon crushed ginger root or mixed whole spices, or 12 cloves into a cheesecloth bag and add the bag to the syrup. Continue to boil the syrup until it registers 222° F. on a candy thermometer, discard the spice bag, and pour the hot syrup over the apples. Seal at once.

APRICOT PRESERVE

Wash, peel, and halve 2 pounds firm-ripe apricots. Put the fruit in a kettle with 3¼ cups sugar in alternate layers and let stand overnight. In the morning add ¼ cup lemon juice, heat slowly until the sugar is dissolved, then boil rapidly until the fruit is clear. Let the fruit stand in the syrup for several hours to plump. Pack the cold fruit into hot jars. Reheat the syrup and boil until it is thick, or until it registers 224° F. on a candy thermometer. Pour the hot syrup over the apricots and seal.

BAR-LE-DUC I (Home Style)

Wash and stem large red or white currants. Measure 4 cups currants into a flat pan and pour over them 1 cup currant juice. Bring the liquid to a boil and simmer for 5 minutes. Add 1½ cups sugar, stir gently, and cook slowly for 5 minutes. Add another 1½ cups sugar and boil rapidly for 5 minutes. Let stand until cold. Skim out the currants and pack them into hot jars. Bring the syrup again to a boil and boil until it jellies, or until it registers 222° F. on a candy thermometer. Pour the hot, thick syrup over the fruit and seal.

BAR-LE-DUC II (French Method)

Wash and stem large red or white currants. Remove the seeds by piercing the bottom of each berry with a toothpick and forcing the seeds through the opening. Measure 2 cups currants into a saucepan. Add 1½ cups strained honey, bring to a boil, and simmer for 5 minutes. Skim the fruit into small hot jars and place the jars in a pan of hot water to keep warm. Simmer the honey until it is reduced to a fairly heavy syrup, pour the syrup over the currants, and seal.

BERRY PRESERVE I

Select uniform berries, large and firm. Sort them carefully and wash lightly by putting them in a colander and letting cold water run over them.

Put 2 pounds berries into a preserving kettle, sprinkle with 1¾ pounds (3½ cups) sugar, and let stand overnight. In the morning heat the berries slowly to the boiling point, then boil rapidly for 10 to 12 minutes, or until the berries are tender and the syrup almost jells (222° F. on a candy thermometer). Skim the surface of the liquid, pour into hot jars, and seal.

BERRY PRESERVE II

(Suitable for Blackberries, Loganberries, Boysenberries, Youngberries, and Currants)

Wash and pick over the berries. Measure 6 cups berries into a preserving kettle and add 5 cups sugar. Mash a few berries in the bottom of the kettle to start the juice flowing. Bring slowly to a boil, then boil rapidly for 8 minutes. Add ½ cup lemon juice and boil rapidly for 8 minutes longer, occasionally stirring gently. Let the fruit stand in the syrup overnight, stirring occasionally while cooling. Pour into jars, paraffin, and seal. **See also sun-cooked strawberry preserve.**

CANTALOUPE PRESERVE

Cut firm-ripe melons crosswise into 1-inch slices. Remove the rind and cut the slices into uniform pieces. Mix 2 pounds of prepared melon with 1½ pounds sugar, cover, and let stand for 12 hours, or overnight, in a cool place. Add the juice of 2 lemons and heat slowly to the boiling point, then boil rapidly until the fruit is tender and clear and the syrup is thick, or until it registers 222° F. on a candy thermometer. Pack into hot jars and seal.

CHERRY PRESERVE

To each pound pitted cherries use from ¾ to 1 pound sugar, depending on the sourness of the fruit. Mix the cherries and the juice saved from the pitting with the sugar and let stand overnight. In the morning, heat the cherries to the boiling point and boil rapidly for 15 to 20 minutes, or until the cherries are tender. Let the cherries stand in the syrup until cold, then pack the cherries in hot jars. Bring the syrup back to the boil and cook until it is thick, or until it registers 224° F. on a candy thermometer. Pour the hot syrup over the cherries and seal. **See also sun-cooked strawberry preserve.**

CHERRY CURRANT PRESERVE

Mix 1 quart each of pitted cherries and stemmed currants with from 7 to 8 cups sugar. Seven cups is plenty if the cherries are sweet. Let stand for 2 to 3 hours. Heat the fruit slowly to the boil, then boil rapidly until the cherries are clear and tender. Pack the fruit into hot jars and continue to boil the syrup until it is thick, or until it registers 224° F. on a candy thermometer. Pour the hot syrup over the cherries and seal.

BRANDIED CHERRIES

Soak 2 pounds cherries in ice water for 30 minutes, then drain and stem. Dissolve 2 cups sugar in 2 cups water, bring to a boil, and boil the syrup rapidly for 5 minutes. Add the cherries, bring again to a boil, and let the syrup boil up 3 times, stirring gently with a long wooden spoon. Fill sterilized pint jars three fourths full of fruit and syrup and cool. When the syrup is almost cool fill each jar to the top with brandy and seal. Turn the jars upside down overnight, then store in a cool, dark place for 3 months before using.

MARASCHINO-TYPE PRESERVED CHERRIES

Wash, stem, and pit light cherries such as Royal Ann. Save the juice and the pits. Place the cherries in a shallow pan and cover them with a syrup made of 2 cups sugar and 1 cup cherry juice for each pound of cherries. If there is not enough juice, use water. Add a few drops of red vegetable coloring to the syrup, bring the syrup to a boil, and simmer for 10 minutes. Remove from the heat and let the cherries plump in the syrup overnight.

In the morning drain the cherries from the syrup and pack them in jars. Measure the syrup, and for each quart of syrup crush ½ cup of cherry pits. Tie the pits in cheesecloth and add them to the syrup. Bring the syrup to a boil and boil until it is thick, or until it registers 222° F. on a candy thermometer. Pour the hot syrup over the cherries and seal.

PRESERVED CHESTNUTS

With a sharp knife slit the shells of large chestnuts. Put the nuts in a saucepan, cover with cold water, and bring the water to a boil. Remove the pan from the fire and, without draining, peel the chestnuts one by one and remove the inner skins while the nuts are still hot. Cover the peeled nuts with water, bring to a boil, and cook for 30 minutes. Drain.

For each quart of nuts, make a syrup of 1 cup sugar, 2 cups honey, and 1 cup water and boil the syrup for 10 minutes. Add the chestnuts and boil them for 10 minutes. Let the chestnuts stand in the syrup overnight, then cook them until tender, adding boiling water if necessary ½ cup at a time to keep the syrup from becoming too thick. Pack the nuts into hot jars, add vanilla to the syrup to taste, and cook the syrup until thick, or until it registers 222° F. on a candy thermometer. Pour the hot syrup over the chestnuts and seal at once. The syrup may be flavored with brandy or rum instead of vanilla. Pour the liquor over the nuts before filling the jars with hot syrup.

CITRON MELON PRESERVE

Citron melon is similar to a small round watermelon, and it belongs to the same species. It should not be confused with the tree-borne citron, the thick spongy rind of which is used extensively for candying.

Cut a citron melon crosswise into ½-inch-thick slices. Trim off the green rind and discard the seeds. Split the slices, keeping the inner and outer sections separate. The two parts should be preserved separately, for the outer, more solid section requires longer cooking.

Weigh out 2 pounds of fruit, cover with water, and bring the water to a boil. Cook the citron for 25 to 35 minutes and drain. Dissolve 2 cups sugar in 4 cups water, bring to a boil, and add the citron. Cook the citron in the syrup for 45 minutes, then let the fruit stand overnight in the syrup.

In the morning add 2 cups sugar and 1 lemon, thinly sliced, and cook until the citron is tender. If the syrup becomes too thick, before

91

the citron is tender, add a little boiling water. Pack the melon into hot jars and continue to boil the syrup until it is thick, or until it registers 222° F. on a candy thermometer. Pour the hot syrup over the fruit and seal.

PRESERVED COCONUT

Combine 1 cup milk from the coconut, 3 cups water, and 3 cups sugar. Bring to a boil and boil for 5 minutes. Add 4 cups grated coconut to the syrup and cook until it is transparent. Pack the coconut and syrup in hot jars and seal.

CRAB APPLE PRESERVE

Select sound, well-colored crab apples. Wash and remove the blossom ends, but leave the stems and skins. In a preserving kettle combine 6 cups sugar and 3 cups water, bring to a boil, and boil for 5 minutes. Add as many crab apples as the syrup will take, but the syrup must cover the apples at all times. Cook the crab apples slowly for about 30 minutes, or until tender and transparent. Pack the apples in hot jars and continue to cook the syrup until it is thick, or until it registers 224° F. on a candy thermometer. Pour the hot syrup over the fruit and seal.

CRANBERRY PRESERVE

Bring to a boil 1⅛ cups sugar and 1½ cups water. Add 1 quart cranberries and cook until the skins crack. Pack the berries into hot jars and continue to boil the syrup until it is thick, or until it registers 226° F. on a candy thermometer. Pour the hot syrup over the berries and seal.

CURRANT PRESERVE

Stem 4 quarts currants. Put 2 quarts currants in a preserving kettle, add ¼ cup water, and simmer the currants gently for 15 minutes, mashing them occasionally with a potato masher during the cooking period. Strain the juice through a jelly bag and measure the juice. Measure 2 cups sugar to each cup juice. Simmer the juice for 10 minutes, skimming frequently, add the sugar, and when the syrup comes to a boil, add the remaining 2 quarts currants. Simmer until the whole currants are tender. Ladle the currants into hot jars and continue to cook the syrup until it is thick, or until it registers

226° F. on a candy thermometer. Pour the syrup over the currants and seal. **See also Bar-le-Duc, cherry currant preserve** and **sun-cooked strawberry preserve.**

FIG PRESERVE

Peel the figs as thinly as possible. For each pound figs, make a syrup of from ¾ to 1 pound sugar, 3 cups water, and 2 tablespoons lemon juice. Bring the syrup to a boil, add the figs, and boil rapidly until the figs are transparent. If the syrup becomes too thick before the figs are clear, add boiling water ½ cup at a time. Let the figs stand in the syrup overnight to plump. In the morning pack the figs in hot jars. Bring the syrup to a boil and boil until it is as thick as honey, or until it registers 224° F. on a candy thermometer. Pour the hot syrup over the figs, seal, and process the jars in a simmering water bath for 15 minutes.

One lemon, thinly sliced, may be substituted for the lemon juice. Spices may also be added to the hot syrup. A good combination is 1 stick of cinnamon and 12 cloves for each pound of fruit. Tie the spice in a cheesecloth bag before adding it to the syrup.

SUN-COOKED FIG PRESERVE

Select figs that are not too ripe and peel them thinly. For each pound of figs, combine 1 pound sugar and 3 cups water and bring to a boil. Add the juice and grated rind of 1 lemon. Put in the figs and simmer slowly for 30 minutes. Turn the figs and syrup into a large, shallow dish, cover with cheesecloth, and set the figs in the sun outdoors or in a sunny window for 2 hours. Next day bring the figs and syrup to a boil, simmer for 30 minutes, and again set them in the sun for 2 hours. Repeat on the third day. The fruit will now be quite transparent and the syrup will be thick. Pack into jars, seal, and process in a simmering water bath for 15 minutes.

BRANDIED FIGS

Sprinkle ½ cup baking soda over 3 quarts firm-ripe figs. Pour 3 quarts boiling water over the figs and let stand for 15 minutes. Drain and rinse the figs in several changes of fresh, cold water. Drain again and dry the figs in the sunshine if possible.

Combine 5 cups sugar and 8 cups water. Bring the liquid to a boil, skim and boil for 10 minutes. Add the figs gradually to the boiling syrup and cook gently for about 1 hour, or until transparent. Ladle the figs into a shallow pan and continue to cook the syrup until it is very thick, or until it registers 222° F. on a candy thermometer. Pour the syrup over the figs and let them stand overnight to plump.

In the morning pack the figs into hot, sterilized pint jars and add ¼ cup brandy to each jar. Return the syrup to the fire and cook until it again registers 222° F. on a candy thermometer. Pour the hot syrup over the figs, seal the jars, and store in a cool, dark spot.

If the cold thick syrup is poured over the figs in the jars, the jars should be sealed and then processed in simmering water for 15 minutes.

FRENCH BRANDIED FRUITS

Wash, scald, and thoroughly dry a 1-gallon porcelain or earthenware crock. Put in the crock 4 cups strawberries, washed, drained, and hulled, 2 cups sweet cherries, stemmed and pitted, 2 cups diced fresh pineapple, and 2 cups peeled, stoned, and quartered peaches. Add 1 stick of cinnamon, 5 cups light brown sugar, and 5 cups granulated sugar. Stir the mixture gently with a long wooden spoon and let it stand for several hours, stirring occasionally until the sugar is melted. Add 16 blanched almonds or peach pits and about 1 quart brandy, or enough to cover the fruit well. Seal the crock and store it in a cool, dry, dark place for 6 months.

BRANDIED FRUIT MÉLANGE

Wash and scald a large, wide-mouthed earthenware jar, fill it with hot water, add ¼ pound washing soda, and let stand overnight. In the morning empty the jar, rinse it several times and wipe dry.

Pour a fifth of good brandy into the jar and add 1 tablespoon mixed spices, such as clove, allspices, and cinnamon bark, and 1 tablespoon grated lemon, orange, or grapefruit rind.

Wash, drain well, and hull 1 quart perfect strawberries, add them to the jar with their own weight in sugar, and let the fruit stand for 1 week. Then add 1 quart each of hulled raspberries and stemmed cherries along with their weight in sugar. Continue to add fruit and sugar as the fruit comes in season, remembering gooseberries, black-berries, peaches, pears, plums, and grapes. Add more brandy from time to time to keep the fruit covered with liquid at all times. Add spices to taste as the jar fills with fruit and sugar. When the jar is full, cover with a plate to hold the fruit under the liquid. Tie down and store in a cool, dry place for 3 months.

Brandied fruit mélange makes an excellent sauce for desserts, ho¹ or cold. It will not spoil if stored in a cool place and kept well covered. If it suits your storage facilities better, pack it into sterile pint jars and seal.

GINGER ROOT PRESERVE

Wash green ginger roots and soak them in cold water for 1 hour. Cover with fresh water, bring to a boil, and boil for 5 minutes. Drain, again cover with fresh cold water, bring to a boil, and boil for 5 minutes. Repeat this process several times, depending on whether a mild- or a strong-flavored preserve is desired. Then boil the ginger until it is tender, and cool in cold water for about 1 hour.

Drain the ginger roots and put them in a syrup made by combining 2 cups sugar and 1 cup water for every pound of ginger roots. Bring the syrup to a boil, boil for 5 minutes, then let the ginger stand in the syrup, submerged by means of a china plate, overnight.

In the morning drain off the syrup, bring it to a boil, and boil for 10 minutes. Pour the syrup over the ginger and let stand for 2 days. Bring syrup and ginger roots to a boil, cook for 5 minutes, and let stand, covered, for 2 to 3 days to plump. By this time the ginger roots should be tender, clear, and bright, and the syrup very thick. Pack the ginger into hot jars and heat the syrup to the boiling point. If the syrup is not as thick as it should be, cook it until it registers 222° F. on a candy thermometer. Pour the syrup over the ginger, seal the jars, and store in a dark, cool spot.

GOOSEBERRY PRESERVE

Make in the same manner as **Bar-le-Duc.**

WHITE GRAPES IN COGNAC

Select large, white California grapes. Wash the firm-ripe fruit and cut each grape in half, extracting the seeds. Cook the seeds in water to cover for 15 minutes, strain, and use this liquid to make the syrup.

For 2 pounds prepared grapes combine 2 cups of the liquid and 2 cups sugar, bring to a boil, and boil for 5 minutes. Add the grapes and cook rapidly until the grapes are tender and transparent. Pack the grapes into pint jars and pour into each jar ¼ cup cognac or *fine champagne*. Continue to cook the syrup until it is thick, or until it registers 222° F. on a candy thermometer, pour the syrup into the jars to overflowing, and seal. Store the jars in a dark, cool place.

GROUND CHERRY PRESERVE

Wash, husk, and drain 2 quarts of "ground" cherries. Combine 6 cups sugar, 3 cups water, and the juice of 2 lemons, bring to a boil, and boil 5 minutes. Cool the syrup, add the cherries, and bring the syrup again to a boil. Boil until the cherries are clear and the syrup is thick. Pack in jars and seal.

GUAVA PRESERVE

Select fine-flavored, thick-meated fruit. If the skins are unblemished, they do not need to be peeled; merely remove the blossom ends. Although the peel is good to eat, the finished preserve looks better if the guavas are peeled. Cut the fruit in half and scoop out the seed center. Save this pulp to make **guava butter.**

For each pound of prepared fruit use from ¾ to 1 pound sugar and ¼ cup water. Add the sugar and water to the fruit and let stand for 3 to 4 hours, or until the sugar is thoroughly dissolved. For a spiced conserve, add ginger root or a few slices of lemon. Bring the syrup and fruit to a boil and cook until the fruit is transparent. Let stand overnight. Bring the fruit again to a boil and pack it hot into jars. If the syrup is not thick enough, concentrate it by further cooking and pour it over the guavas. Seal and process pint jars in simmering water for 5 minutes.

PRESERVED KUMQUATS

Wash 1 pound kumquats in warm, soapy water. Sprinkle them with ½ tablespoon baking soda, pour over them enough boiling water to cover, and let stand for 10 minutes. Pour off the water and rinse the kumquats three times in cold water.

Make 4 deep slits in one end of each kumquat. Place the kumquats in water to cover, bring the water to a boil, and boil for 15 minutes. Drain, add fresh water, and boil for another 15 minutes. Drain, again add fresh water, and repeat the boiling process until the fruit is tender.

Combine 2 cups each of sugar and water, bring to a boil, and boil for 5 minutes. Add the kumquats to the boiling syrup and cook until the fruit is transparent and the syrup registers 222° F. on a candy thermometer. Remove the kettle from the heat and let the kumquats plump in the syrup overnight. Reheat fruit and syrup to the boiling point. Pack the kumquats in jars, strain the syrup over them, and seal the jars while hot.

LOQUAT PRESERVE

Wash 1 pound loquats. Scald the fruit in boiling water, peel, and remove the seeds. Dissolve ¾ pound sugar in 1½ cups water, bring to a boil, and cook for 5 minutes. Add the fruit and cook rapidly until the fruit is transparent and the syrup registers 226° F. on a candy thermometer. Pack in hot jars and seal.

MANGO PRESERVE

Select fruit that is just beginning to show color. Peel the mangoes and cut into sections. For each pound of sliced fruit, dissolve 1 pound of sugar in 4 cups water, bring to a boil, and boil for 5 minutes. Add the mangoes and cook rapidly until the fruit is clear. Let stand until cold. Return to the fire and continue to cook until the syrup registers 222° F. on a candy thermometer. Again let stand until cold. Pack the fruit in jars, cover with the syrup, and seal. Process the jars in simmering water for 15 minutes.

MIXED FRUIT PRESERVE

Wash 1 cup red currants and cook them with 2 tablespoons water until soft. Strain the currant juice through cheesecloth. Wash and drain 2 cups each of strawberries and loganberries. Pit 2 cups sweet cherries. Weigh the berries and cherries and add an equal amount by weight of sugar. Pour the currant juice over the fruit and sugar and let stand overnight in a cool place.

In the morning, heat the fruit slowly to a boil, then boil rapidly for about 12 minutes, or until the syrup registers 222° F. on a candy thermometer. Again let the fruit stand overnight, stirring occasionally as it cools. In the morning, heat fruit and syrup to the scalding point, but do not let it boil, pour hot into hot jars, and seal.

PEACH PRESERVE

Dip peaches into boiling water, peel, and cut them into halves or quarters, discarding the pits. For every 2 pounds prepared peaches combine 3 to 4 cups sugar and 2 cups water, bring to a boil, and boil the syrup for 2 minutes. Cool. Add the peaches, bring the syrup again to a boil, and cook rapidly until the fruit is tender and clear. Let the fruit stand in the syrup for several hours or overnight to plump. Pack the peaches in the jar and cook the syrup until it registers 222° F. on a candy thermometer. Pour the syrup over the peaches in the jars and seal.

BRANDIED PEACHES

Wash and peel the peaches. Halve and pit if desired. Weigh the peaches and measure out 1 pound sugar and 1 cup water for every pound of fruit. If the peaches are unpitted, allow only ½ pound sugar to every pound of fruit.

Combine the sugar and water, bring to a boil, and boil rapidly for 5 minutes. Add a few peaches at a time and cook them for 5 to 10 minutes, or until they can be pierced easily with a straw. Remove the fruit and pack in hot jars. Continue until all the peaches have been cooked. Then continue to boil the syrup until it is thick, or until it registers 222° F. on a candy thermometer. Cool the syrup and add 1 pint brandy for every pint of syrup. Stir well and fill the jars to overflowing with the brandy syrup. Seal the jars at once.

Pears may be brandied in the same way.

PRESERVED PEARS

Wash and peel the pears. Leave them whole or halve or quarter them and remove the cores. For each pound of prepared fruit make a syrup of 1½ cups sugar and 1½ cups water. Add the pears to the syrup, bring to a boil, and cook until the fruit is clear and tender and the syrup registers 224° F. on a candy thermometer. Let the fruit stand overnight in the syrup to plump. In the morning bring the syrup back to a boil and pack the fruit into hot jars. Continue to cook the syrup until it again reaches 224° F., fill the jars to overflowing with the hot syrup, and seal.

A sliced lemon, a few cloves, or a stick of cinnamon may be added to the cooking syrup. Pineapple juice used instead of water adds additional flavor.

GINGERED PEARS

Peel and core 5 pounds hard pears and slice the fruit lengthwise. Add 3 cups water and cook until the pears are tender. Add 5 pounds sugar, ½ cup chopped preserved ginger, and the grated rind and juice of 3 lemons and cook until the fruit is clear and the syrup is thick, or until the syrup registers 222° F. on a candy thermometer. Pack hot into hot jars and seal.

Hard varieties of **apples** are excellent prepared in the same way.

PINEAPPLE PRESERVE

Peel a pineapple and remove the eyes. Slice the pineapple in half, remove the core, and cut the flesh into squares or long sticks. Mix 2 pounds pineapple with 3 cups sugar and let stand overnight. In the morning, bring to a boil and cook until the pineapple is clear and the syrup is thick, or until it registers 224° F. on a candy thermometer. Pack hot in hot jars and seal.

PLUM PRESERVE

Wash and drain the plums. Either cut the plums in half and remove the pits or leave them whole and prick each plum several times with a large darning needle. For every 2 pounds plums combine 1½ cups water and 3 to 4 cups sugar. Add the plums and let them stand for several hours or overnight. Bring the syrup to a boil and cook until the plums are tender and the syrup registers 222° F. on a candy thermometer. Pack hot in hot jars and seal.

PUMPKIN PRESERVE

Quarter a pumpkin and discard the seeds and inner fibers. Slice the pumpkin ¼ inch thick and trim off the outer skin. Then cut the slices into pieces from 1 to ½ inch square. To 5 pounds pumpkin chips add 4 pounds sugar and let stand overnight. In the morning add 3 lemons, thinly sliced, and ½ teaspoon salt, bring the syrup to a boil and cook until the pumpkin is clear and tender and the syrup is thick, or until it registers 222° F. on a candy thermometer. Pack hot in hot jars and seal.

QUINCE PRESERVE

Wash, pare, and core the fruit. The quinces may be left in halves or they may be quartered or sliced. Combine 1¾ cups sugar with 2 quarts water, bring to a boil, and boil for 5 minutes. Add 2 pounds prepared quinces and boil slowly for 1 hour. Let stand for 24 hours. Add 1¾ cups sugar, bring again to a boil, and cook slowly until the fruit is tender and clear and a rich red color. Let stand overnight. In the morning pack the fruit into hot jars. Bring the syrup to a boil and cook until it registers 222° F. on a candy thermometer. Pour the hot syrup over the fruit and seal.

RASPBERRY PRESERVE

Prepare as for **berry preserve** or **sun-cooked strawberry preserve.**

RASPBERRY STRAWBERRY CHERRY PRESERVE

Mix 2 cups each of raspberries, strawberries, and pitted cherries and weigh. Sprinkle the fruit with an equal weight of sugar and let stand overnight. In the morning add ½ cup lemon juice, bring to a boil, and cook rapidly until the fruit is clear and tender. Cover and keep in a cool place overnight. Pack cold into jars and seal with paraffin. The syrup will appear to be too thin, but it will thicken upon standing.

RHUBARB PRESERVE

Combine 3 cups sugar and 1 cup water, bring to a boil, and cook until the syrup reaches the hard-crack stage, or until it becomes brittle when a drop is put into cold water. Add 1 quart diced rhubarb and cook until the fruit is tender and clear and the syrup registers 224° F. on a candy thermometer. Turn into hot jars and seal.

STRAWBERRY PRESERVE

Wash and hull the strawberries and weigh 2 pounds into a preserving kettle. Add 5 cups sugar and let stand for 4 hours. Bring to a boil, add ¼ cup lemon juice, and cook rapidly for 12 minutes. Cover and let stand in a cool place overnight. Pack the berries into jars, bring the syrup again to a boil, and cook until it is thick, or until it registers 224° F. on a candy thermometer. Pour the hot syrup over the berries and seal.

SUN-COOKED STRAWBERRY PRESERVE

Put ½ cup hot water in a kettle, add 2 pounds sugar, and bring to a boil, stirring until the sugar is dissolved. Add 2 pounds cleaned and hulled strawberries and simmer the berries for 2 minutes. The berries will lose their color and shrink. Pour the berries and syrup into a large shallow dish or platter. Cover the platter with glass or netting to keep out insects and let stand in the sun for 3 days, taking them in at night. If the sun is extremely hot, move the preserve into the shade during the noon hours. On the third day the color will return to the berries, they will plump and be firm. The syrup will almost jell. Pack into sterilized jars without reheating. Be careful to deal only with 2 pounds of fruit at a time, but several 2-pound batches may be sunning at the same time.

Other fruits that may be sun-preserved are: **dark pitted cherries, currants, red raspberries,** or a **combination of ⅔ currants and ⅓ raspberries.**

TOMATO PRESERVE

> 5 pounds ripe tomatoes
> 4 pounds sugar
> 2 lemons, thinly sliced
> ¼ teaspoon salt

Scald the tomatoes and slip off the skins. Put the tomatoes in an enamel bowl or crock, add the sugar, and let stand overnight. In the morning drain off the juice and boil it rapidly until it spins a thread. Add the tomatoes and lemons and cook until the fruit is clear and the syrup is thick. The tomatoes should be a rich red in color. Seal in hot jars. A stick of cinnamon and a few pieces of ginger root may be added to the syrup if desired.

GOLDEN TOMATO PRESERVE

> 1 pound yellow pear tomatoes
> 1½ cups sugar
> Grated rind and juice of 1 orange
> 1 lemon, thinly sliced

Scald the tomatoes and slip off the skins, being careful not to crush the fruit. Put the tomatoes and sugar in an enamel bowl, cover tightly, and let stand overnight. In the morning drain off the juice, add the orange juice and rind, and boil until the syrup spins a thread. Add the tomatoes and lemon and cook until the tomatoes are clear and the syrup is thick. Pack into hot jars and seal.

WATERMELON MARBLES

Cut the pink flesh of a watermelon into little balls with a French potato ball cutter and soak them overnight in a very weak alum water, allowing 1 ounce alum to 4 quarts water. In the morning pour off the water. Weigh the fruit and allow three fourths as much sugar as fruit, 1 lemon, thinly sliced and the slices quartered, for each pound of fruit, and 1 ounce ginger root for every 3 pounds fruit. Put all the ingredients into a preserving kettle and add just enough water to melt the sugar. Bring slowly to a boil and add more water if there is not enough syrup to cover the fruit. Cook until the melon balls are clear and pack them into hot jars. Continue to cook the syrup until it is thick, or until it registers 224° F. on a candy thermometer. Pour the syrup over the melon balls and seal.

CRISP WATERMELON RIND PRESERVE

Cut the red portion of the melon from the rind and remove the green outer skin. Cut the white rind into 1-inch pieces and soak them for 3 hours in lime water made by dissolving 1 tablespoon slaked lime (obtainable at your drugstore) in each quart of water needed to cover the rind. Drain and let the rind stand in fresh cold water for 1 hour, changing the water several times. Drain and cook in fresh water for 1½ hours, or until tender. Drain and weigh the rind.

For every 2 pounds watermelon rind make a syrup of 4 cups sugar, 8 cups water, and the juice of 1 lemon and bring to a boil. Add the waterlemon rind and, if desired, 4 small pieces of ginger root and boil gently for about 1 hour. Add 1 lemon, thinly sliced, and continue to cook until the rind is transparent and the syrup is as thick as honey. If the syrup gets too thick before the rind is clear, add boiling water ½ cup at a time. Let stand for several hours to plump, bring again to a boil, and pack hot in hot jars. Seal at once.

SOFT WATERMELON RIND PRESERVE

If watermelon rind is soaked overnight in salted water instead of several hours in lime water the resulting preserve has a texture similar to that of preserved pears.

Cut the red portion of the watermelon from the rind, remove the green outer skin, and cut the white part into small pieces. Soak the rind overnight in a salt solution made by dissolving 2 tablespoons salt to each quart of water needed to cover the rind. In the morning drain and soak the rind for 2 hours in ice water. Drain carefully and dry between towels.

For every 2 pounds of watermelon rind cook 4 cups light brown sugar in 2 cups water for 10 minutes. Add the rind and cook until it is tender but not soft. Remove the rind and pack in hot jars. To the syrup add 2 lemons, thinly sliced, and 1 teaspoon ground ginger and cook until the syrup is thick, or until it registers 222° F. on a candy thermometer. Pour the hot spiced syrup over the rind and seal.

Candying Fruits and Nuts

Candied fruits—either crystallized or glacéed—may be prepared at home, but it is an exacting and lengthy process. They belong in this chapter, for the principles involved are the same as those applied to fruit preserves. The fruits are slowly impregnated with syrup, the syrup is finally concentrated to an even greater density than for preserves, and finally the fruit is dried and either rolled in granulated sugar or dipped in a syrup glaze. Crystallized candied fruits have a coating of tiny sugar crystals, while glacéed candied fruits have a hard smooth shining coat of sugar syrup.

Many fruits are excellent for candying and the technique is basically the same for all of them. Royal Ann, Lambert, and Bing cherries, Bartlett pears, Golden Delicious and Northern Spy apples, Golden Transparent gage plums, Reine Claude plums and Italian plums, Elberta peaches as well as apricots, quinces, pineapples, kumquats, whole figs, whole Seckel pears, crab apples, and watermelon rind are all good.

The fruit is allowed to soak in a thin syrup until the syrup gradually replaces the fruit juice in the cells of the fruit. The fruit will absorb gradually more and more syrup, but care must be taken that the starting syrup is not too heavy, and the density must be increased very slowly. A small amount of corn syrup should be used in the syrup to prevent hard sugar crystals from forming, but too much will make the finished fruit sticky and less flavorful.

Fruits to be candied should be firm-ripe and sound. Too soft fruit will not hold its shape during the processing.

GENERAL METHOD FOR CANDYING FRUITS

1st day *Step 1.* Prepare the fruit. Peel and quarter apples, pears, or quinces and remove the cores. Peel peaches and apricots, halve or quarter, depending on the size, and discard the stones. Halve and stone plums. Stem and pit cherries. Leave figs, Seckel pears, and crab apples whole.

To prevent fruit from discoloring, drop it as soon as it is cut into cold water in which has been dissolved either ½ teaspoon ascorbic acid (**see Index**) or 1 tablespoon salt for each 2 quarts water. Work with not more than 2 pounds fruit in one batch, but several batches or batches of different fruits may be started at the same time.

Step 2. Put 2 pounds prepared fruit into just enough boiling water to cover it. Bring the water to a boil and boil rapidly for 3 minutes. This is sufficient parboiling for most fruits. Quinces, however, should be parboiled from 5 to 8 minutes.

Drain the fruit in a colander, saving the water to make the starting syrup. Make a syrup of 3 cups sugar and 3 cups liquid. If the liquid in which the fruit was cooked is not enough, add hot water to make the required amount. Heat the syrup and as soon as the sugar is dissolved, add the drained fruit and bring just to a boil. Do not boil, for longer cooking would make the fruit too soft. Turn the fruit and syrup into a china or porcelain bowl, which has been rinsed in hot water, place a china plate on top of the fruit to keep it submerged in the syrup, and let stand for 24 hours. The syrup must cover the fruit. Any parts of the fruit exposed to the air will harden and discolor.

2nd day *Step 3*. Drain the syrup from the fruit and add ½ cup each of sugar and corn syrup. Heat the syrup and, as soon as the sugar is dissolved, add the fruit and bring the syrup to a boil. Pour fruit and syrup into the bowl and again let it stand for 24 hours.

3rd day *Step 4*. Drain the syrup from the fruit and add 1 cup sugar. Heat the syrup and, as soon as the sugar is dissolved, add the fruit and bring the syrup to a boil. Pour the syrup and fruit into the bowl and let it stand for 24 hours.

4th day *Step 5*. Repeat Step 4.

5th day *Step 6*. Repeat Step 4, but let the fruit soak in the syrup for 48 hours.

7th day *Step 7*. Repeat Step 6.

9th day *Step 8*. The syrup should now be as thick as honey. If it is not, drain the syrup from the fruit, bring it to a boil, and boil until it registers 228° F. on a candy thermometer. Pour the hot thick syrup over the fruit and let it stand for 7 days.

16 day *Step 9*. Drain the fruit in a colander, saving the syrup, and dip colander and fruit into simmering water for 3 seconds to remove the surface syrup. Place the pieces of fruit on cake racks to dry.

The syrup may be used in place of sugar in canning or preserving or it may be diluted with water and used as the starting syrup for a fresh batch of the same kind of fruit to be candied. *To reuse the syrup for candying:* Dilute 3 parts of the syrup with 1 part water and begin again with Step 2.

DRYING CANDIED FRUITS

The fruit should be dried until no syrup exudes from the center of the fruit. The surface will remain sticky. Drying in the sunshine is the best way, for it preserves the natural fruit color and results in a brighter fruit. If it is necessary to dry the fruit indoors, put the racks in a cool oven (100° F.) for 8 to 10 hours. The oven door must be left open to provide ventilation. Or the fruit may be allowed to dry at room temperature for 2 to 3 days.

FINISHING CANDIED FRUITS

Crystallized fruit is the easiest to finish. Before the fruit is completely dry, roll each piece in granulated sugar and complete the drying.

Glazed fruit—quick method Combine 2¼ cups sugar and ¾ cup water, bring to a boil, and boil for 3 minutes. Lift each piece of candied fruit on a fork and dip it into the syrup. Place on racks to harden and dry at room temperature for 24 hours or in hot sunshine or a cool oven (100° F.) for about 4 hours.

Glazed fruit—long method This method gives the fruit longer keeping qualities. When the fruit is dry after the final heavy syrup, dip the pieces into warm water for 1 second, drain, and dry at room temperature for 24 hours. Then combine 1 cup liquid pectin and 1½ cups warm water. Dip the fruit into the pectin solution, drain, and dry again at room temperature for 24 hours or in hot sunshine or a cool oven (100° F.) for about 4 hours.

Dissolve 3 cups sugar in ¾ cup water, bring the syrup slowly to a boil, and boil until it registers 228° F. on a candy thermometer. Pour a little syrup into a cup, keeping the rest of the syrup tightly covered over hot water. Lift each piece of fruit on a fork and dip it into the syrup in the cup. Place the fruit on wire racks. The minute the syrup in the cup begins to be cloudy, set it aside and pour a little more of the hot clear syrup into another cup. Repeat until all the fruit has been glazed. It is small crystals of sugar that form as the syrup cools that makes the syrup cloudy and unless the dipping syrup is warm and clear, the glaze on the fruit is apt to become translucent instead of transparent.

Dry the dipped fruit at room temperature for 24 hours, in hot sun-

105

shine, or in a cool oven (100° F.) for 4 hours. Turn the fruit occasionally until it is dry on all sides.

Candied fruits may be stuffed with raisins, dates, fondant, or nut meats before they are glazed.

OTHER FINISHES

Candied fruit may be dipped in fondant or in chocolate, in this case the glaze is not necessary. Or they may be dipped in fondant, or stuffed with fondant and glazed, or coated with chocolate.

Fondant

> 3 cups sugar
> 1 cup hot water
> ⅛ teaspoon cream of tartar

Combine the sugar, water, and cream of tartar in a heavy 2-quart saucepan. Stir over a low flame until the sugar is dissolved, then increase the heat and cook rapidly, without stirring, until the syrup registers 238° F. on a candy thermometer, or until a few drops of the hot syrup form a soft ball in cold water. During the cooking wash down the crystals that form on the sides of the pan with a brush moistened with water or with a fork wrapped in a damp cloth.

When the syrup registers 238° F., pour it at once onto an enamel-top table or marble slab to cool. When the center of the fondant is lukewarm to the hand, work the fondant vigorously with a spatula until it becomes white and firm. Then knead the fondant until it is soft and creamy and let it ripen in a tightly covered jar at room temperature for 2 days before using it.

The fondant may be flavored with vanilla, almond, or coffee extract, or with rum, kirsch, kummel, anisette, or cognac, and it may be lightly colored with vegetable colors.

To dip candied fruits in fondant Flavor about 1 cup fondant with any flavoring desired and stir it over a low flame until it is just warm to the touch. The fondant should be just thick enough to coat the candied fruit with a thin layer, yet thin enough to flow smoothly. If it is too thick, stir in a little warm water.

Keep the fondant warm over hot water. With a fork lift the fruit, one piece at a time, and lower it into the fondant. Place the fruit on wax paper to dry for 1 hour or more. If fondant-coated candied fruit is to be dipped in chocolate, the fondant should be allowed to dry and set for several hours.

Chocolate-coated candied fruits About ½ pound of dipping chocolate is needed for every 2 pounds of candied fruit. Melt the chocolate in the top of a double boiler over hot, not boiling, water. The chocolate must not be allowed to get too hot, nor should it be allowed to come in contact with any escaping steam from the lower vessel. Too high temperature or humidity will cause the chocolate coat to be streaked with white when it cools. The chocolate should not be heated over 110° F. and the perfect temperature of the room is between 65° and 70° F.

With a fork lift each piece of candied fruit and dip it into the melted chocolate. Lift it out, let the chocolate drip off until only a thin coat remains, and place the fruit on wax paper to dry.

STORING CANDIED FRUITS

The storage life of candied fruits, even under ideal circumstances, is not over 3 months. Wrap each piece in wax paper and store in wooden boxes lined with wax paper.

CANDIED FRUIT PEEL

Citrus fruit peels may be candied by the **general method for candying fruits.** Orange, lemon, and grapefruit peel must, however, be cooked in boiling water for about 60 minutes, or until tender. For grapefruit peel, several changes of water are necessary to rid the peel of excess bitterness. Corn syrup should replace the sugar in at least 2 steps, to produce a soft, moist product.

Candied orange, lemon and grapefruit peel Select citrus fruit with brightly colored, thick peel, free of blemishes. Wash the fruit and rub the surface with a fine grater to break the oil cells. Remove the peel and cut it into strips. Cover the strips with cold water, bring to a boil, and simmer for 10 minutes. Drain, cover with fresh cold water, and bring to a boil. If the peel is orange or lemon, it needs no further change of water—simply boil it for about 60 minutes, or until it is tender. If the peel is grapefruit, the boiling process must be carried out in several changes of cold water to remove the bitterness. Sometimes as many as 6 or 7 changes of water are needed for a mild-flavored peel. Begin with cold water each time. Finally, when the peel tastes just right, continue to boil it until tender.

For each pound of peel dissolve 1 cup each of sugar and corn syrup in 2 cups water and bring to a boil. If artificial color is desired, add 3 drops of vegetable coloring to the syrup. Boil the syrup until it registers 220° F. on a candy thermometer. Add the peel and cook until it becomes transparent. The syrup should not be allowed to get above 220° F., so it may be necessary to add 1 tablespoon boiling water from time to time. If the peel is cooked too long or if the syrup becomes too concentrated, the peel will become hard. To test the peel for doneness, take a strip from the syrup as soon as it has become transparent, roll it in granulated sugar, and let it cool. If the peel stiffens enough to hold its shape as it cools, it should not be cooked longer.

Remove the peel from the stove, weigh it down with a china plate and let it soak in the syrup for 24 hours. Return the peel to the stove, bring the syrup to a boil, and boil until the syrup registers 226° F. Let the peel soak in the syrup for 48 hours, then pack peel and syrup in jars and store for 4 to 6 weeks.

At the completion of the storage and plumping period, return peel and syrup to the stove, bring to a boil, and boil until the syrup registers 228° F. on a candy thermometer. Place the peel on wire cake racks to drain and dry for several days in the hot sun, or for 24 hours in a cool oven (100° F.). The oven door must be left open to allow for circulation of air. When the peel is almost dry, roll it in granulated sugar and complete the drying. Cool and pack in wooden boxes lined with wax paper.

A quick method to candy grapefruit peel Prepare the grapefruit peel, cover it with a solution of 2 parts water and 1 part lime water, and boil for 30 minutes. Drain, cover with fresh water, and cook for another 30 minutes. Repeat with fresh cold water until the peel does not taste too bitter. About 3 changes of water will give a characteristic bitter flavor. For a mild-flavored peel, change the water 5 or 6 times. Drain and gently press out excess moisture.

For each pound of peel dissolve 1 cup each of sugar and corn syrup in 2 cups water. Add the peel, cook slowly for 1 hour and let the peel soak in the syrup for 48 hours. Bring the syrup again to a boil and boil until the syrup registers 228° F. on a candy thermometer. Drain the syrup from the peel, roll the peel in granulated sugar, and let it dry for several days at room temperature. Store in airtight jars or cans.

CANDIED KUMQUATS

Wash and scrub kumquats in soap and water and rinse thoroughly to remove any trace of soap. Sprinkle 2 tablespoons baking soda over 2 quarts kumquats, cover with water, and let them soak in the soda solution for 20 minutes. Drain, rinse again in several changes of cold water and slit each kumquat on one side through to the seeds.

Dissolve 4 cups sugar in 4 cups water and bring to a boil. Add the kumquats and simmer for 30 minutes. Remove from the fire, weigh the fruit down with a china plate to keep it submerged, and let it cool and plump for 24 hours. Drain off the syrup and add to it 1 cup each of sugar and corn syrup. Bring to a boil, add the fruit, and simmer until the kumquats are plump and transparent. Again submerge the fruit in the syrup and let it plump for 24 hours. Next day boil the kumquats in the syrup for 30 minutes and let cool.

Lift the kumquats from the syrup and place them on racks to dry in hot sun or in a cool oven (100° F.). The kumquats may then be stuffed with fondant or nut meats and rolled in granulated sugar or dipped in glaze.

CANDIED ANGELICA

Gather the stalks in early spring when they are still tender. Discard the leaves and root ends and place the stalks in a flat deep pan. Pour over them a boiling salt solution made by dissolving 1 tablespoon salt in each 2 quarts water. Let the angelica soak for 15 minutes, drain, and rinse several times in fresh cold water. Drain, cover with boiling water, and cook from 5 to 6 minutes, or until tender.

When tender, drain and scrape off the outer skin from the stalks. Make a syrup of 2 cups sugar and 2 cups water, bring to a boil, and boil for 5 minutes. Pour the syrup over the angelica, weigh the stalks down with a china plate, and let them soak for 24 hours.

Continue according to the **general method for candying fruits** beginning with Step 3. At the end of Step 9, remove the angelica from the syrup and place on racks to dry. Dry in the hot sun or in a cool oven (100° F.). When dry, dip the angelica into a syrup glaze (**see section "Finishing Candied Fruits"**) and again dry in the oven or in the hot sunlight. Store in glass jars in a cool, dark, dry spot.

CANDIED CHERRIES

Select firm-ripe sweet cherries, free from blemishes. Napoleon and Royal Ann are the best varieties for candied cherries. The cherries must first be bleached, then dyed to produce a uniformly colored candied cherry. Commercially, the cherries are bleached with sulphur dioxide, but for home methods a brine made of chemicals easily available at a drugstore is more satisfactory.

Ask your druggist to compound for you a mixture of:
180 grains of U.S.P. precipitated chalk
882 grains of sodium bisulphite
1080 grains of U.S.P. citric acid granular
Dissolve these chemicals in 10 cups water to make the bleaching "brine."

Stem the cherries and put them into quart jars. A quart jar will hold about 1 pound of cherries. Cover the cherries with the bleaching solution and close each jar with a rubber ring and the lid. Place the filled jars in a cool place for 6 weeks. At the end of this time the cherries will be yellow instead of red.

Drain the cherries, rinse, and pit them. Boil the cherries for 30 minutes, changing the water several times until it is free from the taste of sulphur. The method for candying cherries is the same as the **general method for candying fruits.** Begin by preparing the starting syrup as in Step 2. Red coloring should be added to this syrup to dye the cherries. For 2 pounds of fruit, add 7 grains of ponceau 3 R certified food color dissolved in a little water. Follow the steps given in the general method for candying fruits through Step 7. Now is the time to flavor the cherries and the flavoring is put into the final syrup. Commercial cherries are flavored with benzaldehyde, but many prefer a mixture of benzaldehyde, oil of neroli, and oil of rose. These flavoring oils are available at a drugstore.

For 2½ quarts cherries and syrup, ask your druggist to mix 30 drops pure benzaldehyde in ½ ounce alcohol. To this mixture may be added, if desired, 2 drops each of oil of neroli and oil of rose.

Drain the syrup from the fruit and stir in flavoring to taste. If the syrup is not as thick as honey, bring it to a boil and boil until it registers 228° F. on a candy thermometer. Pour the hot thick syrup over the cherries and let them stand for 6 or 7 days before drying and coating the fruit with syrup glaze. A special glaze is used for cherries.

Syrup glaze for candied cherries

2 cups sugar
½ cup corn syrup
1 cup water

Combine the ingredients, bring to a boil and boil briskly for 6 minutes, without stirring, or until the syrup registers 310° F. on a

110

candy thermometer. Set the pan containing the boiling syrup into cold water to stop the boiling, then put it into a pan of very hot water while the cherries are being glazed.

Tiny circles of **watermelon rind** may be candied in the same way as cherries. When colored red, they make an excellent substitute for candied cherries.

CANDIED CITRON

The thick, spongy rind of the citron, the fruit of a subtropical evergreen tree, candied and either crystallized or glazed, is used extensively in holiday fruitcakes and plum puddings.

Pick citron that is well developed but still green. Cut the fruit in half or quarters and discard the center. Soak the rind in cold water for 24 hours, changing the water several times. Then soak it for 2 hours in a lime solution made of 2 parts water and 1 part lime water. Bring the lime water to a boil and boil the citron peel for 30 to 40 minutes. Drain, rinse in cold water, and drain again.

Drop the citron into a syrup made of equal amounts of water and sugar, bring to a boil, and boil the citron for 50 to 60 minutes. There must be enough syrup to cover the peel. Remove the citron and weigh it. For each pound of citron add 1 pound of sugar to the syrup. Heat the syrup slowly until the sugar is dissolved, then add the citron, bring the syrup to a boil and boil for 10 minutes. Let the citron plump in the syrup for 24 hours. Drain off the syrup, bring it to a boil, and cook until it registers 228° F. on a candy thermometer. Cool the syrup, add the citron, and let it soak in the syrup overnight. Bring the syrup just to a boil and cool before removing the citron to wire racks to dry.

Dry the citron for several days in the hot sunshine if possible. If not, put it in a cool oven (100° F.) with the oven door open for 24 hours.

BRANDIED CHERRIES IN CHOCOLATE COATING

Wash and dry thoroughly large, perfect sweet cherries. Pack them loosely, stems up, in quart jars and pour over them the following syrup:

Cook together 3 cups sugar and 1 cup water until the syrup registers 228° F. on a candy thermometer. Cool slightly and measure the syrup. For each cup syrup add 1½ cups brandy.

Seal the jars and store the cherries for 6 months.

Drain the cherries, saving the syrup to use with fresh fruit cup. Melt bittersweet dipping chocolate over hot water. Dip the cherries, one by one, into the chocolate and put them on wax paper to harden. Store them in tins, packing them carefully with wax paper strips between layers.

CANDIED CHESTNUTS (Marrons Glacés)

Chestnuts may be candied in the same manner as the **general method for candying fruits.** The chestnuts must first be shelled and the inner skins removed. To do this cut through the shells of large perfect chestnuts with a sharp knife, making a slit around each one. Place them in a saucepan, cover with cold water, and bring the water to a rolling boil. Remove the pan from the fire and, without draining, take the chestnuts from the pan, one by one, and remove the shell and inner skin before the nut has a chance to cool. Drop the chestnuts into fresh cool water to which a little lemon juice has been added and let them soak overnight. In the morning, drain the nuts, cover them with fresh water, and cook for about 30 minutes or until they are tender but still firm. They may then be put into the starting syrup, Step 2 in the **general method for candying fruits,** and the process continued through the 16 days. A little shorter method follows:

For each 2 pounds of cooked chestnuts make a syrup of 3 cups sugar and 3 cups water. Bring the syrup to a boil and boil for 5 minutes. Add the nuts and simmer them for 10 minutes. Remove from the fire and let the nuts stand overnight in the syrup, submerged by means of a china plate. Next day drain off the syrup, add ½ cup each of sugar and corn syrup and a split vanilla bean, and bring the syrup to a boil. Add the chestnuts, heat the syrup again to the boil, and let the nuts cool in the syrup for another 24 hours.

Next day drain the syrup from the nuts, add 1 cup sugar, and heat until the sugar is dissolved. Add the nuts and bring the syrup to a boil. Again let the nuts cool in the syrup for 24 hours.

Finally drain the nuts from the syrup, place them on wire racks, and dry them in a cool oven (100° F.) with the oven door open.

Boil the syrup until it is very thick, or until it registers 228° F. on a candy thermometer. Spoon the syrup over the nuts, little by little until it is all used. Continue to dry the nuts until the syrup is no longer sticky and store in jars until ready to use.

GLAZED NUTS

Combine 1 cup water, ½ cup corn syrup, and 2 cups sugar. Bring the syrup to a boil and boil briskly for 12 minutes, without stirring, or until it registers 310° F. on a candy thermometer. Immediately lower the pan in cold water to stop the boiling, and then put the pan over boiling water to keep hot while the nuts are being glazed. Drop a few nuts into the syrup, pick them out with long tweezers, and place them on oiled platters to dry. If the syrup becomes too thick before all the nuts are glazed, add about 1 tablespoon hot water and again bring the syrup to a boil.

CHAPTER FOUR

Jams, Conserves, Butters, and Pastes

The word "jam" may have originated from the Arabian word *jamad*, for preserved fruit, or from the English "to jam," or "crush together." The controversy has never been settled, but it is of little concern to those of us who simply would like to distinguish one preserve from another. Fruit and sugar, cooked rapidly to a thick consistency, without conscientious effort to retain the shape of the fruit or berry is JAM and, when properly made, is bright, sparkling, easy to spread, and of a jellylike consistency.

Small batches of jam may be easily and quickly prepared from canned or frozen fruits or from fresh fruits at the peak of their harvest, alone, or combined with out-of-season frozen or canned fruits and juices to make new and unusual flavors.

HOW TO MAKE JAM

1. Wash and sterilize jelly glasses and keep them warm.
2. Prepare the fruit. Wash, stem, and crush berries. Peel, stone,

and finely chop or crush whole fruits. Cook solid-fleshed or under-ripe fruits with a little water for about 10 minutes, or until soft.

3. Measure fruit, put it in an enamel preserving kettle, and bring it slowly to a boil. There must be sufficient fruit juice or water to keep the fruit from sticking to the bottom of the kettle.

4. Stir in sugar equal to the amount of the fruit or three fourths as much sugar as fruit and, when necessary, 2 tablespoons lemon juice to each pound of fruit.

5. Boil rapidly, stirring constantly, to the jellying point (see Index), or to 222° F. at sea level (10° F. above the boiling point of water).

6. Pour into the hot glasses and seal with a thin layer of paraffin. Let cool overnight and add a second thin layer of paraffin. (To paraffin, see Index). Wash the outsides and rims of the glasses and cover with the lids, or tie rounds of white paper over the tops.

7. Store in a dark, cool dry place.

A QUICK REFERENCE CHART OF POPULAR JAMS
WILL BE FOUND ON THE PAGES FOLLOWING.

POPULAR JAMS AND THEIR VARIATIONS—WITHOUT ADDED PECTIN

1 quart (2 pounds) fruit purée + 3 cups (1½ pounds) sugar = about 5 8-ounce glasses
1 quart (2 pounds) fruit purée + 4 cups (2 pounds) sugar = about 6 8-ounce glasses

Cook jam rapidly, stirring, to the jellying point (222° F.), or 10° F. above the boiling point of water.

MAIN INGREDIENT	PREPARATION	TO EACH QUART PREPARED FRUIT (2 LBS.) STIR IN	JAM VARIATIONS
APPLES	Pare, quarter, and peel tart apples. Add water to cover parings and cores, cover, and cook 30 minutes. Drain liquid over apples, cook until soft, press through a sieve, and measure.	3 cups sugar Juice and grated rind of 1 lemon or orange	1. APPLE GINGER. Add ¼ cup chopped, preserved ginger.
APRICOTS	Wash, scald, skin, pit, crush, measure, and heat.	3 cups sugar 1 tablespoon lemon juice	1. APRICOT RASPBERRY. Combine 3 cups crushed apricots and 1 cup strained raspberry purée. 2. APRICOT BLACKBERRY. Combine equal parts crushed apricots and strained blackberry purée.

116

BERRIES Boysenberries Dewberries Loganberries Raspberries Youngberries Blackberries	Wash, pick over, crush, and measure. To each quart add ¼ cup water or fruit juice, cook until soft, and press through a fine sieve.	3 to 4 cups sugar
BLACKBERRIES	Wash, pick over, crush, and measure. Add 3 cups sugar to each quart fruit, stir, and let stand for 1 hour before cooking.	2 tablespoons lemon juice	1. BLACKBERRY APPLE. Combine blackberries with half their weight of thinly sliced tart apples.
BLUEBERRIES	Wash, pick over, crush, measure, and heat.	3 cups sugar	1. BLUEBERRY CRAB APPLE. Combine equal quantities crushed blueberries and cooked crabapple purée. 2. SPICED BLUEBERRY. Add the juice of ½ lemon and ¼ teaspoon allspice.
CARROTS	Wash, pare, grate, and measure.	3 cups sugar Juice of 1 lemon	1. ORANGE CARROT. Add the juice and grated rind of 1 orange.
CHERRIES	Wash, stem, pit, crush, measure, and heat.	3 to 4 cups sugar ¼ cup lemon juice	1. CHERRY RASPBERRY. Combine equal parts cherries and strained raspberry purée.

117

MAIN INGREDIENT	PREPARATION	TO EACH QUART PREPARED FRUIT (2 LBS.) STIR IN	JAM VARIATIONS
CRAB APPLES	See Apples		
CRANBERRIES	Mash and cook until soft in just enough water to prevent sticking, press through a sieve, and measure.	3 cups sugar	1. CRANBERRY ORANGE. Add grated rind of 1 orange. 2. CRANBERRY RAISIN. Add 1 cup seedless raisins. 3. SPICED CRANBERRY. Add ½ cup vinegar, ½ teaspoon each clove and allspice, and 1 teaspoon cinnamon.
CURRANTS	Wash, stem, simmer until soft in just enough water to prevent sticking, press through sieve, and measure.	4 cups sugar	1. CURRANT GOOSEBERRY. Combine equal quantities currants and cooked gooseberries, or sieved raspberry purée. 2. SPICED CURRANT. Add 1 cup vinegar, ½ teaspoon clove, 1 teaspoon cinnamon, and ¼ teaspoon each nutmeg and salt.
DAMSON PLUMS	Wash and cook until soft in just enough water to prevent sticking, press through a sieve, and measure.	3 cups sugar	

118

ELDERBERRY	Wash, stem, crush, measure, and heat.	3 cups sugar 2 tablespoons lemon juice or vinegar	
FIGS	Stem and scald ripe figs in boiling water for 5 minutes. Drain, crush or chop, and boil for 20 minutes with just enough water to prevent burning. Measure.	3 cups sugar ¼ cup lemon juice	1. FIG HONEY. Substitute honey for the sugar. 2. FIG LEMON OR ORANGE. Add 1 lemon or orange, thinly sliced. 3. GINGERED FIG. Add ¾ cup chopped nut meats and ¼ cup chopped preserved ginger.
GOOSEBERRIES	Wash, stem, remove blossom end, mash, and measure. Add 1½ cups water to each quart fruit and boil until soft.	3 to 4 cups sugar	1. GOOSEBERRY CURRANT. Add 1 cup red currant juice. 2. GOOSEBERRY BERRY. Combine equal quantities cooked gooseberries and cooked, sieved blackberries or blueberries.
GRAPES	Wash, stem, and press pulp from skins. Chop skins and boil 20 minutes in just enough water to prevent sticking. Cook pulp until soft, press through sieve to remove seeds, combine with skins, and measure.	3 cups sugar	1. GRAPE ORANGE. Add grated rind and juice of 1 orange and ½ cup chopped raisins. 2. SPICED GRAPE. Add 1 cup vinegar and ½ tablespoon each ground cinnamon and clove.

MAIN INGREDIENT	PREPARATION	TO EACH QUART PREPARED FRUIT (2 LBS.) STIR IN	JAM VARIATIONS
GUAVAS	Wash and cook fruit in just enough water to prevent sticking. Press through sieve to remove seeds and measure.	3 cups sugar	
HUCKLEBERRIES	See Blueberries		
LOQUATS	Wash, scald, peel, and seed. Put through food chopper and measure. Add 2 cups water to 1 quart fruit and cook for 10 minutes.	3 cups sugar ¼ cup lemon juice	
MAY HAWS	Wash, stem, and cook until soft with just enough water to prevent sticking. Press through sieve to remove seeds and measure.	3 to 4 cups sugar	
MULBERRIES	Stem. Cover with cold salt water (¼ cup salt to 1 quart water), let stand 5 minutes, and rinse in 3 changes of cold water. Crush, simmer until soft with just enough water to prevent sticking, and measure.	3 cups sugar ¼ cup lemon juice or vinegar	1. SPICED MULBERRY. Add ½ teaspoon cinnamon.

PEACHES	Wash, peel, stone, crush, and measure. Add ¼ cup water or orange juice to each quart fruit and boil 10 minutes.	3 cups sugar 2 tablespoons lemon juice	1. PEACH PINEAPPLE. Combine equal quantities cooked peaches and pineapple. 2. PEACH PLUM. Combine equal quantities cooked peaches and plums.
PEARS	Wash, peel, core, crush, and measure. Add ¼ cup water or orange juice to each quart fruit and boil 10 minutes.	3 cups sugar ¼ cup lemon juice	1. PEAR APPLE. Combine equal quantities cooked pears and cooked tart apples or pineapple and the grated rind of 1 lemon.
PINEAPPLE	Peel, core, and chop fresh fruit and measure. Add ½ cup water to each quart fruit and cook until soft.	3 cups sugar	1. PINEAPPLE RHUBARB. Combine equal quantities cooked pineapple and sliced rhubarb. 2. PINEAPPLE APRICOT. Combine equal parts cooked pineapple and fresh, sliced apricots.
PLUMS	Cut in half and cook until tender. Press through sieve to remove pits and measure.	3 cups sugar	1. PLUM PEACH. Combine equal quantities cooked plum purée and peaches, and 1 lemon, thinly sliced.
QUINCES	Wash, peel, core, chop, and measure. Add ¼ cup water to each quart fruit and boil for 10 minutes.	3 cups sugar	1. GINGERED QUINCE. Add ½ cup chopped crystallized ginger and the rind and juice of 1 lemon.

MAIN INGREDIENT	PREPARATION	TO EACH QUART PREPARED FRUIT (2 LBS.) STIR IN	JAM VARIATIONS
RASPBERRIES	Wash, sort, hull, mash, measure, and heat.	3 cups sugar	1. RASPBERRY CURRANT OR CHERRY. Combine equal quantities mashed raspberries and cooked, sieved currants or cherries.
RED CURRANTS	See Currants		
RHUBARB	Cut stalks into ½-inch slices, add 3 to 4 cups sugar to each quart fruit, and let stand overnight.	Grated rind and juice of ½ lemon	1. RHUBARB STRAWBERRY. Combine equal quantities sliced rhubarb and crushed strawberries.
STRAWBERRIES	Wash, cap, crush, measure, and heat.	3 cups sugar ¼ cup lemon juice or 1 cup red currant juice	1. STRAWBERRY GOOSEBERRY. Combine 3 cups crushed strawberries and 1 cup cooked gooseberries. 2. STRAWBERRY CHERRY OR PINEAPPLE. Combine equal quantities strawberries and crushed cherries or cooked pineapple.
TOMATOES	Peel, chop, heat, press through a sieve, and measure.	3 cups sugar, white or brown, 1 cup vinegar, 1 cup seedless raisins, chopped, and 1 teaspoon each cloves, allspice, and cinnamon tied in a bag.	

APPLE OR GOOSEBERRY AND RAISIN JAM

> 5 pounds apples or gooseberries
> 5 pounds sugar
> 3 oranges, seeded and put through food chopper
> 2 pounds seeded raisins, chopped

Peel apples and put the peeled apples or the gooseberries through a food chopper, saving the juice. Put juice and fruit in a preserving kettle and stir in the sugar and oranges. Bring slowly to a boil, add the raisins, and cook for about 1 hour, or until thick, stirring frequently. Pour into hot jars and seal.

APRICOT PINEAPPLE JAM

> 1 pound dried apricots
> 1 fresh pineapple
> ¾ cup sugar to each cup prepared fruit
> 16 maraschino cherries, halved

Soak the apricots in water to cover until soft. Pare and core the pineapple. Drain the apricots, put apricots and pineapple through a food chopper, saving the juice, and measure fruit and juice.

In a heavy kettle combine fruit, juice, and sugar and stir until the sugar is dissolved. Add the cherries and bring to a boil. Cook over low heat for 25 to 30 minutes, or until the fruit is clear and the jam is thick, stirring occasionally. Pour into hot jars and seal.

BLUEBERRY CURRANT JAM

Put 1 quart blueberries, washed and drained, through a food chopper. Add 1 cup water, bring to a boil, and cook for 6 minutes. Wash 1 pint currants and, without removing the berries from the stems, cook them with 1 cup water very slowly in a covered saucepan for 8 minutes. Press the currant pulp and juice through a fine sieve to remove stems and seeds. Mix the currant pulp and the cooked blueberries, bring to a boil, and cook for 5 minutes. Add 3 cups sugar and boil rapidly until the jam will sheet from the edge of the spoon. Pour into sterilized jars and seal while hot.

CANTALOUPE ORANGE JAM

    5 cups diced cantaloupe
    2 oranges, peeled and sliced
    3 tablespoons lemon juice
    1 teaspoon grated orange peel
    1 teaspoon grated lemon peel
    4 cups sugar

In a heavy kettle combine the cantaloupe, sliced oranges, and lemon juice, bring to a boil, and boil rapidly for 15 minutes. Add the orange and lemon peel and sugar and cook rapidly until the jam is thick and clear, stirring frequently. Pour into hot jars and seal.

SPICED FIG JAM

    5 pounds fresh figs
    3½ cups sugar
    1 lemon, thinly sliced
    4 2-inch sticks cinnamon
    2 teaspoons whole cloves
    2 teaspoons whole allspice
    2 1-inch pieces ginger root

Wash the figs and cover them with boiling water for 1 minute. Drain, rinse in cold water, and peel thinly. Combine the figs, sugar, lemon, and the spices, tied in a bag, in a large preserving kettle. Bring slowly to a boil and cook slowly for about 1 hour, or until the jam is thick, stirring frequently. Discard the spice bag, pour the jam into hot jars, and seal.

GOOSEBERRY CURRANT JAM

Head and tail the gooseberries and pick the currants from the stems. Measure the fruit and put it in a preserving kettle with an equal amount of sugar. Bring to a boil slowly, stirring frequently at first to blend the sugar with the fruit and later to keep the jam from sticking, and cook until the jam is thick. Pour into hot jars and seal.

124

MIXED FRUIT JAM I

  1 quart stoned dark cherries
  1 pint picked red currants
  1 pint stemmed and tailed gooseberries
  1 cup hulled raspberries
  4 pounds sugar

In a heavy preserving kettle combine the fruit and sugar and bring slowly to a boil, stirring frequently to start the juice flowing. Cook slowly, stirring occasionally, until the fruit is clear and the juice is thick. Pour into hot jars and seal.

MIXED FRUIT JAM II

  1 cup rhubarb
  1 cup diced pineapple
  1 cup hulled raspberries
  2 cups sugar

Cook the rhubarb over boiling water until it is soft. Add the pineapple, raspberries, and sugar and cook gently over direct heat, stirring frequently, until the jam is thick. Pour into hot jars and seal.

MIXED FRUIT JAM III

  2 lemons
  2 oranges
  6 apples
  6 pears
  6 peaches
  Sugar

Slice the lemons and oranges thinly, cover them with cold water, and let stand overnight. In the morning bring the water to a boil and simmer the lemons and oranges for 10 minutes. Peel and core the apples and pears; peel and pit the peaches. Dice the fruit and measure. Add the fruit and an equal amount of sugar to the oranges and lemons, bring to a boil, and cook until the jam is thick. Pour into hot jars and seal.

SPICED PEACH JAM

2 pounds peaches
1-inch piece ginger root
½ teaspoon allspice
1 teaspoon crushed cinnamon bark
1 teaspoon whole cloves
½ cup peach juice
1 pound sugar

Peel the peaches, halve them, and discard the pits. Crush the fruit in a preserving kettle, cook until the peaches are soft, and press the fruit through a fine sieve. Tie the spices in a cheesecloth bag and add to the peach pulp with the peach juice or water and the sugar. Bring to a boil and cook until the jam is thick, or until it registers 222° F. on a candy thermometer. Remove the spice bag, turn the jam into jars, and seal.

PEAR HONEY

9 cups sliced ripe pears
1 cup diced pineapple
Grated rind and juice of 1 lime
5 cups sugar

Grind the pears through the fine blade of a food chopper and combine all the ingredients in a preserving kettle. Bring to a boil and cook the jam over a slow fire for about 20 minutes, or until the fruit is clear and the liquid is thick. Pour into hot jars and seal.

GINGERED PEAR JAM

6 pounds Kieffer pears, peeled and cored
6 oranges
2 ounces green ginger root
Grated rind of ½ lemon
Sugar

Grind the pears, oranges, and ginger root in a food chopper, bring to a boil, and cook until the fruit is soft. Measure the fruit, add ¾ cup sugar for each cup fruit and the lemon rind, and cook for about 20 minutes longer, or until thick. Pour into hot jars and seal.

SWEET AND SOUR PEPPER JAM

    1 dozen large red peppers
    1 tablespoon salt
    1½ pounds sugar
    2 cups vinegar

Stem and seed the peppers and chop the flesh finely. Sprinkle the peppers with the salt, let stand 3 to 4 hours, and rinse in cold water. Put the peppers in a preserving kettle with the sugar and vinegar, bring to a boil, and simmer until the jam is thick, stirring frequently. Pour into jars and seal. This jam is delicious served with cream cheese.

NATAL PLUM JAM

Cut Natal plums in half, discard the pits, and chop the flesh. Barely cover the plums with water and cook slowly until the fruit is very tender. Mash the plums with a potato masher and measure the pulp. For every 3 cups of pulp and juice add ½ cup lime juice and bring to a boil. Add cup for cup of sugar and cook, stirring frequently, until thick and clear. Pour into hot jars and seal.

QUINCE AND APPLE HONEY

    6 large quinces
    4 large sweet apples
    Sugar
    6 cups boiling water
    Juice of 2 lemons

Peel and core the quinces and apples and grate the flesh. Measure the pulp and use three-fourths as much sugar as pulp. Dissolve the sugar in the boiling water, add the fruit and lemon juice, and cook slowly until the honey is thick and clear. Pour into hot jars and seal.

ROSE HIP JAM

Gather rose hips before they grow soft and cut off the heads and stems. Slit the hips in half and discard the seeds and pithy flesh. Cover the hips with water, cook until soft, and press through a sieve. Measure the purée.

To each 4 cups rose hip purée add 1 cup finely diced pineapple.

Slice 1 lemon thinly and cook it in ½ cup water for 15 minutes. Drain and add to the rose hip purée. Add 5 cups sugar, bring to a boil, and cook slowly until thick. Pour into jars and seal.

ROSE PETAL JAM

Strip enough petals from fresh red roses to measure 1 pound. Dissolve 2 cups sugar in ½ cup water and stir into the rose petals. Put the petals and sugar in a shallow pan, cover with a sheet of glass, and set in the sun for 8 hours. Then bring to a boil and cook for 20 minutes, stirring constantly. Pour into jars and seal.

RHUBARB FIG JAM

> 2 pounds rhubarb, thinly sliced
> 1 pound fresh figs, chopped
> 4 cups sugar
> 1 cup boiling water
> 2 teaspoons lemon juice

Combine all the ingredients in a preserving kettle, bring to a boil, and cook slowly until the jam is thick. Pour into hot jars and seal. Raisins may be substituted for the figs.

SURINAM CHERRY JAM

> 3¾ cups sugar
> 2 cups water
> 3¾ cups seeded Surinam cherries

Combine the sugar and water, bring to a boil, and add the cherries. Boil the cherries in the syrup for 20 to 25 minutes, or until the juice thickens slightly but does not jelly. Pour into hot jars and seal.

TAMARIND JAM

> 1 quart shelled tamarind pods
> Water
> Sugar

Boil the tamarind seeds and pulp in water to cover until soft and press them through a sieve to remove the seeds. Measure the puréed pulp and add an equal amount of sugar. Bring to a boil and simmer, stirring frequently, until the jam is thick enough to coat a silver spoon. Pour into hot jars and seal.

WINTER JAM

    3 cups cranberries
    1 cup diced apple
    1½ cups water
    Juice and grated rind of 1 lemon
    1 cup finely diced pineapple
    3 cups sugar

Cook the cranberries and apple in the water until tender and press the fruit and juice through a fine sieve to remove the cranberry skins. Add the lemon juice and rind, pineapple, and sugar, mix thoroughly, and boil rapidly until the jam is thick and clear. Pour into hot jars and seal.

Conserves

Conserves are made in exactly the same way as jams, for they really are jams. The distinguishing feature of a conserve is that it is always a blend of two or more kinds of fruit. It usually contains thin slices of citrus fruit or juice and often contains raisins or nut meats or both. Small fruits and berries are frequently left whole, but large fruits are usually sliced or diced. The prepared fruit is measured and mixed with three fourths the amount of sugar. It is then cooked until it is thick but still slightly runny. The nut meats are added during the last few minutes of cooking.

APPLE BLUEBERRY CONSERVE

    4 cups chopped apples
    4 cups blueberries
    6 cups sugar
    ½ cup raisins
    4 tablespoons lemon juice

Mix all the ingredients, bring to a boil, and boil until the conserve is thick. Pour into hot jars and seal.

APPLE CHERRY CONSERVE

    3 cups chopped apples
    8 cups pitted cherries
    2 cups diced pineapple
    11 cups sugar
    ½ teaspoon salt
    1 cup shelled nuts

Mix the fruit and sugar and let stand for 4 to 5 hours. Bring the mixture to a boil and boil until the conserve is thick. Add the salt and nuts 5 minutes before cooking is finished. Pour into hot jars and seal.

APPLE PINEAPPLE COCONUT CONSERVE

    4 cups diced apples
    4 cups chopped pineapple
    2 oranges
    1½ cups grated coconut
    6 cups sugar

Combine the apples, pineapple, the pulp of the oranges and the slivered peel of 1 orange, and 3 cups water. Bring the mixture to a boil and cook until the peel is tender. Add the coconut and sugar and continue to boil almost to the jellying point. Pour into hot jars and seal.

BLUEBERRY CONSERVE

    2 cups water
    4 cups sugar
    ½ lemon, thinly sliced
    ½ orange, thinly sliced
    ⅓ cup raisins
    4 cups blueberries

Bring the water and sugar to a boil. Add the lemon, orange, and raisins and simmer for 5 minutes. Add the blueberries and cook gently until the conserve is quite thick, stirring frequently but being careful not to crush the berries. Pour into hot jars and seal.

CANTALOUPE PEACH CONSERVE

    4 cups chopped cantaloupe
    4 cups chopped peaches
    6 cups sugar
    4 tablespoons lemon juice
    ½ teaspoon nutmeg
    ¼ teaspoon salt
    1 teaspoon grated orange peel
    ½ cup blanched almonds

Mix the cantaloupe and peaches and bring to a boil. Add the sugar and lemon juice and cook until the conserve is thick. Add the nutmeg, salt, orange peel, and almonds and continue to cook for 3 minutes longer. Pour into hot jars and seal.

BLACK CHERRY CONSERVE

    2 oranges
    4 cups pitted sweet black cherries
    3½ cups sugar
    ¼ cup lemon juice
    ¾ cup shredded blanched almonds

Wash and slice the oranges thinly. Cover the slices with cold water, bring to a boil, and cook until soft. Add the cherries, sugar, and lemon juice and continue to boil until the conserve is thick and clear. Add the nuts and cook for 2 minutes. Pour into hot jars and seal.

CHERRY DATE CONSERVE

    5 pounds pitted cherries
    3 cups sugar
    1¼ pounds dates, chopped
    1 cup chopped figs
    2 cups raisins
    ½ teaspoon cinnamon
    ½ teaspoon ground cloves
    1 cup chopped pecans

Drain the juice from the cherries and add the sugar. Bring to a boil and boil until the syrup spins a thread. Add the cherries and cook for 5 minutes. Add the dates, figs, raisins, and spices and continue to cook slowly until the conserve is thick. Add the chopped pecans, cook for 1 minute longer, and pour into hot jars. Seal at once.

CHERRY PINEAPPLE CONSERVE

2½ pounds Royal Ann cherries
2 cups sugar
1 cup canned crushed pineapple
1 cup finely chopped pecans

Wash, halve, and pit the cherries. Combine the cherries and sugar, bring slowly to a boil, and cook for about 20 minutes, or until the cherries are partially tender. Add the pineapple and continue cooking slowly for about 15 minutes longer, or until the conserve is thick and transparent, stirring occasionally. Add the nut meats and cook for 2 minutes more. Pour into hot jars and seal.

CHOP SUEY CONSERVE

1 pound seedless white grapes
12 red plums
1 orange
4 pounds fresh peaches
1 No. 2 can pineapple
Sugar

Halve the grapes. Pit the plums and cut them into small pieces. Slice the orange thinly, discard the seeds, and cut each slice into quarters. Scald the peaches, peel, and slice, discarding the pits. Put the fruit into a large preserving kettle and add the pineapple juice. Bring to a boil and simmer for 30 minutes, stirring frequently. Add the pineapple, diced. Measure the fruit and for each cup fruit add ¾ cup sugar. Bring again to a boil and continue to simmer for about 1 hour, or until the conserve is thick, stirring frequently. Pour into hot, sterilized jars and seal.

CRANBERRY CONSERVE

>Grated peel and pulp of 2 oranges
>2 cups water
>4 cups cranberries
>3 cups sugar
>1 cup raisins
>¼ teaspoon salt
>½ cup chopped nut meats

Cook the orange peel and pulp in the water for 20 minutes. Add the cranberries, sugar, raisins, and salt and boil rapidly to the jellying point. Add the nut meats and cook for 5 minutes longer. Pour into hot jars and seal.

EASTERN CONSERVE

>2 cups maraschino cherries
>2 cups seeded raisins
>2 cups sugar
>Grated rind and juice of 3 oranges
>½ cup chopped preserved ginger

Cut the cherries and raisins in halves and mix them with the sugar, the orange juice, and the ginger. Bring the mixture to a boil and cook slowly until the conserve is thick. Add the grated orange rind and continue to cook for 10 minutes longer. Pour into hot jars and seal.

GOOSEBERRY CONSERVE

>6 cups gooseberries
>1 orange
>4 cups sugar
>1 cup raisins

Wash and drain the gooseberries and remove the stems and tails. Grate the orange peel and chop the pulp. Mix the berries, orange peel and pulp, sugar, and raisins and heat slowly until the sugar dissolves. Then bring to a boil and cook rapidly to the jellying point. Pour into hot jars and seal.

133

GRAPE CONSERVE

>5 pounds Concord grapes
>4 pounds sugar
>Juice and grated rind of 2 oranges
>1 cup raisins
>1 cup nut meats

Pulp the grapes. Cook the pulp until the seeds are loosened and press through a fine sieve to remove the seeds. Put the skins through the coarse blade of a food chopper. Combine the pulp purée, skins, sugar, orange juice and rind, and raisins and bring to a boil. Cook rapidly until the mixture sheets from a spoon, or to 221° F. on a candy thermometer, stirring occasionally. Add the nut meats and cook 2 minutes longer. Pour into hot jars and seal.

If Malaga or Tokay grapes are used, cook the whole grapes and press them through a fine sieve to remove the seeds.

SEEDLESS GRAPE CONSERVE

>1 orange
>1 lemon
>1½ cups water
>3 cups sugar
>3 cups halved seedless grapes

Chop the orange and the lemon finely. Put them in a saucepan with the water, bring to a boil, and cook, covered, for 10 minutes. Add the sugar and grapes, bring again to a boil, and cook, uncovered, until a few drops will jell when dropped on a cold saucer, or to 221° F. on a candy thermometer. Pour into hot jars and seal.

HONEYDEW CONSERVE

>2 limes
>1 cup water
>3 cups sugar
>3 cups diced honeydew melon

Slice the limes and cut the slices into slivers. Put the limes in a saucepan with the water, bring to a boil, and cook, covered, for 10 minutes. Add the sugar and diced honeydew, bring again to a boil, and cook, uncovered, until a few drops will jell when dropped on a cold saucer, or to 220° F. on a candy thermometer. Pour into hot jars and seal.

PEACH CONSERVE

3 pounds peaches, peeled and sliced
1 orange, chopped
1 lemon, chopped
2 cups raisins
½ cup water
1½ pounds sugar
¼ teaspoon salt
1 cup chopped walnuts

Cook the peaches, orange, lemon, and raisins with the water until the mixture is thick. Add the sugar and salt and continue to cook until the fruit is clear. Add the nuts, pour into hot jars, and seal. One half cup chopped maraschino cherries may be added at the same time as the sugar.

Peach Apple Conserve   Use half sliced peaches and half diced apples instead of all sliced peaches in the above recipe.

Peach Apple Rhubarb Conserve   Use one third sliced peaches, one third sliced rhubarb, and one third diced apples instead of all peaches in the above recipe.

PEAR CONSERVE

5 pounds hard pears
10 cups sugar
1 pound seedless raisins
Grated rind of 2 oranges
Juice of 3 oranges and 2 lemons

Peel and core the pears and cut the fruit into small pieces. Add the sugar, mix, and let stand overnight. In the morning add the remaining ingredients, bring to a boil, and cook until the conserve is thick and clear. Pour into hot jars and seal.

135

PINEAPPLE STRAWBERRY CHERRY CONSERVE

        1 quart strawberries
        1 quart cherries
        1 orange
        2 cups diced pineapple
        Sugar

Wash and hull the berries. Wash, stem, and pit the cherries. Slice the orange very thinly or put through a food chopper. Combine all the fruits and weigh. Add an equal weight of sugar and bring to a boil. Cook slowly until the mixture is thick and clear. Pour into hot jars and seal. Delicious with cream cheese.

DAMSON PLUM CONSERVE

        2 pounds Damson plums
        1½ pounds sugar
        1 pound seedless raisins
        Juice and grated rind of 1 lemon
        1 cup chopped nut meats

Pit the plums and chop the fruit. Add the sugar, raisins, lemon juice and rind. Bring to a boil and cook slowly until the conserve is thick and clear. Add the nuts, pour into hot jars, and seal.

QUINCE CONSERVE

        2 cups quince pulp
        2 cups apple pulp
        2 cups cranberry or sour cherry pulp
        Juice and grated rind of 1 orange
        4 cups sugar
        ¾ cup English walnut meats

Cook the fruits separately until soft with just enough water to prevent them from sticking to the pan, press through a fine sieve, and measure the purée. Add the orange rind and juice and the sugar, bring to a boil, and cook until thick and clear. Add the nuts, turn into hot jars, and seal. One cup raisins may be added if desired.

RASPBERRY CONSERVE

4 cups crushed raspberries
1 cup crushed sliced peaches
1 cup seedless raisins
2 oranges, thinly sliced
Juice of 1 lemon
Sugar
½ cup chopped walnut meats

Combine all the fruits and the lemon juice and measure. Add ¾ cup sugar for each cup of the fruit and juice. Bring the mixture to a boil and cook slowly for about 45 minutes, or until the conserve is thick and clear, stirring frequently. Add the chopped nuts, pour into hot jars, and seal.

RHUBARB CONSERVE

2 cups finely sliced rhubarb
2 cups sugar
Juice and grated rind of 1 orange
Juice and grated rind of 1 lemon
½ cup chopped nuts

Combine the rhubarb, sugar, the juice and grated rind of the orange and lemon, and heat slowly until the sugar is dissolved. Bring to a boil and boil rapidly until the conserve is thick and clear. Add the nuts, pour into hot jars, and seal.

RHUBARB CURRANT RASPBERRY CONSERVE

2 cups raspberries
2 cups currants
4 cups sliced rhubarb
Sugar
Grated rind and juice of 2 oranges
Grated rind and juice of 2 lemons
½ cup finely chopped pecans

Combine the raspberries, currants, and rhubarb and weigh. Add ¾ pound sugar for each pound fruit. Add the juice and grated rind of the lemons and oranges, bring to a boil, and simmer until the conserve is thick and clear. Add the pecans and continue to cook for 5 minutes longer. Turn into hot jars and seal.

RHUBARB MINCEMEAT

2 cups diced apples
2 cups sliced rhubarb
Grated rind and pulp of 1 orange
Juice of ½ lemon
1 cup raisins
½ cup currants
¼ cup chopped citron
2½ cups brown sugar
½ cup water
½ teaspoon cinnamon
½ teaspoon ground cloves
½ teaspoon allspice
¼ teaspoon nutmeg

Combine all the ingredients, bring to a boil, and cook for 30 minutes, or until the mincemeat is thick and clear. Turn into hot jars and seal. Makes mincemeat for 1 pie.

RED ROSE CONSERVE

1 pound dried red rose petals
2 cups sugar
2 tablespoons orange flower water
⅔ cup water

Tie the rose petals in a cheesecloth bag, plunge them into boiling water, and drain. In a saucepan combine the sugar, orange flower water, and water, bring to a boil, stirring until the sugar is dissolved, and add the blanched rose petals. Cook until the conserve is thick, pressing the petals under the syrup frequently. Turn into hot jars and seal.

STRAWBERRY CONSERVE

2 pounds strawberries
1 orange
2 pounds sugar
2 cups seedless raisins
1 cup fresh raspberry juice

Wash and hull the strawberries. Slice the orange and run through a food chopper. Combine all the ingredients, bring to a boil, and simmer until the conserve is thick and clear. Turn into hot jars and seal.

TOMATO CONSERVE

> 4 cups peeled, sliced tomatoes
> 1 cup seedless raisins
> 4 cups sugar
> 1 lemon, cut into small pieces
> ½ cup chopped walnut meats

Put the tomatoes, raisins, sugar, and lemon into a preserving kettle, bring to a boil, and simmer until the conserve is thick and clear. Add the walnuts, pour into hot jars, and seal.

WATERMELON PLUM CONSERVE

> 2 cups finely diced watermelon rind
> 2 cups pitted, quartered Damson plums
> 1½ tablespoons lemon juice
> 4 cups sugar
> ½ cup raisins
> 1 orange, diced
> 1 tablespoon slivered orange rind
> ½ cup chopped nuts

Combine the watermelon rind, plums, lemon juice, and sugar and bring to a boil. Stir in the raisins and simmer briskly for 15 minutes, stirring constantly. Reduce the heat and cook for 10 minutes longer. Add the orange and rind and nuts and cook for 5 minutes, stirring constantly. Turn into hot jars and seal.

Fruit Butters

Fruit butters are made by pressing fruit pulp through a fine sieve and then cooking the purée with sugar until it is thick enough to spread.

All fruits should be cooked with a little water until tender before they are pressed through the sieve. Apples and pears do not need to be peeled and cored before they are cooked, for the peel and core add flavor to these fruits and are easily removed when the pulp is sieved. Peaches, however, should be peeled and all the stone fruits such as apricots, peaches, plums, and prunes should be pitted before the fruit is cooked.

Spices—cinnamon, clove, and allspice—are frequently used to flavor the butter; so too are ginger, nutmeg, and occasionally vanilla extract. The blander fruits are improved with a little lemon juice or by combining the purée with the pulp of a more highly flavored fruit such as plums or cherries.

From one half to two thirds as much sugar as fruit is the usual proportion, and the length of time the purée and sugar are cooked together is determined by the consistency of the butter rather than the boiling point. The butter, when cold, should be thick enough to stand on a plate without running, but thin enough to spread easily on bread.

Fruit butters are poured into jars while they are still boiling hot and sealed at once. They need no further processing for preservation. The jars or glasses should be scalded in boiling water and the butter sealed with paraffin (see Index).

APPLE BUTTER

> 5 pounds tart cooking apples
> 7 cups water
> 2 cups apple cider
> 4 cups sugar
> 1 teaspoon ground cloves
> 1 teaspoon allspice
> 1 tablespoon cinnamon
> ½ teaspoon nutmeg

Wash and quarter the apples. Put them in a large preserving kettle with the water and cook for about 15 minutes, or until the apples are soft. Press the apples through a fine sieve to make about 2 quarts apple purée. Boil the cider down to 1 cup and add it to the apple purée with the remaining ingredients. Bring to a boil and cook gently for 30 minutes, stirring frequently. Pour into an oven-proof dish or casserole and bake, uncovered, in a slow oven (250° F.) for about 6 hours, or until thick, stirring occasionally. Pour into hot jars and seal at once.

Equal parts of cooked apple purée and blueberry purée may be used instead of all apple purée.

APPLE GRAPE BUTTER

> 2 cups grape pulp
> 2 cups apple pulp
> 2 cups sugar

Cook the fruits separately in water to cover until soft and press through a fine sieve. Combine the purées and sugar and cook the mixture for about 20 minutes, or until the butter is thick, stirring frequently. Seal in hot jars.

APRICOT BUTTER

> 5 pounds apricots
> 6 cups sugar
> Juice and grated rind of 1 orange

Peel and pit the apricots and cut the fruit into small pieces. Add the sugar and the juice and rind of the orange and cook slowly to the desired consistency. Seal while very hot in hot jars.

One to 2 teaspoons mixed spices per gallon of butter may be added. If whole spices are used the butter will be lighter in color. Tie whole spices in a cheesecloth bag for easy removal.

CARROT, WINTER SQUASH, OR PUMPKIN BUTTER

> 6 pounds carrots, pumpkin, or squash
> 2 tablespoons ground ginger
> 2 tablespoons ground cinnamon
> 1 teaspoon allspice
> 5 pounds light brown sugar
> Juice and grated rind of 5 lemons
> 2 cups water

Peel the vegetable and put the flesh through the fine blade of a meat chopper. Add the spices, sugar, lemon juice and rind and let stand overnight. In the morning, add the water, bring to a boil, and cook gently until the vegetable is soft and clear. Continue to cook until the butter is the desired consistency, pour into hot jars, and seal.

GRAPE BUTTER

Wash and stem the grapes and simmer them in a small amount of water until tender. Press the cooked pulp through a strainer to remove the seeds. Measure the purée and add half as much sugar as purée. Cook the purée until it is thick, stirring frequently. Seal in hot jars.

141

SPICED GRAPE BUTTER

Stem and mash the grapes well. Weigh 4 pounds or measure out 2 quarts of the mashed grapes. Add 10 whole cloves, 12 allspice berries, a stick of cinnamon, and a bit of ginger root and cook until the grapes are soft. Press through a fine sieve and measure the purée. Add ½ cup vinegar and for each 2 cups of the purée add 1 cup sugar. Cook until the butter is thick and pour hot into hot jars. Seal at once.

GUAVA BUTTER

Make in the same manner as **apple butter.**

PEACH BUTTER

Scald, peel, and stone the peaches. Cook the peaches, with just enough water to prevent them from sticking, until soft and press through a fine sieve. Measure the purée and to each cup of purée add ½ cup sugar. Cook until the butter is thick and clear and pour into hot jars. Seal at once. Spices may be added. **Equal parts of cooked peach and plum purée may be used instead of all peach purée.**

PEAR BUTTER

Wash and slice ripe pears and cook, with just enough water to prevent them from sticking, until soft. Press through a fine sieve and measure the purée. To 6 cups pear purée add 3 cups sugar, ¼ cup orange juice, 1 teaspoon grated orange rind, and ½ teaspoon nutmeg. Bring to a boil and cook until the butter is thick, stirring frequently. Pour into hot jars and seal.

PEAR HONEY BUTTER

Cook pears, with just enough water to prevent them from sticking, until soft. Press them through a fine sieve and measure the purée. To 4 cups of the pear purée add 1 cup sugar, 1¼ cups strained honey, and 1 tablespoon lemon juice. Cook for about 1 hour, or until the butter is thick, stirring frequently. Pour into hot jars and seal.

PLUM OR PRUNE BUTTER

> 2 pounds fresh ripe prunes or plums
> 1 cup brown sugar
> 1 teaspoon each ground cloves, allspice, and cinnamon

Wash the fruit, pit, and cut the flesh into quarters. Cook the fruit with a little water until tender and press through a fine sieve.

To the purée add the sugar and spices and cook for about 1 hour, or until the butter is thick, stirring frequently. Pour into hot jars and seal.

TOMATO BUTTER

Wash and core firm-ripe tomatoes and cook them until soft. Press the tomatoes through a sieve and drain off the excess juice. To 12 cups of the tomato purée add 7 cups sugar, ¼ cup lemon juice, 1 teaspoon cinnamon, ½ teaspoon ginger, and ¼ teaspoon cloves and boil until the bitter is thick. Pour into hot jars and seal. **Four cups of cooked apple purée may be substituted for an equal amount of tomato purée.**

Fruit Pastes

Fruit purées may be cooked with sugar and dried in a breeze to make unusual fruit confectionaries. Almost any fruit or a combination of different fruits may be used. Press the fruit pulp through a fine sieve to make a purée. The harder fruits must be cooked in enough water to cover until they are soft. For each 2 cups of cherry, plum, strawberry, raspberry, currant, or gooseberry pulp allow 2 cups of sugar. For each 2 cups of apricot, peach, apple, or quince purée allow 1½ cups sugar. Stir the sugar into the purée and cook over low heat, stirring frequently, until the mixture is thick. Then cook over boiling water for 30 minutes longer. Raisins, chopped nut meats, chopped candied fruits or peel may be added. Pour the paste ½ inch thick onto oiled china plates and dry in a warm breeze or under the current from an electric fan for several days. Cut the paste into squares, roll the squares in granulated sugar, and pack in tin boxes.

PEACH LEATHER

Measure ½ cup sugar for each pound of peeled, stoned peaches. Put the fruit and sugar in a preserving kettle, bring slowly to a boil, and simmer until most of the moisture from the fruit has cooked away, mashing the peaches to a smooth paste as they cook.

Oil a large china platter and spread the cooked peaches on it in a thin sheet. Put the paste in the sun until thoroughly dry. Roll the paste up, wrap it in cloth, and store it in a cool, dry place.

Fruit leather, sometimes called fruit roll, may be melted in hot water and used as a sauce or glaze.

FRUIT CANDY

Mix 2 tablespoons powdered apple pectin with 1 tablespoon sugar and ¼ cup corn syrup. Bring to a boil 1 cup fruit juice and stir the hot juice into the pectin mixture. Return the mixture to the stove and heat it slowly for 2 minutes, stirring constantly to prevent it from burning. Stir in 2 tablespoons cornstarch dissolved in ¼ cup fruit juice and continue to heat for 2 more minutes, stirring constantly. Add 2 cups sugar and continue to cook the candy for 12 minutes, stirring constantly. Pour the candy into a large flat tin and chill in the refrigerator. When cold, cut the candy into squares and roll the squares in sifted confectioners' sugar.

About 2 tablespoons fruit purée or ½ cup chopped nut meats may be stirred into the candy 2 minutes before it is taken from the fire.

QUINCE CHEESE

Peel, core, and coarsely chop 5 ripe quinces. To each pound of the chopped fruit measure ½ pound sugar. Cover the cores and parings with water and cook, covered, until soft. Strain the water over the sugar, bring to a boil, and boil to a thick syrup, skimming the surface frequently. When no more scum rises, add the quinces and simmer over a very low fire, stirring and mashing the fruit frequently with a wooden spoon, until the paste is thick and smooth. Pour into buttered pans or dishes and let stand until cold. Turn the paste out and cut it, like cheese, into slices or cubes. Store the quince cheese in a dry cool place or dust the pieces liberally with confectioners' sugar and pack loosely into fruit jars.

CHAPTER FIVE

Jellies and Marmalades

No other type of preserving is quite so rewarding as the making of sparkling jellies and marmalades. A perfect jelly is clear, transparent, and bright. It has captured the original flavor of the fruit, and when turned from the glass is tender and quivering, not syrupy or sticky. It should cut with a clean, smooth edge.

A true marmalade is a preserve in which slices of fruit or peel are suspended in a clear jelly.

In Elizabethan England, any sweet preserve was designated by the name "marmalade." The word was derived from the Portuguese word for quince—*marmelo*—and quince "marmelade" was a favorite of Elizabethan housewives who, in summer and fall, boiled down fruit juice with sugar to relieve the monotony of the long winter diet of salted flesh and bread. They tackled huge quantities of fresh fruit juice, boiled it mercilessly for hours until the delicate flavor and aroma of the fruit were lost forever. It is not hard to imagine the sweet, sticky, caramelized results.

Today we know that jelly making is a scientific process. Merely boiling fruit juice and sugar does not give satisfactory results. We know that most fruits contain pectin in varying amounts and that, if we combine a fruit juice lacking it with another high in pectin, the jelly will set without hours of destructive boiling. We know that slightly underripe fruit contains more pectin than the sweeter, riper, fruit. We know that some fruits, such as strawberries, peaches, and cherries, are so deficient in pectin that they need the acid juice of red currants, gooseberries, or crab apples or the addition of commercial pectin to make jelly. We know that a certain amount of acid is necessary to render soluble the available pectin and that pectin, acid, and sugar must all be present in proper proportion to one another to make a bright-colored, sparkling, tender, flavorful jelly.

We know that jellies and marmalades may be made from:
1. Underripe fruit
2. Fully ripe fruit and acid
3. Fully ripe fruit and commercial pectin

Pectin　Pectin is a substance in fruit that, when combined with fruit acid and heated with sugar, causes the fruit juice to "jell." Some fruits contain little or no pectin, but most fruits and some vegetables contain it in varying amounts, and it is more abundant in underripe fruits than it is in the fully ripe.

Fruits that make the best jelly are those that contain both pectin and acid. If the pectin is extracted from fruits known to contain it in large amounts—apples, plums, or quinces—and combined with the juice of a fruit low in pectin, the resulting juice will jell. So too will the juice of sweet apples, rich in pectin but low in fruit acid, by the simple expedient of adding lemon juice.

To test for pectin　Mix 1 tablespoon cooked unsweetened juice with 1 tablespoon grain alcohol. Wood or denatured alcohol may be used, but they should not be tasted as they are poisonous.

Juice rich in pectin will form a large clot.

Juices moderately rich in pectin will form a few smaller clots.

Juices poor in pectin will form small flaky sediment.

Adding the right amount of sugar　The amount of sugar to be added will depend on the pectin and acid content of the juice. The only home method to determine the acid content of fruit juice is to taste it. If the juice is sweet, lemon or lime juice should be added.

To juices rich in pectin add ¾ cup sugar per cup of juice.

To juices poor in pectin add only ½ cup sugar per cup of juice.

The juice should be boiling when the sugar is added and the juice and sugar should be cooked as rapidly as possible until the jellying point is reached.

Test for the jellying point Dip a spoon into the boiling syrup. As the boiling fruit and sugar mixture nears the jellying point it will drop from the side of the spoon in two drops. When the drops run together and slide off the spoon in a sheet the jelly is finished and should be taken from the fire immediately.

Thermometers are excellent for consistently good results, but the sheet test should also be used, since the jellying point is not always the same. The range of temperature may vary from seven to ten degrees about the boiling point, or 212° F. at sea level.

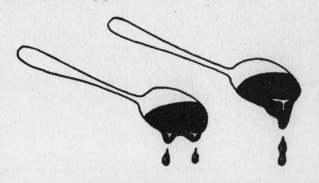

JELLY-MAKING PROPERTIES OF FRUITS

RICH IN ACID AND PECTIN	RICH IN PECTIN BUT DEFICIENT IN ACID	RICH IN ACID BUT DEFICIENT IN PECTIN	DEFICIENT IN BOTH ACID AND PECTIN
Sour apples	Sweet apples	Pomegranates	Raspberries
Blackberries, sour	Quinces	Apricots	Elderberries
Crab apples		Cherries	Peaches
Cranberries		Pineapples	Overripe fruits
Currants, red		Strawberries	
Gooseberries			
Grapefruit			
Grapes			
Guavas, sour			
Lemons			
Loganberries			
Oranges, sour			
Plums (most varieties)			

Apple
Apple and Strawberry
Apricot and Plum
Blackberry
Crab Apple
Crab Apple and Cherry
Crab Apple and Raspberry
Currant
Currant and Apple
Currant and Apricot
Currant and Pear
Currant, Peach, and Pineapple
Fig and Lemon
Grape
Grape and Apple
Grape and Apricot
Grape and Orange
Grapefruit
Grapefruit and Cherry
Lemon
Lemon and Cherry
Lemon and Raspberry
Loganberry
Loganberry and Pineapple
Orange
Orange and Apple
Orange and Pineapple
Orange and Plum
Peach and Lemon
Peach and Apple
Peach and Quince
Pineapple and Quince
Plum
Plum and Raspberry
Quince
Quince and Apple
Quince and Apricot
Raspberry
Raspberry and Currant
Roselle

Making Homemade Jelly

GENERAL METHOD

1. Select a mixture of ripe and slightly underripe fruit, or combine fully ripe fruit or fruit low in pectin (such as figs, pears, cherries, or peaches) with one quarter the amount of fruit or fruit juice high in acidity (such as sour apples, plums, red currants, cranberries, gooseberries, or citrus fruit) to render soluble the available pectin.

2. Wash the fruit thoroughly, discarding any spoiled parts. Drain, hull, stem, and cut or crush the fruit before measuring. Cut hard fruit such as crab apples, quinces, and apples into pieces. Do not remove the skins, cores, and seeds unless the recipe states that they should be discarded. Berries and currants should be slightly crushed.

3. Cook no more than 2 quarts fruit at one time. The smaller the batch, the better the product. Several small batches give better results than cooking a large quantity. Just enough water should be

148

added to the fruit to obtain the greatest yield of juice and pectin. Juicy fruits such as currants, berries, and grapes require no water. The hard fruits such as apples and quinces need from half to an equal volume of water, or from 1 to 2 cups for each pound of fruit. Citrus fruits, because of the longer boiling period needed to make the rind tender, usually require twice the volume of water.

Caution If too much water is added to the fruit the resulting juice will be so diluted that it will need long cooking to reduce it before it can be made into jelly. On the other hand, if too little water is used there is danger of burning the fruit.

Boil the fruit until it is tender, but do not overcook it. Prolonged cooking destroys the jellying qualities of the fruit and results in inferior jellies.

4. Pour the hot cooked fruit into a jelly bag suspended over a kettle or use 4 layers of cheesecloth stretched and tied over the top of a deep pan, and let the juice drip into the container beneath.

There are two methods of extracting the juice—the long method and the shorter, more modern way. The old method insists that the juice be allowed to drip quietly through the jelly bag or cheesecloth until all the juice is extracted. Squeezing or pressing the bag to force out the juice and shorten the process is not recommended as this tends to make the juice cloudy.

The shorter method lets the juice drip twice through a bag. The juice is first strained through a wet jelly bag or clean sugar sac and the bag is squeezed and pressed to expel the juice as fast as possible. This naturally results in a cloudy juice. But then the extracted juice is put into a wet flannel bag, nap side in, to drip for 2 to 4 hours, yielding a clear, sparkling juice in less than half the time.

The pulp remaining from either method may be put through a sieve and used to make fruit butter. Some fruits such as crab apples, currants, or wild grapes are rich enough in pectin and sufficiently distinctive in flavor to stand two extractions. After draining, a small amount of water is added to the pulp and the mixture is cooked for a few minutes. The juice is then drained off the pulp and either mixed with the juice from the first extraction or made separately into jelly.

IN GENERAL: 1 pound juicy fruit will make 1 cup juice
1 cup juice and ¾ cup sugar will make 1 cup jelly

5. Boil jelly glasses and the lids for 10 minutes and invert them on a clean, warm surface to dry.

6. Measure the juice and sugar. Put the juice into a saucepan and bring it to a boil. Add the sugar and stir until the sugar is dissolved.

149

The amount of sugar added is determined by the pectin and acid content of the juice. Sugar must be present in sufficient quantity to preserve the jelly. Too much sugar can overpower the flavor of the fruit and cause crystallization, while too little sugar can result in spoilage. Three fourths as much sugar as fruit or, in the case of extremely sour fruits, equal quantities of sugar and fruit is the general rule. **See Index for "Adding the right amount of sugar."**

7. Fruit high in acid content makes bright, attractive jelly if care is taken in the preparation and cooking of the fruit, and most jellies improve in color, flavor, and consistency if 2 tablespoons lemon juice are added to each pound of fruit before it is cooked. Interesting flavors may be made by combining two, three, four, or as many as five different fruits.

8. Fruit and sugar should be cooked rapidly if the jelly is to be flavorful and bright in color. Boil the juice and sugar rapidly until two drops on the side of a spoon run together and slide off the spoon in a sheet, or to 220° to 222° F. on a candy thermometer. The jellying point at sea level is 222° F., or 10° F. above the boiling point of water. **See Index for "Test for the jellying point."**

9. Remove the jelly from the heat and skim the surface if necessary. Pour the hot jelly into the sterilized glasses to within ½ inch of the top. Hold the saucepan about 1 inch above the glass while pouring to avoid spilling the jelly on the glass.

10. **Seal with paraffin.** As soon as the jelly is set and cool it is ready to seal. With a damp cloth remove any jelly that may be on the glass above the surface of the jelly. Melt the paraffin in a small saucepan or an aluminum measuring cup over boiling water. It should not be allowed to get too hot. Pour a thin layer of the paraffin over the jelly and slightly rotate the glass as soon as the paraffin is poured on so that it will stick to the glass above the surface of the jelly. Place the dry lid on the jelly glass, label, and store the jelly in a cool, dry place.

APPLE JELLY

Use tart, hard-ripe fruit. Wash the fruit and discard the stems and blossom ends. Slice the fruit and put it in a kettle with water barely to cover (2 cups water to 4 cups fruit). Bring the water to a boil and simmer the fruit until it is soft. Turn fruit and juice into a jelly bag or several layers of cheesecloth and let the juice drip into a container placed below. Measure the juice and bring it to a rolling boil. Add ¾ cup sugar to each cup of juice and stir until the sugar is thoroughly dissolved. Then boil rapidly until the jellying point is reached. Skim and pour into hot jelly glasses to within ¼ inch of the top. When the jelly is cool and set, cover with a thin layer of hot paraffin. Cover with tin lids, label, and store.

Apple Geranium Jelly Put 2 rose geranium leaves in the bottom of each jelly glass and fill with hot apple jelly.

COMBINATIONS OF APPLE JUICE AND OTHER JUICES THAT MAKE FINE JELLY

KIND OF JUICE	PROPORTION OF JUICE	NO. OF CUPS	CUPS OF SUGAR TO ADD
Apple Rhubarb	1 cup each	2	1⅓
Apple Blueberry Rhubarb	1 cup each	3	2
Apple Black Raspberry	1 cup each	2	1⅓
Apple Quince	1 cup each	2	1¼
Apple Pineapple	1 cup each	2	1⅓
Apple Peach	1 cup each	2	1
Apple Strawberry	1 cup each	2	1
Apple Quince Cranberry	1 cup each	3	2
Apple Blueberry	1 cup each	2	1¼
Apple Blackberry	1½ ½	2	1¼
Apple Cherry	1½ ½	2	1⅓

APPLE PECTIN

Cover 2 pounds of apple skins and cores with 4 cups water. Add the juice of 1 lemon, bring to a boil, and simmer for 40 minutes. Strain the juice through a jelly bag, bring the juice to a boil, and boil rapidly for 15 minutes. Seal the apple pectin in hot sterilized jars and use for making jelly from fruits such as peaches, strawberries, or cherries that are lacking in pectin. Usually ¾ cup sugar to 1 cup of combined juices is the right amount to add.

BEACH PLUM AND APPLE JELLY

Combine equal quantities of ripe beach plums and quartered cooking apples. Just cover with water, bring to a boil, and simmer until the fruit is soft. Strain the juice through a jelly bag all night. In the morning measure the juice, bring it to a boil, and boil briskly for 10 minutes. Stir in 1 cup sugar for each cup juice and boil rapidly to the jelly stage.

BERRY JELLY

Blackberries, dewberries, loganberries, elderberries, and **youngberries** all make excellent jellies. Use from one third to one half slightly underripe berries. Wash, stem, and crush the berries. If the berries are very juicy no water is necessary, but if they seem a little dry add from ¼ to 1 cup water for each 4 cups berries. Bring the liquid to a boil and simmer the berries for 15 minutes. Drain the juice through a jelly bag or several layers of cheesecloth and measure.

Bring the juice to a rapid boil and add ¾ cup sugar for each cup juice. Stir until the sugar is dissolved, then boil rapidly without stirring or skimming until the juice sheets from a spoon, or to 222° F. Remove from the fire, skim, and pour immediately into hot jelly glasses.

CRAB APPLE RHUBARB JELLY

Wash and remove the blossom end from crab apples and cut the fruit into quarters, without peeling. Barely cover the apples with water, bring to a boil, and simmer until the fruit is tender. Strain the juice through a jelly bag. Wash rhubarb, discard the leaves, and cut the stalks into 1-inch pieces. Add a small amount of water to start the rhubarb cooking, bring to a boil, and cook until tender. Strain the juice through a jelly bag. Combine equal quantities of the juices and bring to a boil. Add ¾ cup sugar for each cup juice and boil rapidly to the jellying point.

SPICED CURRANT JELLY

5 pounds currants
1 ounce stick cinnamon
1 tablespoon whole cloves
Sugar

Wash the currants, drain, and mash. Cook the currants slowly until they look white and strain through a jelly bag. Tie the spices in a cheesecloth bag and boil it in the juice for 10 minutes. Discard the spices and measure the juice. Add ¾ cup sugar for each cup juice and boil rapidly to the jelly stage.

GRAPE JELLY

Wash, stem, and crush the grapes. Add a small amount of water, bring to a boil, and simmer for 15 minutes. Strain the juice through a jelly bag and let the juice stand overnight in a cool place to let any formation of tartaric acid crystals settle to the sides and bottom of the container. In the morning pour the juice carefully off the sediment in the bottom, measure, and bring to a boil. For each cup of juice add ¾ cup sugar and boil rapidly to the jelly stage.

GRAPE, LEMON, OR LIME JELLY

5 pounds grapes
3 lemons or limes
Sugar

Wash the grapes and slice the lemons or limes thinly. Put the fruit into a preserving kettle, bring slowly to a boil, and cook slowly, stirring often, until the skins have separated from the pulp. Strain the juice through a jelly bag. Measure the juice and bring it to a boil. Add ¾ cup sugar for each cup juice and boil rapidly to the jelly stage.

HERB JELLIES

The best herb jellies are made with a base of tart apple juice. Bring the apple juice to a boil and stir in ¾ cup sugar to each cup apple juice. Add a few herb leaves such as lemon verbena, sage, bay leaf, tarragon, sweet basil, thyme, or marjoram and cook the juice rapidly for about 15 minutes, or until the jelly sheets from the edge of a spoon. Pour into hot jelly glasses, with a leaf of herb in the bottom of each glass.

LOQUAT JELLY

Gather loquats when they are still hard and have only partially turned color. Wash, remove the blossom ends, and add water barely to cover. Bring the water to a boil and simmer the loquats until very soft. Strain the juice through a jelly bag, bring the juice to a boil, and simmer until it is thick and cherry-colored. Then measure the juice and add 1 cup sugar for each cup juice. Boil rapidly to the jelly stage.

MAY HAW JELLY

Wash 1 pound ripe May haws and put them in a preserving kettle with 4 cups water. Bring the water to a boil and simmer the May haws until they are tender. Strain the juice through a jelly bag. Bring the juice to a boil, stir in 2 cups sugar, and boil rapidly to the jelly stage.

MINT JELLY

Pour 1 cup boiling water over 1 cup firmly packed mint leaves and let stand for 1 hour. Press the juice from the leaves. To each cup of apple juice add 2 tablespoons of the mint extract and bring to a boil. Add ¾ cup sugar for each cup of apple juice and boil rapidly to the jelly stage. Tint the jelly with a few drops of green food coloring and pour into hot jelly glasses.

ORANGE LEMON JELLY

> Juice of 6 lemons
> 6 oranges, sliced
> Sugar

Measure the lemon juice and add 3 times as much water. Add the sliced oranges and let stand overnight. In the morning bring the mixture to a boil, boil until the fruit is tender, and strain the juice through a jelly bag. Measure the juice and bring to a boil. Add 1¾ cups sugar to each 2 cups juice and boil rapidly to the jelly stage.

ORANGE PECTIN

Grind ¼ pound of the white portion of orange peel and mix it with 2 tablespoons lemon juice and 1 cup cold water. Let stand for 4 hours, add 2½ cups cold water, and let stand overnight. In the morning bring the liquid to a boil and boil for 10 minutes. Cool and strain the juice through a jelly bag.

PASSION FRUIT JELLY

Wash and slice 5 quarts fully ripe passion fruit. Add 1½ cups cold water, bring to a boil, and simmer for 15 minutes, crushing the fruit occasionally with a potato masher. Strain the juice through a jelly bag and measure. Bring the juice to a boil and add 6 cups sugar to each 4 cups juice. Boil rapidly for 1 minute. Add ½ cup liquid commercial pectin and remove from the fire. Stir well, skim the surface quickly, and pour into hot jelly glasses.

PEACH JELLY

Peel and stone the peaches. Barely cover the fruit with water, bring to a boil, and cook until the juice is well extracted. Strain the juice through a jelly bag and measure. Combine 2 cups each of the peach juice and **apple pectin.** Add the juice of ½ lemon and bring to a boil. Add 3 cups sugar and boil rapidly to the jelly stage.

PINEAPPLE JELLY

Peel and core a fresh pineapple and chop the flesh. Partially cover the fruit with water, bring to a boil, and simmer until the fruit is tender. Strain the juice through a jelly bag. Combine 2 cups of the pineapple juice with 2 cups tart apple juice and bring to a boil. Add 3 cups sugar and boil rapidly to the jelly stage.

PLUM ORANGE JELLY

Wash 5 pounds plums and cover them with water. Add 6 oranges, thinly sliced or chopped, bring to a boil, and simmer until the plums are soft. Strain the juice through a jelly bag, bring it to a boil, and boil for 15 minutes. Measure the juice and to every 4 cups juice add 3½ cups sugar. Boil rapidly to the jelly stage.

QUINCE ORANGE JELLY

Wash and quarter quinces and discard the cores. Barely cover the fruit with water, bring to a boil, and simmer for about 45 minutes, or until the fruit is tender. Strain the juice through a jelly bag, measure, and add an equal quantity of orange juice and a little of the grated rind. Bring the juice to a boil and simmer for 20 minutes. Stir in ¾ cup sugar for each cup of the combined juices and boil rapidly to the jelly stage.

RASPBERRY CURRANT JELLY

Wash 4 quarts each of red raspberries and red currants. Put them in a preserving kettle and mash well. Bring the juice to a boil and simmer the fruit for 30 minutes. Strain the juice through a jelly bag. Measure the juice and bring to a boil. Boil rapidly for 5 minutes, stir in 1 cup sugar for each juice, and boil rapidly for about 5 minutes longer, or to the jelly stage.

ROSELLE JELLY

Only the fleshy calyxes of the Florida cranberry are used to make jelly. After the blossoms have formed pods that resemble rose hips, remove the calyxes from the seed pods. Measure the calyxes into a preserving kettle and add twice the amount of water. Bring the water to a boil and simmer the calyxes for 10 minutes. Cover the kettle and let the calyxes cool in the liquid. Strain the juice through a jelly bag and to each cup of roselle juice add ¼ cup **orange pectin.** Bring the juice to a boil and stir in 1 cup sugar for each cup of mixed roselle juice and orange pectin. Boil rapidly to the jelly stage.

STRAWBERRY JELLY

Combine 1 cup each strawberry juice and **apple pectin.** Bring to a boil, stir in 1 cup sugar, and boil rapidly to the jelly stage.

STRAWBERRY RHUBARB JELLY

Wash and chop 1 pound pink rhubarb and add just enough water to keep it from burning. Add the juice and grated rind of 1 lemon and 1 orange, bring to a boil, and simmer until the rhubarb is tender.

Add 1 quart hulled strawberries and simmer for 10 minutes longer. Strain the juice through a jelly bag. Measure the juice and bring to a boil. Stir in 1 cup sugar for each cup juice and boil rapidly to the jelly stage.

SURINAM CHERRY JELLY

Wash underripe Surinam cherries and crush them lightly. Add enough water barely to cover the fruit, bring to a boil, and simmer for 20 minutes, or until the cherries are soft. Let stand 20 minutes, then strain the juice through a jelly bag. Measure the juice and bring to a boil. Add 1 cup sugar for each cup juice and boil rapidly until the jelly sheets off the edge of a spoon, or to 221° F.

SPICED WILD GRAPE JELLY

Remove the stems from 1 peck of wild grapes. Put the grapes in a preserving kettle with 2 cups vinegar, ¼ cup whole cloves, and ¼ cup stick cinnamon. Bring to a boil and cook until the grapes are soft. Strain the juice through a jelly bag and let stand in a cool place overnight. In the morning pour the juice carefully off the sediment in the bottom of the container, bring to a boil, and boil for 20 minutes. Measure the juice and add 1 cup sugar for each cup juice. Boil rapidly to the jelly stage.

Marmalades

In the wonderland of preserves, there is little differentiation between jams and marmalades. Jams are generally made from crushed fruit, while marmalades are usually made from sliced fruits or small berries. Marmalades, nevertheless, rightfully belong in the jelly chapter, for a true marmalade contains pieces of fruit suspended in a clear, sparkling jelly. And so the principles of jelly making apply to marmalades.

As in the making of most preserves, working with small quantities gives the best results. This is one reason why better marmalades can be made in the home kitchen than in a commercial factory. No factory in the world could afford to cook 2 cups fruit and juice with the required amount of sugar to the jellying point, yet this is the quantity that is recommended for really superior marmalades. When this small amount of fruit and sugar is cooked vigorously in a wide kettle, evaporation is rapid and it does not take long for the syrup to reach the jellying point. Several small batches may be made at the same time with, of course, constant supervision.

The old method of making marmalades was to boil all the ingredients for hours until the excess moisture was evaporated and the syrup jelled. By today's quicker method, the fruit is cooked in its own juice or with a little water until the fruit is tender. Then the sugar is added, and rapid boiling is only a matter of minutes.

The jellying point is the same as for jellies (**see Index**). Once this point is reached the marmalade should be poured into clean, hot but dry jelly jars and covered immediately with a thin layer of paraffin.

The only exceptions to this rule are marmalades that contain whole berries or sliced fruits, which have an exasperating inclination to float to the surface of the syrup. Then the marmalade should be cooled for a few minutes and stirred thoroughly. This corrects the floating foolishness, providing the syrup has been cooked to the right consistency.

The most inexpensive marmalades are made from citrus fruits— from one variety only or from a combination. The fruit should be washed but not peeled, and cut into paper-thin slices. The larger slices cut from oranges or grapefruit should be halved or quartered.

Citrus Marmalade Cook the sliced fruit in three times the amount, by weight or measure, of water for about 10 minutes, or until the peel is tender. Let the fruit stand in the liquid overnight. In the morning measure 2 cups of the fruit and liquid into a wide kettle and stir in from 1½ to 2 cups sugar. Bring to a boil and cook vigorously for 12 to 18 minutes, or until the syrup gives the jelly test. When thick reluctant drops sheet from the spoon, the marmalade is ready to be poured into jars to within ¼ inch of the top. Cover immediately with paraffin.

Sealing with paraffin A small china teapot makes a perfect container in which to melt, and from which to pour, the paraffin. The paraffin should not be too hot, so melt it over simmering water. With a damp cloth remove any particles of marmalade that may be on the glass above the surface of the marmalade. Pour a thin layer of melted paraffin over the marmalade and slightly rotate the jelly jar so the paraffin will stick to the glass above the surface of the marmalade. This makes a good seal. When the marmalade is cool, repeat with another thin layer of melted paraffin. Place a clean dry lid on the jars, label, and store in a cool, dry place.

AMBER MARMALADE

1 orange
1 lemon
1 grapefruit
Sugar

Wash and cut the fruit into small pieces, discarding the seeds. Put the fruit through the fine blade of a food chopper, saving the juice. Mix the ground fruit and juice and measure it. Pour three times the amount of water over the fruit and juice and let stand for 24 hours. Bring the mixture to a boil, cook for 30 minutes, and measure again. To each cup liquid and fruit allow 1 cup sugar. Mix well and again let stand for 24 hours. Then bring to a boil and simmer until thick.

CARROT ORANGE MARMALADE

6 oranges
4 lemons
4 cups water
6 cups chopped carrots
5 cups sugar

Remove the peel from the oranges and lemons. Chop the peel of all the oranges and 2 of the lemons and soak the peel overnight in the water. Drain, reserving the liquid. Chop the orange pulp, add the peel and the carrots, and cook until tender in as little water as possible to prevent the fruit and carrots from burning. Add the sugar and the reserved liquid from the peel and cook until the marmalade is thick and clear. Add the juice of the lemons and cook for 5 minutes longer.

CARROT PINEAPPLE GINGER MARMALADE

4 cups finely ground carrots
Grated rind and juice of 2 lemons
Grated rind and juice of 3 oranges
1 teaspoon ground ginger
½ cup water
3½ cups sugar
1 cup diced pineapple
1 cup pineapple juice

159

Cook the carrots, grated rind and juice of the lemons and oranges in as little water as possible for about 40 minutes, or until the carrots are tender. Add the ginger, water, sugar, pineapple, and pineapple juice and cook until the marmalade is thick and clear. Add the lemon juice and cook for 5 minutes longer.

CHERRY MARMALADE

> 2 oranges
> 4 cups pitted sweet cherries
> 4 tablespoons lemon juice
> 3½ cups sugar

Chop the orange peel and pulp separately. Cover the peel with water and bring to a boil. Boil for 15 minutes and drain. Mix the orange pulp and peel with just enough fresh water to cover, boil until the rind is soft, and cool. Add the cherries, lemon juice, and sugar, bring again to a boil, and boil rapidly to the jellying point. If sour cherries are used, add only 2 tablespoons lemon juice.

CITRON MELON MARMALADE

> 6 cups sugar
> 6 cups water
> A 6-pound citron melon
> 6 lemons, thinly sliced
> 6 ounces ginger root

Combine the sugar and water, bring to a boil, and simmer for 20 minutes, skimming when necessary. Peel the melon, discard the seeds, and cut the fruit into thin slices. Add the melon, lemons, and ginger root, tied in a bag, to the syrup and simmer for about 1 hour, or until the fruit is clear and tender.

GRAPEFRUIT MARMALADE

> 1 grapefruit
> Sugar
> 4 cups water

Wash the grapefruit and peel it. Slice half the peel thinly and cut the pulp into chunks. Cover the slivered peel and the pulp with the water and let stand for 12 hours, or overnight, in a cool place. Bring to a boil and simmer until the peel is tender. Measure and add 1 cup sugar for each cup fruit and juice. Bring to a boil and boil to the jellying point.

GREEN GRAPE MARMALADE

4 cups young green grapes
1 cup water
4 cups sugar
Juice of 1 lemon

Wash and stem the grapes. Any large grapes should be halved and the seeds discarded. Add the water to the grapes, bring to a boil, and simmer until the grapes are tender. Add the sugar and boil to the jellying point. Add the lemon juice and boil for 5 minutes longer.

KUMQUAT MARMALADE

24 kumquats
2 oranges
6 tablespoons lemon juice
Sugar

Wash the kumquats and slice them paper-thin, discarding the seeds. Chop the orange peel and pulp, combine with the kumquats, and measure the fruit. Add 3 cups water for each cup fruit and let stand for 12 to 18 hours in a cool place. Bring the liquid to a boil and simmer until the peel is tender. Measure fruit and water. Add the lemon juice and 1 cup sugar for each cup fruit and water and boil to the jellying point.

LEMON MARMALADE

4 cups thinly sliced, seeded lemons
3 quarts water
9 cups sugar

Put the lemon slices and water in a preserving kettle, bring to a boil, and cook rapidly for about 20 minutes, or until the lemon rind is tender. Drain and measure the liquid. Add enough water to make 3 quarts of liquid, return the liquid and the lemons to the kettle, and stir in the sugar. Bring again to a boil and cook rapidly until the mixture sheets from a spoon, or to 221° F. on a candy thermometer.

Lime Marmalade Follow directions for **lemon marmalade,** using 3 cups sliced limes and 1 cup sliced lemons.

ORANGE MARMALADE

>6 oranges
>2 lemons
>Sugar

Wash the fruit and slice thinly or sliver the peel and cut the pulp into small pieces. Cover the fruit with 6 cups water, bring to a boil, and simmer for 5 minutes. Let stand in a cool place for 12 to 18 hours, then bring again to a boil and simmer until the peel is tender. Measure the fruit and water and add 1 cup sugar for each cup fruit. Boil rapidly to the jellying point.

Orange Lemon Marmalade   Follow the recipe for **orange marmalade,** using 4 oranges and 4 lemons.

ORANGE PEACH MARMALADE

>12 peaches
>3 oranges
>1½ tablespoons lemon juice
>Sugar

Peel, stone, and chop the peaches. Sliver half the peel of the oranges, cover with water, and boil until the peel is tender. Drain. Add the cooked orange peel, the orange pulp, and the lemon juice to the peaches and measure. Add ¾ cup sugar for each cup fruit and boil rapidly for 25 to 30 minutes, or until thick, stirring frequently to prevent burning.

ORANGE PINEAPPLE MARMALADE

>6 oranges
>1 lemon
>1 pineapple
>Sugar

Wash the oranges and lemon, discard the seeds, and put the fruit through a food chopper. Weigh the fruit and to each pound fruit add 1 quart water. Bring the water to a boil and simmer for 1 hour. Set aside for 20 minutes. Peel and core the pineapple and grate the flesh. Add the pineapple to the other fruit and continue to cook until the pineapple is tender. Cool and weigh again. Add an equal amount of sugar, bring again to a boil, and boil rapidly until the marmalade is thick.

Orange Apple Marmalade   Follow the recipe for **orange pine-apple marmalade,** using 4 large tart apples, peeled and cored, in place of the pineapple.

BITTER ORANGE MARMALADE

Weigh a preserving kettle. Cut 6 bitter oranges in half, squeeze out the juice and seeds, and strain the juice into the kettle. Put the seeds into a small bowl, just cover them with warm water, and let stand overnight. With kitchen scissors, cut the orange peel into fine slivers along with any bits of pulp adhering to it. Add the peel to the juice and weigh. Add 3 cups water for every pound of juice and peel and let stand overnight.

In the morning drain all the jelly off the seeds into the juice and peel. Keep spooning the liquid in the kettle over the seeds until no jelly remains on them and they no longer feel slippery. Bring the mixture in the kettle to a boil and simmer for 2 hours. Do not boil hard or too much moisture will be evaporated. Weigh again and to every pound of juice and peel add 1 pound sugar. Bring again to a boil and boil rapidly for about 30 minutes to the jellying point, or until a candy thermometer registers 220° F.

PEACH MARMALADE

    3 pounds peaches
    2 oranges
    4 tablespoons lemon juice
    3½ cups sugar

Peel, stone, and cut the peaches into ¼-inch slices. Grate the rind from the oranges, discard all the white membrane, and slice the fruit thinly. Combine the peaches, orange rind and pulp, lemon juice, and sugar, bring to a boil, and cook rapidly for about 30 minutes, or until the syrup is thick and the fruit is transparent, stirring frequently.

PEACH AND PEAR MARMALADE

    3 large firm-ripe pears
    3 large freestone peaches
    1 orange
    3 cups sugar
    Juice of 1 lime

Peel the pears and peaches and chop the flesh finely. Sliver the orange peel and cut the orange pulp finely, discarding the seeds. In a preserving kettle combine the orange peel and pulp and 1 cup water, bring to a boil, and cook until the orange peel is tender and the water is reduced to half. Add the peaches and pears, sugar, and lime juice and cook rapidly until the marmalade is thick.

GINGERED PEAR MARMALADE

4 pounds firm-ripe pears
2 pounds sugar
2 ounces preserved ginger, chopped
4 lemons, thinly sliced

Peel, core, and quarter the pears. Put them in a kettle with the sugar and ginger and let them stand overnight. In the morning, stir the fruit and sugar well and add the lemons. Bring slowly to a boil and simmer for about 2 hours, or until thick.

PRICKLY PEAR MARMALADE

2 oranges
1 cup thinly sliced lemons
4 cups water
4 cups chopped prickly pears
Sugar

Chop the orange peel and pulp, combine it with the lemons, and add the water. Let stand for 12 to 18 hours in a cool place. Bring the water to a boil and simmer until the peel is tender. Cool and add the pears. Measure the fruit and water and add 1 cup sugar for each cup fruit and water. Bring to a boil and boil rapidly to the jellying point.

PINEAPPLE MARMALADE

1 pineapple
3 cups sugar
Grated rind and juice of 3 lemons
1 cup raisins

Peel and core a pineapple and cut the flesh into small cubes. Add the sugar and rind and juice of the lemons, bring to a boil, and simmer for 30 minutes, or until thick. Add the raisins and cook for 5 minutes longer.

164

PINEAPPLE APRICOT MARMALADE

        1 large pineapple
        6 dozen fresh apricots
        Sugar

Pare, core, and cut the pineapple into small cubes. Peel and halve the apricots and discard the stones. Combine the fruit, measure it into a preserving kettle, and add 3 cups sugar to every 4 cups fruit. Heat slowly to the boiling point and cook gently until the marmalade is thick and the fruit is clear.

QUINCE APPLE MARMALADE

        6 quinces
        Water
        3 tart apples
        Sugar

Wash, peel, and chop the quinces, discarding the cores. Cover with water, bring to a boil, and simmer until tender. Peel, core, and chop the apples. Add the apples to the quinces and cook for 10 minutes longer. Measure the fruit and liquid. Add ¾ cup sugar to each cup fruit and water and boil rapidly to the jellying point.

RASPBERRY CURRANT MARMALADE

        4 cups raspberries
        2 cups currants
        4½ cups sugar

Wash and drain the raspberries and stem and crush the currants. Cook the currants slowly until the juice flows freely, then add the raspberries and bring to a boil. Add the sugar and cook rapidly to the jellying point.

RED PEPPER MARMALADE

        6 sweet red peppers
        3 oranges, thinly sliced
        Juice and grated rind of 1 lemon
        Sugar

Remove the stems from the peppers and discard the seeds and white veins. Cut the flesh into thin slivers, cover with a very little water, and cook for 10 minutes, or until tender. Add the oranges and the juice and rind of the lemon and measure. Add ⅔ cup sugar for each cup of the red pepper and fruit mixture and cook to the jellying point.

RHUBARB MARMALADE

> 4 pounds rhubarb, chopped
> Slivered rind and juice of 1 lemon
> Slivered rind and juice of 1 orange
> 1 pound seedless raisins, finely chopped
> 3 pounds sugar

In a preserving kettle combine the rhubarb, rind and juice of the lemon and orange, and the raisins and let stand for 30 minutes. Stir in the sugar, bring slowly to a boil, and cook for about 1 hour, or until the marmalade is thick, stirring occasionally.

SCOTCH MARMALADE

Use Seville oranges if possible, otherwise sour or wild oranges. Wash the fruit, remove the peel, discarding two thirds of it and retaining the third most free of blemishes. With kitchen scissors cut the peel into slivers and put the slivers in a kettle with 4 times the amount in weight of water. Bring the water to a boil, simmer for 10 minutes, and drain. Repeat the process three times, the last time cooking the peel until it is tender.

Cut the fruit of the oranges into small pieces, weigh it, and add 4 cups cold water to every pound of fruit. Bring to a boil and simmer until the fruit pulp is very soft. Strain the liquid through a jelly bag, pressing well, then strain the juice again through a flannel cloth wrung out of cold water without pressing.

Combine the juice and peel and weigh. To every pound of the mixture add 1½ pounds sugar, bring to a boil, and boil rapidly to the jellying point, or until the marmalade sheets from the edge of a spoon.

YELLOW TOMATO MARMALADE

> 1 quart small yellow tomatoes
> 1 small pineapple
> 2 pounds sugar
> Juice and grated rind of 2 lemons

166

Peel the tomatoes and quarter them. Peel and core the pineapple and cut the flesh into fine dice or shreds. Add enough water to the pineapple barely to cover it and simmer for 5 minutes. Add half the sugar and the tomatoes and cook until the fruit is tender. Add the remaining sugar and the juice and grated rind of the lemons and cook until the marmalade sheets from the edge of a spoon.

WILD CHERRY MARMALADE

2 oranges
1 quart pitted wild cherries
4 tablespoons lemon juice
3½ cups sugar

Peel the oranges, discard the white membrane from the peel, and cut the peel into slivers. Cut the orange pulp into small pieces, mix with the rind, and measure. Add an equal measure of water, bring to a boil, and simmer until the rind is tender. Add the cherries, lemon juice, and sugar and cook rapidly to the jelling point.

CHAPTER SIX

Pickling and Brining

When Caesar went into Egypt to conquer the Egyptian empire and remained to be conquered by the Queen of the Nile, he learned of the merits of pickles from Cleopatra, for the ancient nations were familiar with the use of salt and vinegar, and alchemists were curious about the mystery of fermentation. Many of their early experiments with fermentation established the elementary principles that are the basis of today's modern pickling methods.

The Greeks thought highly of their pickles, consisting of herbs, roots, flowers, and vegetables prepared with utmost care in a solution of brine, vinegar, and oil, and stored in cylindrical widemouthed vases. The Romans drank vinegar, tempering its acrimony with water and sugar, and they fed pickles daily to their gladiators to keep them in condition. Even now our present-day biochemists assure us that pickles perk up the appetite and aid digestion.

There are innumerable kinds and flavors of pickles. There are sour pickles, sweet pickles, mustard pickles, dill pickles, tarragon pickles—so named for the predominating flavor of the pickle; and

168

there are ketchups, chowchows, chili sauces, relishes, and chutneys —which names designate types of pickles rather than flavors. A relish, a chowchow, or a piccalilli is usually a combination of finely chopped, spiced vegetables. Ketchups and sauces are made from a strained or puréed mixture, and the word "chutney" conveys the connotation of a hot, highly seasoned condiment.

EQUIPMENT FOR PICKLING

The best container to use for curing or fermenting pickles is a stone crock, but clean paraffined wooden containers may also be used. A 2- or 4-gallon container is the best size for home use and may easily be cleaned. To cook pickles or to heat a pickling solution, use a kettle of enamelware, glass, or stainless steel. Don't use iron, copper, or zinc kettles. Iron darkens pickles, copper turns them green, and zinc destroys the color. The long-handled spoons used for stirring should be made of wood or stainless steel.

Glass jars with glass tops are the best containers for storing pickles. Avoid metal tops, for the acid and salt in the pickles may corrode them.

An inexpensive scale is an asset in any home kitchen, and is particularly important in the curing of cucumbers. The salt should be weighed rather than measured to insure the correct amount in the brine needed to cure cucumbers properly.

DO'S AND DON'T'S OF PICKLING

1. Use only firm, fresh, unbruised fruits and vegetables of the best quality. Cucumbers and tomatoes are best if they are pickled within twenty-four hours from the time they are harvested. Fruits may be slightly underripe.

2. Wash the fruits or vegetables carefully and thoroughly. Most fruits and vegetables should be peeled, but the skin is usually left on green tomatoes. Most fruits should be cored or pitted. Slice, dice, or chop the fruit or vegetable according to directions in the recipe, but cut them to uniform size, not merely for the sake of appearance but because the pickling liquid will cure uniform pieces more evenly.

3. Use modern pickle recipes. The vinegar of twenty years ago was weaker than today's vinegar, so old-time recipes probably call for more vinegar than is required for the best results.

4. Follow the recipes within reason. But *do* taste the pickle before turning it into containers for storage. The finished pickle may need

a little more salt, sugar, or spice to please your individual taste. *Don't* try to make any adjustments to the recipe in the beginning, for shriveled pickles owe their unattractive appearance to the use of too strong a salt or sugar or vinegar solution. On the other hand, too weak a brine may cause some pickles to spoil. Garlic may be added to or deleted from any recipe.

5. Keep vegetables below the brine at all times. If they are exposed to the air, the pickles may become soft or slippery.

6. Remove the scum from the top of the brine every day to keep the top layer of vegetables from spoiling. But if spoilage begins, remove the spoiled parts and add enough fresh brine of the same strength to cover the lower layers.

INGREDIENTS FOR PICKLING

Salt Use pure granulated salt. Do not use free-flowing or iodized table salt, for the chemicals added to these salts interfere with the brining and pickling processes. Most stores carry pickling salt.

Vinegar A clear vinegar, free from sediment, must be used to make good pickles. The acid content of the vinegar should be from 4 to 6 per cent. Most of the bottled vinegars on the market are of this strength, but read the label to be sure. Cider vinegar is preferred in pickling because of its special flavor, but white vinegar should be used to preserve the natural light color of such vegetables as cauliflower and onions.

Sugar Cane or beet sugar, granulated or brown, may be used, but it is best to use granulated white unless the recipe specifies brown. Honey or corn syrup may replace from one third to one half the amount of sugar called for in any recipe for sweet pickles.

Spices For full flavor, use spices of the very best quality. Spices should be renewed each year, for unless last year's spices were stored in airtight containers much of the flavor will have been dissipated. Unless the recipe specifies the use of ground spices, use whole spices, and tie them in a cheesecloth bag. The bag should be large enough to let the pickling liquid flow freely through the spices. Discard the bag before packing the pickles in jars.

Water Use soft water if possible, especially for long-process pickles, for the minerals in hard water interfere with the curing process. If the water is very hard, boil it, cool, and strain through several thicknesses of fine cloth.

Alum   Alum is used to make pickles crisp, but it may also make them bitter. In general, avoid the use of alum except where called for in specific recipes.

WHAT CAUSES PICKLES TO SPOIL?

Soft or slippery pickles   There are many reasons why pickles become soft or slippery. Too weak a curing brine is the most common, but failure to keep the pickles submerged under the brine and failure to remove the scum promptly from the surface of the brine are other reasons. Still others are the use of too weak vinegar; storing pickles in a warm place; or boiling pickles in the pickling liquid.

Shriveled pickles   Too much salt or sugar or too strong vinegar used at the beginning of the pickling process will cause pickles to shrivel.

Hollow pickles   Cucumbers that are too mature or that are allowed to stand for more than 24 hours off the vine are apt to be hollow before they are ever pickled. Hollow pickles usually float and should be set aside when the cucumbers are sorted and washed. They may be used for relish or chunks. Faulty curing will also result in hollow pickles.

Discolored pickles   The minerals, especially iron, in hard water may cause pickles to darken and discolor. The use of iron, copper, or zinc utensils in making pickles will also cause discoloration or abnormal coloring. A darkening of pickles should be expected when certain ground spices are specified in the recipe, or when cider vinegar is used with light-colored fruits and vegetables; this discoloration is in no way harmful.

Pickling Vegetables

There are usually two stages in making pickles: the **curing,** or **brining,** during which the vegetables are soaked in salt brine or sprinkled with dry salt and usually allowed to ferment, and the **finishing,** at which stage the vinegar, sugar, and spices are added. But many pickles and relishes are made without any cure at all;

171

others, such as the popular dill pickle, are cured and finished in a single operation. Some vegetables are preserved solely in brine, with no further treatment, and some types of pickles are both brined and finished.

Brining or curing   The chief purpose of brining is to change the physical structure of the vegetable so that it can more easily absorb the sugar, vinegar, and flavorings. When a vegetable is placed in a salt brine, the salt first draws out the water from the vegetable and changes the texture of the cells so that the substances essential to the growth of fermentation bacteria may pass out into the brine. The bacteria convert the sugars into acid, which cures the vegetable, and the acid, along with the salt, acts as a preservative. This process is well illustrated in the making of **sauerkraut,** in which the acid is the main preservative.

For practical purposes there are four types of brining: *low* and *high dry salting,* and *low* and *high wet salting.* Low dry salting is practiced in making sauerkraut, where from 2 to 2½ per cent dry salt in proportion to cabbage is used. But sometimes as much as 15 to 20 per cent salt is added dry to vegetables to preserve them. In this case enough water is drawn from the vegetables to make a brine to cover them, and little or no fermentation takes place.

Wet brining is used for vegetables that do not contain enough moisture to make sufficient brine. Small amounts of salt are used for the wet brining of dill pickles, cucumbers, peppers, green tomatoes, and a few other vegetables when some fermentation is desired. Larger amounts of salt—from 15 to 20 per cent—are used on cauliflower, onions, corn, peas, and lima beans, when no fermentation is desired. These vegetables are soaked, or freshened, in clear water to remove the salt, and are converted or *finished* into mixed pickles or relishes.

Finishing   This stage of pickling is essentially a matter of giving the pickle its distinctive quality by the addition of sugar, vinegar, and spices. The pickles are heated in a spiced vinegar to prevent the growth of yeasts and harmful bacterias, and to destroy the enzymes which, if allowed to remain active, would cause the pickles to soften.

Vegetables in strong brine   Pack the vegetable loosely in a crock and cover with a brine made by dissolving 3¾ cups salt in 6 quarts water. Cover with a plate, weigh the plate down, and let stand for 24 hours. On the second day add 1 pound of salt for every 10 pounds of the vegetable. Put the salt on top of the plate so that the brine will gradually dissolve it, otherwise it will sink to the bottom. At the end of 1 week, add ¼ pound of salt and repeat every week for 5 weeks. Skim off the white scum if it forms.

Vegetables fermented in weak brine Prepare the vegetable as you would for table use. Blanch string beans in boiling water for 5 minutes and cool in cold water. Wash greens in several changes of cold water to remove the sand. Wash but do not slice carrots, beets, or tomatoes. Pack the vegetables loosely in a clean crock, cover them with a cloth, and place a plate and a weight on top. Make a brine by dissolving ½ pound, or ¾ cup, salt and 1 cup vinegar in 1 gallon soft water. Pour the brine over the vegetables to cover the plate and set in a cool place. Remove the white scum, wash the plate, and weight and change the cloth every other day.

In 2 to 4 weeks, when fermentation has ceased, pack the vegetables firmly in clean jars and fill the jars to overflowing with the brine. Adjust the lids and process in a boiling-water bath:

  Pints: 25 minutes
  Quarts: 30 minutes

Do not taste brined vegetables until after they have been processed. The vegetable will have a characteristic sour, salty flavor. To prepare the vegetable for the table, rinse in cold water and cook in fresh water. To reduce the salt and sour flavor, soak the vegetable in cold water for several hours.

SAUERKRAUT

Select solid mature heads of cabbage. Remove the outer leaves, cut the heads into quarters, and cut out the cores. Weigh the cabbage accurately, allowing from 40 to 50 pounds of cabbage and 1 pound of salt to a 5-gallon crock.

Shred the cabbage finely on a kraut cutter, weigh 5 pounds shredded cabbage into a bowl, and with the hands mix in 2 ounces, or 3½ tablespoons, pickling salt. Put the salted cabbage in a crock or a tight wooden keg, and tamp it down firmly with a wooden masher to extract the juice and force out the air. Repeat until the cabbage comes to within 4 inches of the top of the container and juice covers the cabbage.

Cover the cabbage with a layer or two of clean white cloth, tucking it down around the edge, and place on top a plate or round wooden board small enough to fit snugly inside the container. Weigh the plate or board down with a clean rock or brick. A jar filled with water makes a good weight. Set the crock in a warm place, from

70° to 75° F. Every other day, remove the scum that forms on top, wash and dry the cloth, and wash the plate and weight.

The kraut will be fermented or cured in 10 to 20 days, depending on the temperature at which it is stored. Its appearance and taste will tell you when it is fermented. Move the crock, with the cloth and weighted cover, to a cold place and it will keep for several months. Or the kraut may be packed in jars, covered with brine, sealed, and stored in a cool place. It will keep for several months. If longer storage is desired the kraut should be processed.

To preserve sauerkraut   Pack the kraut in glass jars. If extra brine is needed to fill the jars to overflowing, dissolve 1½ tablespoons salt in 1 quart soft water. Adjust the jar lids and set the jars in a pan of cold water with water up to the shoulders of the jars. Bring the water slowly to a boil, cover, and process for 30 minutes. Complete the seal on the jars, if necessary.

Small quantity sauerkraut   Weigh 10 pounds of finely shredded cabbage and mix it thoroughly with 4 ounces, or 7 tablespoons, salt. Pack the kraut firmly into quart jars, tamping it to draw out the juice. A quart jar will hold 2 pounds of shredded cabbage. Cover the kraut in each jar with rounds of cheesecloth and insert a wooden splint to hold the cabbage under the brine. Adjust the jar lids loosely and set the jars on a tray to catch any juice that might overflow during fermentation. Remove the scum as it forms each day and keep the jars at room temperature (70° F.) for 10 days to 2 weeks.

To store, make a brine by dissolving 1 tablespoon salt in 3 cups water. Fill the jars to overflowing with the brine, seal, and store in a cold place, where the kraut will keep for several months. For longer storage periods, or if the kraut is to be stored in a warm kitchen, process it as above.

Mild sauerkraut   Shred solid heads of cabbage and pack it firmly into quart jars. Do not use the self-sealing type jars. Add 1 teaspoon salt to each jar and fill the jars to overflowing with water that has been boiled and cooled to lukewarm. Seal the jars and keep in a warm place for 2 days. Tighten the seal and store in a cold place.

PRESERVING OLIVES

Gather the olives when they have attained their full size but before they have begun to change to their ripening color. Sort them according to size and quality and in order to prevent bruising drop them immediately into pails containing water.

Wash the olives thoroughly and put them into stone crocks or tight wooden kegs. Cover them with a solution made by dissolving 2 ounces soda lye, 1 ounce lime, and 1 ounce pickling salt in 1 gallon water. The solution should cover the fruit by 2 inches. Place a weighted board or plate on top to keep the olives submerged. This lye treatment is necessary to remove the excess bitterness from the fruit, and it will take from 8 to 10 hours, depending on the size, variety, and ripeness of the olives. Stir the olives frequently.

The lye changes the color of the olive to a yellowish green, and the lye should be allowed to penetrate the olive almost but not quite to the pit. If the penetration is not deep enough the olives will still be bitter, but if the penetration is allowed to go too far the flavor, color, and texture of the finished olives will be destroyed. The penetration of the lye solution is clearly indicated by a dark ring in the flesh. Cut away the tip portion of one of the largest of the olives. When the dark ring has progressed about two thirds of the way to the pit, the treatment is complete.

Remove the olives from the lye solution immediately and let them stand in cold water for several hours, stirring the fruit occasionally and changing the water several times. All traces of the lye must be removed before the olives are brined, and the only sure way of determining this is to press red litmus paper against the cut surface of a few of the washed olives. The litmus paper will turn blue if any trace of lye remains. Litmus paper is available at any drugstore.

As soon as the olives are free of lye they should be brined.

Dissolve 2 ounces pickling salt in 1 gallon water. Bring the brine to a boil, cool, and pour it over the olives. The next day drain the olives and cover them with a similar brine made with 4 ounces salt and 1 gallon water. The next day drain the olives and cover them with a boiled and cooled brine made of 8 ounces salt and 1 gallon water and let them stand in a cool place for 24 hours.

Then pack the olives into jars, fill the jars to overflowing with the brine, and adjust the jar lids. Process the jars in a simmering-water bath (180° F.) for 30 minutes. Tighten the jars if necessary and store the olives in a cool, dark place.

Fermented olives   After the olives are washed to rid them of any trace of lye, put them in a brine made by dissolving 1 pound salt in 9 pints water and let them ferment for several weeks. When fermentation is complete the olive flesh will be a yellowish green all the way to the pit.

CURING CUCUMBERS

1. The **long cure** takes from 8 to 10 weeks. The cucumbers are heavily salted and can be stored for several months before they are freshened and made into a specific kind of pickle.

2. The **short cure** takes from 7 to 10 days, and the cucumbers need not be freshened before they are made into pickles. They must, however, be pickled immediately after the fermentation period or they will spoil.

3. The **24-hour cure** is really a soaking in brine rather than a cure, since little or no fermentation takes place.

Long or short cure begins in the same way   Wash the cucumbers well to remove all sand and dirt, weigh them, and pack them into a 4-gallon crock or container. The crock should be filled to not more than 4 inches from the top.

For 12 pounds cucumbers, make a brine by dissolving 15 ounces pickling salt (1½ cups) in 6 quarts soft water. For each additional 2 pounds cucumbers, make 1 quart more brine (2½ ounces salt per quart of water).

Cover the cucumbers with the brine, cover with a plate or round board that will fit snugly down inside the crock, and place on it a weight to keep the cucumbers submerged below the surface of the brine. Then tie a clean cloth over the crock to keep out the dust and set the cucumbers in a warm place to ferment. The ideal temperature is between 65° and 70° F.

Do not stir the brine during the fermentation period. If the plate fits closely and the weight on the plate holds the cucumbers below the surface of the brine, no scum should form. If scum does form, remove it immediately and thoroughly.

Short-cured pickles   At the end of a week or 10 days, take the cucumbers from the brine, wash them to remove the salt brine, and make them into pickles according to the recipes in the section **"Vegetable Pickles."**

Long-cured pickles   At the end of a week place ½ pound salt on top of the plate or board for 12 pounds cucumbers; ¾ pound salt for 16 pounds cucumbers; 1 pound salt for 20 pounds cucumbers. The salt will gradually be dissolved into the brine. Place the crock in a cool place.

Repeat the addition of salt at the end of the second, third, fourth, and fifth weeks.

Fermentation is complete when the brine stops foaming. Very large cucumbers may take as long as 2 months. To test, slice a

176

cucumber in half. A cucumber that is completely fermented is free from whitish spots, is transparent, firm, crisp in texture, and dark olive-green in color.

If the long-cured cucumbers are sealed from the air and kept cool they will keep for several months. Skim the surface of the brine carefully, cover the surface with a layer of mineral oil, and replace the cover and weight. Place in a cold cellar or basement. Or pack the cucumbers in glass jars, cover with brine, seal, and store.

Freshening long-cured cucumbers Before long-cured cucumbers can be made into pickles they must be freshened in lukewarm water. Take the cucumbers from the brine and cover them with fresh lukewarm water. Let them soak in a warm place for 6 to 12 hours, changing the water two or three times. For sweet pickles, cucumbers should be almost free of saltiness; for other pickles they may be slightly salty. Test by tasting.

Freshened pickles may be made into **sweet** or **sour pickles, dill pickles, bread and butter pickles,** and many other favorites. Use very small cucumbers, or gherkins, for **sweet** or **sour pickles.** Cut slightly larger cucumbers in half lengthwise for **spiced pickles, sweet** or **sour.** The next larger size are made into **dill pickles** or sliced for **bread and butter pickles.** If still larger, they are used for **dill pickles,** cut into squares for chunk pickles, or ground for chowchows.

To use short- or long-cured cucumbers in pickle recipes Omit the 24-hour brining period in pickle recipes and follow the remaining instructions. Remember, short-cure cucumbers may be used directly from the brine. Long-cure cucumbers MUST be refreshed before use.

Vegetable Pickles

SWEET GHERKINS

> 2 quarts small cucumbers, or gherkins, from 1 to 2 inches long
> 3 cups sugar
> 1 quart vinegar
> 2 tablespoons whole allspice
> 1 tablespoon celery seeds
> 2 tablespoons broken cinnamon sticks
> 2 tablespoons whole cloves
> ½ cup white mustard seeds

Brine the cucumbers: dissolve ½ cup salt in 2 quarts water, pour the solution over the cucumbers, and let them stand for 24 hours in a cool place. Drain.

Put the cucumbers in a clean crock. Dissolve 1 cup of the sugar in the vinegar and add the spices, tied in a bag. Bring the vinegar to a boil, boil for 5 minutes, remove the spice bag, and pour the boiling-hot syrup over the cucumbers.

Next day, drain off the syrup, add 1 cup sugar, and bring to a rolling boil. Pour the boiling-hot syrup over the cucumbers. Repeat this step the following day, adding the last cup of sugar.

Next day, drain the syrup from the pickles and pack the pickles into hot, sterilized jars. Heat the syrup to a rolling boil and fill the jars. Remove any air bubbles trapped in the jar by running the blade of a knife up and down the sides of the jar. Add more syrup if necessary to cover the pickles completely and seal at once.

To use short- or long-cure cucumbers   Omit the brining process. Freshen **long-cure cucumbers.**

ONE-DAY SWEET GHERKINS

        2 quarts gherkins
        ½ cup salt
        2 quarts water
        6 cups brown sugar
        1 quart cider vinegar
        1 tablespoon whole allspice
        1 tablespoon whole cloves
        ½ tablespoon celery seeds
        ½ tablespoon mustard seeds
        1 stick cinnamon
        Bay leaves

Wash the gherkins and soak them overnight in a brine made of the salt and water. In the morning, drain the gherkins, rinse them in hot water, and drain again. In a preserving kettle bring the brown sugar and vinegar to a boil. Add the gherkins and the spices, tied in a cheesecloth bag. Take the kettle from the heat and let the gherkins cool in the pickling syrup. Remove the spice bag. Pack the pickles in pint jars and add 1 bay leaf to each jar. A small hot red pepper may also be added. Heat the syrup to the boiling point, fill the jars to overflowing, and seal.

To use short- or long-cure cucumbers   Omit the brining process. Freshen **long-cure cucumbers.**

SWEET CHUNK PICKLES

1 gallon medium or large cucumbers
1 cup salt
1 gallon water
8 cups sugar
4 cups vinegar
2 tablespoons mixed pickling spices

Wash the cucumbers, put them in a crock, and cover them with a brine made by dissolving the salt in the water. Let them stand in the brine for 24 hours and drain.

Cut the cucumbers into chunks and put them in a clean crock. Combine 2 cups of the sugar and the vinegar and add the spices, tied in a bag. Bring the vinegar to a boil, boil for 5 minutes, and pour the boiling-hot syrup over the cucumbers. Discard the spice bag. Next day, drain off the syrup, add 2 more cups of the sugar, and bring the syrup to a rolling boil. Pour the boiling-hot syrup over the cucumbers. Repeat this step for two more days, adding 2 cups of sugar each day.

Next day, drain the syrup from the pickles and pack the pickles into hot, sterilized jars. Heat the syrup to a rolling boil and fill the jars. Remove any trapped air with a knife, add more syrup if necessary to cover the pickles completely, and seal.

To use short- or long-cure cucumbers Omit the brining process. Freshen **long-cure cucumbers.**

OLD-FASHIONED CUCUMBER CHUNKS

1 gallon cucumber chunks
1½ cups salt
1 gallon water
9 cups cider vinegar
5 cups sugar
2 tablespoons mixed pickling spices
1 teaspoon powdered alum

Put the cucumber chunks into a stone jar or enamel kettle. Dissolve the salt in the water and pour the brine over the cucumbers. Place a weighted plate on the top to keep the cucumbers submerged and let stand for 36 hours. Drain. Pour 4 cups of the vinegar over the cucumbers, add enough water to cover, and bring to a boil. Simmer for 10 minutes and drain.

Combine 2 cups of the sugar with 3 cups water and the remaining vinegar. Add the spices, tied in a bag, bring to a boil, and simmer for 10 minutes. Discard the spice bag and pour the spiced vinegar over the cucumbers. Let stand for 24 hours. Drain the liquid into a kettle and add the remaining sugar and the alum. Bring to a boil, pour over the cucumbers, and let stand for 24 hours. Pack the pickles into hot jars. Bring the syrup to a boil, pour it boiling hot over the pickles to cover, and seal.

To use short- or long-cure cucumbers Omit the brining process. Freshen **long-cure cucumbers.**

CUCUMBER CHIPS

> 24 slender cucumbers 5 inches long
> ½ cup salt
> 7 cups vinegar
> 5 cups water
> 1 tablespoon turmeric
> 2 cups white sugar
> 1 tablespoon white mustard seeds
> 1 piece ginger root
> 2 sticks cinnamon
> 1 teaspoon cloves
> 2 cups brown sugar
> 1 teaspoon powdered alum

Slice the cucumbers thinly, mix the slices with the salt, and let stand for 3 hours. Drain thoroughly. Combine 3 cups of the vinegar, 4 cups of the water, and the turmeric and bring to a boil. Pour the liquid over the cucumbers, let stand until cool, and drain.

Combine the white sugar, the remaining water and vinegar, and the spices, tied in a bag, and bring to a boil. Boil for 15 minutes, discard the spice bag, and pour the spiced vinegar over the cucumbers. Let stand for 12 to 24 hours. Drain the liquid from the cucumbers, stir in the brown sugar, and bring to a boil. Add the cucumbers and simmer for 10 minutes. Pack the cucumbers into hot jars. Add the alum to the syrup, heat again to a boil, and pour the boiling-hot syrup over the cucumbers. Seal at once.

To use short- or long-cure cucumbers Omit the salting process. Freshen **long-cure cucumbers.**

SENF GURKEN

12 large cucumbers
½ cup salt
4½ cups water
6 cups cider vinegar
3 cups brown sugar
6 cloves garlic
12 teaspoons grated horseradish
6 teaspoons mustard seeds
6 small hot red peppers

Peel the cucumbers, slice them in half lengthwise, and scoop out the seeds. Cut the halves into strips 1 inch thick and 2 inches long and soak them overnight in a brine made of the salt and water. In the morning drain the cucumbers and put them in a preserving kettle with the vinegar and sugar. Bring the liquid to a boil and simmer the cucumbers for 5 minutes, or until tender. Pack the strips in hot pint jars with 1 clove garlic, 2 teaspoons horseradish, 1 teaspoon mustard seeds, and 1 hot pepper in each jar. Seal immediately.

To use short- or long-cure cucumbers   Omit the brining process. Freshen **long-cure cucumbers.**

FRENCH CUCUMBER PICKLES

Cut large cucumbers into strips about the length and width of a finger, sprinkle them generously with salt, and let them stand for 24 hours. Then drain thoroughly and dry the strips on a towel.

Into each pint jar put ½ teaspoon sugar, 1 teaspoon mustard seeds, ½ teaspoon white peppercorns, a spray of dill, and 1 teaspoon each of minced shallots and horseradish. Pack the cucumber strips in the jars and cover them with cider vinegar, heated to a boil and cooled. Place the lids on the jars and let the jars stand in a cool place for 48 hours. At the end of this time, drain the liquid from the cucumbers, bring it to a boil, cool, and cover the cucumbers in the jars. Repeat this procedure twice more, each time after an interval of 48 hours, and seal the jars.

To use short- or long-cure cucumbers   Omit the salting process. Freshen **long-cure cucumbers.**

CRISP BREAD AND BUTTER PICKLES

4 quarts thinly sliced cucumbers
8 white onions, peeled and sliced
½ cup salt
5 cups sugar
1½ teaspoons turmeric
1 teaspoon celery seeds
2 tablespoons mustard seeds
5 cups cider vinegar

Mix the cucumbers and onions with the salt and 2 quarts cracked ice and let them stand, covered with a weighted lid, for 3 hours. Drain thoroughly and put the vegetables in a large kettle. Add the sugar, spices, and vinegar and bring almost to a boil, stirring often with a wooden spoon, but do not let boil. Pack the pickles into hot jars and seal.

To use short- or long-cure cucumbers Omit the salting process. Freshen **long-cure cucumbers** before slicing them.

SPICED BREAD AND BUTTER PICKLES

4 quarts medium-sized cucumbers
2 green peppers, seeded
8 small white onions, peeled
½ cup salt
5 cups sugar
5 cups cider vinegar
1½ teaspoons turmeric
⅛ teaspoon ground cloves
2 tablespoons mustard seeds
2 teaspoons celery seeds

Wash the cucumbers carefully and slice them thinly into a large bowl. Slice the peppers and onions and add them to the cucumbers. Add the salt, mix well, and cover with ice cubes. Cover the bowl and let the vegetables stand for 3 hours. Drain well.

In a saucepan combine the sugar, vinegar, turmeric, cloves, mustard seeds, and celery seeds, bring the vinegar slowly to a boil, and boil for 3 minutes. Add the drained vegetables and bring almost to a boil but do not boil. Pack into hot sterilized jars and seal.

To use short- or long-cure cucumbers Omit the salting process. Freshen **long-cure cucumbers** before slicing them.

SOUR PICKLES

>4 quarts cucumbers
>1 cup salt
>1 gallon water
>6 cups vinegar
>1 cup sugar
>½ tablespoon whole cloves
>½ tablespoon mustard seeds
>½ tablespoon peppercorns
>½ tablespoon celery seeds

Wash the cucumbers and put them in a clean crock. Cover them with a brine made by dissolving the salt in the water. Let the cucumbers stand in the brine for 24 hours and drain.

Cut the cucumbers in half lengthwise or in strips, according to their size, and put them in a clean crock. Combine the vinegar and sugar and add the spices, tied in a bag. Bring to a boil and boil for 5 minutes. Remove the spice bag and pour the boiling-hot syrup over the cucumbers. Let stand for 24 hours.

Drain the syrup off the cucumbers and pack the cucumbers in hot sterilized jars. Heat the syrup to a rolling boil and fill the jars. Remove any trapped air bubbles with a knife and seal.

To use short- or long-cure cucumbers Omit the brining process. Freshen **long-cure cucumbers.**

FERMENTED DILL CUCUMBERS OR GREEN TOMATOES
(Large Quantity Method)

>16 pounds medium-sized or large cucumbers or green tomatoes
>¾ cup mixed pickling spices
>Fresh dill
>1¼ pounds (2 cups) salt
>2 gallons water

Wash and drain the vegetables. Place half the pickling spices and a good layer of dill in a 5-gallon crock or stone jar. Fill the crock with cucumbers or green tomatoes to within 4 inches of the top.

Dissolve the salt in the water and pour it over the vegetables. Add the remaining pickling spices and put a layer of dill over the top. Cover with a large plate or wooden lid that just fits within the top of the crock and weight it down to bring the brine to the cover but not over it. Be sure all the vegetables are submerged. Keep the crock at room temperature (65° to 70° F.) for 2 to 4 weeks, remov-

183

ing any scum that forms each day. The pickles are ready to use when they are well flavored with dill and are clear when cut, with no white spots.

Pack the cured pickles in hot, sterilized jars. Strain the pickling brine, bring it to a rolling boil, and pour it over the pickles to fill the jars. Seal and store in a cool, dark place.

Sour Dills   Add ¼ cup vinegar to each quart jar.

Garlic Dills   Add ½ pound peeled garlic cloves to the curing crock.

A variety of flavors   A little imagination will add variety to pickles as well as to many other preserves. Try adding 3 tablespoons whole white peppercorns or cloves, a handful of bay leaves or fresh tarragon, summer savory or sweet basil, ½ pound fresh sliced horseradish, or ¼ pound fresh sliced ginger to the curing crock.

KOSHER DILL PICKLES (Quick Method)

> 4 quarts medium-sized cucumbers
> 4 cups vinegar
> 1 cup salt
> 3 quarts water
> FOR EACH QUART
> 2 sprays dill
> 1 clove garlic
> 1 small hot red pepper

Wash the cucumbers and let them stand in cold water overnight. Put a spray of dill in the bottom of each jar, and pack the cucumbers into the jars, being careful not to bruise them. Add a clove of garlic and a hot red pepper to each jar and place a spray of dill on top. Combine the vinegar, salt, and water and bring to a rolling boil. Fill the jars to overflowing with the vinegar brine, seal the jars, and store in a cool dark place.

GARLIC DILL PICKLES

> Dill
> Garlic
> Small hot red peppers
> Cucumbers
> Salt
> Vinegar

184

In the bottom of sterilized quart jars put a large spray of dill, 1 clove garlic, and 1 hot pepper. Pack firm cucumbers, washed and dried, in the jars and fill the jars with a brine made of 1 cup salt and 1 cup cider vinegar to each 14 cups cold water. Top each jar with another spray of dill and a clove of garlic. Seal the jars, and store in a dark, cool spot for 4 to 6 weeks before using.

SWEET DILL PICKLES

6 large dill pickles
2 cups sugar
½ cup tarragon vinegar
3 cloves garlic, halved
2 tablespoons mixed pickling spices

Cut the pickles into slices ¼ inch thick and pack them in jars. Combine the sugar, vinegar, and the garlic and pickling spices, tied in a bag. Bring to a boil and cool. Discard the spice bag. Pour the cool syrup over the pickles in the jars and seal. Store in the refrigerator for at least 1 week before using.

FIVE-DAY SWEET DILL PICKLES

4 quarts medium-sized cucumbers
4 cups sugar
2 cups vinegar
2 cloves garlic
2 tablespoons broken stick cinnamon
2 tablespoons whole cloves
2 tablespoons peppercorns

Slice the cucumbers ½ inch thick and put them in a clean crock. In a saucepan combine 1 cup of the sugar and the vinegar. Add the garlic and the spices, tied in a bag, bring to a boil, and boil for 5 minutes. Pour the syrup over the cucumbers and let stand for 24 hours. On the next three successive days drain off the syrup and add another cup of the sugar. Bring the syrup to a rolling boil and pour it over the cucumbers.

On the fifth day, drain off the syrup and pack the cucumbers into hot sterilized jars. Bring the syrup again to a boil, pour it over the cucumbers to fill the jars, and seal.

RIPE CUCUMBER PICKLES

    12 large ripe yellow cucumbers
    ½ cup salt
    1½ cups sugar
    4 cups vinegar
    ½ cup water
    4 tablespoons mixed pickling spices

Wash and dry the cucumbers and slice them or cut into chunks. Sprinkle with the salt and let stand about 18 hours. Drain, rinse in cold water, and drain again. Combine the sugar, vinegar, and water. Add the spices, tied in a bag, and bring to a boil. Add the cucumbers and simmer for 15 minutes. Discard the spice bag and pack boiling hot into hot jars and seal.

SWEET RIPE CUCUMBER STRIPS

    12 large ripe cucumbers
    ½ cup salt
    3 pounds sugar
    4 cups cider vinegar
    2 tablespoons mustard seeds
    1 whole stick cinnamon
    1 tablespoon whole cloves

Cut the cucumbers in half lengthwise and scrape out the seeds with a silver spoon. Sprinkle with the salt and let stand in a cool place for about 18 hours. Drain and dry the cucumbers.

Combine the sugar and vinegar, add the spices, tied in a bag, and bring slowly to a boil, stirring until the sugar is dissolved. Add the cucumbers and simmer for about 20 minutes, or until they are glossy. They must remain crisp. Discard the spice bag. Pack cucumbers and syrup in jars and seal.

CUCUMBER OIL PICKLES

    4 quarts thinly sliced slender cucumbers
    4 cups thinly sliced onions
    ½ cup salt
    ⅔ cup olive oil
    ¼ cup mustard seeds
    ½ teaspoon crushed hot red peppers
    1 quart white vinegar

Mix the cucumbers and onions in a large bowl, sprinkle them with the salt, and let stand for 6 to 8 hours. Drain well and pack the slices in clean hot pint jars to within about 1 inch of the top.

Mix the olive oil, mustard seeds, and red peppers in a saucepan and slowly stir in the vinegar. When well blended, pour the liquid over the cucumbers and onions to fill each jar to overflowing, making sure that some of the seeds and peppers are in each jar. Seal and store in a cool, dark place for 2 weeks before using. The oil rises to the top and seals the pickles. To use, shake the jar to distribute the oil; once a jar is opened it must be stored in the refrigerator.

ICE-WATER PICKLES

> 3 pounds 4-inch cucumbers
> 5 medium-sized onions
> 1 tablespoon mustard seeds
> 1 quart cider vinegar
> 1 cup sugar
> ¼ cup salt

Wash the cucumbers, quarter them lengthwise, and soak in ice water for 2 hours. Slice the onions and pack the onions in the bottoms of 5 sterilized pint jars. Pack the cucumbers lengthwise in the jars. Combine the mustard seeds, vinegar, sugar, and salt, bring to a boil, and boil for 1 minute. Fill the jars to overflowing with the boiling-hot syrup and seal.

CURRY PICKLES

> 24 medium-sized cucumbers, thinly sliced
> ½ cup salt
> 2 quarts water
> 1 teaspoon curry powder
> 2 cups vinegar
> 2½ cups sugar
> ¼ cup mustard
> 1 tablespoon celery seeds

Put the cucumbers in a bowl, add the salt and water, and let stand for 5 hours. Drain and rinse the cucumbers well. Combine the remaining ingredients and bring to a boil. Add the cucumbers and heat just to the boiling point. Pack into hot sterilized jars and seal.

To use short- or long-cure cucumbers Omit the brining process. Freshen **long-cure cucumbers** before slicing them.

MIXED PICKLES

4 cups cut cucumbers
2 cups cut carrots
2 cups cut celery
2 sweet red peppers, seeded and chopped
1 pod hot red pepper
1 cauliflower, broken into flowerets
2 cups pickling onions, peeled
1 cup salt
1 gallon water
1½ cups sugar
5 cups vinegar
4 tablespoons mustard seeds
2 tablespoons celery seeds

Mix the prepared vegetables, sprinkle them with the salt, and add the water. Let the vegetables soak in the brine for 18 hours, then drain. Combine the sugar and vinegar, add the seeds, tied in a bag, and bring to a boil. Boil for 3 minutes, add the vegetables, and simmer until the vegetables are heated through. Bring to a boil, discard the seed bag, pack, boiling hot, in jars, and seal.

END-OF-THE-SEASON PICKLES

1 cup sliced cucumbers
1 cup chopped sweet peppers
1 cup chopped cabbage
1 cup sliced onions
1 cup chopped green tomatoes
½ cup salt
2 quarts water
1 cup chopped carrots
1 cup Frenched string beans
2 tablespoons mustard seeds
1 tablespoon celery seeds
1 cup chopped celery
2 cups cider vinegar
2 cups sugar
2 tablespoons turmeric

Combine the cucumbers, peppers, cabbage, onions, and tomatoes and cover them with a brine made by dissolving the salt in the water. Let the vegetables soak overnight, then drain. Cook the carrots and string beans separately in water to cover until tender and drain. Mix the prepared vegetables with the remaining ingredients, bring to a boil, and simmer for 10 minutes. Seal in hot sterilized jars.

ARTICHOKE PICKLES

Small or medium-sized artichokes
2 quarts cider vinegar
1 tablespoon mixed pickling spices
1 tablespoon whole cloves
1 stick cinnamon, broken
⅛ teaspoon mace
½ teaspoon thyme
2 cups sugar

Remove the leaves and chokes from the artichokes. Trim the hearts and drop them immediately into water acidulated with 2 tablespoons vinegar or the juice of 1 lemon.

In a preserving kettle bring the vinegar to a boil with the spices, tied in a bag. Set aside and let the spices steep in the vinegar for 45 minutes. Then stir in the sugar, bring to a boil, and simmer for 20 minutes. Add the artichoke hearts, a few at a time, and boil for 1 minute. Remove the hearts with a skimmer and put them into hot sterilized jars. Continue cooking the hearts until they are all packed in jars. Discard the spice bag. Fill the jars to overflowing with the boiling-hot spiced vinegar and seal.

JERUSALEM ARTICHOKE PICKLES

1 gallon Jerusalem artichokes
Small hot red peppers
2 quarts vinegar
1 cup brown sugar
½ cup salt

Wash and scrub the artichokes, dry them with a cloth, and pack them into sterilized jars. Add a hot pepper to each jar. Bring the other ingredients to a boil and boil for 5 minutes. Fill the jars to overflowing with the boiling-hot syrup and seal.

DILLED GREEN BEANS

Wash and trim the beans and pack them upright in hot pint jars. To each jar add ½ teaspoon red pepper, 2 cloves garlic, and a large spray of dill. Combine 2 cups each of water and vinegar, add ¼ cup salt, and bring to a boil. Pour the boiling-hot solution over the beans and seal.

CAULIFLOWER PICKLES

    2 cauliflowers
    2 cups pickling onions
    1 cup salt
    1 cup sugar
    3 cups white vinegar
    2 tablespoons white mustard seeds
    1 tablespoon celery seeds
    1 small hot red pepper

Wash the cauliflowers and break them into flowerets. Scald, cool, and peel the onions. Mix the vegetables with the salt, add just enough water to cover, and let stand about 18 hours. Drain, rinse in cool water, and drain again. Dissolve the sugar in the vinegar, add the seeds and the hot pepper, and bring to a boil. Add the vegetables and simmer for 10 minutes, or until the vegetables are barely tender. Pack the vegetables hot into hot jars, fill the jars with the boiling-hot liquid, and seal.

"MANGOES" (Stuffed Peppers, Green Tomatoes, Cucumbers, Cantaloupe, et cetera)

Wash and drain the vegetables. Cut and reserve the tops from the peppers, tomatoes, or cantaloupes; cut and reserve the ends from the cucumbers. Scoop out the centers. Dissolve 1 cup salt in 1 gallon cold water, pour the brine over the vegetables, and let stand in a cool place for 24 hours. Drain, rinse in fresh, cool water, and drain again. Fill the shells with any **vegetable relish** desired, replace the tops, and fasten with toothpicks. Pack the stuffed vegetables into hot jars, fill the jars with boiling-hot vinegar, spiced and sweetened to taste, and seal.

MUSHROOM PICKLES

    ⅞ cup white vinegar
    1 bottle dry white wine (⅘ quart)
    5 pounds mushrooms, peeled
    5 cloves garlic
    2 teaspoons salt
    Bay leaves
    Cloves

Two days before pickling the mushrooms, combine the vinegar and wine and let stand in an open vessel, covered with 3 layers of

190

cheesecloth. Simmer the mushrooms for 10 minutes in salted water to cover; drain and dry the mushrooms in a cloth. In a kettle combine the wine-vinegar mixture, the garlic, and the salt and bring to a rolling boil. Add the mushrooms, a few at a time so that the liquid will not stop boiling, and boil rapidly for 5 minutes. Pack the mushrooms into hot sterilized jars with 1 bay leaf and a few cloves in each jar, fill the jars to overflowing with the boiling-hot liquid, and seal.

PICKLED ONIONS I

>4 quarts small onions
>1 cup salt
>1 quart boiling water
>1 quart white vinegar
>6 tablespoons whole allspice
>2 tablespoons peppercorns
>Small hot red peppers

Peel the onions, cover them with cold water, and let stand overnight. In the morning drain and pour over them a hot brine made by adding the salt to the boiling water. Let the onions stand in a cool place for 24 hours. Then drain and rinse thoroughly. Heat the vinegar slowly to a boil with the allspice and peppercorns, tied in a bag. Add the onions, bring the vinegar again to a boil, and pack the onions in sterilized jars. Discard the spice bag. Add 1 small red pepper to each jar, fill to overflowing with the hot vinegar, and seal.

PICKLED ONIONS II

>1 gallon pickling onions
>1 cup salt
>1 to 2 cups sugar
>5 cups white vinegar
>3 tablespoons white mustard seeds
>2 tablespoons horseradish
>Hot red peppers
>Bay leaves

Scald the onions for 2 minutes in boiling water, dip into cold water, and peel. Sprinkle the onions with the salt, add cold water to cover, and let stand for 12 hours, or overnight. In the morning drain the onions, rinse them in cold, fresh water, and drain again. Combine the sugar, vinegar, mustard seeds, and horseradish, bring to a boil, and simmer for 15 minutes. Pack the onions into sterilized jars. Add 1 small pepper and 1 bay leaf to each jar, fill the jars with the boiling-hot liquid, and seal.

PICKLED PEPPERS

    1 gallon long sweet peppers, red, green, or yellow
    1½ cups salt
    1 gallon water
    5 cups vinegar
    1 cup water
    2 tablespoons sugar
    1 tablespoon grated horseradish
    1 clove garlic

Wash the peppers, cut 2 small slits in each pepper, and sprinkle them with the salt. Pour the gallon of water over the peppers and let stand for 12 to 18 hours. Drain the peppers, rinse them in fresh, cold water, and drain again. Combine the vinegar with the cup of water, the sugar, horseradish, and garlic. Bring to a boil and simmer for 15 minutes. Discard the garlic. Pack the peppers into hot jars and fill the jars to the top with the boiling-hot pickling liquid. Seal immediately.

PICKLED STUFFED PEPPERS

    24 green peppers
    2 quarts finely shredded cabbage
    2 cucumbers, chopped
    4 red peppers, chopped
    4 onions, chopped
    ½ cup grated horseradish
    ¼ cup salt
    ¼ cup mustard seeds
    ¼ cup celery seeds
    24 cloves garlic
    Vinegar

Cut a slice from the stem end of each green pepper and set the slices aside. Discard the seeds and white membranes from the peppers and pack them firmly with a mixture of the cabbage, cucumbers, red peppers, onions, horseradish, and spices. Press a clove of garlic into the center of each pepper, replace the tops of the peppers, and fasten them securely with toothpicks. Pack the stuffed peppers into sterilized 2-quart jars and fill the jars to overflowing with mild vinegar. Store the jars in a cool, dark place for 3 to 4 weeks before using them.

TOMATO AND ONION PICKLES

>1 gallon green tomatoes
>6 onions
>½ cup salt
>1½ cups sugar
>4 cups vinegar
>1 tablespoon mustard seeds
>1 tablespoon celery seeds
>1 tablespoon grated horseradish
>1 tablespoon allspice
>1 tablespoon peppercorns

Wash, drain, and slice the tomatoes. Peel and slice the onions. Combine the vegetables, sprinkle with the salt, and let stand for 12 hours, or overnight. In the morning combine the sugar and vinegar. Add the remaining ingredients, tied in a bag, bring to a boil, and boil for 5 minutes. Drain the vegetables and add them to the spiced vinegar. Simmer for 20 minutes. Discard the spice bag. Pack boiling hot into hot jars and seal.

GREEN TOMATO PICKLES

>7 pounds green tomatoes, sliced
>2 cups slaked lime
>2 gallons water
>5 pounds sugar
>6 cups vinegar
>1 teaspoon cloves
>1 teaspoon ginger
>1 teaspoon allspice
>1 teaspoon ground celery seeds
>1 teaspoon mace
>1 teaspoon cinnamon

Put the tomatoes in a stone crock or earthenware bowl. Dissolve the lime in the water, pour the solution over the tomato slices, and let stand for 24 hours. Drain and soak the slices in fresh cold water for 4 hours, changing the water every half hour. Drain well. Combine the sugar, vinegar, and spices (all ground), bring to a boil, and

193

pour the syrup over the tomatoes. Let stand overnight. In the morning bring tomatoes and syrup to a boil and simmer for 1 hour. Seal in hot sterilized jars.

DILL GREEN TOMATOES

Select small, firm green tomatoes. Pack the tomatoes into sterilized jars and to each quart jar add 1 clove garlic, 1 stalk celery, several strips of green pepper, and a large spray of dill. Bring to a boil 2 quarts water, 1 quart vinegar, and 1 cup salt and boil for 5 minutes. Pour the hot brine over the vegetables in the jars and seal. The pickles will be ready to use in about 4 weeks.

HERBED GREEN TOMATOES

Wash and drain firm green tomatoes and pack them in sterilized quart jars. To each jar add 1 clove garlic and 2 sprays of dill. In a saucepan combine 2 quarts cider vinegar and 1 quart water. Add 2 tablespoons salt and a handful each of fresh dill, sweet basil, and tarragon and a few sprays of orégano and marjoram. Bring the liquid to a boil, simmer for 2 minutes, and fill the jars to overflowing. Seal and store.

SWEET PICKLED CHERRY TOMATOES

> 4 pounds firm cherry tomatoes
> 3½ pounds sugar
> 4 cups water
> 1 fresh ginger root, grated
> Juice and grated rind of 2 lemons
> 1 teaspoon salt

Wash the tomatoes and prick each one in several places with the tines of a fork. Dissolve the sugar in the water, bring to a boil, and boil rapidly for 5 minutes. Add the tomatoes and cook for 10 minutes. Remove the tomatoes and to the syrup add the ginger root, lemon juice and rind, and salt. Simmer the syrup for 15 minutes, return the tomatoes to the syrup, and cook for about 30 minutes longer, or until the syrup is thick and the tomatoes are transparent. Turn into hot jars and seal.

194

PICKLED WALNUTS

100 green walnuts
4 pounds salt
1 gallon water
2 tablespoons peppercorns
2 tablespoons allspice
½ tablespoon ground cloves
½ tablespoon nutmeg
1 teaspoon mace
2 tablespoons mustard seeds
4 quarts cider vinegar

Pick the walnuts in September while they are still green and young. Prick them with a needle to be sure they are not woody. They should be easily pierceable and uniform in size. Scald the walnuts and rub off the outside fuzz. Put them in a crock, cover them with a brine made of the salt and water, and let them stand for 10 days, changing the brine every 3 days and keeping the nuts completely covered with the brine. On the tenth day, drain the walnuts and sponge each one dry. Pierce each walnut in several places with a darning needle. Mix the spices and pack the walnuts in jars in layers with a sprinkling of the mixed spices between the layers. Bring the vinegar to a boil, boil for 3 or 4 minutes, and fill the jars to overflowing. Seal and let stand in a cool, dark place for at least 6 weeks before using them.

Mustard Pickles, Chowchows, and Relishes

Commercial pickling companies make many good products, but one they don't make is a really fine-flavored mustard pickle or chowchow.

The best mustard pickles are made with pure cider vinegar and the best quality dry mustard and spices; the sauce is thickened with a little flour or cornstarch. Any single vegetable or a combination of vegetables may be pickled in mustard sauce. The procedure is the same, but spices and flavorings may be varied to suit the individual. In this book my favorite mustard pickles are entitled exactly that, to distinguish the recipe from the many others. It is the recipe made by my mother that she learned from her mother, and it was always the favorite condiment in our house. All the vegetables remained crisp and flavorful in the sauce, but the crispest and most flavorful were the little onions. Everyone seemed to single out the onions from the rest of the vegetables. I could never get enough of them, and it was difficult to restrain myself from monopolizing what I considered the choicest morsels on the pickle platter.

When I had my own home, and the making of my mother's mustard pickles became a yearly ritual, I decided to do something about it. I simply eliminated all the other chunk vegetables from the recipe and substituted an equal quantity of tiny onions! Now I have all the mustard onions I can eat.

You can do the same. You can adjust the sugar content, making the relish sweeter or sourer. You can vary, increase or decrease the spices according to preference. You can substitute one vegetable for another. In other words you can take liberties with mustard pickles and relishes that you can't take with many other preserves.

ARTICHOKE MUSTARD PICKLES I

> 3 quarts Jerusalem artichokes, peeled and sliced
> 1 quart onions, peeled and sliced
> 1 large cauliflower, broken into flowerets
> 6 green peppers, seeded and chopped
> 1½ cups salt
> 1 gallon water
> 1 cup flour
> 6 tablespoons dry mustard
> 1 tablespoon turmeric
> 4 cups sugar
> 2 quarts cider vinegar

Mix the vegetables with the salt, add the water, and let stand overnight. In the morning drain the vegetables well. Combine all the dry ingredients with enough of the vinegar to make a smooth thin paste. Bring the remaining vinegar to a boil and gradually stir in the paste. Cook, stirring constantly, until the sauce is smooth and thickened. Add the vegetables, bring again to a boil, and seal hot in hot jars.

ARTICHOKE MUSTARD PICKLES II

> 1 gallon Jerusalem artichokes
> ½ cup olive oil
> ½ cup dry mustard
> 2 quarts cider vinegar
> 3 cups sugar

> 1 tablespoon mustard seeds
> 1 tablespoon celery seeds
> 1 teaspoon turmeric
> 1 small hot red pepper
> 1 tablespoon peppercorns

Scrub the artichokes with a wire brush and soak them for 3 days in a brine made by dissolving 2 tablespoons salt to each quart of water. Drain, rub dry with a cloth, and pack in sterilized jars. Mix the oil and mustard to a smooth paste. Stir in half the vinegar and the sugar. Gradually add the remaining vinegar and the spices. Bring to a boil and fill the jars to overflowing. Seal and let the pickles stand for 6 weeks before using them.

ARTICHOKE RELISH

> 3 quarts Jerusalem artichokes
> 2 heads cabbage, shredded
> 3 pounds pickling onions, peeled
> 2 bunches celery, chopped
> 1½ cups salt
> 1 gallon water
> ½ cup dry mustard
> 3 tablespoons turmeric
> 3 tablespoons curry powder
> 1½ cups flour
> 3 cups brown sugar
> 3 quarts cider vinegar

Wash and peel the artichokes and mix them with the other vegetables and the salt. Add the water and soak overnight. In the morning drain the vegetables well. Combine the mustard, turmeric, curry powder, flour, and sugar and stir in the vinegar gradually. Bring slowly to a boil, stirring constantly, add the mixed vegetables, and bring again to a boil. Pack into hot jars and seal.

BEET RELISH

> 4 cups chopped cooked beets
> 4 cups chopped cabbage
> 1 cup chopped onions
> 1 cup chopped sweet red peppers
> 2 tablespoons grated horseradish
> 1½ cups sugar
> 3 cups vinegar
> 1 tablespoon salt

Mix all the ingredients, bring to a boil, and boil for 10 minutes. Pack into hot jars and seal at once.

MUSTARD CABBAGE PICKLE

> 4 pounds cabbage, shredded
> 3 bunches celery, chopped
> 4 cups peeled and chopped onions
> ½ cup salt
> 1 pound sugar
> 6 tablespoons dry mustard
> 1 tablespoon cornstarch
> 1 tablespoon powdered celery seeds
> 1 tablespoon turmeric
> 2 quarts cider vinegar

Mix the vegetables and salt. Mix the dry ingredients with enough of the vinegar to make a smooth, fairly thin paste. Bring the remaining vinegar to a boil, gradually stir in the paste, and continue to cook, stirring constantly, until the sauce is smooth and thickened. Add the vegetables, bring again to a boil, and simmer for 10 minutes. Seal hot in hot jars.

CABBAGE RELISH

> 4 cups chopped cabbage
> 2 cups chopped onions
> 2 cups chopped sweet red peppers
> 2 cups chopped sweet green peppers
> ½ cup salt
> 8 cups water
> 4 cups vinegar
> 1 cup sugar
> 3 tablespoons mustard seeds
> 2 tablespoons celery seeds

Mix the vegetables and sprinkle with the salt. Add the water and let the vegetables soak in the brine for 1 hour. Drain, rinse in clear cold water, and drain again. Add the vinegar, sugar, and seeds, bring to a boil, and simmer for 20 minutes. Pack boiling hot into hot jars and seal.

CABBAGE TOMATO RELISH

4 quarts green tomatoes
¼ cup salt
8 cups chopped cabbage
6 cups cider vinegar
1¼ cups chopped onions
1¼ cups chopped sweet green peppers
¼ cup chopped sweet red peppers
3 cups sugar
1 tablespoon celery seeds
1 tablespoon mustard seeds
1 teaspoon bruised peppercorns
1 stick cinnamon
2 teaspoons whole cloves

Wash and chop the green tomatoes, mix with the salt, and let stand in a cool place overnight. In the morning drain, rinse in fresh cold water, and drain again. Add the cabbage and vinegar, bring to a boil, and boil for 25 minutes. Add the onions, peppers, sugar, and seeds, and the peppercorns, cinnamon, and cloves, tied in a bag, stir well, and simmer for 20 minutes, stirring frequently. Remove the spice bag. Turn into hot jars and seal.

CRISP CELERY RELISH

4¾ quarts diced celery
⅔ cup celery leaves, chopped
4 sweet green peppers, seeded and chopped
4 sweet red peppers, seeded and chopped
12 medium-sized onions
6 cups sugar
4 cups white vinegar
¼ cup salt
1 teaspoon turmeric
⅓ cup mustard seeds

Mix the vegetables, cover them with boiling water, and let stand for 10 minutes. Drain well. Combine the sugar, vinegar, salt, turmeric, and mustard seeds and bring to a boil. Add the vegetables and simmer for 5 minutes. Pack boiling hot into hot jars and seal.

CELERY AND TOMATO RELISH

>2 cups chopped celery
>2 dozen ripe tomatoes, peeled and chopped
>4 green peppers, seeded and chopped
>2 chili peppers, seeded and chopped
>4 onions, peeled and chopped
>1 cup sugar
>2 cups cider vinegar
>2 tablespoons mixed pickling spices, tied in a bag

Put all the ingredients into a preserving kettle, bring to a boil, and simmer for about 2 hours, or until the relish is thick. Season to taste with salt when cooking time is almost finished. Discard the spice bag and seal in hot jars.

CHOWCHOW

>2 cups whole tiny cucumbers
>2 cups chopped cucumbers
>2 cups small pickling onions, peeled
>2 cups chopped onions
>2 cups quartered green tomatoes
>6 red peppers, seeded and chopped
>2 cups Frenched string beans
>2 cups chopped celery
>2 cups cauliflower flowerets
>½ cup salt
>1½ quarts cider vinegar
>4 tablespoons flour
>1 cup sugar
>1 teaspoon turmeric
>3 tablespoons dry mustard

Combine the vegetables and salt and add enough cold water to cover. Let stand overnight and in the morning drain, rinse with fresh water, and drain again. Put the vegetables in a preserving kettle and add the vinegar. Bring slowly to a boil. Combine the rest of the ingredients with enough water or vinegar to make a smooth paste and stir the paste gradually into the boiling vegetables. Simmer for 5 minutes, stirring constantly. Seal in hot jars at once.

PENNSYLVANIA DUTCH CHOWCHOW

8 cucumbers, sliced or diced
1 quart small pickling onions
1 bunch celery, chopped
2 heads of cauliflower, broken into flowerets
1 quart quartered green tomatoes
1 cup salt
1 gallon water
1 cup flour
6 tablespoons dry mustard
1 cup sugar
1 tablespoon turmeric
2 quarts vinegar

Mix the vegetables and salt, add the water, and let stand overnight in a cool place. In the morning bring to a boil and drain through a coarse sieve. Mix the flour, mustard, sugar, and turmeric with enough water to make a smooth paste. Bring the vinegar to a boil, stir in the paste, and cook, stirring constantly, until the sauce is smooth and thickened. Add the vegetables, bring again to a boil, and pack hot in hot jars. Seal and store.

GREEN TOMATO CHOWCHOW

1 head cabbage, chopped
1 quart chopped onions
1 quart chopped sweet peppers
1 gallon chopped green tomatoes
1 cup salt
2 tablespoons turmeric
4 tablespoons flour
3 tablespoons dry mustard
2 quarts vinegar
3 cups sugar
2 tablespoons white mustard seeds
1 tablespoon celery seeds

Mix the vegetables and salt and let stand overnight. In the morning drain well. Mix the turmeric, flour, and mustard with enough water to make a smooth paste. Bring the vinegar to a boil, stir in the paste gradually, and add the sugar, seeds, and drained vegetables. Bring to a boil and simmer for 10 minutes. Seal hot in hot jars.

CORN RELISH

2 quarts cooked, cut corn
4 cups shredded cabbage
1 cup chopped onions
2 cups chopped sweet peppers, red, green, or mixed
4 cups vinegar
1 cup water
1½ cups sugar
2 tablespoons dry mustard
1 tablespoon mustard seeds
1 tablespoon celery seeds
1 to 2 tablespoons salt
1 tablespoon turmeric

In a large kettle combine all the ingredients and bring slowly to a boil. Simmer for 20 minutes and pack boiling hot into hot jars. Seal at once.

SPICY CORN RELISH

2 cups chopped sweet red peppers
2 cups chopped sweet green peppers
2 cups chopped celery
1 cup chopped onions
1 cup sugar
1 quart cider vinegar
2 tablespoons salt
2 teaspoons powdered celery seed
2 tablespoons dry mustard
¼ cup flour
1 teaspoon turmeric
½ cup water
2 quarts cooked, cut corn

Into a large preserving kettle put the peppers, celery, onions, sugar, vinegar, salt, and celery seed. Bring to a boil and boil for 15 minutes, stirring occasionally. Combine the mustard, flour, and turmeric and stir in the water to make a smooth paste. Stir the paste gradually into the relish, add the corn, and bring again to a boil. Boil for 5 minutes, stirring constantly. Seal hot in hot jars.

CORN AND CELERY RELISH

6 large ears corn
2 cups chopped celery
3 sweet green peppers, seeded and chopped
4 onions, peeled and chopped
1 small head cabbage, chopped
4 cups cider vinegar
2 cups brown sugar
3 tablespoons dry mustard
2 tablespoons salt

Blanch the corn on the cobs for 2 minutes and cut off the kernels. Combine all the ingredients, bring to a boil, and simmer for about 25 minutes, or until the vegetables are tender, stirring occasionally. Pack into hot jars and seal.

CORN AND TOMATO RELISH

12 ears sweet corn
1 quart onions
1 quart ripe tomatoes
1 quart cucumbers
3 sweet green peppers
3 sweet red peppers
6 small hot red peppers
1 bunch celery
2 tablespoons turmeric
2 quarts vinegar
2 tablespoons mustard seeds
1 cup sugar
¼ cup salt

Cut the corn from the cobs. Peel the onions, tomatoes, and cucumbers and chop. Remove the seeds and veins from the peppers and chop. Discard all but the heart and tender stalks of the celery and mince. Dissolve the turmeric in a little of the vinegar and add the mustard seeds. Dissolve the sugar and salt in the remaining vinegar. Combine all the ingredients, bring to a boil, and simmer for 1 hour. Pour into hot jars and seal.

CUCUMBER RELISH

2 quarts small whole cucumbers
2 onions, sliced
2 sweet red peppers, seeded and chopped
¼ cup salt
1 cup brown sugar
2 teaspoons white mustard seeds
2 teaspoons grated horseradish
½ teaspoon turmeric
Vinegar

Mix the cucumbers, onions, red peppers, and salt and let stand overnight. In the morning drain, rinse in clear water, and drain again. Stir in the sugar, mustard seeds, horseradish, and turmeric and add just enough vinegar to cover the vegetables. Bring to a boil and seal at once in hot jars.

CHOPPED CUCUMBER RELISH

8 cups chopped cucumbers
2 cups chopped sweet red peppers
2 cups chopped sweet green peppers
1 cup chopped onions
1 tablespoon turmeric
½ cup salt
8 cups water
4 cups vinegar
1 to 2 cups brown sugar
1 tablespoon mustard seeds
2 sticks cinnamon
2 teaspoons whole cloves
2 teaspoons whole allspice

Combine the chopped vegetables and sprinkle with the turmeric and salt. Pour the water over the vegetables and let stand for 3 hours. Drain, cover with fresh cool water, and let stand for 1 hour. Drain.

In a large kettle combine the vinegar and sugar. Add the spices, tied in a bag, and bring to a boil. Add the vegetables and let stand in a cool place for 12 hours, or overnight. In the morning bring to a boil and simmer for 3 minutes. Remove the spice bag. Pack boiling hot into hot jars and seal.

CUCUMBER AND ONION RELISH

18 cucumbers, thinly sliced
6 onions, thinly sliced
1 cup salt
2 cups cider vinegar
½ cup sugar
½ cup water
2 tablespoons mustard seeds
3 small hot red peppers, minced
4 bay leaves
1 tablespoon celery seeds

Mix the cucumbers, onions, and salt and let stand in a cool place overnight. In the morning drain and press out the excess moisture. Combine the remaining ingredients and bring to a boil. Boil for 3 minutes. Add the cucumbers and onions and bring again to a boil. Cook for 2 minutes. Turn into hot jars and seal.

TWO-WEEK MUSTARD CUCUMBERS

Use cucumbers fresh from the vine. The small cucumbers are best, but all should be of a uniform size. Pack the cucumbers into clean jars. Combine 1 cup salt, 1 cup sugar, 1 cup prepared mustard, and 1 gallon vinegar. Fill the jars to the top with this spiced vinegar and seal. The pickles will be ready to eat in 2 weeks. Makes about 8 quart jars.

FRUIT RELISH

4 pears
4 peaches
4 ripe tomatoes
1 onion
1 green pepper
¾ cup sugar
1½ cups cider vinegar
2 teaspoons salt
¼ teaspoon cayenne pepper
⅛ teaspoon ground cinnamon
⅛ teaspoon ground cloves

Wash and peel the fruit, tomatoes, and onion. Core the pears; pit the peaches; seed the pepper. Put all the fruit and vegetables through the medium blade of a food chopper. Mix the ground fruit and vegetables with the rest of the ingredients, bring to a boil, and simmer for about 1½ hours, or until the relish is thick, stirring frequently. Pour into hot jars and seal.

GRAPE RELISH

Wash 7 pounds grapes. Separate the skins and the pulp. Cook the pulp until tender and press through a fine sieve to remove the seeds. Cook the skins with 1 cup water until wilted. Combine the pulp and skins with 6 cups sugar and 1 cup vinegar. Add 1 teaspoon each of ground cinnamon, cloves, and allspice, bring to a boil, and cook slowly until the mixture is the thickness of ketchup. Turn into hot jars and seal.

HOT DOG RELISH

    3 pounds sweet red peppers
    3 pounds sweet green peppers
    3 pounds onions
    4 cups cider vinegar
    ½ cup sugar
    1 teaspoon mustard seeds
    1 teaspoon dry mustard
    1 teaspoon celery seeds
    2 tablespoons salt

Wash the peppers, remove the seeds and stems. Peel the onions. Put the vegetables through the medium blade of a food chopper. Cover the vegetables with boiling water, let stand for 5 minutes, and drain well. Add the remaining ingredients, bring to a boil, and cook for 10 minutes, stirring occasionally. Turn into hot jars and seal.

INDIA RELISH

    12 medium-sized cucumbers
    6 green tomatoes
    2 ripe tomatoes
    2 sweet green peppers
    2 sweet red peppers
    2 onions
    ¼ cup salt
    4 cups vinegar

1 cup water
4 tablespoons sugar
1 teaspoon ground cinnamon
1 teaspoon turmeric
¼ teaspoon ground cloves
½ teaspoon ground allspice
2 tablespoons white mustard seeds

Slice the cucumbers and green tomatoes. Peel and slice the ripe tomatoes. Seed and chop the peppers; peel and finely chop the onions. Mix the vegetables with the salt and let stand overnight. Drain the vegetables, add 2 cups of the vinegar and the water, bring slowly to a boil, and drain again. Mix the sugar, cinnamon, turmeric, cloves, and allspice to a smooth paste with a little of the vinegar. Bring the remaining vinegar to a boil, stir in the paste, and add the white mustard seeds and the vegetables. Bring to a boil and cook for 20 minutes, stirring constantly. Turn into hot jars and seal.

MUSTARD PICKLES I

36 tiny cucumbers, or gherkins
1 cauliflower, cut into flowerets
6 green tomatoes, cut into wedges
2 cups pickling onions, peeled
3 sweet green peppers, seeded and chopped
3 sweet red peppers, seeded and chopped
1 cup salt
1 gallon water
½ cup prepared mustard
1 tablespoon turmeric
5 tablespoons flour
5 cups vinegar
1 to 2 cups sugar

Mix the vegetables, sprinkle them with the salt, and add the water. Cover and let stand for 12 hours, or overnight. In the morning drain the vegetables, rinse them in clear cold water, and drain again, pressing out the excess moisture. In a large kettle mix the mustard, turmeric, flour, and ½ cup of the vinegar to a smooth paste. Stir in the sugar and the remaining vinegar, bring to a boil, stirring, and cook until the sauce coats the spoon. Add the vegetables, bring to a boil, and simmer for 15 minutes. Pack boiling hot into hot jars and seal at once.

MUSTARD PICKLES II

40 small pickling cucumbers, or gherkins
1 quart sliced cucumbers
5 cups cauliflower flowerets
2 cups thinly sliced green pepper rings
1 pound small pickling onions
1 gallon water
2 cups salt
1 cup flour
6 tablespoons dry mustard
1 tablespoon turmeric
½ cup sugar
2 quarts cider vinegar

Soak the vegetables overnight in a brine made with the water and salt. In the morning bring the brine to a boil, then drain the vegetables thoroughly. Make a smooth paste of the flour, mustard, turmeric, sugar, and 2 cups of the vinegar. Heat the rest of the vinegar, gradually stir in the paste, and cook, stirring constantly, until the sauce is smooth and thickened. Add the vegetables, bring to a boil, and simmer for about 5 minutes. Seal in hot jars.

FAVORITE MUSTARD PICKLES

2 quarts medium-sized cucumbers
1 quart medium-sized onions, peeled
6 red peppers, seeded
2 quarts gherkins
2 quarts tiny pickling onions, peeled
2 heads cauliflower, broken into bite-sized flowerets
1½ cups salt
8 cups sugar
8 cups cider vinegar
1¼ cups flour
½ cup dry mustard
3 tablespoons turmeric
2 tablespoons celery salt

Chop finely or grind through the medium blade of a food chopper the medium-sized cucumbers and onions and the red pepper and put each ground vegetable in a separate bowl. Also put into separate bowls the gherkins, pickling onions, and cauliflower flowerets. Sprinkle each vegetable with the salt, using about ¼ cup to each bowl. Cover the gherkins, pickling onions, and cauliflower with cold water and let all the vegetables stand overnight. In the morning drain the chopped vegetables in a colander. Drain the whole vegetables and dry them on a towel. Mix the vegetables in a preserving kettle, stir in the sugar, and 6 cups of the vinegar, and bring the mixture to a boil. Combine the flour, mustard, turmeric, and celery salt and mix them to a smooth paste with the remaining vinegar. Stir the paste gradually into the vegetables and continue to stir until the sauce is slightly thickened. Turn the pickles into jars and seal at once.

MUSTARD RELISH

2 quarts green tomatoes
7 large onions
6 sweet yellow peppers
6 sweet red peppers
¼ cup salt
2 bunches celery
2 cups cider vinegar
2 cups sugar
2 tablespoons prepared mustard
1 teaspoon turmeric
⅓ cup flour
½ cup water

Wash the vegetables, peel the onions, seed the peppers. Grind the tomatoes and onions through the medium blade of a food chopper and sprinkle with half the salt. Grind the peppers into a separate bowl and sprinkle with the rest of the salt. Let stand overnight. In the morning drain well and add the celery, finely chopped. Turn the vegetables into a large kettle and add the vinegar, sugar, mustard, and turmeric. Bring to a boil and simmer for 15 minutes. Mix the flour and water to a paste, gradually stir the paste into the relish, and simmer for 10 minutes longer. Seal in hot jars.

SWEET MUSTARD PICKLES

1 quart chopped green tomatoes
1 quart chopped cabbage
1 quart tiny pickling onions
1 quart chopped sweet green peppers
1 quart chopped cucumbers
¼ cup salt
3 cups sugar
1 cup flour
½ cup dry mustard
2 teaspoons turmeric
2 quarts cider vinegar

Mix the vegetables and salt and let stand overnight. In the morning drain well. In a kettle mix the sugar, flour, mustard, and turmeric with a little of the vinegar to make a smooth paste. Gradually stir in the remaining vinegar and bring to a boil, stirring constantly. Add the vegetables and bring again to a boil, stirring. Turn into hot jars and seal.

PALMETTO MUSTARD PICKLE

    2 quarts diced heart of palm
    2 tablespoons salt
    1 quart water
    1 quart vinegar
    1 tablespoon celery seeds
    1½ tablespoons mustard seeds
    1½ tablespoons dry mustard
    1½ cups sugar
    Juice of 1 lemon
    1 tablespoon turmeric
    ¾ cup flour
    ½ teaspoon cayenne pepper

Trim the heart of a palmetto palm to the tender white part in the center and cut it into small pieces. The upper portion is usually used for pickles, but the lower portion, though slightly bitter, may also be used. Soak the heart of palm in a brine, made by dissolving the salt in the water, for 2 days and drain. Rinse in clear cold water and drain again. Mix all the remaining ingredients in a kettle, bring slowly to a boil, stirring, and cook for 10 minutes. Add the heart of palm, bring again to a boil, and seal in hot sterilized jars.

PEAR RELISH

    3 pounds Bartlett pears, peeled and cored
    1½ pounds small white onions, peeled
    7 sweet green peppers, seeded
    1 sweet red pepper, seeded
    ¼ cup salt
    2 cups sugar
    2 cups white vinegar
    1 tablespoon mustard seeds
    1 teaspoon turmeric
    ¼ teaspoon cayenne pepper

Put the pears through the medium blade of a food chopper and measure 4⅔ cups into a large bowl. Put the onions and peppers through the medium blade of a food chopper, mix, and measure 6½ cups. Add the peppers and onions to the pears, stir in the salt, and let stand for 4 hours. Rinse the pear and pepper mixture three times in cold water, draining well after each rinsing. In a large preserving kettle combine the sugar, vinegar, and spices, bring to a boil, and boil for 5 minutes. Add the pear and pepper mixture and simmer for 5 minutes longer. Turn into hot jars and seal.

HOT PEAR RELISH

> 3 quarts peeled, cored, and chopped pears
> 1 quart chopped onions
> 4 sweet green peppers, seeded and chopped
> 5 small hot red peppers, minced
> 1 cup salt
> 1 quart vinegar
> 2 cups sugar
> 1 tablespoon prepared mustard
> 1 tablespoon turmeric

Combine the pears, onions, and peppers, mix with the salt, and let stand overnight in a cool place. In the morning drain, rinse three times in cold water, and drain well after each rinsing. Put the pear mixture in a large kettle with the remaining ingredients, bring to a boil, and simmer for 5 minutes. Increase the heat and boil briskly for 10 minutes longer. Pour into hot jars and seal.

PEPPER RELISH

> 12 red peppers, seeded
> 12 green peppers, seeded
> 12 onions, peeled
> 2 tablespoons salt
> 2 cups sugar
> 4 cups cider vinegar

Put the vegetables through the medium blade of a food chopper. Pour boiling water over the vegetables, let stand for 10 minutes, and drain. Add the salt, sugar, and vinegar, bring to a boil, and simmer for 20 minutes. Seal in hot jars.

For a **hot pepper relish,** add 1 or 2 hot red peppers, chopped.

For a **spiced pepper relish,** add 1 or 2 tablespoons mixed pickling spices, tied in a bag. Discard the bag before sealing.

SWEET PEPPER RELISH

    7 cups chopped sweet red peppers
    2 tablespoons salt
    6 cups sugar
    4 cups vinegar

Mix the peppers and salt, let stand for 3 hours, and drain well. Add the sugar and vinegar, bring slowly to a boil, and boil until the relish is as thick as jam. Seal hot in hot jars.

UNCOOKED PEPPER RELISH

    2 cups finely chopped sweet red peppers
    2 cups finely chopped sweet green peppers
    4 cups shredded cabbage
    2 cups finely chopped onions
    4 cups cider vinegar
    4 cups sugar
    4 tablespoons mustard seeds
    1 tablespoon celery seeds
    3 small hot red peppers, chopped
    4 tablespoons salt

Mix all the ingredients and let stand in a cool place overnight. In the morning pack in sterilized jars and seal.

PICNIC RELISH

    12 sweet green peppers, seeded
    12 onions, peeled
    12 green tomatoes
    ½ cup salt
    4 cups cider vinegar
    6 cups sugar
    2 teaspoons dry mustard
    1 teaspoon allspice
    ¼ teaspoon red pepper

Put all the vegetables through the medium blade of a food chopper, sprinkle with the salt, and let stand 4 hours. Drain, rinse in clear water, and drain again.

In a kettle combine the vinegar and sugar. Bring the liquid to a boil and add the vegetables and spices. Boil for 10 minutes and seal in hot jars.

PICCALILLI I

6 pounds green tomatoes, chopped
2 cups small cucumbers, chopped
2 onions, chopped
1 green pepper, seeded and chopped
½ cup salt
4 cups vinegar
1 cup sugar
1 tablespoon peppercorns
1 tablespoon celery seeds
1 tablespoon mustard seeds
1 teaspoon whole cloves

Mix the vegetables and salt and let stand in a cool place for 12 hours, or overnight. In the morning drain and press out the excess moisture. Combine the vinegar and sugar, add the spices, tied in a bag, and bring slowly to a boil. Add the vegetables and bring again to a boil. Discard the spice bag. Pack into hot jars and seal.

PICCALILLI II

1 quart chopped green tomatoes
2 red peppers, seeded and chopped
2 green peppers, seeded and chopped
2 large onions, peeled and chopped
1 small head cabbage, shredded
½ cup salt
3 cups cider vinegar
2 cups brown sugar
3-inch stick cinnamon
1 teaspoon cloves
1 teaspoon allspice
1 teaspoon mustard seeds

Combine all the vegetables and the salt and let stand overnight. In the morning drain the vegetables, pressing out the juice. Add the vinegar and sugar and the spices, tied in a bag, bring to a boil, and simmer until the vegetables are clear and the syrup is thickened. Discard the spice bag and seal the piccalilli in hot jars.

PICCALILLI III

    1 gallon green tomatoes
    2 large onions, peeled and chopped
    3 sweet peppers, seeded and chopped
    1 head cabbage, shredded
    ¼ cup salt
    4 cups vinegar
    1½ cups brown sugar
    2 tablespoons mustard seeds
    1 tablespoon celery seeds
    1 tablespoon grated horseradish

Wash, core, and chop the tomatoes. Mix all the vegetables with the salt and let stand for 3 hours. Drain well, pressing to remove excess liquid. Add the vinegar, sugar, and seasonings, bring to a boil, and simmer for 15 minutes. Pack boiling hot into hot jars and seal.

SPANISH PICCALILLI

    4 pounds green tomatoes
    4 pounds ripe tomatoes
    3 onions, peeled
    3 sweet red peppers, seeded
    3 sweet green peppers, seeded
    1 large cucumber
    2 bunches celery
    ½ cup salt
    6 cups cider vinegar
    4 cups brown sugar
    1 teaspoon dry mustard
    1 teaspoon white pepper

Slice or chop the vegetables coarsely, sprinkle them with the salt, and let stand for 12 hours, or overnight. Drain well and add the vinegar, sugar, mustard, and pepper. Bring the mixture to a boil and simmer for 30 minutes. Seal in hot jars.

RED AND GREEN TOMATO RELISH

    2 quarts green tomatoes
    2 quarts red tomatoes
    1 bunch celery
    3 large onions
    1 small head cabbage

    2 cucumbers
    3 sweet green peppers
    ½ cup salt
    6 cups vinegar
    1 teaspoon mustard

214

Prepare and chop all the vegetables, mix them with the salt, and let them stand overnight. In the morning drain off the juice and add the vinegar and mustard. Bring to a boil, simmer for 30 minutes, and seal in hot sterilized jars.

TOMATO FRUIT RELISH

> 30 ripe tomatoes
> 6 pears
> 6 peaches
> 6 apples
> 4 large onions
> 2 cups cider vinegar
> 4 cups sugar
> 2 tablespoons salt
> 2 tablespoons mixed pickling spices

Peel and finely chop the tomatoes, pears, peaches, apples, and onions. Mix with the remaining ingredients, bring to a boil, and cook until the relish is thick. Pour into hot sterilized jars and seal.

GREEN TOMATO MINCEMEAT I

> 2½ quarts chopped green tomatoes
> 2½ quarts peeled, cored, and chopped tart apples
> 1 pound cooked, pitted, and chopped prunes
> 1 whole orange, ground
> ½ pound seeded raisins, ground
> ½ pound seedless raisins
> ½ cup ground suet
> 1 pound brown sugar
> ½ cup molasses
> ½ tablespoon salt
> 1 tablespoon cinnamon
> ½ tablespoon nutmeg
> 1 teaspoon ground cloves
> 1 cup vinegar

Combine all the ingredients in a large kettle, bring to a boil, and simmer for about 1 hour until the mixture is thick and the flavors are well blended, stirring frequently. Seal in hot sterilized jars.

GREEN TOMATO MINCEMEAT II

3 pounds green tomatoes
1 tablespoon salt
3 pounds tart apples, peeled, cored, and chopped
2 cups brown sugar
2 pounds seedless raisins
1 cup ground suet
½ cup vinegar
2½ tablespoons cinnamon
1 tablespoon nutmeg
1 tablespoon grated lemon rind
2 teaspoons ground cloves

Wash the tomatoes and put them through the medium blade of a food chopper. Mix the ground tomatoes with the salt and let stand for 1 hour. Drain the tomatoes, add water just to cover, and bring to a boil. Simmer the tomatoes for 5 minutes and drain. Add the remaining ingredients, bring to a boil, and simmer for 1 hour, stirring frequently. Seal in hot sterilized jars.

GREEN TOMATO RELISH

6 pounds green tomatoes
3 medium-sized onions
4 tablespoons salt
5 thin slices lemon
¾ cup finely chopped sweet red peppers
1½ cups brown sugar
1½ cups vinegar
2 teaspoons white peppercorns
2 teaspoons whole allspice
2 teaspoons whole cloves
2 teaspoons celery seeds
2 teaspoons mustard seeds
2 teaspoons dry mustard

Wash and core the tomatoes; peel the onions. Slice the tomatoes and onions thinly, mix with the salt, and let stand overnight. In the morning drain thoroughly. Put the tomatoes and onions in a large kettle and add the lemon slices, peppers, sugar and vinegar, and the spices and mustard, tied in a bag. Bring to a boil and cook for about 30 minutes, or until slightly thickened, stirring occasionally. Discard the spice bag and turn the relish into hot jars. Seal at once.

RIPE TOMATO RELISH

½ peck red tomatoes
3 sweet green peppers, seeded
3 sweet red peppers, seeded
4 Bermuda onions
½ cup chopped cabbage
2 cups cider vinegar
1 cup sugar
3 tablespoons salt
1 tablespoon celery seeds
4 teaspoons mustard seeds
1 teaspoon ground cloves
¼ teaspoon cayenne pepper

Wash and peel the tomatoes and mash them to a pulp. Run the peppers and onions through the medium blade of a food chopper and add them to the tomatoes. Add the remaining ingredients, mix well, and let stand overnight in a cool place. In the morning bring the relish to a boil and cook for 10 minutes. Seal in hot jars.

UNCOOKED TOMATO RELISH

4 quarts peeled and chopped ripe tomatoes
5 onions, peeled and chopped
3 sweet red peppers, seeded and chopped
2 cups chopped celery
¼ cup grated horseradish
½ cup salt
4 tablespoons white mustard seeds
4 cups vinegar
2 to 3 cups sugar, brown or white
Horseradish leaves

Combine the vegetables, horseradish, and salt and let stand overnight in a cool place. In the morning drain thoroughly and add the remaining ingredients. Mix well and pack in sterilized jars with a horseradish leaf on top. Seal and store.

MIXED VEGETABLE RELISH

8 cups chopped green tomatoes
4 cups chopped ripe tomatoes
3 cups chopped onions
4 cups chopped cabbage
2 cups chopped celery

1 cup chopped sweet red peppers
1 cup chopped sweet green peppers
1 cup chopped cucumbers
½ cup salt
8 cups vinegar
4 cups brown sugar
1 tablespoon celery seeds
1 tablespoon mustard seeds
1 tablespoon broken stick cinnamon
1 piece ginger root
1 teaspoon whole cloves
2 cloves garlic

Mix the vegetables and salt and let stand in a cool place for 12 hours, or overnight. In the morning drain well and press out the excess moisture. Add the vinegar and sugar and the spices and garlic, tied in a bag. Bring to a boil and simmer for 30 minutes. Discard the spice bag, pack boiling hot in hot jars, and seal.

Chutneys

What would chicken curry—or any other curry dish, for that matter—be without its accompanying chutney, that hot, spicy condiment that originated in India? The classic chutney includes among its ingredients the mango, a fruit native to tropical Asia. It also contains onions, peppers, garlic, ginger, and tamarinds, the large flat seed pods of the giant African tamarind tree. The pods contain a sweet-sour pulp and several hard glossy seeds. The pods are steeped in warm water until the seeds can easily be extracted, and the pulp is added to chutneys and other preserves.

The exotic fruits that go into chutney are grown now in almost every warm clime, but they are often difficult to find, even in their season. In the home kitchen more common fruits—tomatoes, apples, gooseberries, peaches, bananas—give generously of their flavor to many American versions that retain the characteristic texture and quality of the classic Indian chutney.

218

APPLE CHUTNEY

8 cups chopped apples
1 cup chopped onions
2 cloves garlic, chopped
2 sweet red peppers, seeded and chopped
2 pounds seeded raisins, chopped
2 pods hot peppers, chopped
4 cups brown sugar
4 cups vinegar
2 tablespoons white mustard seeds
2 tablespoons black mustard seeds
2 tablespoons ground ginger
2 teaspoons allspice
2 teaspoons salt

In a large kettle combine all the ingredients. Bring slowly to a boil and boil until the vegetables are tender and the chutney is thick. Pour boiling hot into hot jars and seal.

APPLE AND GREEN TOMATO CHUTNEY

12 tart apples, peeled and chopped
24 small green tomatoes, peeled and chopped
4 onions, thinly sliced
1 pound seedless raisins
1 quart vinegar
1 pound brown sugar
2 tablespoons salt
½ teaspoon red pepper
1½ tablespoons curry powder
2 tablespoons pickling spices, tied in a bag

Combine all the ingredients in a preserving kettle, bring to a boil, and simmer until the syrup is thick and the apples are transparent. Discard the spice bag. Pack in hot jars and seal while hot.

APRICOT CHUTNEY

½ pound dried apricots
½ pound pitted dates
2 pounds sour red cherries, pitted
1 cup seedless raisins
2 cloves garlic
1 small hot red pepper, seeded
1 tablespoon salt

½ cup preserved ginger, chopped
½ cup honey
1 cup brown sugar
1 cup wine vinegar

Soak the apricots in water to cover for 1 hour. Drain and reserve
the liquid. Chop the apricots along with the dates, cherries, raisins,
garlic, and hot pepper. Add the salt and ginger, mix well, and let the
mixture stand for 1 hour. Then add the honey and brown sugar, 1
cup of the reserved apricot liquid, and the vinegar. Bring the mixture to a boil and simmer for 45 minutes, or until the chutney is very
thick, stirring frequently. Seal in hot sterilized pint jars.

ENGLISH CHUTNEY

24 ripe tomatoes, peeled and chopped
4 green peppers, seeded and chopped
12 peaches, peeled and chopped
4 onions, peeled and chopped
½ pound seedless raisins
1 cup preserved ginger in syrup
4 cups brown sugar
1 tablespoon salt
3 cups vinegar

Combine the ingredients in a preserving kettle, bring to a boil,
and cook slowly for about 3 hours, or until the chutney is thick,
stirring frequently. Seal in hot jars.

GOOSEBERRY CHUTNEY

3 pounds gooseberries
1 cup seedless raisins
4 onions, chopped
3 cups brown sugar
1 teaspoon crushed mustard seeds
½ teaspoon cayenne pepper
¼ teaspoon turmeric
2 tablespoons salt
3 cups vinegar

Combine the ingredients, bring to a boil, and cook gently for
about 2 hours, or until the chutney is thick. Turn into sterilized
bottles or jars and seal.

GRAPE CHUTNEY

    1 quart unripened grapes, seeded
    1 quart peeled, cored, and sliced tart apples
    1 tablespoon chopped garlic
    1 tablespoon grated horseradish
    1 tablespoon chopped preserved ginger
    1 tablespoon dry mustard
    1 tablespoon salt
    ½ teaspoon cayenne pepper
    1 pint cider vinegar
    1 cup brown sugar
    ½ cup blanched, sliced almonds
    ½ cup seedless raisins

In a preserving kettle combine the grapes, apples, garlic, horse-radish, ginger, mustard, salt, cayenne pepper, and vinegar. Bring to a boil and simmer until the grapes are soft. Mash the fruit, stir in the sugar, almonds, and raisins, and continue to cook for about 1 hour longer, or until the chutney is thick. Turn into sterilized bottles or jars and seal.

INDIAN CHUTNEY

    5 pounds mangoes, peeled and sliced
    2 pounds apples, peeled and quartered
    1 pound preserved ginger
    ½ pound pitted dates
    ¼ pound Sultana raisins
    1 large onion, finely chopped
    2 tablespoons salt
    Juice of 2 lemons
    1 tablespoon cayenne pepper
    ½ teaspoon nutmeg
    3 bay leaves
    1 quart cider vinegar
    4 pounds sugar
    2 tablespoons lime juice

In a large kettle combine all the ingredients except the sugar and lime juice and let stand for 3 hours. Bring the mixture to a boil and simmer until the fruits are tender. Stir in the sugar and lime juice and continue to cook until the syrup is thick. Seal in hot jars. This chutney is better after it has matured for several months.

MANGO CHUTNEY

2 cups vinegar
¾ pound brown sugar
1 pound peeled, sliced mangoes
½ pound currants
¼ pound raisins
¼ pound blanched almonds
3 ounces sliced green ginger
1 tablespoon salt
½ tablespoon white mustard seeds, tied in a bag
½ cup chopped onions
½ cup chopped sweet peppers
1 ounce chili peppers or hot peppers

Combine the vinegar and sugar and bring to a boil. Add all the other ingredients and cook for about 30 minutes, or until the syrup is thick and the fruit is clear. Discard the spice bag and seal in hot jars.

MANGO PAPAYA CHUTNEY

5 pounds green mangoes, peeled and thinly sliced
2 large onions, chopped
2 green peppers, chopped
4 ounces chopped preserved ginger
1 cup chopped firm-ripe papaya
1 lime, seeded and chopped
2 cloves garlic, chopped
1 cup seedless raisins
½ cup pitted dates
1 tablespoon cinnamon
1 teaspoon ground cloves
1 teaspoon allspice
2 teaspoons salt
3 cups brown sugar
4 cups vinegar
¼ teaspoon cayenne pepper
6 tamarind pods

In a preserving kettle combine all the ingredients except the tamarind pods. Bring to a boil and cook until the fruit is tender.

Shell the tamarind pods and let the seeds and pulp stand in water to cover until the seeds can be easily removed. Add the pulp to the mixture and taste for seasoning. Add more brown sugar if the chutney is too tart and boil gently for 1 hour longer, stirring often. Turn into sterilized bottles or jars and seal.

PEACH CHUTNEY

½ cup chopped onions
½ pound seedless raisins
1 clove garlic
4 pounds peaches, peeled, stoned, and chopped
⅜ cup preserved ginger
2 tablespoons crushed mustard seeds
1 tablespoon chili powder
1 tablespoon salt
1 quart vinegar
1¼ pounds brown sugar

Combine all the ingredients, bring to a boil, and simmer for about 1 hour, or until the chutney is thick. Pour into hot jars and seal at once.

PEAR CHUTNEY

3½ pounds firm-ripe pears
3 cups seedless raisins
3 cups sugar
1 cup vinegar
Grated rind and juice of 2 oranges
1 teaspoon cinnamon
1 teaspoon ground cloves
1 teaspoon allspice
1 cup broken pecans

Peel, core, and chop the pears coarsely. Combine the pears with the rest of the ingredients except the pecans, bring to a boil, and simmer for about 2 hours, or until the chutney is thick. Add the pecans 2 minutes before taking the chutney from the fire. Turn into hot bottles or jars and seal.

PINEAPPLE CHUTNEY

3 fresh pineapples
1½ teaspoons salt
1½ pounds plums, stoned and chopped
3 sweet red peppers, seeded and chopped
¼ pound preserved ginger, chopped
3 cloves garlic, minced
1 small hot red pepper, minced
3 tablespoons sugar
1 tablespoon vinegar
2 cups boiling water
1 tablespoon ginger syrup

Peel, core, and shred the pineapples. Sprinkle them with the salt and let stand overnight. In the morning add the plums, sweet peppers, and ginger, and mix well. In a saucepan combine the garlic, hot pepper, sugar, vinegar, water, and ginger syrup. Bring the mixture to a boil and simmer for 5 minutes. Add the pineapple mixture and simmer for about 1 hour, or until the chutney is thick, stirring frequently. Seal in hot sterilized pint jars.

PLUM CHUTNEY

    3 pounds plums, stoned and quartered
    1 pound tart apples, peeled, cored, and finely chopped
    2 large onions, finely chopped
    1 pound seedless raisins
    1 quart cider vinegar
    2 cups sugar
    2 tablespoons salt
    1 teaspoon ground cloves
    1 teaspoon cinnamon
    1 teaspoon ginger
    1 teaspoon allspice

Combine all the ingredients in a preserving kettle, bring to a boil, and simmer until the chutney is thick. Turn into hot jars or bottles and seal.

RHUBARB CHUTNEY

    4 pounds rhubarb
    1 pound apples
    1 pound seedless raisins
    4 onions
    1 pound sugar
    3 cups vinegar
    1 tablespoon salt
    2 tablespoons allspice
    2 tablespoons ginger
    1½ tablespoons crushed mustard seeds

Trim the rhubarb and cut the stalks into ½-inch pieces. Peel and core the apples and grind them with the raisins and onions through the fine blade of a food chopper. Mix all the ingredients in a preserving kettle and simmer gently for about 2 hours, or until thick. Pour while hot into hot jars and seal.

SUN-COOKED CHUTNEY

½ pound chili peppers
1 cup mustard seeds
6 cloves garlic
1 pound seedless raisins
½ pound preserved ginger
½ pound blanched, whole almonds
2½ pounds green mangoes, peeled and sliced
½ pound sliced blanched almonds
¼ pound sugar, or to taste
8 cups cider vinegar
Salt to taste

Combine the chili peppers, mustard seeds, garlic, half the raisins, the ginger, the whole almonds, and the mangoes and grind the mixture several times through the fine blade of a food chopper. Stir in the remaining ingredients, adding sugar and salt to taste. Put the mixture in bottles and cork tightly. Place the bottles on a sunny porch or in a sunny window for 6 weeks, turning the bottles every few days so that all sides will be exposed to the sun.

TOMATO CHUTNEY

12 ripe tomatoes
3 onions
3 sweet red peppers
1 small hot red pepper
1 cucumber
6 tart apples
1 cup seedless raisins
1 clove garlic
3 cups brown sugar
3 cups vinegar
1 tablespoon ginger
1 teaspoon cinnamon
2 teaspoons salt

Wash and drain the vegetables. Peel and core the tomatoes, peel the onions, seed the peppers, peel and core the apples. Chop all the vegetables and the raisins. In a large kettle combine all the ingredients, bring slowly to a boil, and boil until the vegetables are tender and the chutney is thick. Pour boiling hot into hot jars and seal.

225

WATERMELON RIND CHUTNEY

1 small watermelon
1 teaspoon alum
4 tablespoons salt
1 pound tart apples, peeled, cored, and diced
3 onions, chopped
Vinegar
2 tablespoons mustard seeds
2 teaspoons celery seeds
3 cloves garlic
1 cup preserved ginger, chopped
1 cup white sugar
2 cups brown sugar
1 lemon, sliced
½ cup lemon juice
1 pound seedless raisins
2 teaspoons cayenne
2 teaspoons cinnamon
2 teaspoons ground cloves
2 teaspoons allspice

Wash the watermelon and remove the flesh and seeds. Peel the green from the rind and cut the rind into 1-inch squares or thin slices. Put the rind in a saucepan with water to cover, the alum, and 2 tablespoons of the salt and cook for about 10 minutes, or until the rind is almost tender. Drain.

Mix together the apples and onions. Add vinegar to cover and stir in the remaining salt. Add the cooked rind and let the mixture stand for 2 to 3 hours. Drain off the vinegar and add more to make 1 quart.

In a mortar pound the mustard seeds, celery seeds, and garlic. Put the spice mixture in a saucepan and add the ginger, sugars, lemon, lemon juice, raisins, spices, and vinegar. Bring to a boil, stirring until the sugar is dissolved, add the diced mixture, and cook until the rind is clear and the syrup is thick. Let stand overnight. In the morning taste for flavor and add more seasoning if necessary. Bring again to a boil, pour into hot jars, and seal.

Pickled Fruits

Pickled fruits contribute variety to a condiment tray, and are especially good served with cold meats or poultry. Almost any fruit can be pickled in the same spiced syrup, although there are many variations on the basic theme.

Prepare the fruit: wash and peel and leave whole or cut into halves or quarters. Then make the basic syrup:

BASIC SYRUP FOR PICKLING FRUITS

>   3 cups sugar
>   2 cups cider vinegar
>   2 cups water
>   1 tablespoon whole cloves
>   1 tablespoon whole allspice
>   3-inch stick of cinnamon

In a saucepan combine the sugar, vinegar, water, and the spices, tied in a bag. Bring the syrup to a boil and boil for 5 minutes.

Add the prepared fruit to the boiling syrup a few at a time and cook gently until it is partially tender but not soft. The fruit should be removed from the syrup as soon as it is cooked and packed into hot sterilized jars. When all the fruit is cooked, discard the spice bag, fill the jars to overflowing with the spiced syrup, and seal at once.

Apricots   Leave whole or halve and pit. Cook 5 minutes. 4 pounds or 35 to 40 medium apricots make 4 pints.

Crab Apples   Leave stems on but cut out blossom ends. Cook 10 minutes, or until almost tender. 2½ pounds or 2½ quarts crab apples make 5 pints.

Peaches   Scald and peel; leave whole or cut in halves and pit. If using clingstones, loosen the pit by cutting around it with a knife, but do not remove. Cook 5 to 8 minutes. 4 pounds or 12 to 16 medium-sized peaches make 5 pints.

Apples   Peel, quarter, and core. Cook for about 10 minutes, or until almost tender. 2½ pounds apples make 5 pints.

Pears Peel, leaving stems intact. Remove the cores from the blossom end and cook for 5 to 10 minutes, or until almost tender. 4 pounds or 12 to 16 medium pears make 4 to 5 pints.

Another basic syrup for pickling fruit is made with honey. The quantity is sufficient for 2 or 3 pints of fruit—pears, apricots, apples, pineapple, or peaches.

HONEY SYRUP FOR PICKLING FRUITS

> 2 cups strained honey
> 1 cup cider vinegar
> 1 cup water
> 16 whole cloves
> 3-inch stick of cinnamon

Bring the honey, vinegar, and water to a boil. Add the spices, tied in a bag, and boil for 5 minutes. Add the prepared fruit, a few at a time, and simmer gently until the fruit is almost tender. Remove the fruit with a skimmer to hot sterilized jars and continue to cook the fruit until it is all in jars. Discard the spice bag. Fill the jars to overflowing with the syrup and seal.

SWEET PICKLED APPLES

Peel, quarter, and core enough apples to measure 1 gallon. If crab apples are used, do not peel them or remove the stems. Wash them well, drain, and run a large darning needle through each apple to prevent it from bursting. Combine 5 cups sugar, 4 cups vinegar, and 3 cups water. Add 2 sticks cinnamon, 1 tablespoon whole cloves, and 2 pieces ginger root, tied in a bag, and bring slowly to a boil. Add the apples and simmer until the apples are tender. Let stand in a cool place for 12 hours, or overnight. In the morning bring the apples and syrup again to a boil. Discard the spice bag. Pack the apples in hot jars and fill the jars to the top with the boiling syrup. Seal immediately.

PICKLED BLUEBERRIES

> 2 cups blueberries
> ½ cup water   ½ teaspoon crushed stick cinnamon
> ¼ cup vinegar   ⅛ teaspoon whole cloves
> 1 cup sugar   ⅛ teaspoon whole allspice

In a saucepan combine the blueberries, water, vinegar, and sugar. Tie the spices in a bag, add them to the berries, and bring to a boil. Cook rapidly until the syrup reaches the jellying point. Remove the spice bag, pour into hot jars, and seal.

CANTALOUPE PICKLE

3½ pounds cubed cantaloupe meat
2 cups water
2 cups vinegar
3½ cups sugar
Pinch of salt
⅛ teaspoon oil of cinnamon
⅛ teaspoon oil of cloves

Put the cantaloupe in a crock or bowl. Combine the water, vinegar, sugar, salt, oil of cinnamon, and oil of cloves and bring to a boil. Pour the hot syrup over the cantaloupe and let stand overnight. In the morning pour off the syrup, bring it to a boil, and pour it over the cantaloupe. Again let stand overnight. Repeat this process on 2 more consecutive mornings, then heat both cantaloupe and syrup together until the syrup boils. Turn into hot jars and seal.

SPICED BLACK CHERRIES

Wash, stem, and pit firm black cherries. Measure the cherries into a deep kettle and add an equal amount of sugar and one third as much vinegar. Add a spice bag containing 1 stick cinnamon, 3 cloves, and 1 ginger root, bring to a boil, and simmer for about 30 minutes, or until the syrup is very thick. Discard the spice bag, pour into hot jars, and seal.

PICKLED SOUR CHERRIES

3 pounds sour red cherries, pitted
½ cup vinegar
3 pounds sugar

Put the cherries in a crock, add the vinegar, and let stand for 24 hours. Drain and add the sugar. Let stand in a cool place for about 6 days, stirring every day until the sugar is completely dissolved. Pack the cherries into hot jars. Heat the syrup to the boiling point, pour the boiling-hot syrup over the cherries, and seal.

SPICED CURRANTS

2 quarts currants
1 cup vinegar
2 cups sugar
½ teaspoon allspice
½ teaspoon cloves
1 teaspoon cinnamon

Stem and wash the currants. Combine the vinegar, sugar, and spices, bring to a boil, and boil rapidly for 5 minutes. Add the currants and continue to cook until the syrup is thick and the currants are clear. Seal in hot jars.

SWEET PICKLED FIGS

3½ pounds ripe figs
1 cup vinegar
3 cups sugar
1 teaspoon whole cloves
1 teaspoon allspice

Stem the figs, wash them, and wipe dry with a soft cloth. Cover the figs with water, bring to a boil, and simmer for 20 minutes. Drain. Combine the vinegar, sugar, and spices, tied in a bag, bring to a boil, and boil for 5 minutes, or until the syrup spins a fine thread. Drop in the figs and cook for 10 minutes longer, or until the figs are tender. Discard the spice bag. Turn into hot jars and seal.

SPICED GRAPES

4 pounds Concord grapes
1½ cups vinegar
2 pounds sugar
2 sticks cinnamon
½ ounce whole cloves
1 blade mace

Wash the grapes and separate the skins from the pulp. Cook the pulp with the vinegar until the pulp is soft. Press the pulp through a fine sieve to remove the seeds. Add the skins to the pulp purée, bring to a boil, and add the sugar and the spices, tied in a bag. Cook until thick, remove the spice bag, and seal in hot jars.

SPICED GREEN GRAPES

    5 pounds large grapes
    3 pounds sugar
    1 cup vinegar
    ½ cup water
    1 tablespoon crushed stick cinnamon
    1 tablespoon whole cloves
    1 pound seedless raisins

Wash the grapes, cut them in half lengthwise, and discard the seeds. Bring the sugar, vinegar, and water to a boil. Add the spices, tied in a bag, and the grapes and simmer for about 30 minutes, or until the syrup is thick and the grapes are transparent. Add the raisins and cook for 5 minutes longer. Discard the spice bag and seal in hot jars.

LEMON ACHAR

    4 ounces mustard seeds
    4 ounces black peppercorns
    1 ounce cumin seeds
    4 ounces fennel seeds
    ½ ounce chili powder
    1 ounce salt
    2 dozen thin-skinned lemons
    2 quarts mustard oil

Grind all the spices in a mortar. Cut the lemons halfway down in four sections, spread the sections apart, and stuff each lemon with some of the ground spice mixture. Bring the mustard oil to a boil, remove it from the fire, and place the lemons in it. Cover closely and let stand for 1 week, or until the lemons are soft. Seal in jars.

PICKLED LIMES

Select fully matured limes with thick rinds, before the rinds have turned yellow. Wash and rinse them and slit them in quarters without cutting them all the way through. Fill the slits with salt, packing it in carefully, and place the salted limes upright in a shallow pan for 4 to 5 days, or until the salt has dissolved. Leave the limes in the brine, turning them every day until they are tender. Transfer both the limes and the brine to a preserving kettle and pour over them enough boiling spiced vinegar to cover them generously. Bring the vinegar to a boil and cook the limes for 5 minutes. Pack the limes in hot pint jars, fill the jars with the hot vinegar, and seal at once. Store in a cool, dry, dark place.

SPICED ORANGES

 8 whole, unpeeled oranges
 4 cups sugar
 4 cups water
 ½ cup vinegar
 12 cloves
 1 stick cinnamon

Simmer the oranges in water to cover for about 20 minutes, or until they may be easily pierced with a fork. Drain and cut the oranges into halves or quarters for convenience in packing. Combine the sugar, water, and vinegar and bring to a boil. Add the oranges and the spices, tied in a bag, and simmer for 30 minutes. Discard the spice bag and seal in hot jars.

PICKLED PEACHES OR PEARS

 7 pounds firm-ripe fruit
 Whole cloves
 4 cups cider vinegar
 6 cups sugar
 1 tablespoon broken stick cinnamon
 1 tablespoon whole allspice

Peel the fruit and stick 4 whole cloves in each. Combine the vinegar and sugar and the spices, tied in a bag, bring to a boil, and drop in the fruit one by one so that the boiling is not stopped. Cook for about 10 minutes, or until the fruit can be pierced easily with a fork. Discard the spice bag. Pack the fruit in hot jars, fill the jars to overflowing with the boiling syrup, and seal.

WHOLE SPICED PEACHES

 5 pounds peaches
 2½ pounds sugar
 ½ cup cider vinegar
 1 tablespoon each allspice, cloves, and cinnamon

Peel the peaches and leave them whole. Combine the sugar and vinegar. Add the spice, tied in a bag, and the peaches, bring the liquid to a boil, and cook until the peaches are tender. Remove the fruit and continue to boil the syrup until it is thick, or to 224° F. on a candy thermometer. Return the peaches to the syrup and let them cool in the syrup. Pack in wide-mouthed jars and seal.

SLICED PICKLED PEACHES

    5 pounds peaches
    1 tablespoon grated nutmeg
    1 ounce stick cinnamon, broken into bits
    3½ pounds brown sugar
    6 cups cider vinegar

Peel the peaches and slice the flesh from the pits. Put the slices into a stone jar with the spices. Combine the sugar and the vinegar, bring to a boil, and boil for 10 minutes. Pour the hot syrup over the peaches and let stand overnight. In the morning drain the syrup from the peaches, bring to a boil, and again pour the syrup over the peaches. Repeat this process on 2 more consecutive days. Then bring fruit and syrup to a boil and simmer the peaches for 10 to 15 minutes, or until the fruit is clear and tender and the syrup registers 224° F. on a candy thermometer. Pack in jars and seal.

SWEET PICKLED PEACHES

    6 pounds firm-ripe clingstone peaches
    3 pounds sugar
    2 cups water
    2 cups vinegar
    4 ounces stick cinnamon
    2 ounces whole cloves
    1 ounce whole ginger

Peel the peaches and drop them a few at a time into a boiling syrup made of 2 pounds of the sugar and the water. Cover, simmer for 10 minutes, and let the fruit cool in the syrup, basting occasionally. Drain off the syrup into a saucepan and add the remaining pound of sugar, the vinegar, and spices. Bring slowly to a boil and boil for 15 minutes. Add the peaches, simmer for 10 minutes, and let stand in the syrup overnight. In the morning drain off the syrup again, bring it to a boil, and boil for 20 minutes. Again add the peaches and cook for 15 minutes. Cool again, then bring to a boil, and simmer until the peaches are clear and the syrup is thick. Pack the peaches into hot jars and garnish each jar with small pieces of the cinnamon. Cover with the strained syrup and seal.

STUFFED PICKLED PEACHES

> 10 freestone peaches, peeled
> 6 tablespoons minced onion
> 2 teaspoons minced sweet red pepper
> 2 teaspoons cinnamon
> 5 cups sugar
> 1½ cups water
> 1 cup white vinegar
> 12 cloves, tied in a bag

Remove the peach stones from the stem end, leaving the peaches whole. Mix the onion, pepper, and cinnamon and fill the centers. In a kettle combine the sugar, water, vinegar, and cloves. Bring the liquid to a boil, add the peaches, and simmer for about 10 minutes, or until just cooked through. Discard the cloves, pack the peaches into hot jars, fill almost to the top with the boiling syrup, and seal.

PICKLED PEARS

> 3 pounds firm pears
> 4 cups sugar
> 3 cups vinegar
> 5 cups water
> 1 piece ginger root
> 1 tablespoon mixed whole spices
> Stick cinnamon
> Cloves
> Grated rind of 1 lemon

Peel the pears and leave them whole. Make a syrup of the sugar, vinegar, and water. Tie the ginger root, mixed whole spices, 1 stick of cinnamon, and a few whole cloves in a bag and add to the syrup. Bring the syrup to a boil, add the pears and the grated lemon rind, and cook until the pears are tender and clear and the syrup registers 222° F. on a candy thermometer. Let the fruit stand in the syrup overnight, then remove the spice bag and pack the fruit in jars, adding 1 stick cinnamon to each jar. Bring the syrup to a boil, pour it over the fruit in the jars, and seal.

PLUMS IN VINEGAR

> 4 pounds firm blue prune plums
> 12 cloves
> 2 sticks cinnamon, broken
> 5 cups red wine vinegar
> 8 cups sugar

Wash the plums and prick each one in several places with a large needle. Put the plums close together in an earthen dish and sprinkle them with the cloves and cinnamon. Combine half the vinegar and half the sugar, bring to a boil, and boil for 5 minutes, skimming the scum from the surface as it rises. Pour the syrup over the plums, cover tightly, and let stand for 2 days. Drain off the liquid and reserve it. Repeat the operation with the rest of the sugar and vinegar and let the plums stand for 1 day. Then combine all the liquid, bring to a boil, and add the plums. When the plums are heated through and the syrup is again simmering remove the plums to hot jars. Continue to boil the syrup for 5 minutes longer and cool. Fill the jars to overflowing with the syrup and seal.

SWEET PICKLED QUINCES

 4 pounds quinces, peeled, cored, and diced coarsely
 2 pounds sugar
 1 cup vinegar
 1 teaspoon whole allspice
 1 teaspoon whole cloves
 ½ ounce stick cinnamon

Cook the quinces until tender in just enough water to prevent them from burning. Combine the sugar and vinegar, add the spices, tied in a bag, and bring to a boil. Boil the syrup for 5 minutes, skimming well. Pour the hot syrup over the fruit and let stand overnight. In the morning drain off the syrup and boil it until as thick as honey. Add the quinces and cook until the quinces are heated through. Remove the spice bag. Pack into hot jars, fill the jars to overflowing with the syrup, and seal.

CRISP WATERMELON RIND PICKLES

Peel and remove all the green and pink portions from the rind of a large watermelon. Cut the rind into cubes or slices and measure 1 gallon. Drop the rind into a kettle of boiling water, boil 5 minutes, and drain. Cool. Dissolve 4 tablespoons slaked lime (obtainable at your drugstore) in 2 quarts cold water. Pour the solution over the watermelon rind and let stand for 3 hours. Drain and rinse thoroughly. Cover the rind with clear cold water, bring to a boil, and boil until the rind is tender. Drain. Combine 4 cups sugar, 2 cups vinegar, and 8 cups water. Add 2 tablespoons each of whole allspice and whole cloves, 4 sticks cinnamon, and 2 pieces ginger root, all tied in a bag, bring to a boil, and boil for 5 minutes. Add the rind, bring again to a boil, and simmer for 30 minutes. Let the rind stand in the syrup in a cool place for 12 to 24 hours. Add 6 cups vinegar and from 4 to 8 cups sugar according to taste, bring to a boil, and simmer until the rind is transparent. If the syrup becomes too thick before the rind is clear add ½ cup hot water from time to time as needed. Discard the spice bag, pack the rind and syrup, boiling hot, into hot jars, and seal.

SOFT WATERMELON PICKLE

> 3 quarts peeled, diced white watermelon rind
> 3 tablespoons salt
> 3 quarts water
> 3 tablespoons powdered alum
> 1 quart white vinegar
> 9 cups sugar
> ¼ cup whole cloves
> 2 2-inch sticks cinnamon

Let the rind stand for 24 hours in a solution of the salt and 2 quarts of the water. Drain thoroughly and let stand another 24 hours in a solution of the alum and the remaining quart of water. Drain thoroughly, add fresh water to cover, and let stand for 24 hours. Then bring to a boil and cook for about 30 minutes, or until the rind is tender.

In a large kettle combine the vinegar, sugar, and the spices, tied in a bag. Add the rind and cook for about 20 minutes, or until it is clear. Pack the rind into hot jars. Boil the syrup for 15 minutes longer, discard the spices, and fill the jars with the hot syrup.

FIVE-DAY PICKLED WATERMELON

> 5 pounds cut watermelon rind
> 4 teaspoons powdered alum
> 8 cups sugar
> 4 cups cider vinegar
> 1 tablespoon whole cloves
> 2 sticks cinnamon, broken

Put the watermelon rind in a kettle and cover with cold water. Bring the water to a boil and cook the rind for about 20 minutes, or until tender. Remove from the fire, stir in the alum, and let stand overnight.

Next day rinse the watermelon rind well under cold running

water and drain thoroughly in a colander. In the same kettle combine the sugar, vinegar, and the spices, tied in a bag, and bring to a boil, stirring. Add the rind and cook for 10 minutes. Let stand overnight. Every day for 5 consecutive days, bring the rind and syrup to a boil, boil for 10 minutes, and let stand overnight. Discard the spice bag. Finally bring once more to a boil, pack the rind in hot jars, and fill to overflowing with the boiling syrup. Seal and let stand for 3 weeks before using.

Ketchups and Sauces

When the tomatoes hang heavy on the vine, it's time to make one of the most popular of all the pickles known as sauces—chili sauce. Chauvinistic Americans are apt to consider chili sauce a strictly American condiment, but the truth is that chili sauce was appearing on Continental tables at a time when Americans were still calling the tomato a love apple and artistic gardeners were using the plant for decorative garden borders. American housewives were quick to duplicate the European sauce to produce America's best-loved relish.

But this is only a beginning. All of Indian summer's vegetables find their way eventually into the preserving kettle in chopped or puréed form to supply innumerable appetite-provoking sauces for winter use.

APPLE CHILI SAUCE

> 2 tart apples
> ½ cup sugar
> 6 large ripe tomatoes
> 2 medium-sized onions
> 1 sweet green pepper
> 1 sweet red pepper
> ½ cup vinegar
> ½ teaspoon celery seeds
> ½ teaspoon cinnamon
> ¼ teaspoon black pepper
> ¼ teaspoon ground cloves
> 1 teaspoon salt
> ¼ teaspoon dry mustard

Core the apples, put them through a food chopper, and stir in the sugar. Cook the apples and sugar until the apples are tender. Peel the tomatoes and onions and seed the peppers. Run these vegetables through a food chopper and mix with the apples. Add the remaining ingredients and cook for about 1 hour, until the sauce is thick, stirring occasionally. Seal in hot sterilized jars.

APPLE KETCHUP

>12 tart apples
>1 cup sugar
>1 teaspoon pepper
>1 teaspoon ground cloves
>1 teaspoon mustard
>2 teaspoons cinnamon
>1 tablespoon salt
>2 onions, finely chopped
>2 cups cider vinegar

Wash, core, and quarter the apples. Put them in a saucepan, cover with boiling water, and simmer until the apples are soft. Rub the apples through a fine sieve and measure the purée. Put 1 quart of the apple purée into a kettle and add the remaining ingredients. Bring to a boil and simmer for about 1 hour, or until the ketchup is thick. Seal in hot sterilized jars.

CHILI SAUCE I

>25 large ripe tomatoes
>3 sweet red peppers, seeded and chopped
>1 small bunch celery, chopped
>6 onions, chopped
>3 cloves garlic, minced
>2 tablespoons whole allspice, tied in a bag
>2 cups cider vinegar
>1½ cups light brown sugar
>2 tablespoons salt
>1 teaspoon pepper
>1 teaspoon dry mustard

Scald, peel, core, and quarter the tomatoes. Squeeze out the seeds and excess juice and chop the pulp finely. Put the pulp in a large kettle, bring to a boil, and boil rapidly until the tomatoes are soft. Ladle off the clear liquid that comes to the top of the tomatoes while they are cooking. Add the remaining ingredients and cook for 30 minutes. Discard the spice bag and continue to cook for about 1 hour longer, or until thick, stirring occasionally. Seal in hot sterilized jars.

CHILI SAUCE II

4 quarts ripe tomatoes, peeled and chopped
1 cup chopped onions
1½ cups chopped red peppers
1½ cups chopped green peppers
1½ teaspoons whole allspice
1½ teaspoons whole cloves
2 sticks cinnamon
2 cups vinegar
1 cup sugar
3 tablespoons salt

In a large preserving kettle combine the tomatoes, onions, and peppers. Add the spices, tied in a bag, bring the mixture to a boil, and cook until it is reduced to half its volume, stirring frequently. Add the vinegar, sugar, and salt and boil rapidly for 5 minutes, stirring constantly. Discard the spice bag. Pour into hot jars and seal.

CHILI SAUCE III

1 gallon ripe tomatoes
2 cups chopped onions
2 cups chopped sweet red peppers
1 small hot red pepper
1 cup sugar
3 tablespoons salt
1 tablespoon mustard seeds
1 tablespoon celery seeds
3 tablespoons mixed pickling spices
2½ cups cider vinegar

Scald, core, peel, and chop the tomatoes. Mix the vegetables with the sugar and salt, bring slowly to a boil, and boil for 45 minutes. Add the spices, tied in a bag, and continue to boil until the sauce is very thick, stirring frequently. Add the vinegar, correct the seasoning to taste, and boil until the sauce is the desired consistency. Discard the spice bag and seal in hot sterilized jars.

239

GREEN CHILI SAUCE

       8 pounds green tomatoes, cored
       6 medium-sized onions, peeled
       6 sweet green peppers, seeded
       1¾ cups sugar
       3 tablespoons salt
       3 cups cider vinegar
       4 teaspoons whole cloves
       4 teaspoons whole allspice
       2 sticks cinnamon, broken

Chop the tomatoes, onions, and peppers finely and add the sugar, salt, vinegar, and the spices, tied in a bag. Bring the mixture to a boil and simmer for 2½ to 3 hours, or until quite thick. Discard the spice bag and seal in hot, sterilized jars.

CRANBERRY KETCHUP

       2½ pounds cranberries
       Vinegar
       2⅓ cups sugar
       1 tablespoon cinnamon
       1 teaspoon ground cloves

Wash the cranberries and just cover them with vinegar. Bring to a boil and cook until the berries are soft. Press the mixture through a fine sieve. Add the remaining ingredients and simmer until the ketchup is thick. Seal in hot sterilized jars or bottles.

CUCUMBER KETCHUP

       1 quart large ripe cucumbers
       1 cup small onions
       2 sweet green peppers, seeded
       ½ cup water
       2 cups vinegar
       1 cup sugar
       2 tablespoons white mustard seeds
       1 tablespoon salt
       ¼ teaspoon cayenne pepper

Peel and quarter the cucumbers and discard the seeds. Chop the flesh coarsely. Chop the onions and peppers. Combine the vegetables in a kettle, add the water, and cook until the vegetables are tender. Press the vegetables through a fine sieve. To the purée add the vinegar, sugar, the mustard seeds, tied in a bag, the salt and cayenne pepper, bring to a boil, and cook until the ketchup is thick and clear. Discard the spice bag and seal in hot sterilized jars.

CUCUMBER CHILI SAUCE

    1 quart ground cucumbers
    1½ tablespoons salt
    ½ cup grated onion
    2 cups vinegar
    1 teaspoon white pepper
    ⅛ teaspoon cinnamon
    ⅛ teaspoon dry mustard
    ¼ cup brown sugar

Mix the ground cucumbers and salt thoroughly, let stand for 30 minutes, then drain off the liquid, pressing to extract as much excess moisture as possible. Mix the cucumbers and onion. Combine the vinegar, spices, and sugar, bring to a boil, and simmer for 5 minutes. Add the mixed vegetables, bring to a simmer, and simmer for 5 minutes. Seal in hot sterilized jars.

ELDERBERRY KETCHUP

    2 quarts ripe elderberries
    Vinegar
    1 cup sugar
    1 tablespoon cinnamon
    1 tablespoon allspice
    ¼ teaspoon cayenne pepper
    1 tablespoon ground cloves

Cook the elderberries until soft in just enough vinegar to cover and rub the mixture through a fine sieve. Add the sugar and spices and simmer until the ketchup is thick. Seal in hot sterilized jars or bottles.

Grapes or **plums** may be substituted for the elderberries.

GRAPE KETCHUP

    5 pounds Concord grapes
    2 cups cider vinegar
    6½ cups sugar
    1½ teaspoons salt
    1 stick cinnamon, broken
    1 tablespoon whole cloves
    1 tablespoon whole allspice
    2 pieces whole mace
    2 ginger roots

241

Wash and stem the grapes, put them in a large preserving kettle, and simmer until tender, stirring frequently. Press the grapes through a sieve and to the grape pulp add the vinegar, sugar, salt, and the spices, tied in a bag. Bring to a boil and simmer for about 35 minutes, or until the consistency of ketchup, stirring frequently. Discard the spice bag and seal in hot sterilized jars or bottles.

MUSHROOM KETCHUP

> 10 pounds mushrooms
> ½ cup salt
> 1 small onion, chopped
> 1 teaspoon grated horseradish
> 1 teaspoon allspice
> 1 teaspoon ground cloves
> ¼ teaspoon cayenne pepper
> 1 cup vinegar

Trim the stem ends of the mushrooms, wipe them with a damp cloth, and chop coarsely. Mix the mushrooms thoroughly with the salt and let them stand overnight. In the morning add the onion, spices, and vinegar, bring to a boil, and simmer for about 30 minutes, stirring frequently. Press the mixture through a fine sieve and thin with a little more vinegar if the sauce is too thick. Return the sauce to the heat and bring again to a boil. Seal boiling hot in hot jars.

RED HOT PEPPER SAUCE

> 24 long hot peppers
> 12 ripe tomatoes
> 4 cups vinegar
> 1 cup sugar
> 1 tablespoon salt
> 2 tablespoons mixed pickling spices

Wash and drain the vegetables. Seed and chop the peppers. Core and chop the tomatoes. Put the vegetables in a kettle with 2 cups of the vinegar, bring to a boil, and boil until soft. Press the mixture through a fine sieve. Add the sugar and salt and the spices, tied in a bag, and boil until the sauce is thick. Add the remaining vinegar and continue to boil for about 15 minutes, or until the sauce is the desired consistency. Discard the spice bag and seal boiling hot in hot jars.

PERUVIAN SAUCE

24 large ripe tomatoes
3 large onions, peeled and chopped
3 sweet green peppers, seeded and chopped
1 small hot red pepper
6 tart apples, peeled and chopped
1 clove garlic
3 cups brown sugar
1 tablespoon salt
1 tablespoon whole allspice
1 tablespoon mustard seeds
1 teaspoon broken cinnamon
3 cups vinegar

Scald, core, and peel the tomatoes. Combine the vegetables, apples, and sugar, bring to a boil, and boil until the sauce is thick. Add the spices, tied in a bag, and the vinegar and continue to cook until the sauce is the desired consistency. Discard the spice bag and seal boiling hot in hot, sterilized jars.

PLUM KETCHUP

6 pounds stoned plums
2 cups vinegar
4 cups brown sugar
3 tablespoons cinnamon

½ tablespoon paprika
½ tablespoon ground cloves
½ tablespoon mace
½ tablespoon salt

Cook the plums until soft in just enough water to keep them from sticking and press through a fine sieve. Add the remaining ingredients to the plum purée and simmer until the ketchup is thick, stirring constantly. Seal in hot sterilized jars.

TOMATO KETCHUP I

16 pounds ripe tomatoes
3 sweet red peppers, seeded
2 onions, peeled
2 tablespoons salt
⅓ cup sugar
2 teaspoons celery salt
2 teaspoons dry mustard
1 teaspoon paprika
1 tablespoon whole allspice
1 tablespoon whole cloves
1 tablespoon broken cinnamon
2 cups cider vinegar

243

Chop the tomatoes, peppers, and onions, put them in a kettle, and cook until soft. Press the mixture through a fine sieve and measure the purée. There should be 4 quarts purée. To the purée add the salt, sugar, celery salt, mustard, and paprika and the whole spices, tied in a bag, bring to a boil, and cook rapidly for 1 hour. Discard the spice bag. Add the vinegar and continue to cook until the ketchup is thick. Seal in hot sterilized jars or bottles.

TOMATO KETCHUP II

1 gallon ripe tomatoes
1 cup chopped onions
1 tablespoon salt
1 cup sugar
½ tablespoon celery seeds
1 teaspoon mustard seeds
½ teaspoon whole allspice
1 stick cinnamon, broken
1 to 1½ cups vinegar
1 tablespoon paprika

Wash, drain, core, and chop the tomatoes. Cook the tomatoes and onions until soft and press the mixture through a fine sieve. Return the purée to the heat and cook until it is reduced to about half its original quantity. Add the salt, sugar, and the spices, tied in a bag, and boil until the ketchup is thick. Add the vinegar and paprika and continue to cook for about 5 minutes longer, or until the ketchup is the desired consistency. Discard the spice bag and seal boiling hot in hot jars.

TOMATO COCKTAIL SAUCE

16 pounds ripe tomatoes
8 bay leaves
½ cup celery seeds
¼ cup fresh onion juice
½ cup fresh carrot juice
¼ cup brown sugar
4 teaspoons salt
¼ teaspoon cayenne pepper

Wash, core, and quarter the tomatoes. Put them in a kettle and cook until soft. Drain the juice into a saucepan, add the bay leaves and celery seeds, tied in a bag, and boil briskly until the juice is reduced to one fourth its original quantity. Press the tomato pulp through a fine sieve to remove the skins and let the purée simmer gently. Discard the spice bag and stir the juice into the purée.

Squeeze the juice from halved onions as you would lemons. Grind carrots through the fine blade of a food chopper and strain the juice through a fine sieve lined with cheesecloth. Add the onion and carrot juice to the tomato mixture, add the remaining ingredients, and simmer until the sauce is the desired consistency. Pour boiling hot into hot sterilized jars to within ½ inch of the top. Adjust the glass lids on the jars and process in a boiling-water bath for 5 minutes.

SPICY TOMATO KETCHUP

> 8 pounds ripe tomatoes
> 1 cup cider vinegar
> 3 tablespoons salt
> 2 tablespoons allspice
> 1 tablespoon dry mustard
> ½ tablespoon ground cloves
> 1 teaspoon black pepper
> ¼ teaspoon red pepper

Coarsely chop the tomatoes, cook them until soft, and strain through a fine sieve. This should make 2 quarts tomato purée. Put the purée in a kettle with the remaining ingredients, bring to a boil, and simmer for about 4 hours, stirring frequently. Seal in hot sterilized jars or bottles.

UNCOOKED TOMATO SAUCE

> 8 pounds firm-ripe tomatoes
> ¼ cup salt
> 2 cups sugar
> 2 cups cider vinegar
> 2 ounces mustard seeds
> 1 teaspoon cinnamon
> 1 teaspoon ground cloves
> 1 teaspoon black pepper
> ¼ teaspoon cayenne pepper
> 2 tablespoons grated horseradish
> 3 green peppers, seeded and finely chopped

Peel, core, and finely chop the tomatoes, stir in the salt, and let stand overnight. In the morning drain and add the remaining ingredients. Mix thoroughly until the sugar is completely dissolved and seal in sterilized jars.

TOMATO CELERY SAUCE

7 pounds ripe tomatoes, peeled
2 bunches celery
2 sweet green peppers, seeded
10 onions, peeled
4 cups cider vinegar
3 cups sugar
4 teaspoons salt
6 small hot red peppers

Put the tomatoes, celery, peppers, and onions through the medium blade of a food chopper. Combine all the ingredients in a large kettle, bring to a boil, and simmer for about 2 hours, or until thick, stirring occasionally. Discard the hot peppers and seal the sauce in hot sterilized jars.

CHAPTER SEVEN

Smoking and Curing

The smoking and curing of meat and fish are among our most ancient and primitive methods of preserving food. Early man, who hunted the lion, the bear, and the woolly-haired rhinoceros with weapons of rough stone and made his home in a cave or in the shelter of rocks, one day discovered that meat hung from the roof of his dwelling over a smoky fire not only had longer lasting qualities but was greatly improved in flavor. The flavor and staying power were further increased by first rubbing the meat with salt, and so, from early man's will to survive, the brining and smoking of meat and fish became for many centuries the major ways of preserving protein foods, and the methods have come down to us with little alteration.

Before the perfection of canning and the advent of quick freezing, when smoking was a necessity, almost every American farm was equipped with a smokehouse, from which came the family's supply of succulent hams, golden slabs of bacon, and spiced haunches of beef. In this year of grace man has been relieved of the actual necessity to smoke meat and fish, but during those many years before quick freezing man cultivated a decided taste for smoked foods which he is unwilling to forgo, even though an alternative method of preservation has been discovered. Had there been no necessity to apply smoke to food, however, it is unlikely that present-day palates would even like the smoked, burned flavor.

In order to smoke foods you first need a smokehouse. It may be simply constructed or elaborately designed and built. For small amounts of foods you can buy a manufactured smoke-cooking unit that may be used outdoors or fitted into an indoor fireplace. In all cases the method of smoking is the same.

HOW TO BUILD A BARREL SMOKEHOUSE

Knock both ends out of a large barrel and set it over a hole in the ground about 2 feet deep and a little narrower than the diameter of the barrel. Nail wooden strips inside the barrel on two sides, a few inches below the top of the barrel. The ends of the sticks on which food will hang rest on these strips. Put a loose-fitting cover on top. About 12 feet away from the smokehouse pit dig a fire pit, also about 2 feet deep, and connect the fire pit to the smokehouse pit by means of a trench with a terra-cotta drainpipe placed in the trench. The fire pit and the pit below the smokehouse may be lined with brick. The fire pit should be covered with a lid which serves as a draft when it is partly raised. Always dig the fire pit on the side from which the prevailing winds usually come.

HOW TO BUILD A SHED SMOKEHOUSE

The pit below the smokehouse and the fire pit are dug in the same way as in the construction of the **barrel smokehouse.** The fire pit, dug on the side from which the prevailing winds come, should be about 12 feet from the pit beneath the smokehouse, both pits should be lined with brick, and the two pits connected with a terra-cotta drainpipe.

The shed itself should be 7 feet high and 4 feet square, inside measurements. About 12 inches above the ground, place a false bottom with 1-inch auger holes at 2-inch intervals. On the sides of the shed nail wooden battens at 1-foot intervals, the first one about 18 inches below the top. The ends of the smoke sticks on which the food to be smoked will be hung rest on these battens. The entire front of the smokehouse is a hinged door. On both sides, a few inches below the roof, cut 3 or 4 holes, 2 inches square, fitted with slide covers to act as drafts or ventilators.

Fuel for the smokehouse   Only hardwoods should be used in smoking. Soft, resinous woods should never be used, for they give an unpleasant flavor to the foods. Oak, hickory, beech, and sweet bay are excellent woods to use. Manzanita roots are used in California, while in the Southern states palmetto roots and buttonwood are used. Apple wood and other dry, fruit-tree woods make fine fuel and give an especially good color and flavor to the food. Sawdust and wood chips from these hardwoods are better to use than larger pieces as they smolder more slowly and give a denser smoke.

Use kindling and charcoal to start the fire, let it burn down to glowing embers, then smother it with the sawdust or wood chips. The sawdust may be dampened slightly if it begins to burn too fast.

METHODS OF SMOKING

There are two general methods of smoking: hot smoking, or barbecuing, and cold smoking. In hot smoking the food is hung fairly close to a fire—usually not more than 3 or 4 feet from a fire—and smoked at temperatures of 150° to 250° F. or more, so that they are partially or wholly cooked. Hot-smoked foods are appetizing, require no further preparation, but will keep for only a short time. In cold smoking the food is hung at some distance from a smoldering fire and smoked at a temperature below 100° F. The degree of preservation resulting from smoking depends on the length of time the food is exposed to the smoke. Foods smoked for only a few hours will have an agreeably mild smoke flavor but will keep only a short time. They should be kept under refrigeration. If foods are to be kept for a long period, the food must be cold-smoked for several days or a week or more.

Smoked Fish

HOT SMOKING OF FISH

Almost any fish may be hot-smoked and, once smoked, may be used immediately without any further cooking or may be kept under refrigeration for a short time.

The favorite fish for hot-smoking are mullet, shad, Spanish mackerel, mackerel, alewives or river herring, herring, lake herring, whitefish, or king mackerel.

Split the fish along the back, just above the backbone, so that it will open from the back, leaving the belly solid. Scrape out the viscera, blood, and membranes. In the larger fish, cut out the forward three quarters of the backbone. Wash the fish thoroughly and soak them for 30 minutes in a brine made by dissolving ½ cup salt in each quart of water. This preliminary soaking draws the blood out of the flesh.

Then make a saturated salt solution by dissolving 2½ pounds salt in 1 gallon of water. To this brine add 1 pound sugar, 2 tablespoons saltpeter, 2 tablespoons crushed peppercorns, and about 1 ounce crushed bay leaves. Put the fish in this brine for 2 to 4 hours, depending on the size and thickness of the fish and the desired amount of cure—light or heavy. The exact length of the cure can be determined only by experiment. Rinse off the fish in fresh water and hang them outside in a cool, shady, but breezy place to dry for about 3 hours. Before hanging the fish in the smokehouse they must be dried until a thin shiny "skin" has formed on the surface.

Hang the fish in the smokehouse in which a low fire is smoldering. The temperature of the smokehouse must not be higher than 90° F. Smoke the fish at this temperature for 8 hours. Then build up a very dense smoke and smoke the fish at this temperature for 4 hours longer. Increase the fire until the temperature in the smokehouse is between 130° and 150° F. and continue to smoke the fish for 2 to 3 hours, or until the surface is brown and glossy.

Remove the fish from the smokehouse to cool for 2 to 3 hours. Then wrap each fish separately in moistureproof paper and store in a cool, dry place.

COLD SMOKING OF FISH

Small fish such as sea herring, alewives, or butterfish may be smoked in the round—that is, with both back and belly uncut. Make a slash just below the gills and pull out the gills, heart, and liver. This is known as gibbing. Fish larger than 1 pound should be split along the back and opened flat in a single piece, leaving the belly uncut. Scrape out the viscera, blood, and membranes. The head may be removed if desired, but in this case leave the hard bony plate that lies just below the gills, as it will be needed to carry the weight of the fish when it is suspended in the smokehouse.

Wash the fish thoroughly and put them in a brine made by dissolving 1 cup salt in 1 gallon water. Let the fish soak in this brine for 30 minutes to draw the blood out of the flesh. Rinse in fresh cold water and drain.

Drop each fish singly into a shallow box containing fine pickling salt and dredge well. Pick the fish up with as much salt as will cling to the body, and pack them in even layers in a wooden tub. Leave the fish in the salt for from 1 to 12 hours, depending on the size of the fish, the fatness, and the degree of cure desired.

When the cure is completed, rinse the fish thoroughly and scrub off all particles of salt. Hang the fish outside in a cool, shady spot to dry for about 3 hours, or until a thin shiny "skin" has formed on the surface. The use of an electric fan will speed up the drying process.

A low smoldering fire should be burning in the smokehouse, and the fire should not give off too much smoke during the initial smoking period.

If the fish are to be kept for about 2 weeks, give them an initial smoking at a temperature of between 70° and 90° F. for 8 to 12 hours. If the fish are to be kept for longer than 2 weeks, this initial smoking should continue for 24 hours. If a thermometer is not used to control the smokehouse temperature, insert the hand in the smokehouse and if the air feels distinctly warm the temperature is too high.

At the end of the initial smoking build up a dense smoke in the smokehouse, but the temperature should still remain between 70° and 90° F. If the fish are to be kept for 2 weeks, smoke them densely for another 12 to 16 hours. The total smoking period should be 24 hours. For fish to be kept longer than 2 weeks, the smoking should continue for 5 days or more.

During the entire smoking period the fire must be kept low and steady, and it must not be allowed to die out at night. It cannot be built up for the night, but must be tended regularly both night and day.

When the fish are smoked, cool them, wrap each separately, and store in a cool, dry place.

SMOKING FILETS

Any white-fleshed, lean fish producing filets that weigh a pound or more may be smoked. Cut the fish into filets and discard the backbone and skin. Soak the filets for 2 hours in a brine made by dissolving 2¼ pounds of salt in 4 quarts of water. Remove the filets, drain, and dry them thoroughly for 2 to 3 hours in the air. Place the filets in the smokehouse on oiled racks or hang them over strips of wood about 3 inches in width. Lightly smoke the filets at 90° F. for 4 hours. Turn the filets and lightly smoke for 4 hours longer. Then smother the fire to obtain a thick dense smoke and continue to smoke for about 6 hours, or until the filets are a deep straw color, turning them once or twice so that both sides will be evenly smoked. Cool, wrap each filet separately, and store in a cool, dry place, where they will keep for about 10 days.

SMOKING FISH INDIAN FASHION

This method of smoking is often used by sportsmen who wish to preserve part of their catch, and when facilities for immediate freezing are not at hand. The fish will keep for 2 weeks to 1 month in good condition, and the method of smoking is especially recommended for trout, pike, or pickerel.

Head and gut the fish. Cut out most of the backbone, leaving only a small piece in the tail section. Spread the fish open flat in one piece, and score the flesh longitudinally from head to tail about ¼ inch deep at intervals of 1 inch. Wash the fish thoroughly, wipe them dry, and rub them inside and out with a mixture of 1 ounce (2 tablespoons) pepper and 1 pound salt. Store the fish in a cool place overnight and in the morning rinse thoroughly. Thread the fish on pointed green-wood sticks, keeping them spread open, and hang the fish in a breezy place to dry for several hours, or until a thin shiny "skin" has formed on the surface.

Meanwhile dig a shallow fire pit, about 3 feet in diameter, and in the pit start a fire. Let the fire burn down to a good bed of red coals, and feed it with any hardwood such as hickory, oak, maple, beech, birch, or alder. The wood should be green so that it smokes and smolders. Fasten each fish to the forked end of a green-wood stick about 5 feet long. Thrust the other end of the stick into the ground at an angle so that the fish hangs over the smoking fire. Build a tripod of poles around the sticks and cover the tripod with a thick bedding of green boughs and grasses. Smoke the fish from 8 to 18 hours, depending on the size and degree of smoke cure desired. Cool the fish before wrapping them, and store in a cool, dry place.

SMOKED SALMON OR LAKE TROUT

Salmon may be cold-smoked like any other fish, but the following method results in a superior product.

Remove the head and clean the fish. Force the shoulder of the fish down on a sharp nail protruding from a board to keep the fish from slipping, and make a short incision above and below the backbone under the anal fin. Hold the fish firmly by the shoulder and insert a sharp knife at the shoulder just above the backbone. Keep the knife steady and slant the blade downward at a slight angle touching the backbone. With one sweep of the knife remove the top side of the fish. Then insert the knife at the shoulder just under the backbone with the blade slanted slightly upward and touching the backbone, and cut off the other side. A thin line of backbone edge should run down each side.

Wash the sides thoroughly, trim off the ragged edges, and remove all blood clots. Soak the fish for 60 to 90 minutes in a cold brine made by dissolving 2½ pounds salt in 1 gallon ice water. Remove the fish to drain for 20 minutes.

For 20 pounds of fish mix together 2 pounds salt, 1 pound brown sugar, 2 tablespoons saltpeter, 2 tablespoons white pepper, and 1 ounce each of crushed bay leaves, allspice, cloves, and mace. Dip the fish, one side at a time, in the spice mixture and rub the mixture gently into the flesh. Pick up the sides with as much of the curing mixture as will cling to the flesh and pack them in a wooden tub. Place a loose-fitting cover on top and weigh it down.

Leave the fish in the curing mixture for 8 to 12 hours, then rinse in cool water and scrub the sides to remove all traces of the salt and spices.

Attach the fish to hangers and let them dry in the air for about 6 hours. Then hang the fish in the smokehouse and lightly smoke them at a temperature of not more than 100° F. for 8 hours. Build up a dense smoke and continue to smoke the fish at a temperature not more than 70° F. for from 16 to 24 or for 48 hours for maximum preservation qualities. Cool the fish for several hours, brush with vegetable oil, and store in a cool, dry place.

HOT-SMOKED CATFISH

Clean and skin the catfish and discard the backbone and head. Small catfish may be left whole, but catfish weighing more than 3 pounds should be cut into 1½-pound pieces. Place the fish in a brine for 3 to 6 hours, depending on the size, made by dissolving 2½ pounds salt in 1 gallon cold water. Rinse the catfish and scrub them to remove any slime or dirt. Arrange the fish on oiled wire trays. Small catfish may be strung on rods, which should go through the backbone near the tail. Let the fish hang in a cool, drafty place to dry for several hours, or until a thin shiny "skin" forms on the surface. Place the fish in the smokehouse and smoke them lightly at a temperature of about 80° F. for 7 to 12 hours. Then build up the fire to create a dense smoke and increase the temperature in the smokehouse. Hot-smoke the fish for 1 hour at 170° to 180° F. or for 30 minutes at 250° F.

Cool the fish thoroughly before wrapping it if it is not to be eaten immediately. Stored in a cool place or under refrigeration, it will keep about 10 days.

SMOKED SHRIMP

Clean and devein 2 pounds shrimp, removing the heads but leaving the shells intact. Simmer the fish for about 3 minutes, or until the shrimp turn pink in a **court bouillon** made by simmering 1 onion, 1 carrot, and 3 stalks celery, all chopped, 1 bay leaf, 2 sprays of parsley, 6 peppercorns, and 2 cloves in 2 quarts water for 30 minutes. Remove the fish, drain thoroughly, and dry them on absorbent paper. Arrange the shrimp on oiled smoking racks, taking care that the shrimp do not overlap. When the fish feel dry to the touch, cold-smoke them lightly at a temperature of 90° F. for 35 to 40 minutes. The smokehouse draft should be fully open during the first 15 minutes of smoking, then half closed, and finally three fourths closed. If a smokier flavor is desired, build up a dense smoke and continue the smoking at the same temperature for 15 minutes longer.

Cool the shrimp, wrap them in moistureproof paper, and store them in the refrigerator, where they will keep for 1 week or more.

SMOKED OYSTERS

Shuck fresh oysters, drain them thoroughly, and dry them on absorbent paper. Place the oysters on an oiled smoking rack, without overlapping, and cold-smoke them for about 1 hour, or until the oysters have taken on color and their edges are curled and golden brown.

Smoked Poultry

A full-scale smokehouse is needed for long cold smoking of ducks, geese, and turkeys. But a fine effect can be produced by hot-smoking poultry of all kinds, with the possible exceptions of chicken and game birds. Squabs, ducks, and other small birds may be smoked whole. Turkeys and geese should be halved or quartered. The poultry may be soaked for a few hours in a flavorful marinade. A good marinade is made from dry wine, soy sauce, honey, garlic, and thyme. Hang whole birds by the neck in the smokehouse; place halved or quartered birds on oiled racks. Cold-smoke the poultry for 4 to 6 hours or overnight. Then raise heat in the smoke chamber to 350° F. and hot-smoke until the poultry is cooked and golden brown in color. Whole squab will take about 45 minutes; whole ducks 1½ hours. The temperature, of course, need not be as high as 350° F., but if less, the hot-smoking period will be proportionally greater. For a glazed effect, baste the bird several times during the smoking period with a honey marinade.

COLD-SMOKED DUCK

Clean a small tender duck and truss it as for roasting. In a kettle combine 5 quarts water, 4 pounds pickling salt, 1 cup sugar, ½ cup saltpeter, 6 crushed bay leaves, 1 tablespoon crushed peppercorns, and 6 whole cloves. Bring the water to a boil, cool to lukewarm, and submerge the duck in this brine. Keep the duck in the brine, in the refrigerator, for 5 days, turning it occasionally. After 5 days, remove the duck, drain it thoroughly, and wipe it dry with absorbent paper. Cold-smoke the duck for 7 days at a temperature of 90° F., preferably, over a fire made of olive-tree chips.

After smoking place the duck in a saucepan and cover it with half water and half dry white wine. Bring the liquid to a boil and simmer the duck for 15 minutes. Cool thoroughly, wrap in moisture-proof paper, and store in the refrigerator, where it will keep for months.

SMOKED TURKEY

Truss a turkey as for roasting and submerge it in a brine made of 2 cups pickling salt to 3 quarts water. Leave the turkey in the brine for 8 hours or overnight, under refrigeration. Remove the turkey from the brine, press out the excess liquid gently, and dry with absorbent paper. Hang the bird in a cool, drafty place to dry for several hours, or until the flesh is completely dry to the touch. Then densely smoke the turkey at a temperature of 90° to 100° F. for about half as many hours as the number of pounds the turkey weighs. Raise the temperature gradually to 200° F. and hot-smoke for the same amount of time again or more, until the bird is cooked and golden red in color.

Halfway through the smoking, the bird may be brushed several times with a honey glaze.

Smoked Meats

Smoking adds a great deal of flavor and palatability to meats that have first been cured in brine, and increases their lasting qualities. To preserve meat by smoke, cold smoking is generally the method used, and the temperature inside the smokehouse must be watched very carefully. Too much heat will cook the meat and too little heat and smoke will not dry the meat and flavor it properly.

Hot smoking of meats is really barbecuing in smoke and is done only when the meat is to be eaten immediately. The meat, in this case, does not need any preliminary brining or curing, but for extra flavor it may be marinated for an hour or so in olive oil with salt and coarsely ground black pepper, or in an herb-wine marinade. A 2½-inch-thick steak, hot-smoked, will be cooked rare in about 30 minutes at temperatures ranging from 300° to 350° F. Hamburgers will take from 10 to 15 minutes at a temperature of 300° F. Lamb steaks need from 25 to 30 minutes at 300° F., depending on the thickness of the meat, and pork chops require from 40 to 50 minutes at 350° F.

PASTRAMI FOR THE SMALL SMOKEHOUSE

Submerge a 1½-pound steak of choice shoulder beef, cut about 1½ inches thick, in a brine made of 4 cups water, 14 teaspoons salt, 6 teaspoons brown sugar, 4 teaspoons minced parsley, ½ teaspoon black pepper, a dash of cayenne pepper, 2 onions, chopped, 2 teaspoons pickling spices, 3 whole cloves, 2 cloves garlic, and 1 teaspoon saltpeter. Keep the meat in this brine, under refrigeration, for 1 week, turning the meat every day. Remove the meat from the brine, wipe it dry with absorbent paper, and let it hang in a breezy spot until it is completely dry to the touch. Cold-smoke the meat for 3 hours at a temperature of 90° to 100° F. Raise the temperature gradually to 180° F. and hot-smoke for another 2 to 3 hours. Serve hot from the smokehouse, or cool, wrap, and store in the refrigerator.

PASTRAMI FOR THE LARGE SMOKEHOUSE

The smokehouse should be approximately 5 feet deep, 3 feet wide, and 12 feet high. There should be at least 6 feet between the meat and the fire, and heat should be furnished by a floor gas-heating system.

The entire shoulder of kosher cattle may be used in making large quantities of pastrami, or the rib or round steak of ordinary beef may be used.

Bone the meat and trim away the excess fat. Place the meat in a refrigerator for 24 hours before putting it in the cure. The cure consists of 5 pounds pickling salt and 2¾ ounces sodium nitrate to each 100 pounds meat. Sprinkle the bottom of a curing vat with this mixture and pack a layer of meat in the vat. Cover the meat with curing mixture and sprinkle with ground black pepper and ground garlic. Add another layer of meat and treat it in the same way. Continue adding layers of meat, curing mixture, pepper, and garlic until the vat is full, taking care that the layers are tightly and compactly packed. At the end of 24 hours, weight the meat down with heavy wooden covers. The meat now begins to form its own brine, which should cover the top layer. If there is not enough brine formed by the meat, add a brine made of 2¼ pounds salt dissolved in 6 quarts water. Leave the meat in the brine for 60 days at a temperature of 36° to 40° F.

Remove the meat from the vat, dry each piece with absorbent paper, and rub each piece heavily with a mixture of 65 per cent black pepper and 35 per cent allspice. Another spice mixture is made of 60 per cent coriander, 25 per cent allspice, 7½ per cent white pepper, and 7½ per cent garlic powder. Put the meat under refrigeration overnight after rubbing it with the spice.

Next day insert a hanging post in each piece of meat and attach it to smoke sticks. Place the meat in the smokehouse and roast and smoke it at a temperature of 320° F. for 6 to 7 hours.

SMOKED PORK LOIN

Bone fresh loin of pork and trim away the excess fat. Cut the meat into ½-pound pieces. Submerge the meat in a brine made of 4½ cups water, 1½ cups dry white wine, 8 tablespoons salt, 4 tablespoons brown sugar, 1 teaspoon each of black pepper and allspice, and 10 juniper berries. Let the meat stand in the brine in the refrigerator for 24 hours. Then drain and dry thoroughly. Smoke the meat lightly for 1 hour at 100° F., with the chimney wide open. Smother the fire to create a dense smoke, half close the chimney, and cold-smoke for another hour. Then gradually increase the temperature inside the smokehouse and hot-smoke the meat with the chimney three fourths closed until the interior temperature of the meat reaches 170° F. To form a golden crust, brush the meat several times during the hot-smoking period with honey.

SUGAR-CURED HAMS, SHOULDERS, AND BREAKFAST BACON

For every 100 pounds meat mix together thoroughly 8 pounds salt, 2 pounds brown sugar, 2 ounces saltpeter, 3 ounces black pepper, and 2 ounces red pepper. Dampen the meat on the side away from the skin and rub the spice mixture well into this side, the edges and ends. With hams, press some of the mixture into the openings around the bones in the shank. Sprinkle the bottom of a large crock or barrel with salt. Place a piece of pork skin side down in the container and sprinkle it lightly with the salt mixture. Continue until all the meat is used and sprinkle the remaining salt mixture on top. Store the crock at a temperature of 35° to 38° F. If the temperature is allowed to go over 40° F. for any length of time, spoilage is apt to occur. Every 7 days the crock should be unpacked and the pieces rubbed again and repacked in the same salt mixture.

Bacon 1 inch thick should be cured for 15 days; bacon 1½ inches thick for 22 days; a 15-pound ham will need 30 days. In general, allow 2 to 3 days of curing per pound weight of the piece of meat.

Remove the meat when it is cured, wash it thoroughly, and hang it in the smokehouse to drain and dry for 24 hours. The meat should be suspended about 6 feet above the fire. Start a slow fire with green hickory or other hardwood chips and smother the flame, if any, with hardwood sawdust or corn cobs. The meat should be warmed gradually with a cool, dry smoke and smoked continuously for 5 to 10 days or for 5 to 6 hours each day for 6 consecutive days, until a light chestnut in color. The temperature of the smokehouse should not go above 100° F. When well smoked, let the meat cool. Wrap it in paper, then in muslin, and hang in a cool, dry dark place to age for 3 to 6 months.

BRINE-CURED HAMS, SHOULDERS, AND BACON

Rub the pieces of pork with salt and pack them in a tight keg or barrel or crock with a layer of salt in the bottom. Pack the hams and shoulders in the bottom and the bacon on top. Pack all the meat skin side down, except for the top layer.

For 100 pounds meat mix together 9 pounds salt, 2 pounds brown sugar or 4 pounds molasses, and 2 ounces saltpeter. Add 4 gallons warm water, cool, and pour the brine over the meat. Leave the meat in the cure for 2 to 3 days per pound weight of the piece of meat and, when it is cured, remove it from the brine, wipe dry, and hang it in the smokehouse for 24 hours to dry thoroughly. Then smoke it over a low, cool fire. See smoking direction in recipe for sugar-cured hams.

SMOKED COUNTRY SAUSAGE

21 pounds lean pork, chopped
3½ pounds beef, chopped
½ pound pickling salt
1 ounce black pepper
½ ounce red pepper
½ ounce mace
½ ounce marjoram

Blend all the ingredients and run through the fine blade of a food chopper several times. Pack the meat in a crock, cover, and let it stand in a cool place for 24 hours. Moisten the mixture with a little vinegar, red wine, or water, mix thoroughly, and pack it into casings. Hang the sausage in the smokehouse and smoke lightly over a cool fire for 1 to 2 hours. Increase the density of the smoke and continue to smoke until the sausages are dark mahogany in color. The temperature in the smokehouse should not be allowed to go over 100° F. When smoked, cool and store in a cold place until used. Cook the sausage well before eating.

BOLOGNA SAUSAGE

15 pounds ground beef
½ pound salt
1 tablespoon black pepper
10 pounds ground fat pork
½ ounce mace
¼ ounce cayenne pepper
¼ ounce coriander
10 cups water

Mix the beef thoroughly with the salt and pepper, pack it into a stone crock, and let it stand in a cool place for 24 to 36 hours to cure. Grind the cured beef through the fine blade of a food chopper, add the pork and spices, and mix well. Stir in the water and stuff the mixture into large casings, 10 to 12 inches long. Tie each end of the casing and tie the ends of the casings together to form a ring of sausages. Hang the bologna in a cool place for 2 hours to dry, then smoke over a cool smoke for 3 to 5 hours, or until dark mahogany in color. The smoke should be light during the first hour, then the density increased for the remainder of the smoking period. The temperature in the smokehouse should not exceed 100° F.

After smoking, the sausages must be cooked in simmering water for 45 minutes to 1½ hours, depending on their size, or until they rise to the surface of the water. Squeeze a sausage in the hand and release the pressure. If the sausage is cooked it will squeak. Cool the sausages in cold water for 30 minutes, then hang them in a cool dry place to store.

Pickled and Preserved Meats, Fish, and Eggs

Smoking is not the only way to preserve protein foods. Many people like the piquant flavor of pickled meats, and the methods for making such products as corned beef, pickled pork, or pickled eggs have, along with the smoking procedures, come down to us through the generations.

Salt, sugar, saltpeter, and spices are used in the cure. The salt or brine extracts the water from the cells; the saltpeter speeds up this curing process; and the sugar and spices add flavor.

While most smoked foods are given a preliminary cure in dry salt or brine before they are smoked, it is an equally general rule that cured or pickled protein foods may be subjected to a smoke treatment, if one prefers a smoky flavor.

PICKLED EGGS

24 fresh eggs	½ tablespoon coriander seeds
6 cups cider vinegar	½ tablespoon cardamom seeds
2 tablespoons peppercorns	½ tablespoon cloves
1 tablespoon whole allspice	10 small hot red peppers
½ tablespoon mace	2 tablespoons sugar

Cook the eggs in boiling water for 12 minutes. Plunge them into cold water, remove the shells, and pack the eggs in sterilized jars. In a kettle combine the vinegar, spices, and sugar, bring to a boil, and simmer for 5 minutes. Cool, pour over the eggs, and seal.

PICKLED HERRING

Cut off the heads and clean the herring thoroughly. Cut away the strip of thin belly flesh on each side and remove the dark streak next to the backbone. Wash the fish thoroughly and drain well. Put the fish loosely in a crock and cover them with a pickling solution made by mixing 1 quart water, 1 quart white vinegar, and ⅝ cup pickling salt. The fish are cured in this solution from 3 to 7 days, the exact time depending on the size of the fish and the temperature. Should the skin of the fish start to wrinkle or lose color, remove the fish from the brine immediately.

When the herring are cured, repack them more tightly in a crock with a little salt sprinkled between the layers, and cover them with a pickling solution made of 2 quarts water, 1 quart white vinegar, and ⅝ cup salt. Store the crock in a cool place, where it may be kept for 2 to 3 weeks but no longer. The fish may be freshened for 8 hours, or overnight, in cold water and used immediately.

SPICED HERRING

Cut **pickled herring** across the body into strips 1 to 1½ inches wide. Pack the herring in a crock in layers with sliced onions, bay leaves, and mixed pickling spices between the layers.

Combine 1 quart white vinegar, 2 cups water, 6 tablespoons whole allspice, 4 tablespoons broken bay leaves, 4 tablespoons mustard seeds, 1 onion, sliced, a few small hot red peppers, 1 teaspoon whole cloves, and 1 tablespoon each of black peppercorns and sugar. Pour the mixture over the herring and let them stand for 24 hours before using.

To preserve the spiced herring, pack them with the spiced pickling solution in jars, cover, and store in the refrigerator, where they will keep for 6 months or more.

PICKLED PIKE OR PICKEREL

Clean the fish, cut them into filets, and discard the backbones. Wash 5 pounds of the filets thoroughly and cut them into 2-inch lengths. Dredge the pieces in fine pickling salt and pack them in a crock for 12 hours. Rinse off the salt and soak the fish in fresh cool water for 30 minutes.

In a kettle combine 1½ pints vinegar, 1½ cups water, 1 cup chopped onions, 2 cloves garlic, 1 tablespoon each of whole allspice, mustard seeds, and broken bay leaves, and 1 teaspoon each of whole cloves and peppercorns. Bring the liquid to a boil and simmer for 10 minutes. Add the fish and simmer for 10 minutes longer. Pack the fish in hot sterilized jars, adding a little chopped onion, a few pickling spices, a small hot red pepper, and a slice of lemon to each jar. Strain the spiced liquid, bring it again to a boil, and fill the jars to overflowing. Seal the jars immediately and store in a cool, dark place.

POTTED HERRING

Remove the heads from the herring. Clean the fish, wash them well, and drain. Wipe the fish dry and rub the belly cavities with pickling salt and ground black pepper. Arrange the fish in an earthenware baking dish with a few bay leaves, cloves, peppercorns, and allspice and half cover the fish with vinegar. Bake the fish in a slow oven (300° F.) for 1½ to 2 hours. Cool and store in the refrigerator, where they will keep for 2 weeks.

PICKLED SARDINES

Wash and scale 10 pounds of small herring. Remove the gills and pull out the intestines through the gill opening without tearing the belly. Wash the fish thoroughly and pack them in a crock. Cover them with a mixture of 3 parts white vinegar and 1 part water, and let them stand for 12 hours, or overnight.

Mix 2 pounds fine pickling salt with 1 pound fine granulated sugar, 2 tablespoons each of ground allspice and pepper, and 1 tablespoon each of saltpeter, crumbled bay leaves, ground cloves, ginger, and nutmeg.

Remove the fish from the brine and drain thoroughly, then dredge them in the spice mixture, and pack them in layers in a crock, belly side up. Pack the layers at right angles to each other, and pack the top layer back side up. Put the remaining spice mixture over the top layer and cover with a weighted cover to keep the sardines submerged in the brine when it forms. Let the fish cure for 10 days to 2 weeks before using, and store in a cool, dark place. If kept under refrigeration or in cold storage they will keep for many months.

ROLLMOPS

Cut **pickled herring** into two filets, discarding the backbone. Roll each filet around a small piece of dill pickle and fasten with a toothpick. Pack the rolls on end in a crock in layers.

In a saucepan combine 1 quart white vinegar, 2 large onions, sliced, 12 whole cloves, and 2 tablespoons each of mustard seeds, black peppercorns, broken stick cinnamon, cracked whole ginger, and bay leaves. Bring the vinegar to a boil, simmer for 45 minutes, and cool. Pour the spiced cooled pickling solution over the rollmops and let stand for 2 to 3 days before using.

Rollmops will keep for 2 weeks in summer and 6 weeks in winter at ordinary temperatures. For longer storage, keep the rollmops in the refrigerator.

PICKLED EELS

Clean and skin the eels and cut them into chunks ¾ inch thick. Wash, drain, and dredge the pieces in fine pickling salt. Rinse off the salt and wipe the pieces dry. Melt some butter with a crushed clove of garlic, brush the eels with the butter, and broil a few inches from the broiler flame until the pieces are lightly browned on all sides. Drain on absorbent paper, cool, and pack the pieces in a crock with sliced onion, whole allspice, bay leaves, mustard seeds, whole cloves, and peppercorns scattered between the layers. Put a weight on top of the fish and let stand for 24 hours. Cover the eels with a mixture of 3 parts white vinegar to 1 part water, cover the crock tightly, and let stand for 48 hours before using.

PICKLED SALMON, MACKEREL, OR SHAD

Cut 10 pounds filets into serving pieces and dredge the pieces well in fine pickling salt. Let them stand for 30 minutes, then drain and simmer the pieces in water for 15 to 20 minutes, or until done. Drain and pack the fish in a crock.

In a saucepan sauté 1 cup sliced onions in ½ cup olive oil until the onions are soft but not browned. Add 1 quart white vinegar, 1 quart water, 1 tablespoon each of peppercorns and mustard seeds, and ½ tablespoon each of cloves and crushed bay leaves. Bring the liquid to a boil and simmer for 45 minutes. Cool and pour the spiced vinegar over the fish, making sure that all the pieces are covered. Let stand in a cool place for 24 hours before using.

ESCABECHE (for Mackerel, Kingfish, or Tuna)

Wash 10 pounds fish filets and cut into small serving portions. Soak the pieces for 30 minutes in a strong brine made by dissolving 1¼ pounds salt in 2 quarts water. Drain and wipe dry. In a large heavy kettle heat 2 cups olive oil with 1 clove garlic, minced, 6 bay leaves, and a few small hot red peppers. Sauté the fish in the oil until lightly browned on both sides and set aside to cool.

To the oil remaining in the kettle add 2 onions, sliced, and cook until the onions are soft. Add 1 tablespoon black peppercorns, ½ tablespoon cumin seeds, 1 teaspoon marjoram, and 1 quart vinegar, bring the vinegar to a boil, and simmer for 15 minutes. Cool.

Pack the fish in sterilized jars with a couple of bay leaves and small hot red peppers in each jar. Fill the jars to overflowing with the spiced vinegar and seal. Escabeche will keep for about 3 weeks in the summer, and much longer if stored in the refrigerator.

PICKLED CLAMS, OYSTERS, OR MUSSELS

Scrub the shells well with a stiff brush and steam the shellfish just long enough to open the shells. Reserve the liquor and take the meats from the shells. Cool both meats and liquor. Pack the meats in sterilized jars with a few bay leaves, whole cloves, and a slice of lemon in each jar.

Strain the liquid, measure, and to each quart add 1 cup white vinegar, ½ tablespoon each of whole cloves, whole allspice, and hot red peppers, and 1 teaspoon cracked whole mace. Bring the liquid to a boil and simmer for 45 minutes. Cool, fill the jars to overflowing, and seal. Store in a cool, dark place.

PICKLED SHRIMP

Peel, devein, and wash the shrimp. In a kettle combine 2 quarts water, ½ cup salt, 1 cup white vinegar, ½ tablespoon each of hot red peppers and white peppercorns, 3 bay leaves, and 1 teaspoon each of whole cloves, whole allspice, and mustard seeds. Bring the liquid to a boil and simmer for 30 minutes. Add the shrimp, bring the liquid again to a boil, and simmer the shrimp for 5 minutes. Remove the shrimp and cool. Pack the shrimp in sterilized jars with a few mixed pickling spices and a slice of lemon in each jar. Fill the jars to overflowing with a solution made of 4 cups water, 2 cups white vinegar, and 1 tablespoon sugar. Seal the jars tightly and store in a cool, dark place.

PRESERVED GOOSE (Confit d'Oie)

Clean and draw a goose. Remove the fat and cut it into small pieces. Cut the goose into 4 sections, rub each piece lightly with salt, and let stand in the refrigerator for 24 hours. In a large skillet render the goose fat over a very low flame. Wipe the pieces of goose, place them in the rendered fat, and poach them very slowly for 1 to 1½ hours. In order to keep the fat from becoming too hot, a small amount of boiling water should be added from time to time, and the pieces of goose must be covered with the fat at all times. If there is not a sufficient quantity of goose fat, add some leaf lard. Cook the goose until no pink juice runs from the thigh when it is pricked with a large needle. Put the goose in a clean stone crock.

Strain the cooking fat through several layers of cheesecloth and discard every trace of water and meat juices. Cover the goose with the clarified fat, adding melted leaf lard if there is not enough fat to cover the goose completely. Cool and cover the lard with a round of parchment paper. Seal the crock airtight and store in a dark cool place.

When the crock is opened for use, any remaining pieces of goose should be stored, covered with the fat, in the refrigerator. Serve cold, in slices, or use in *choucroute* or *cassoulets*.

PRESERVED BONED GOOSE

Follow the directions for **preserved goose,** adding to the fat 2 cloves garlic, split, 2 whole cloves, 1 bay leaf, and 8 peppercorns, tied in cheesecloth. Discard the bag after the goose has cooked for 45 minutes.

When the goose is cooked, remove it from the fat, cool, and discard the bones and skin. Pour half the clarified fat into a crock and let it cool and set. Arrange the pieces of boned goose on the fat, being careful that the meat does not touch the sides of the crock. Cool the remaining fat to lukewarm and pour it over the goose, covering it completely. Cool and set in a cool place for 2 days. Then pour hot lard over the top to seal all the air pockets, and when this is set, cover with parchment paper, cover the crock, and store in a dark cool place.

CORNED BEEF

The cheaper cuts of beef—the plate, rump, cross ribs, and brisket —are usually used for corned beef, but the best of these is the brisket. The meat should be pickled as soon as possible after the animal is slaughtered and the carcass is thoroughly cooled and chilled. Frozen meat should not be used.

This recipe is for a large quantity of meat but may be applied to smaller quantities by proportionately reducing the ingredients that go into the brine.

For 100 pounds meat, measure 8 pounds pickling salt.

Sprinkle a layer of the salt ¼ inch deep in the bottom of a clean crock or tight barrel. Pack closely in the container a layer of the meat about 6 inches thick, and cover the meat with a layer of salt. Repeat these layers until all the meat and salt have been packed, reserving enough of the salt to make a good layer on top. Let meat and salt stand in a cool place overnight. Then make a brine by dissolving in 1 gallon lukewarm water 4 pounds sugar, 2 ounces baking soda, and 4 ounces saltpeter. Pour the brine over the meat and add about 3 gallons more water to the crock, or enough to cover the meat. Place a board cover over the meat and weigh the cover down with a clean, heavy stone to keep the meat submerged in the brine. Store the meat in a cool place for 28 to 40 days before using.

When the meat is thoroughly cured, it may be canned to avoid any risk of losing it from spoilage, and this should be done if the storage temperature is apt to rise. If kept at a temperature of 35° to 38° F. it will keep well all winter.

SMALL QUANTITY CORNED BEEF, JEWISH STYLE

Dissolve ½ teaspoon saltpeter in ¼ cup lukewarm water. Add 2 tablespoons brown sugar, 2 cloves garlic, sliced, 1 tablespoon mixed pickling spices, and 1 cup salt dissolved in 2 quarts warm water. Pour the brine over a 5- to 6-pound brisket of beef in a stone crock and cover the meat with a weighted plate to keep it under the brine. Let the meat stand in the brine in a cool place for about 3 weeks, turning the meat occasionally.

Tongue may be pickled in the same way.

To cook corned beef   Remove the meat from the brine. Cover the meat with fresh cold water, bring to a boil, and simmer for 1 hour. Drain, cover with fresh cold water, and add 4 bay leaves, 1 teaspoon cloves, and 1 onion, sliced. Bring the liquid to a boil and simmer gently until the meat is tender.

SPICED CHRISTMAS BEEF

Remove the bones and gristle from a 8- to 10-pound flank of beef. Combine 1 ounce saltpeter, 2 tablespoons each of ginger, freshly ground black pepper, and allspice, ½ tablespoon ground cloves, and ¼ tablespoon mace. Rub the beef all over with this spice mixture and put the meat, with any remaining spice mixture, in a stone crock. Sprinkle the beef with 6 tablespoons salt and ½ cup sugar, brown or white, and store the beef in a cool place for 2 weeks, turning it and rubbing it well each day.

To cook spiced beef Remove the beef from the crock, roll it tightly, and tie it with string. Put it in a roasting pan with 1 cup water and ½ pound suet, cover, and bake the meat for about 6 hours in a moderate oven (350° F.), basting occasionally. Remove the meat from the pan to cool and serve cold.

PICKLED TRIPE

Clean the tripe thoroughly and rinse it several times in cold water. Pour steaming-hot water over it, let it stand for 5 minutes, then scrape away the inside lining of the stomach. Drop the tripe into boiling water and simmer for about 3 hours, or until the tripe is tender. Drain, drop immediately into cold water, scrape the fat from the outer side, and peel off the membrane.

Scald a stone crock and put the cleaned, cooked tripe in it. Cover the tripe with a strong brine made by dissolving 2½ pounds salt in 6 quarts water. Place a weighted plate on top to keep the tripe under the brine and let it stand in a cool place for 3 to 5 days. Remove the tripe, rinse it in several changes of cold water, and drain. Pack the tripe in clean, sterilized jars and fill the jars to overflowing with cider vinegar. Pickling spices may be added if desired. Keep the tripe beneath the vinegar by means of wooden splints, seal, and store in a cool place.

DRY-CURED LAMB OR MUTTON

Cut lamb or mutton into large, uniform pieces and weigh. For 25 pounds meat mix 1½ pounds salt, 1 pound sugar, and ¾ tablespoon saltpeter. Rub the mixture into the meat and pack the meat into a clean stone crock. Sprinkle the remaining mixture on top and store in a cool place. It may be stored safely at a temperature of 35° to 38° F. Should the storage conditions be unfavorable, pack the cured meat in jars, seal, and process at 15 pounds pressure for 45 minutes.

CORNED LEG OF LAMB OR MUTTON

Other cuts of lamb and mutton may be corned, but the leg is delicious.

Rub 10 pounds meat thoroughly with 1½ cups salt, covering every portion, and let stand for 24 hours. Place the meat in a stone crock and pour over it a solution made of ½ tablespoon baking soda, 1 tablespoon saltpeter, ¾ cup brown sugar, and 1 quart lukewarm water. Add enough water to cover the meat completely and let the meat stand in the brine for 3 to 4 days. If stored in a cool place the corned meat will keep in good condition for many months.

SALT PORK OR PICKLED PORK

The fat back of pork or other thin pieces of fat pork are used for salting or pickling. Cut the meat into pieces 6 inches square, rub each piece well with pickling salt, and pack tightly in a clean crock. Let the meat stand overnight. In the morning, for each 25 pounds meat dissolve 2½ pounds salt and ½ ounce saltpeter in 4 quarts boiling water. Cool and pour the brine over the meat. Place a weighted cover on top to keep the meat under the brine and store at a temperature of 35° to 38° F. Keep the pork in the brine until used.

CHAPTER EIGHT

Drying

Every fall when I drive to Westchester to visit my favorite farm and enter my favorite kitchen, I find hanging above the range, suspended from a narrow rod, bunches of freshly gathered herbs—sweet basil, parsley, marjoram, orégano, thyme, tarragon, and dill. The sun is shining outside; the air is clear and dry, and all that is needed to dry those herbs for winter use is the little additional warmth that emanates from the stove during the hours it is used to cook the family meals.

Drying is the oldest means of preserving food. It is nature's way of suspending the germination of seeds throughout the cold winter months. The grain that was stored in Egyptian granaries thousands of years ago would not have kept had not the heat and drying power of the sun removed the excess moisture, leaving the grain dry and suitable for storage.

The Indians and our early settlers dried their surplus corn, beans, and peas, the fruit from the trees and the berries that grew wild. They even dried meat and fish, but these products were usually dried

269

by means of smoke. Pioneer housewives depended on dried foods to nourish them from one growing season to the next.

Today, except in time of war, there is little reason for us to preserve foods by drying. There are many brands of beautifully dried herbs, attractively packed, in stores throughout the country. Dried corn, for those who have acquired a taste for this product, and other vegetables, scientifically dehydrated and correctly packed in moisture-vaporproof packages, are also available to carry along on extended camping or hunting trips. And our own states of California, Oregon, and Washington produce in great quantity, and of a quality much superior to anything produced in the home kitchen, all the dried apples, peaches, figs, apricots, and raisins that we can possibly consume.

However, for those few who wish to dry foods in limited quantities, this chapter is included, for no book about the preservation of our country's food would be complete without it.

Herbs may be dried in a warm, breezy spot, fruits may be dried in the sun, and vegetables may be dried in a warm oven, in trays or racks placed over the kitchen stove, or in an especially constructed drier. For the best results it is necessary to have the heat as high as possible without injuring the fruit or vegetable, and to keep the air circulating to drive off the moisture.

In the beginning stage, a fairly high heat may be employed to draw the moisture from the center of the fruit or vegetable, but the surrounding air should be kept moist to prevent a hard crust or "case" from forming on the outside of the fruit or vegetable. If this "case hardening" is allowed to take place, the moisture in the center of the food cannot escape and, although the food may appear dry on the outside, it will certainly spoil on the inside.

Several varieties of driers or dehydrators suitable for home use may be purchased, or one may be fairly simply constructed.

HOW TO BUILD A SIMPLE DRIER

A simple box drier 24 by 15 inches and 36 inches in height can be constructed in such a way that currents of heated air will pass over the product and up and out of the drier, gathering moisture as it moves. The upper and lower trays must be exchanged several times throughout the drying process so that the food will dry uniformly.

The boxlike drier should rest on a 6-inch base of galvanized sheet iron. The base should flare out at the bottom and two small openings should be made on each of the four sides for ventilation. The box itself may be constructed of wood or sheet iron, with a hinged door in front that opens wide. The bottom of the drier should be made of perforated galvanized sheet iron, and 2 inches above this should be placed a solid sheet of galvanized iron that is 2 inches shorter in length and width than the perforated sheet. Support the solid sheet by means of cleats. This solid sheet is to prevent the product from coming in contact with direct heat, yet it allows the heated air to pass freely through the drier. Eight trays, 21 by 15 inches, are placed at intervals in the drier, resting on cleats 3 inches apart. The first tray should be placed 3 inches above the solid galvanized iron base. The trays may be constructed of perforated galvanized iron or stainless steel, or they may be simple wooden frames covered with galvanized screen wire. The trays are made 3 inches shorter than the depth or width, as the case may be, of the drier so that they may be staggered in the drier to allow a freer current of air. The first tray should be placed flush with the door or left side of the drier; the second tray should be placed flush with the back or right side of the drier and so on. A ventilator opening must be left in the top of the drier through which the moist air can escape. The ventilator should be equipped with a sliding metal cover, which can be kept closed or partially or fully open.

How to use a homemade drier Fill the drier with prepared fruits or vegetables and place it over gentle heat—a hot radiator, an electric hot plate, or the flame of a gas stove. Place a thermometer in the middle of the lowest tray. The temperature must be closely watched and the trays changed at intervals. In the beginning, the temperature may be allowed to rise to as high as 180° F., if the ventilator is kept closed or only partially open, so that the moist air will not escape too fast. When the product is half dry the temperature should be lowered to around 130° F., and the ventilator should be almost completely open. As the product in the drier loses moisture, the temperature in the drier will rise quickly and must be carefully watched to prevent burning the product. Toward the end of the drying period, the temperature should be still lower, and the ventilator should be fully open.

Vegetables and most fruits should be dried until they are brittle and will rattle on the tray. They should be packed in moistureproof containers.

The specific temperatures in the following procedures are only approximate, and they have been kept purposely low. Through experimenting you may find that drying time can be shortened by the use of higher temperatures, but much depends on the type of home drier and how it is constructed.

Drying Fruits

Only ripe, fresh fruits in perfect condition should be dried. With the exception of pears, the fruit or berries should be allowed to remain on the tree or bush until it is fully ripe in color and flavor.

In very dry climates fruits are often sun-dried, although commercial drying concerns have almost entirely converted to the use of long tunnel dehydrators. For home drying and on very hot sunny days, the fruit may be placed in the sun until it begins to wrinkle, and the drying is then completed in a home drier.

The moisture content of dried fruit should not exceed 20 per cent. At this point the fruit is pliable and leathery, but no moisture can be pressed from a cut surface. Dried fruits will appear softer and less dry when warm than when they are cooled.

For home preservation of dried fruits it is wiser to keep the moisture content below 20 per cent, drying the fruit until it is almost brittle.

Many fruits discolor unattractively in the drying process unless they are first treated with the fumes of burning sulphur.

Sulphuring fruit For home drying a simple sulphuring box may be made from a packing box or wooden crate that is large enough to cover the stack of trays. The lowest tray must be raised several inches off the ground. A little sulphur is placed in a heavy metal container and ignited. The smoking sulphur is placed beneath the stack of trays and the trays are covered with the box or crate. The fruit is allowed to remain in the sulphur box, exposed to the fumes of the burning sulphur, for 10 to 15 minutes, depending on the size of the pieces of fruit. The sulphuring should always be done out of doors.

The use of sodium sulphite An alternative, though slightly less effective, method for treating fruit with sulphur is by soaking the sliced fruit in a solution made by dissolving 1½ teaspoons of either sodium sulphite or sodium bisulphite in 1 gallon of cold water. Weigh the fruit down with a plate to keep it submerged in the solution. Your druggist can supply these chemicals.

APPLES

Early apples lack firmness and flavor and should not be dried. Any good tart cooking apple makes a fine dried product.

Peel and core the apples and remove any bruised or spoiled spots. Cut the fruit into rings, or into quarters or eighths, and drop the sliced fruit directly into a solution made by dissolving 1 teaspoon ascorbic acid in 1 quart cold water. Let the fruit soak in the solution for about 10 minutes, then drain and arrange the fruit in a single uniform layer on the trays.

Apples will have a superior color if they are exposed to the fumes of burning sulphur for 15 minutes before they are dried.

To sun-dry, place the trays in the hot sun for 3 or 4 days, or until dry, bringing them in each night and returning them to the sun in the morning.

To dry indoors, place the trays in a drier placed over the heat, and dry the fruit for 3 to 6 hours at a temperature of not more than 140° F. Test the fruit and, if it is not dry, reduce the temperature in the drier to 120° F. and continue to maintain this heat until the fruit is dry. The dried fruit should be soft and pliable but not wet in the center.

APRICOTS

Cut the apricots in half, remove the stones, and drop the fruit immediately into a solution containing 1 teaspoon ascorbic acid to 1 quart water. Drain and spread the apricot halves in a single uniform layer on the drying trays.

Apricots will have a superior color if they are exposed to the fumes of burning sulphur for 20 minutes before they are dried.

Dry the fruit at 150° F. for about 3 hours. Rearrange the trays in the drier and turn the fruit on the trays. Continue to dry at 140° F. for 6 to 12 hours longer, or until the fruit is dry.

BERRIES

Wild or cultivated blackberries or strawberries, black or red raspberries, loganberries, huckleberries, blueberries, dewberries, and gooseberries all dry well, although considerable care must be taken with the softer varieties of berries.

Pick the berries and prepare them immediately for the drier. They should not be allowed to stand overnight. Sort them, discarding any that are bruised or spoiled. Wash them lightly and remove the surface moisture by drying them between towels or in the hot sun. Spread them in a single layer on the drying trays, and place the trays immediately in a preheated home drier. Dry the berries for 2 hours at a temperature of about 120° F. Raise the temperature to 130° F. and continue drying for 2 hours longer, or until the berries are about half dry. Shake each tray carefully to redistribute the berries, and spread out any clumps that may have formed. The temperature may now be raised to as high as 140° F. to complete the drying.

CHERRIES

Both sweet and sour varieties of cherries may be dried. Wash and pit the cherries and spread them in a single layer on the trays. Dry the cherries for 1 hour at 120° F. to remove the excess moisture, then raise the temperature to 145° F. and continue the drying process for 3 to 6 hours, or until the cherries are dry.

FIGS

Select well-ripened, sound, unbruised figs. Sort them carefully, discarding any that are split, overripe, or defective in any way. Drop the figs for 1 minute into a boiling lye solution made by dissolving 2 tablespoons caustic soda in 2 quarts water. Lift out the figs and wash them in several changes of cold water to remove every trace of lye. Drain the fruit and remove the surface moisture by drying the fruit with towels or in the hot sun. Arrange the fruit in a uniform layer on the trays. Dry the fruit for 1 hour at a temperature of 120° F. Then increase the temperature to 145° F. and continue the drying process for 3 to 4 hours, or until the figs are dry. Turn the figs several times during the drying to prevent them from sticking to the trays.

After rinsing the figs and before drying them, they may be cooked until clear in a boiling syrup made of equal amounts of sugar and water.

PEACHES

Select firm tree-ripened peaches. Peel the peaches, halve, and remove the pits. Drop the halves immediately into a solution made by dissolving 1 teaspoon ascorbic acid in 1 quart cold water. Arrange the peaches, cut surface up, in a single uniform layer on the drying trays.

Peaches retain a better color if they are exposed to the fumes of burning sulphur for 10 to 15 minutes before they are dried.

Dry the fruit for 1 hour at 120° F. to remove the surface moisture. Raise the temperature in the drier to 140° F. and let the fruit dry for 6 hours, or until half dry. Then turn the fruit and rearrange the trays in the drier. Increase the heat in the drier to 160° F. and maintain this temperature until the fruit is dry.

PEARS

Peel, halve, and core firm-ripe pears. Cut the halves into thin lengthwise slices. Drop the cut fruit immediately into a solution made by dissolving 1 teaspoon ascorbic acid in 1 quart water, and let them soak for 30 minutes. Drain and spread the slices on trays.

Pears will have a lighter, more attractive color if they are exposed to the fumes of burning sulphur for 10 to 15 minutes before they are dried.

Dry off the surface moisture in the drier for 1 hour at a temperature of 110° F. Increase the temperature to 130° F. and dry for 2 hours longer, or until half dry. Turn the slices on the trays and rearrange the trays in the drier. Raise the temperature to 150° F. for another 3 hours, or until the pears are dry. The dried fruit should be leathery, but it should be impossible to press any moisture from a cut surface.

After sulphuring and before drying, the fruit may be cooked until almost tender in boiling syrup made of twice as much water as sugar.

PLUMS

Cover firm-ripe plums with boiling water and let them stand for 10 minutes. Drain and arrange them in a single uniform layer on the drying trays.

Remove the surface moisture by drying the plums for 1 hour at a temperature of 110° F. Increase the temperature in the drier to 130° F. and continue to dry the plums for 3 hours, or until half dry. Turn the plums on the trays and rearrange the trays in the drier. Raise the temperature to 150° F., and maintain this temperature in the drier for another 3 hours, or until the plums are dry.

Large, thick-fleshed plums may be halved and pitted before they are dried. They should then be placed on the trays cut side up and exposed to the fumes of burning sulphur for 15 to 20 minutes to preserve their color.

PRUNE PLUMS

Select sweet tree-ripened prune plums and prepare them immediately for the drier.

To remove the waxy coating on the prunes so that the moisture can escape, the prunes must be treated with lye. Drop the prunes for 15 to 20 seconds in a boiling lye solution made by dissolving 2 tablespoons caustic soda in 2 quarts water. Wash the fruit in several changes of cold water to remove any trace of lye and drain well. Place the prunes in a single uniform layer on the drying trays and dry them at 120° F. for about 4 hours, or until the skin is wrinkled. Turn the prunes and rearrange the trays in the drier. Increase the temperature to 160° F. and maintain this temperature for another 2 hours, or until the prunes are dry. No moisture should show when the cut surface of a prune is pressed tightly in the fingers.

Drying Vegetables and Herbs

The drying of only a few vegetables, and of course herbs, should be attempted in the home kitchen. Potatoes, cabbage, onions, and most root vegetables should be left to experienced commercial dehydrators. During the last war great technical advances were made in the drying of vegetables, but these processes are much too complicated to be transferred to the limited conditions of the home. How well I know, for eight years of my life were spent dehydrating vegetables in specially designed and constructed stainless-steel dehydrating cabinets, with scientifically controlled humidity, temperatures, and air flow, for our armed forces.

Some vegetables, however, may be quite simply and successfully dried at home. Corn, green peppers, parsley, celery leaves, and herbs are some of these, so let's begin with corn.

CORN

Many people consider dried corn superior in flavor to canned corn.

Select young tender corn that has not been off the stalks for more than 4 hours. If you are fortunate to be able to harvest it from your own garden, so much the better. Husk the ears immediately and trim them with a sharp knife. Drop the ears into boiling water, cover the kettle, and let the corn poach in the water for 3 minutes.

Keep the water near the simmering point but do not let it boil. Remove the ears, cool slightly, and cut the corn from the cob. Use a sharp knife and cut halfway through the kernels; scrape off the part of the kernels adhering to the cobs. Spread the kernels on drying trays to a depth of about 1 inch.

The corn may be dried either in the sun or in a home-made drier. To dry in the sun, put the corn in a moderate oven (350° F.) for 10 minutes, then place the trays in the hot sun to finish the drying. A better, lighter-colored product is produced with a home drier. Dry the corn at a temperature of 110° F. for 1 hour. Stir the corn on the tray to equalize the moisture and break up any masses, increase the temperature to 120° F., and dry for 2 hours longer. Again stir the corn, raise the temperature to 140° F., and maintain this temperature for 2 to 3 hours, or until the corn is dry, stirring it frequently.

CELERY AND PARSLEY LEAVES

Dry the leaves in a home drier for about 2 hours at 110° F. or spread the leaves thinly on a screen and put the screen in a slow oven, with the door open. An electric fan placed near the entrance of the oven will create a circulation of air to speed up the drying process.

PARSLEY CLUSTERS

A superior product will result if the clusters of parsley are dipped for 30 seconds in rapidly boiling water. Drain the clusters between towels, pressing out the surface moisture, place in a thin layer on a screen covered with cheesecloth, and put the screen in a slow oven with the door open until dry. When dry remove the leaves from the stems and pack in airtight containers.

The leaves may be removed from the stems before they are dried and finely chopped. Tie the chopped parsley in a cheesecloth bag and lower it into rapidly boiling water for 1 minute. Squeeze out the excess moisture and spread the chopped parsley on a cheesecloth-covered screen. Place the screen in a warm spot and it will dry in a few hours.

PEPPERS, RED OR GREEN

Cut out the pepper stems, halve the peppers, and discard the seeds and white membranes. Cut the peppers into thin strips or dice and spread them on drying trays. Dry the peppers for several hours at 120° F. until dry and crisp, stirring frequently to redistribute the moisture.

Small varieties may be spread in the sun until wilted, and the drying completed in the home drier. Or they may be simply hung in a warm sunny place until dry.

DRYING FLOWERS

Cut the flowers early in the morning when the blossoms are fully opened. Spread them on a screen and put them in a shady, airy spot or in a dry warm attic until thoroughly dry. Strip the heads from the stalks and store the flowers in tightly sealed moistureproof containers.

DRYING LEAVES

Strip only perfect, tender leaves from the stalks and spread them in a thin layer on a screen in a shady spot. A current of air should be allowed to flow under as well as over the screen. Turn the leaves once a day and they should be ready to pack in 3 or 4 days.

DRYING PETALS

Cut fully opened flowers early in the morning, when the dew has evaporated. Pluck the petals from the calyx and spread them in a single layer on a screen. Put the screen in a shady, airy spot where air can circulate under and over the petals until the petals are dry. Pack the dry petals in airtight containers and watch them carefully for 1 week. If beads of moisture appear inside the container, turn the petals out on a baking sheet and dry them for 1 or 2 hours in a lukewarm oven. Keep the door of the oven open so that the petals will not burn, and stir them frequently.

DRYING ROOTS

Wash the roots thoroughly, scraping them if necessary to remove the dirt. Large roots should be sliced or split lengthwise. Place the roots in a thin layer on a wire screen and put the screen in a dry, shady spot outdoors. Turn the roots once a day and bring them indoors each night. The drying will take from 3 to 6 weeks. When almost dry place the screen in a very low oven with the door open to finish the drying.

DRYING SEEDS

Gather the seed pods when the stalks are dry and spread them in a thin layer on a screen lined with cheesecloth. Place the tray in a warm, dry spot for 5 to 6 days, stirring the pods each day. When dry rub the pods in the palms of the hands in a breezy place so that the chaff will blow away. Spread the seed on the cheesecloth-covered tray to dry for about a week longer, stirring them gently once or twice a day. Store in tight containers and watch carefully for 1 week. If moisture appears inside the containers, remove the seeds immediately and dry them for several days longer.

HERBS

Garden herbs should be gathered for drying when the plant begins to flower but the leaves are still green and tender. The young leaves at the tip of the plant have more flavor than the larger, older leaves.

For finest flavor gather the herbs on a sunny morning and dry them rapidly in a dry, dark, well-ventilated room. The tender-leaf herbs such as sweet basil, tarragon, lemon balm, and the mints especially need rapid drying, out of the sunlight, to hold their color and flavor and to prevent molding. The thicker, tougher herbs such as rosemary and sage, thyme and summer savory have a lower moisture content and may be dried partially in the sun and finished in a lukewarm oven.

Cut the stems of the herbs 4 or 5 inches from the tip. If the leaves are gritty or dirty, rinse them lightly in cold water and drain them thoroughly. Tie the stems in small bunches and hang them to dry or spread them thinly on a screen in a dark airy spot for about 4 days. As soon as the leaves are dry, separate them from the stems and pack them in airtight containers. If glass jars are used they should be stored in a dark place or the color will fade from the leaves.

Drying Fish and Meats

The drying of fish and meats by air alone is seldom practiced in this country, for it is a treacherous business at best and requires great experience and skill. Little skill is needed, however, to dry salted fish, and fish cured in this way keep for a considerable time; the exact time is dependent on the storage temperature, the amount of moisture remaining in the fish, and the care used in the preparation and storage. Almost all varieties of fish may be preserved by salting and drying, although fatty fish keep for a shorter period.

As soon as the fish is caught, slash the throat, remove the gills, and let the fish bleed thoroughly. Wash the fish well and cut off the head, but leave the hard bony plate just below the gills to keep the fish from pulling apart during the curing. Cut down the left side of the backbone, with the knife slanted slightly down against the bone, and remove the upper section in one piece. Then insert the knife blade under the backbone, with the knife slanted slightly up against the bone, and cut down to the tail. Discard the backbone. Remove any bits of viscera, blood clots, and membranes from the belly cavity, and scrub the fish in water with a stiff vegetable brush, then soak the fish for 20 minutes in a brine made by dissolving 1 cup salt in 1 gallon cold water, and drain well.

Dip the fish into a shallow box of fine pickling salt and dredge each piece thoroughly. Pick up the fish with as much salt as will cling to the body and arrange the fish, alternating heads and tails, in rows on boards placed in a spot where the brine formed may drain off. Pile the fish flesh side up except for the top layer, which should be stacked skin side up. About 1 pound of salt should be used for every 4 pounds of fish.

The fish should remain stacked for 48 hours to 1 week, depending on their size and on the weather. In warm weather, suitable for drying, the salting period is short.

Scrub the fish in water to remove the excess salt, and let them drain for 20 minutes. Frames of wood covered with chicken wire, standing on legs about 4 inches high, are used to dry the fish. The fish should not be dried in direct sunlight, but should be placed in the shade under an open-walled shed where there is good cross ventilation. Place the fish on the racks skin side down, and turn them three or four times the first day. A smoke smudge under the drying racks may be necessary on the first day of drying to keep away the flies. The smudge should be built of hard green wood. Resinous woods such as pine or fir must not be used.

The fish must be gathered and taken in each night. They should be stacked in piles no more than 2 feet high, alternating heads and tails, flesh side up except for the top layer. The fish should be piled on a rack to keep them from contact with the floor and each stack should be weighted down evenly to press the moisture out of the flesh.

About 6 good drying days are needed to remove enough moisture to preserve the fish. If the weather is unfavorable for drying, the fish should be left indoors in the stacks, but they must be repiled each day, placing the top layers of fish at the bottom and scattering a small amount of fine salt between the layers.

After 5 or 6 days of drying, press the thick part of the flesh between the thumb and forefinger. If no impression is left, the fish are sufficiently dry. Wrap the fish in wax paper, pack in wooden boxes, and store in a cool, dry place.

RACKLING

Nordic fishermen prepare rackling from lean fish such as flounder, halibut, hake, rock cod, or cusk. Remove the head of the fish, leaving the collarbone intact, and split the fish into two sides, discarding the backbone. Cut the fish lengthwise into long, narrow strips about 1 inch wide, leaving them joined at the collarbone. Wash the fish thoroughly and soak it for 1 hour in a strong brine made by dissolving 2½ pounds salt in 1 gallon water. Then hang the fish out to dry in a breezy but shaded place for 1 to 2 weeks. Do not expose the fish to direct sunlight.

Rackling is eaten dry, like jerked beef, with no preliminary preparation. It may, however, be soaked for a few hours and made into fishcakes or loaves, or creamed.

DRIED SHRIMP

Wash the shrimp thoroughly and drain. Bring to a boil a salt brine made of 1 cup salt and 2 quarts water. Put in the shrimp and let them simmer for about 10 minutes, or until the meat is separated from the shell. Spread the shrimp in a layer not more than 1 inch deep in the direct sun, and turn them every half hour during the first day of drying. Gather the shrimp at night or at the first sign of rain and store them in a dry, well-ventilated place.

About 3 days of good sunny weather is needed to dry shrimp, but longer, of course, if the weather is unfavorable. When the shrimp are dry, put them in a sack and store them in a dry, cool spot.

To use, soak the shrimp in water for a few hours, wipe them dry, and sauté them in butter. They may also be added to soups, stews, and curries, and are used in various Chinese dishes.

281

JERKED VENISON

Cut the flank of the venison with the grain of the meat into strips 1 inch wide, ½ inch thick, and any length possible. Soak the meat for 2 days in a brine made by dissolving 32½ ounces salt in 6 quarts water. The brine should be so strong that it will float an egg. Remove the meat from the brine, wipe it dry, and hang it in the sun to dry.

PEMMICAN

Meat that has either been salted and sun-dried or dried by means of smoke may be made into pemmican. The meat must be so dry that it can be pounded into a powder. Hot fat is then added and kneaded into the powdered meat to make a thick dough. Often dried fruits—such as currants, raisins, or apricots—are pounded with the meats before the fat is added. The dough is formed into a round loaf or a sausage shape, wrapped in heavy canvas, and dipped into warm paraffin. Pemmican will keep indefinitely if it is properly made and kept dry.

CHAPTER NINE

Freezing

Your home freezer is modern man's latest contribution to the preservation of food. It is not simply a storage vault for bushels of fruit and vegetables, nor a place to hoard large quantities of meat. Rather, it is a miraculous appliance with unlimited possibilities; it can revolutionize your eating habits, give your family better meals, and allow you new freedom and leisure to enjoy other interests.

The purchase of your freezer is probably the biggest step you have taken to make your home more complete and efficient since you bought your first mechanical refrigerator.

How much pleasure and economical use you derive from your freezer depends upon you. It varies with each individual. To some the home freezer may mean larger storage space for commercially frozen foods. To those who live in the suburbs, or on a farm, it may mean an easier way to preserve the surplus from the garden, the liberty to slaughter at the most economical time of the year, or the elimination of frequent trips to the nearest food center. To others it may mean that meals can be planned well in advance, saving last-minute fuss or confusion, affording, too, the comforting knowledge that the utmost in hospitality may be shown to guests at any moment.

To everyone, the freezer should mean a new and better way of life.

Freezing food is the simplest method of food preservation, but it is by no means the least expensive. The cost of freezing 1 pound of food, when you consider equipment cost and depreciation, electricity, and the containers and wrapping materials for proper storage, is several times more than if you canned it.

On the other hand, there are no jars to sterilize and no standing over a hot stove for hours in summertime, for freezing is extraordinarily easy and consumes a minimum of time and labor. You don't save money, but you do save time and work. And foods properly wrapped and frozen are more nearly like fresh foods than if they were preserved by any other method.

What size and kind of freezer to buy   The space that you have available may well be the determining factor in the size of the home freezer you decide to buy. Before you make your final choice you should consider the number of people in your family; the extent of entertaining that you do; whether you have your own garden and wish to freeze the surplus crops. To help you make your decision, you should know that

> 1 cubic foot of freezer space will accommodate 54 rectangular pint containers, 70 twelve-ounce packages of commercially frozen foods, or 12 frying chickens.
> 2 cubic feet will accommodate a loin or round of beef.
> 3 cubic feet will accommodate a quarter of beef.

There are three principal types of home freezers:

1. The **chest-type freezer** ranges in size from 2 to 22 cubic feet, with storage capacities of 70 to 780 pounds. It may be square or rectangular with a top opening. Most single-compartment chest freezers provide both freezing and storage in the same area. Those that have several compartments provide a separate area for freezing.

2. The **upright freezer** ranges in size from 6 to 55 cubic feet, with capacities from 210 to 2000 pounds of food. It requires no more floor space than a refrigerator and has a front-opening door. This type of freezer usually includes several zero storage compartments, and some provide a special quick-freezing compartment.

3. The **walk-in freezer** is really suitable only for farms or for commercial use where more than 20 cubic feet of space is required. It is seldom practical for average-family needs. Some walk-in freezers have a chilling compartment, about 32° F., for holding meat, or for rapidly cooling freshly slaughtered animals. Others include a storage area for root crops and winter fruits.

Points to consider when shopping for your home freezer:

1. All-steel construction will give longer service.

2. The steel cabinet should be given some rust-resistant treatment before the exterior finish is applied.

3. Plastic door gaskets are resistant to grease and last longer.

4. Baked-on enamel does not chip and is easy to keep clean.

5. Rounded corners in the interior of the freezer are easier to clean.

6. The opening should be well insulated, and it should swing up or out easily, on ball-bearing hinges. It should close tightly and have a cushion gasket surrounding the opening to prevent warm air from leaking into the freezer.

7. Inorganic insulation from 3 to 4 inches deep is vitally important to the maintenance of a constant temperature with a minimum of electric power. This is also important in the event that the power becomes interrupted. A well-insulated freezer will keep foods safely at zero temperature for as long as 36 hours with the electric current off.

8. A fast-freezing compartment is not necessary, but it is desirable.

9. Special features are patented by the different manufacturers, and it is up to you to decide which of these special features make one freezer more attractive to you than another.

Where to place your freezer   Before you buy your home freezer you will, naturally, give some thought to where you are going to put it.

The first choice is the kitchen where you prepare the food to be frozen and later cook the frozen food. The temperature of the room does not affect the constant zero temperature within your freezer and certainly the kitchen is the logical place. Common sense would motivate you to select a spot away from the stove, radiator, or the direct rays of the sun.

The next best place would be the breakfast room, pantry, or porch, as close to the kitchen as possible.

Finally, the cellar or garage must be used if there is no room nearer the kitchen. Even so, a home freezer is worth these extra steps.

Check with your electrician to make sure that the electrical circuit for your freezer is not already overloaded. A level, solid floor is important.

If you are planning to remodel or to build a new home, provide adequate space for a home freezer even if your present budget does not allow one. It may not be long before it will!

How to care for your home freezer   Specific directions for the care of your freezer are supplied by the company from whom you bought it. The following are general:

A home freezer is the simplest of all household appliances to operate. The best care you can give it is to leave it strictly alone most of the time. It automatically controls the zero temperature in the storage compartment and below-zero temperature in the quick-freeze compartment. When food to be frozen is placed in the freezer, the automatic control provides the additional refrigeration necessary to freeze it quickly.

DEFROSTING: How often your freezer must be defrosted depends on the moisture content of the air inside the freezer, how many times the door is opened to withdraw or put in packages, and how moisture-vaporproof your packaging of the food has been. But once or twice a year should be sufficient.

When frost accumulates to a depth of about ¼ inch, it should be scraped off with a smooth-edged, hard plastic or wooden paddle. Sharp tools or wire brushes should not be used. Remove the food from your freezer and wrap it in several thicknesses of paper. If your freezer has a drain, the frost may be melted easily by putting saucepans filled with boiling water in the freezer and repeating after 15 minutes if the frost has not melted. Otherwise, scrape the frost onto layers of newspaper so that it can be lifted out easily. Work as quickly as possible and return the frozen food as soon as the frost has been removed.

CLEANING: Once a year your freezer should be thoroughly cleaned, and the logical time to do this is in the spring, when your supply of frozen food is at its minimum. It is also logical to clean your freezer at a time when it needs defrosting as well. Turn off the current and place all the packages from the freezer in a box thickly lined with newspapers and dry ice. Defrost the freezer and wash each compartment with a solution of 2 tablespoons baking soda dissolved in each quart of warm water. Soap or caustic solutions must never be used. Dry the inside of the compartments thoroughly before turning on the power and return the food as soon as the interior reaches zero.

DOES THE MOTOR NEED OILING? That depends entirely on the make of freezer you own. Many home freezers have the units hermetically sealed with a lifetime of lubrication.

WHAT HAPPENS IF THE POWER FAILS? *Don't open the door until the power is restored*, or if the power remains off for more than 48 hours, open the door just long enough to put dry ice into the compartments. It is a wise precaution to locate a source of supply of dry ice near your home in case of emergency. Usually your local dairy or ice plant can supply you. Handle the dry ice with gloves and pack about 10 pounds into each compartment. Fifty pounds of dry ice will hold the temperature in a 20-cubic-foot cabinet with a full load of frozen food for about 4 days. If the freezer is only partially filled with frozen food, the danger point will be reached in 2 to 3 days. A 6-cubic-foot freezer needs only 15 pounds of dry ice to protect food in an emergency.

Dry ice is not really ice at all, for it contains no water. It is a harmless, non-toxic carbon dioxide gas, first liquefied, then frozen to a temperature of 109° *below* zero. As it melts and absorbs heat, it evaporates to its natural gaseous state, leaving behind it no moisture.

SHOULD AN ALARM BE INSTALLED? Definitely! Sometimes the door to your freezer is accidentally left open. A temperature-operated alarm sounds a warning if, for any reason, the temperature in your freezer rises to the danger point. Many freezers on the market today are already equipped with this device. Be sure to have the alarm batteries checked occasionally.

Operation cost How much will a freezer cost to operate? That depends on many things—the cubic-foot capacity, the kind and thickness of insulation, the type of construction, the horsepower of the motor on the freezing unit, the quantity of foods frozen, the temperature of the food to be frozen, the length of time, how frequently the freezer is opened, and the temperature at which the cabinet is held for storage. But your freezer is going to cost you money, so be prepared for your next electric bill. Even the smallest, most economically operated home freezer will add at least $3.00 per month to your bill.

There are a few rules for the most efficient and economical operation of your freezer, and I list them here:

1. Keep your freezer in a dry place away from sunny windows, radiators, and stoves.

2. Avoid freezing too large a quantity of food at one time.

3. Keep the packages well organized in the most convenient place, so you can find them quickly and easily.

4. Defrost when necessary. Thick layers of frost inside your freezer reduce efficiency and make the maintenance of zero temperatures more difficult.

5. Chill all foods before putting them into your freezer. Warm foods raise the temperature inside the freezer and cause unnecessary use of electricity.

6. Two freezers are more economical than one. For instance, if you decide you need 20 cubic feet of freezer space, two 10-cubic-foot freezers are more economical than one large one. The use of one may be discontinued during periods when your supply of frozen foods is at a minimum. Again, one may be reserved for those foods that you intend to store for a considerable period. The other may be kept exclusively for foods such as butter, coffee, cream, bread, rolls, et cetera, that are used every day.

EQUIPMENT FOR FREEZING

Except for a good supply of packaging materials, very little equipment other than that found in a moderately equipped kitchen is needed. You should have:

1. Sharp knives for slicing and preparing vegetables.

2. Measuring cups and spoons.

3. A large spoon or scoop.

4. A nest of bowls.

5. Two 6-quart cooking kettles with tight-fitting lids.

6. A square funnel, or a tin can with ends removed and sides flattened, for filling bags.

7. A carton holder for easier packaging and sealing.

8. A fine-meshed wire basket or cheesecloth for scalding vegetables.

9. A pitcher for syrup.

10. A thermostatically controlled hand iron, or a curling iron, for sealing packages.

11. A labeling pencil.

PACKAGING MATERIALS

Much of the success of home-frozen foods depends upon proper packaging materials and how foods are wrapped and sealed for storage, so the importance of this phase of freezing cannot be over-emphasized. There must be no exchange of moisture or air between the frozen food and the air inside the cabinet. Cold air is dry air and dry air will draw the moisture from the foods unless they are protected by moisture-vaporproof materials, which are readily available and which were designed expressly to exclude the air and prevent the escape of moisture from frozen foods.

The meaning of *moisture-vaporproof* should not be confused with the word "waterproof." Ordinary wax or oil papers, gift-wrap cellophanes, and ice cream cartons, while waterproof, still permit the exchange of moist air through their pores and should not be used. It is false economy to buy improper wrappings and containers, for if the moisture is taken from foods in zero storage that are not carefully wrapped in moisture-vaporproof wrappings, or if the covering becomes torn during storage, the foods will be dry and of inferior quality. They will lose flavor, color, and food value.

Loss of moisture in frozen foods also means that the food is exposed to the oxygen in the air. Exposure to oxygen hastens the rancidity of fats. Grayish-white spots are apt to develop on the surface of meat which is inadequately protected. This is known as "freezer burn." Actually the meat has not been burned at all; rather, it has been robbed of its moisture, or dehydrated, and oxidation has taken place. Though still edible, the meat is definitely of poor quality.

Besides resisting the passage of moisture-vapor and protecting the food from contact with the air inside the freezer, packaging materials must protect the food from leakage and the possibility of an exchange of flavors between one food and another. Fish, butter, cheese, and pastries are all stored side by side, and if an exchange of flavors is permitted, the results could be disastrous. Butter, for example, will pick up other flavors if given the slightest opportunity.

Packaging materials should be odorless, tasteless, flexible, and easy to handle, seal, and label. They should be strong enough to stand considerable handling without cracking, durable enough to resist puncturing by bones or sharp edges, and they must not become brittle at zero temperature.

Packaging materials should be relatively inexpensive and economical of storage space. Square or rectangular cartons stack easily and use a minimum of space. They are available in pint and quart sizes, and you should select the size that is most suited to your family needs. A quart container will give you 6 to 8 servings of a vegetable or 8 to 10 servings of fruit. One cubic foot of freezer space will house about 24 rectangular or square cartons, but only 16 round or slope-sided cartons.

Sheet wrappings

ALUMINUM FOIL is easy to use, as it may be fitted snugly around the food, expelling the excess air, and does not require taping or heat-sealing. When two surfaces of aluminum foil are pressed tightly together, the package is sealed. It punctures easily and must be protected by an outside wrap, but it is excellent for wrapping roasts, poultry, and large fish.

MOISTURE-VAPORPROOF CELLOPHANE needs an overwrap to protect it from puncturing. It must be soft and pliable. Should it become brittle from age, place it in the refrigerator for 46 hours and it will regain its pliability. It may be used to wrap steaks, chops, poultry, and fish.

PLIOFILM is heavier and sturdier than cellophane. It is excellent for wrapping irregular-shaped foods and makes a handsome, air-free package because of its rubberlike quality. It needs a protective covering.

POLYETHYLENE is a plastic film that will stand more handling than either cellophane or pliofilm. It is particularly strong and pliable and needs no overwrap.

SARAN is an excellent transparent plastic film that clings closely to food, eliminating air pockets. It is moisture-vaporproof, pliable, strong, and reusable.

LAMINATED PAPERS are made of two sheets of different materials held together by a flexible adhesive. It may be pliofilm laminated to aluminum foil, or glassine or cellophane laminated to heavy paper. The lamination makes the paper moisture-vaporproof. Laminated papers are perfect for wrapping roasts. The packages may be tied simply with string and need no outer protection.

Containers

FLAT, TOP-OPENING, HEAVILY WAXED PAPER CARTONS with moisture-vaporproof liners or overwraps are ideal for such vegetables as asparagus, corn on the cob, and broccoli. They are also good for chops, hamburgers, croquettes, fish filets, and disjointed poultry. They are easy to stack and freeze faster because they are flat.

LEAKPROOF PARAFFINED CONTAINERS are good for moist foods, soups, stews, sauces, and semiliquid foods such as butter and ice cream. The square ones save storage space.

PLASTIC CONTAINERS are also liquid-tight and easy to fill. They are excellent for ground meats, butter, ice cream, and semisolid foods that can be pressed into them, eliminating air pockets. They are especially suitable for leftovers and although they are fairly expensive compared with other cartons on the market, they can be used indefinitely.

GLASS FREEZER JARS have been specially designed to withstand extreme changes in temperature. They have wide mouths and tapered sides to facilitate the removal of the frozen contents. The rustproof metal screw caps make a leakproof, airtight seal. The cap was ingeniously devised to bulge so the jar won't shatter in case insufficient head space was left in the jar. Glass jars are excellent for fruit purées, juices, stews, soups, sauces, and leftovers, and they may be reused.

Additional basic packaging needs
OUTER WRAPPINGS give added strength to packages and prevent the moisture-vaporproof coverings from tearing during storage.

STOCKINETTE material is a tubular, loosely knitted cotton fabric that may be stretched over odd-shaped foods for added protection.

LOCKER PAPER, BUTCHER PAPER, NYLON STOCKINGS, or CHEESECLOTH may also be used to overwrap. The great value of polyethylene or laminated papers is that they do not need this extra protection.

You should also have on hand LOCKER TAPE—a special tape that will hold even in the zero temperatures of your freezer for any length of time. Use it to seal edges, to cover accidental punctures, and to attach labels. You will need a HEAT SEALER of some type and a CHINA MARKING PENCIL that will label clearly all types of papers and cartons.

HOW TO PACKAGE FOODS FOR YOUR FREEZER

The way food is wrapped for the freezer is just as important in maintaining the quality of frozen food as the wrappings and containers that you buy. No matter how moisture-vaporproof the wrappings may be, if they are carelessly sealed so that the air can get in and the moisture of the food can get out, you might just as well never have wrapped it at all.

Whether you are packaging in containers or wrapping in paper, exclude as much air as possible from the package. Air pockets between the food and the packaging material collect moisture from the food. Package in amounts that are suitable for your family needs. Label accurately and informatively and freeze at once.

The **drugstore fold** is the easiest way to make a close, tight wrap with any suitable sheet wrappings and is recommended for irregularly shaped foods such as poultry and cuts of meat. Place the food in the center of a large sheet of flexible, durable paper. Bring the ends of the paper above the meat and fold them over and over downward in a lock seal, drawing the paper as tightly to the food as possible. Then fold the ends, fitting and pressing the paper close to the food to avoid air pockets. Use low-temperature locker tape to seal the edges of the folds.

The **butcher wrap** is also used for the inner and outer wrap of sheet wrappings, or for a single wrap if laminated paper is used. Place the food diagonally across one corner of a large sheet of freezer paper. Fold over the sides and roll the package over and over until the food is completely covered. Wrap tightly to exclude the air and keep the package flat. Seal the edges carefully with low-temperature locker tape.

Folding cartons with heat-sealing liners Open the moisture-vaporproof liner completely, including the corners, with the hand, and insert it in the opened carton. The use of a block of wood on which to form packages is a time saver. Fill the carton by means of a square funnel, or a tin can slightly flattened, to keep the top of the bag dry. The sealing edge must be perfectly dry and clean if you are going to have a perfect heat seal.

Press out the air from the liner and seal the liner part way across close down to the packaged food. Press out the remaining air and finish the seal. Then draw the iron upward toward the end of the bag. A wooden platform may be made to hold the package upright as you seal the liner. Another easy method of getting a seal close to the food is by resting a wide strip of heavy cardboard on top of the carton. Fold the bag over it at the point where the seal can be made snugly against the contents, press out the air from the liner, and move the iron over the cardboard. Use just enough heat and pressure to melt the plastic film or wax until it seals. Too much heat will scorch the liner and cause an imperfect seal.

Head space must be left when packing liquid or semiliquid foods to allow for expansion during freezing and to prevent bulging of containers, leaking, or breakage of glass. The more liquid the product, the greater the expansion and the more head space needed. Ideally, just enough space should be left so that the food will expand flush with the top, leaving no air pockets in the container, but this takes experience. In general, leave ½ inch head space for most foods and 1 inch for juices. If ordinary glass jars are used for freezing, leave 1 inch in pints and 1½ inches in quarts.

Labeling   Every package in your freezer should be identified as to the kind of food, the weight or the number of servings, the date of storage, and the intended use of the contents.

Freeze immediately   The more quickly packaged foods get into your freezer the better they will be when cooked. Check your freezing compartment to make sure it can accommodate the amount of food you are preparing. Freeze at one time only the number of packages advised by the manufacturer of your freezer. Place the packages in contact with the freezer lining, with air space between them.

WHAT TO FREEZE

Practically every type of food can be preserved by freezing except vegetables to be eaten raw and crisp, such as lettuce, celery, radishes, cucumbers, tomatoes, cabbage, onions, and green peppers. Tomatoes may be frozen as juice or purée, or in ready-made dishes. Cabbage may be frozen and used as a cooked vegetable, but it will not retain its crispness.

Everything else freezes well—beef, lamb, pork, veal, and variety meats; chicken, ducks, turkeys, guinea hens, and geese; game birds, rabbits, squirrels, and venison; fish and shellfish; ice cream, sherbets, butter, cheese, and eggs; fruit juices and fruit purées; cakes, cookies, pies, puddings, bread, rolls, stews, soups, and ready-made dishes.

Your freezer space is limited no matter what size you have, and if you are going to get the most from your freezer, every cubic inch must be strictly and wisely budgeted so that a variety of foods can be stored to satisfy the personal preferences of your entire family.

Your approach to daily living and where you live will naturally affect your decision as to what and how much you want to freeze. If you have a garden, naturally you will want to conserve the fruits and vegetables that cannot be eaten. Frozen fruits and vegetables are good, but they are never as good as when they are fresh, and for most city dwellers there is very little reason to freeze vegetables at all. Why freeze onions, turnips, beets, carrots, celery, green peppers? There is seldom a time throughout the year that these vegetables cannot be bought at your local vegetable store. Who would fill up her freezer with potatoes, just because she happened to have some spare time and felt in the mood to peel a peck? Certainly it makes sense to have a few packages of potato croquettes or French fried potatoes on hand. French fried onions are good too. But it makes no more sense to fill your freezer with potatoes or onions than to fill it with loaves of bread. Yet everyone should have a couple of loaves of French bread and a few packages of rolls and biscuits in the freezer for an emergency.

How difficult to resist filling the freezer with luscious frozen strawberries, raspberries, or peaches when they are in season! But resist you must, if you are going to use your frozen storage space to best advantage. It is so easy to fill the space in your freezer with the first products of spring—asparagus, peas, or strawberries—leaving scant room for the broccoli and spinach that follow later. A fine crop of late vegetables or fruits and no place to put them can cause regret. Don't forget that you can always buy fruits and vegetables, as you need them, meticulously prepared and properly packaged and frozen by reliable commercial freezers.

Also, just because you are the proud owner of a home freezer, don't lose sight of the fact that there *are* other excellent ways (and in certain specific instances *better* ways) to preserve foods. Don't forget to make some of your fruit into jams and jellies. Dill your cucumbers; use your peppers and cauliflower in chowchow. Eat your fresh vegetables while they are in season. Buy the few frozen vegetables you need for winter use, or enjoy those underestimated root crops—beets, turnips, and parsnips—that keep so well in the cellar.

Don't hoard large quantities of meat and poultry in your freezer. There is little to be gained. Let your freezer work for you by keeping the space in constant use. Store wise quantities of meat and poultry. Eat the foods from your freezer, use them up quickly, plan a constant turnover, and make replacements with a fresh supply.

Fish, like vegetables, are never as good as when they are strictly fresh. You don't have to eat broiled lobster or oysters on the half shell every week. Eat them only when you can buy them alive at your fish market. Eat lots of fish when it is in season and store only as much as you will consume in 3 or 4 months.

Ready-cooked foods and entire meals may be frozen to have on hand at a moment's notice. Never make just a single recipe of your favorite dishes. Double or triple it and freeze what you don't eat that day for a quick and delicious meal next week.

It's just as easy to prepare and make chicken *cacciatore,* beef *bourguignonne,* fish chowder, or shrimp Newburg for 12 as it is for 4. This applies not only to stews, goulashes, casseroles, and soups but to breads and pastries. Don't freeze sliced apples. Make 4 apple pies, bake and eat one, and freeze the other 3.

PLANNING AND INVENTORY

Plan in advance what you are going to freeze and how much, depending on the preferences of your family, to avoid overloading with the first crops of the season. Peak seasons for fruits and vegetables vary from one state to another.

A supply of meat can be put into the home freezer at any time of the year. The greatest supply, however, is available at the time when prices are lowest, normally during the late fall, winter, and early spring months. This is the time when farmers usually butcher. The harvest has been brought in and farmers have more time for butchering from November 15 to March 15. Also, at this time the weather is cold and the carcasses can be quickly chilled.

The logical way to fill the freezer with meat is once in the fall and again in early spring. Stocking up on meats only twice a year leaves more space for the seasonable fruits, vegetables, and poultry.

Poultry is in season most of the year, but from May to November the supply is at its greatest.

A well-organized freezer holds more packages. It may take a little more time than just throwing packages in haphazardly, but an orderly freezer is much more convenient to use. Bad planning often results in a scramble through the entire contents of the freezer in order to find a certain package, or it may mean that the last frozen are the first to be used, leaving some packages deep within the freezer much longer than they should be stored for best quality. Group the same kinds of foods together, assigning certain sections to vegetables, fruits, meats, poultry, and ready-cooked dishes. Place newly frozen packages at the bottom or back of their section so that the older ones will be the first used.

Keep a running inventory An elaborate inventory is not necessary, but some system that will keep you informed at all times as to what and how much of the different foods you have on hand is absolutely essential if you are going to get the best use from your freezer.

Some like a series of recipe cards in a file box or a loose-leaf binder, each item with its own page or card. I prefer a good-sized slate blackboard and a piece of chalk. This is probably the simplest and most effective method of keeping an up-to-date record of the contents of your freezer, but make sure you keep it away from mischievous children!

295

HOW LONG CAN FOODS BE STORED AT ZERO?

Many people have the misconception that a freezer preserves food indefinitely. *This is not true.* Freezing simply slows down the destructive action of the organisms that cause food spoilage—it does not destroy these organisms. The length of time that a food can be stored in your freezer without losing quality and flavor depends on the particular food, and the maximum storage times given in this chapter should be taken seriously if you are going to get the greatest enjoyment from your frozen foods.

Certainly no food should be kept longer than from one growing season to another, but most foods should be kept for much shorter periods. Your freezer should not be treated like a revered, almost untouchable hope chest. It should be made an active source of your daily food supply.

A great deal of research and experimentation has been done by the manufactureres of home freezers, by the United States Department of Agriculture, and by the many state colleges in order to determine the maximum storage life of various foods. As a result, we have learned that many factors affect the keeping qualities of food and that not all foods have the same storage life.

We know that the variety and the maturity of fruits and vegetables and the speed and care given to them in their preparation are important. We know that the proper scalding of vegetables is vital to their frozen life.

We have discovered that bacon and salt pork must not be kept in the freezer very long because the salt used in curing these meats accelerates the development of rancidity in the fat.

We know that ground and sliced meats have a relatively short storage life, because a greater amount of surface is exposed to the destructive chemical process of oxidation. Fat is the bad actor in zero storage and for this reason fat meat such as pork and fatty fish should not be kept longer than their recommended storage period.

A DOZEN BASIC RULES FOR HOME FREEZING

1. Select top quality. You get nothing better out of your freezer than you put in. Freezing retains quality, but it does not improve it. Meats should be top grade and properly aged; poultry should be young and tender; fish, fresh. Vegetables should be full-flavored, young, and firm; picked at their peak of perfection. Fruits are right when they are ready to eat out of hand. *Don't waste freezer space with inferior foods.*

2. Choose varieties of fruits and vegetables best adapted to freezing. Some freeze better than others. The varieties vary according to locality, so consult your local state college.

3. Work quickly. Two hours from field to freezer is a good rule.

4. Prepare foods carefully.

5. Follow directions. The instructions in this chapter are the result of the latest and most authoritative research on freezing combined with personal experience. *Vegetables must be scalded.*

6. Freeze small batches at a time. Don't overestimate your energy. Handle only the amount that can be processed quickly and don't burden your freezer with too many unfrozen packages at one time.

7. Chill foods before freezing. Scalded vegetables should be instantly cooled in ice water. Meat, fish, and poultry should be chilled to make sure that all the body heat has been dispersed.

8. Wrap snugly in moisture-vaporproof materials and seal perfectly. All foods must be protected from air, the escape of moisture, and an exchange of flavors.

9. Label every package intelligently and informatively.

10. Freeze packaged foods immediately.

11. Keep a running inventory.

12. Observe recommended storage periods. Plan a constant turnover of the contents of your freezer so that no food will be given the opportunity to lose quality and flavor.

CAN YOU REFREEZE FOODS?

In general, refreezing is not a good idea, as the food suffers a loss of flavor and quality. Completely thawed poultry, meats, and non-acid vegetables, which are subject to attack by harmful bacteria, should not be refrozen. Fruits and acid vegetables, however, are not prey to such bacteria and may be safely refrozen.

Any food only partially thawed may be tucked away again at zero temperature without a qualm.

Freezing Fruits, Fruit Juices, and Fruit Purées

Of all the foods that freeze well, fruits win the blue ribbon. Freezing, better than any other method of preservation, captures the tree- or vine-ripened fresh flavor of fruits, so essential a part of a healthful diet, and retains their bright color and firm texture. Happily, no other home method of preservation is so easy as freezing fruits.

Whole fruits, fruit juices, and purées are unusually easy to pack for year-round use in desserts and salads and for cold drinks, puddings, ice cream, and ice cream toppings. And even, if you wish, for jelly and jam making *in midwinter,* when there is more time for creative homemaking than during the carefree summer and busy, holiday-packed fall and early winter months.

Fruits need no scalding, but are simply packed in sugar syrup or with dry sugar, or sometimes they require nothing added at all. They may be served while they are still frosty from the freezer.

Fruits are such delightfully superior foods to both eye and palate that it is very hard to restrict oneself to the space limitations of a freezer. If your freezer is a small one, you may wish to store only the fruits that your family is especially fond of. Or you might choose to freeze some of the more exotic fruits that reach our markets at various times of the year, such as persimmons, papayas, or fresh figs, which are not packed by commercial freezing companies, depending upon the reliable frozen food companies to supply your daily needs of orange juice, strawberries, peaches, raspberries, apples, et cetera.

Almost all fruits, including berries and melons, can be successfully frozen, but some freeze better than others. And certain varieties of fruits retain their flavor, color, and texture in freezing better than other varieties. Your state agricultural experiment station or your local seed houses can give you information on the fruit varieties grown in your locality that are best suited to home freezing.

Selection is important Fruits ripened on the bush or tree or vine have more flavor and better color for freezing. Select or pick the fruits that are fully ripe yet firm. Overripe fruits will freeze to a mush and those that are not ripe enough lack flavor and sweetness. And be sure to taste fruits before you buy them. Blushing peaches and luscious ripe-red berries may look beautiful and yet be watery and tasteless.

PREPARATION

Fruits and berries lose quality very quickly if they are allowed to stand at room temperature for any length of time. If a delay is unavoidable, store them on trays in the refrigerator until the first free moments. Even then, don't keep the fruits waiting too long for frozen storage.

Work with a small amount of fruit at a time. Clean and sort it carefully and very gently, for all fruits bruise easily. Discard all parts that are blemished, overripe, or green. Wash the fruit carefully in cold running water. It should not be allowed to soak in water, for berries, in particular, will readily exchange valuable and flavorful juice for water. The juices will leach out and water will fill the cells, dissipating the wonderful fruit flavor. Extremely cold water or ice water is best for washing fruit. It helps to prevent "waterlogging" and keeps the fruit firm. Drain off all the excess water and stem, pit, peel, hull, or slice fruit in exactly the same manner as you would prepare it for the table.

Larger fruits are generally sliced before they are packed. Berries may be left whole, sliced, or crushed. Many fruits can be made into purée or juice.

With only a few exceptions, fruits and berries are packed for freezing either mixed with dry sugar or covered with a sugar syrup. The amount of sugar used depends on the tartness of the fruit, the way you plan to serve it, and personal taste.

Fruits may be packed without sugar or sugar syrup, but usually they are not so satisfactory. For fruits, like vegetables, contain chemical substances called enzymes that continue their work of destruction after the product is harvested. While vegetables are scalded to retard the enzymatic action, fruits are packed with sugar. The sugar performs the same service to fruits as the boiling-water bath does to vegetables—it slows down the action of the enzymes. In addition to this the syrup, whether it is prepared and poured over the fruit or formed by the juice drawn from the fruit combining with the dry sugar, keeps the air away from the fruit and retards oxidation.

Dry pack The few exceptions to the sugar-pack rule in freezing fruits are cranberries, boysenberries, gooseberries, loganberries, raspberries, currants, youngberries, and rhubarb. These are fruits that can be washed and prepared without danger of rupturing the skin and that do not darken easily upon exposure to the air. The dry-pack method of packing fruit is usually used for fruits that are to be made into pies, puddings, or preserves.

Wash the fruit carefully and sort it, cutting away any bruises or blemishes and discarding any fruit that is overmature or underripe. Drain the fruit thoroughly between layers of absorbent paper to remove surface moisture and to prevent the fruit from freezing in a solid mass.

Pack the fruit in moisture-vaporproof containers, leaving ½ inch head space, and seal tightly. Label each package with the name of the fruit, the date of storage, and the way it is to be used, and freeze.

Dry sugar pack Fruits packed in dry sugar are excellent for making into pies or for other cooking purposes because they are less liquid. But this method should not be used for fruits that discolor readily. It is especially suitable for juicy fruits that are sliced or crushed, as the natural fruit juices quickly blend with the sugar to form a protective syrup.

Wash the fruit carefully, sort, and drain it. Prepare the fruit as you would for the table. Work with a small amount of fruit at a time. Spread about 1 quart of fruit in a large, flat pan and sift sugar over it, distributing it as evenly as possible. Four parts fruit to 1 part sugar by weight or volume gives adequate protection and is not too sweet for most palates and purposes. The sugar may vary, however, according to the tartness of the fruit. Anywhere from 3 to 5 parts fruit to 1 part sugar is the recommended proportion.

Fruit and sugar are best measured by a kitchen scale, but lacking this, the weight must be estimated on the basis that 1 cup tightly packed fruit weighs about as much as 1 cup sugar. For a 4-to-1 pack, then, you should measure 4 cups or 1 quart tightly packed fruit to 1 cup sugar.

Mix the sugar through the fruit gently with a wooden spoon until each piece is coated with sugar.

The sugar may be added to the fruit as the fruit is packed. Fill the package about one fourth full and sprinkle in one fourth of the sugar. Continue to fill the container in this way, shaking the container occasionally to distribute the sugar through the fruit.

Package sugared fruits in liquid-tight, moisture-vaporproof containers, leaving ½ inch head space. Be certain that the top seal on the bags is complete so there is no danger of the juice leaking out. Label with the name of the fruit, the date of storage, and quantity of sugar added, and the way in which you propose to use it. Freeze and store.

Syrup pack Syrup pack is used for packing fruits that have little juice of their own and is especially valuable for those particular fruits, such as peaches, apricots, plums, and pears, that quickly discolor when the flesh is exposed to the air.

Forty per cent sugar syrup is generally sweet enough for any fruit; however, a higher or lower percentage may be used according to individual taste. A less sweet syrup is better for mild-flavored fruits such as cantaloupe balls or pineapple wedges, because the sugar does not mask the delicate flavor, while a heavier syrup may be preferred for very sour fruits such as sour cherries.

Place the prepared fruit in liquid-tight, moisture-vaporproof containers and cover it with syrup, leaving ¾ inch head space for expansion during freezing. Each pint of fruit will require about ⅔ cup of syrup.

SUGAR SYRUPS: Add the required amount of sugar to clear, cold water and stir until the sugar is completely dissolved. Keep the syrup in the refrigerator until ready to use, but do not store for longer than 2 days.

PERCENTAGE OF SYRUP	AMOUNT OF SUGAR	AMOUNT OF WATER
20% (Very Light)	1 cup	4 cups
30% (Light)	2 cups	4 cups
40% (Medium)	3 cups	4 cups
50% (Heavy)	4 cups	4 cups
60% (Very Heavy)	6 cups	4 cups

Part of the sugar used to make a sugar syrup may be replaced by white corn syrup. As a matter of fact, many fruits are superior in flavor if packed in the sugar and corn syrup mixture rather than in all sugar syrup. Dissolve the sugar in the water, add the corn syrup, and mix well.

PERCENTAGE OF SYRUP	AMOUNT OF SUGAR	AMOUNT OF CORN SYRUP	AMOUNT OF WATER
40% (Medium)	2 cups	2 cups	5 cups
50% (Heavy)	3 cups	2 cups	4 cups

Honey may also be used to replace one fourth of the sugar in the syrup for freezing fruit, but the honey will impart a distinctive flavor to the fruit and should be used only if the family likes honey flavor, as it may mask the flavor of the fruit.

Controlling discoloration Many of the light-colored tree fruits such as apples, peaches, pears, apricots, and nectarines have a tendency to turn dark when their cut surfaces are exposed to the oxygen in the air during preparation or frozen storage, or, more frequently, when the fruit is thawed. This can be partially prevented by slicing the peeled fruit directly into a container partly filled with syrup. But the most effective way to prevent discoloration is by the use of ascorbic acid.

HOW TO USE ASCORBIC ACID: Ascorbic acid is actually another name for vitamin C, which is one of the major vitamins essential to good health. It not only prevents fruit from oxidizing but enriches its vitamin C content. Ascorbic acid may be purchased from your drugstore in powdered or crystalline form and is better than tablets, which contain a filler. To use ascorbic acid, simply add it to the syrup just before the syrup is combined with the fruit. Stir just long enough to dissolve the powder and stir gently to avoid mixing air into the syrup. Use 1 teaspoon ascorbic acid in 1 quart prepared syrup.

To use ascorbic acid with dry sugar packs, dissolve ¼ teaspoon ascorbic acid in 2 tablespoons cold water and drip the solution over the fruit before adding the sugar.

HOW TO USE CITRIC ACID OR LEMON JUICE: An alternative method to the ascorbic-acid treatment of fruit is the use of citric acid or lemon juice, but it is less effective than ascorbic acid and adds tartness to the fruit. Citric acid in powder or crystals is available at your drugstore.

Dissolve 1 teaspoon citric acid in 1 gallon cold water and immerse the sliced fruit in this solution for 1 minute. Drain the fruit well before packing it, whether with dry sugar or in sugar syrup. Three tablespoons lemon juice may be substituted for the citric acid.

HOW TO USE SODIUM SULPHITE: Of all the fruits that discolor quickly when exposed to the air, apples are probably the worst offenders. The use of sulphur to prevent the rapid browning of the cut surfaces has been known for many years, in the preservation of apples by drying or dehydration. It is used now in freezing apples, and it is unfortunate that the flavor of sulphur can be detected in the thawed product if it is not used discreetly and accurately.

Ask your druggist to give you chemically pure sodium sulphite or sodium bisulphite. Put 1 gallon cold water in an earthenware, glass, stainless steel, or enameled container. Add 1½ teaspoons of either sodium sulphite or sodium bisulphite and stir until the chemical is dissolved. Add sliced apples, weigh them down with a plate to keep them submerged in the solution, and let them soak for 5 minutes. Drain immediately. The same solution can be used to treat three or four batches of apples.

Packaging fruit Heavily waxed tubs with snap-in lids, cartons with cellophane or plastic liners, or glass jars are all good for packaging fruits. But the containers, no matter what you use, must be not only moisture-vaporproof, to prevent air leakage that would destroy the quality and appearance of the fruit, but liquid-tight, so none of the juice can escape.

Select the size container that is best suited to your needs. A quart-size container will supply fruit for a well-filled 9-inch pie. A quart of strawberries or peaches will make 4 generous individual short-cakes or 1 large shortcake. If used as an ice cream or pudding topping, 1 pint of fruit will serve from 4 to 6 people.

Pack the fruit firmly into the container, but don't use enough pressure to crush the fruit that you want to remain whole, and leave ½ inch head space for dry packs and ¾ inch head space for syrup packs.

Seal the packages tightly and label each package, with either waterproof ink or a china marking pencil, with the name of the fruit, the date of storage, the quantity of sugar or the percentage of syrup added to the fruit, and the intended use.

To thaw frozen fruit Always thaw fruit in the sealed container in which it was frozen to preserve the best color and turn the container several times during the thawing to keep the fruit bathed in the juice. On the refrigerator shelf a 1-pound package of fruit will thaw in 6 to 8 hours. At room temperature it will defrost in 2 to 3 hours. To thaw fruit quickly, place the package in cool running water for 30 minutes. Fruit packed with dry sugar will thaw a little more quickly than that packed with syrup.

Frozen fruit loses texture and flavor very quickly after it is thawed. So it is best to cook any leftover frozen and defrosted fruit and serve it in a compote, pudding, or other cooked dessert.

Serve berries while they still contain a few ice crystals. And the texture of peaches and most other fruits is better when they are served very cold. On the other hand, the flavor is improved by more complete thawing.

Most frozen fruits may be used in the same way as fresh fruit. They make excellent desserts served alone, or combined with ice cream. Or they may be used in pies, shortcakes, puddings, muffins, cobblers, upside-down cakes, or made into jams, jellies, and pre-serves.

APPLES FOR PIE

Select only firm-ripe sour apples in prime condition for eating. Peel, core, and cut apples into slices for pie. Small apples should be sliced into eighths and large ones into twelfths. Peel only a few apples at one time, as the cut surfaces of apples discolor rapidly on exposure to the air. The browning may be prevented in either of two ways:

1. Drop the apple slices directly into a solution made by dissolving 3 teaspoons salt in 2 quarts cold water, or 3 tablespoons lemon juice or 2 tablespoons citric acid dissolved in 2 quarts cold water. Remove the apples from the solution after 1 minute and drain. Then scald the slices in steam for 90 seconds and cool them in ice water.

2. Submerge the apple slices for 5 minutes in a solution made by dissolving 1½ teaspoons sodium sulphite in 1 gallon cold water. Be sure to mix the solution in an earthenware, glass, stainless-steel, or enameled container.

Drain the apple slices on absorbent paper. Package without sugar, or sugar may be added in the proportion of 1 pound sugar to 4 pounds fruit. Seal and freeze immediately. A quart of apple slices makes a 9-inch pie.

APPLESAUCE

Select fine-flavored apples. Stem the apples, cut away any bruises or bad spots, and cut them into eighths. Put them in a saucepan with only enough water to prevent the apples from sticking to the bottom of the pan and bring to a fast boil. Reduce the heat and simmer for about 10 minutes, or until the apples are mushy. Force the apple pulp through a sieve and stir in sugar to taste. Cool the applesauce over ice water, package, and freeze promptly.

Apple compote Peel, core, and slice apples and stew them in sugar syrup in the usual way. A stick of cinnamon or any other favorite spice may be added. Cool the stewed apples, package with the syrup, and freeze.

Baked apples Bake apples according to your favorite recipe, filling the centers with raisins or nuts, brown sugar, butter, and spice. Cool them over ice water and wrap individually in freezer paper. Package as many as you will need for one meal in a carton, seal, and freeze. Defrost in a moderate oven (350° F.) for 30 minutes, basting them occasionally with a little melted butter and sherry or rum.

APRICOTS

Select tree-ripened fruit, brightly colored, richly flavored, with no trace of green and with easily removable pits. Wash the apricots thoroughly and remove the stems. Plunge about 12 apricots at a time in boiling water for 30 seconds to loosen the skins. Remove and plunge them into ice water to cover for 1 minute. Peel the apricots, cut them into halves, and remove the pits. Pack the apricot halves in containers and cover them with a 50 per cent syrup to which has been added ¼ teaspoon ascorbic acid to each cup of syrup (**see Index**). Place a crumpled piece of freezer paper on the fruit under the top of the container to keep them submerged in the syrup. Seal and freeze at once.

AVOCADOS (purée only)

Select avocados that are just ready to be eaten. They should not be hard or mushy. The small dark-skinned Calavos have a nuttier and better flavor. Wash the avocados, cut them in half, and remove the pits. Scoop the pulp from the rind and mash the pulp with 2 teaspoons lemon or lime juice and 1½ teaspoons sugar for each avocado. Refill the shell with the purée, wrap individually in moisture-vapor-proof paper, and freeze immediately.

Avocados prepared in this way are delicious served for dessert and very colorful too if a fluted border of whipped cream is piped all around near the shell. Sprinkle the center with finely chopped pistachio nuts.

Do not store longer than 1 month.

The velvety-smooth texture of avocado purée lends itself to creamy frozen desserts, ices, and ice creams. The avocado gives a delicate nutty taste to the ice cream, blends well with other fruit flavors, and, because of the large amount of oil in the pulp, adds richness to the cream.

BERRIES (Blackberries, Boysenberries, Dewberries, Loganberries, Nectarberries, and Youngberries)

Select firm, sweet, plump, fully ripened berries with fine flavor. If the berries are from your own garden crop, do not pick them after a heavy rain or during extremely hot weather. Pick over the berries and discard any that are bruised, underripe, poorly colored, badly formed, or overseedy. Wash a few at a time in ice water and drain them in a colander or on absorbent paper.

Syrup pack Place the berries in moisture-vaporproof, liquid-tight containers and cover them with a **40 to 50 per cent syrup,**

305

leaving ¾ inch head space. Berries packed in syrup are good for a dessert sauce or an ice cream topping.

Sugar pack Sprinkle 4 pounds berries with 1 pound sugar and mix lightly with a wooden spoon until the fruit is coated with the sugar. Use for pies or in the making of preserves.

Package and freeze immediately. A quart of berries makes a 9-inch pie.

BLUEBERRIES

Select large, tender-skinned blueberries with a sweet flavor. Wash the blueberries thoroughly, discard the leaves and berries that are immature or shriveled, and drain.

Dry pack This is the best method if the blueberries are to be used in pies, muffins, or pancakes.

Sugar pack Place blueberries in a dish, sprinkle them with sugar in the proportion of 5 parts berries to 1 part sugar, and mix well, crushing them slightly. For use in blueberry shortcake, as a fruit sauce, in ice creams and frozen desserts, or as an ice cream topping.

Package, seal, and freeze.

CANTALOUPE (also Papaya)

Select firm-fleshed but well-ripened melons with fine flavor. The deep yellow varieties are best. Cut the melons in half and discard the seeds. Scoop out the flesh with a French potato-ball cutter, or peel the melons and cut the flesh into uniform slices or cubes. Drain well.

Dry pack the melon balls, slices, or cubes in layers, separating each layer with two pieces of freezer paper, so that the pieces may be easily separated for serving, before they are completely thawed, in fruit cups or salads. Package in moisture-vaporproof containers, seal, and freeze.

CHERRIES, SOUR

Select tender-skinned, bright red cherries with a characteristic tart flavor. Wash the cherries in ice water, stem, and pit.

Sugar pack Mix 1 pound sugar with 4 pounds cherries. Package in moisture-vaporproof, liquid-tight containers, seal, and freeze promptly. Frozen sour cherries are delicious made into pies and cobblers. Frozen cherry juice is excellent in punches and sherbets.

CHERRIES, SWEET

Select firm, fully ripe, tree-ripened berries with rich flavor. Wash the cherries in ice water, stem, and pit if desired, depending on how you wish to serve them.

Syrup pack Whether pitted or whole, cherries should be packed in a **40** to **50 per cent syrup** to which has been added ¼ teaspoon ascorbic acid for each cup of syrup. Sweet cherries are excellent for an ice cream sauce, if slightly crushed, or for cherries Jubilee. Package in moisture-vaporproof, liquid-tight containers, seal, and freeze immediately.

COCONUT

Unsweetened coconut, grated and mixed with its own milk, makes an excellent frozen product for use in curry sauces, desserts, cake frostings, or ice creams. Or 1 part sugar may be added to every 8 parts shredded coconut. Stir in the coconut milk for extra flavor. Package in moisture-vaporproof, liquid-tight containers, seal, and freeze.

CRANBERRIES

Select deep red, glossy-skinned cranberries with a mealy texture. Wash and sort the cranberries and discard any that are soft or poorly formed. Drain.

Dry pack Cranberries need no sugar or syrup. They are packed with nothing added, available at any time to make into sauce or jelly, or they may be made into a sauce by your favorite recipe and the sauce frozen in advance for holiday meals. Dry-packed cranberries may be packed in moisture-vaporproof, heat-sealing bags, but the sauce must be packaged in liquid-tight containers. Seal and freeze

CURRANTS

Select bright red, well-ripened berries. Stem the currants, wash, and drain.

307

Dry pack is good for jelly making later in the season, when you might like to combine them with apple or raspberry juice.

Sugar pack for use in pies, tarts, and cobblers. Crush the currants lightly and mix 3 parts fruit with 1 part sugar.
Package, seal, and freeze.

FIGS

Select figs with tender skins and soft flesh. Wash the figs carefully and discard any that are split or show signs of internal rot or souring. Figs may be peeled, if desired, halved, sliced, or left whole.

Syrup pack Cover the figs with a **40** to **50 per cent syrup.** Package according to family needs in moisture-vaporproof, liquid-tight containers, allowing 3 or 4 figs per serving. Seal and freeze immediately.

GOOSEBERRIES

Select fully matured, ripe berries with just a little red color. Wash the gooseberries in cold water, drain, and remove the stems and blossom ends.

Sugar pack Mix the gooseberries with 1 part sugar to 3 parts berries. Package, seal, and freeze.

GRAPEFRUIT AND ORANGE SECTIONS

All varieties of oranges freeze well. Select them for their fine flavor. Thin-skinned grapefruit that section easily are preferable, but again it is better to select grapefruit for flavor and sweetness.

Chill the fruit in the refrigerator. Peel, removing all the white skin, and cut the sections free from the membranes. Discard the seeds. Package in layers with two sheets of freezer paper between the layers so the sections may be separated, while still partially frozen, for use in fruit cups and salads. Grapefruit sections may be sprinkled with sugar to taste, if you wish.

Orange and grapefruit sections may also be packaged in combination with other fruits, such as cantaloupe, grapes, papaya, unpitted cherries, watermelon, and pineapple.

GRAPES

Select firm, ripe table grapes with tender skins and sweet flavor. Wash, sort, discard any soft or shriveled grapes, and drain.

Dry pack or syrup pack   Cover with **40 per cent syrup** for use in fruit cocktails and salads.

Concord grapes for pie   Separate the pulp and hulls. Simmer the pulp for 5 minutes, press through a fine sieve, and discard the seeds. Simmer the hulls for 20 minutes to soften them, combine puréed pulp and hulls, and stir in 1 part sugar to 3 parts by weight of the combined pulp and hulls. Package in moisture-vaporproof, liquid-tight containers in quart size, which is sufficient for a 9-inch pie.

HUCKLEBERRIES. See BLUEBERRIES

PEACHES (also Nectarines)

Select peaches that are just right for eating. They should be juicy, tree-ripened fruit with firm, fine-grained flesh. The freestone types with red-colored pit cavities make the most attractive frozen product.

Place 12 peaches in a wire basket and plunge them into boiling water to cover for 30 seconds, then plunge them into ice water and peel. Slice the peaches directly into cold syrup in moisture-vapor-proof, liquid-tight containers. The syrup should be made in advance by dissolving 3 cups sugar in each 4 cups water. Chill the syrup and, when ready to use, gently stir 1 teaspoon ascorbic acid into each quart of the syrup. Press the fruit down in the container and add enough cold syrup to cover it, leaving ½ inch head space in pints and 1 inch in quarts. Place a crumpled piece of freezer paper on top of the fruit, under the container top, to hold the fruit under the syrup. Seal and freeze.

Frozen peaches make delicious pies, shortcakes, and upside-down cakes. They may be served as fresh fruit or as an ice cream topping when only partially thawed.

Peaches and nectarines that are crushed or puréed without first being poached in syrup should also be mixed with ascorbic acid (½ teaspoon per pint of purée) to retain the color during frozen storage. Stir the ascorbic acid into the purée with 1 part sugar to 3

309

parts purée. Stir gently until the sugar is dissolved, being careful not to whip in any air. Delicious for ice creams, mousses, soufflés, and filling for tiny thin pancakes.

PEARS

Select tender, juicy, fine-fleshed pears. Peel, halve, and core the pears. Slice them lengthwise about ½ inch thick directly into cold syrup in moisture-vaporproof, liquid-tight containers. The **syrup** should be from **40** to **50 per cent,** with ¼ teaspoon ascorbic acid per cup. Or the sliced pears may be immersed in boiling syrup for 2 minutes, then packed in the containers and covered with cold syrup, leaving ½ inch head space in pints and 1 inch head space in quarts. Place a crumpled piece of freezer paper over the fruit, under the lid of the container, to keep the fruit covered with the syrup. Seal and freeze. After thawing, pears can be used in pies, cobblers, fruit cocktail, or salads.

PINEAPPLE

Select ripe pineapple with a fragrant odor and sweet flavor. Cut the pineapple into slices ¾ inch thick, remove the outer skin and the eyes from each slice, and cut out the core. The pineapple slices need neither sugar nor syrup, and they may be frozen whole in rigid tubs or containers with two pieces of freezer paper between slices so they can be separated easily while still frozen. Or they may be stacked on moisture-vaporproof paper with two layers of freezer paper between layers and the re-formed pineapple wrapped carefully in the paper. Shredded pineapple or cubes may be packed in a light syrup for use in dessert sauces.

PLUMS AND PRUNES

Select fully ripened plums. Wash and sort the plums. Discard any that are bruised or damaged, immature or overripe. Cut the plums in half, remove the pits, and drop them directly into cold syrup in moisture-vaporproof, liquid-tight containers. The **syrup** should be from **40** to **50 per cent** with ¼ teaspoon ascorbic acid per cup. Seal and freeze.

310

RASPBERRIES, RED

Select large, ripe berries. Raspberries are exceptionally fragile and care must be taken in handling them or they will bruise. Wash only a few at a time in ice water and drain them on absorbent paper.

Sugar pack Pack berries directly into moisture-vaporproof, liquid-tight containers. Use 1 cup sugar to 4 cups berries. When the container is one fourth full, add one fourth of the sugar and continue to alternate layers of berries and sugar until the container is full. Raspberries will make their own syrup when sugar is added. Seal and freeze promptly.

RHUBARB

Select tender, deep red-colored stalks early in the spring before the rhubarb has become tough. Wash rhubarb well under running water and cut the stalks into 1-inch pieces.

Dry pack Rhubarb does not need sugar or sugar syrup. Simply pack it in moisture-vaporproof cartons or bags.

Sugar pack Rhubarb may be packed with 1 part by weight of sugar to every 4 or 5 parts by weight of rhubarb. Use liquid-tight containers.

Seal and freeze. Rhubarb may also be stewed or steamed according to your favorite method, sweetened to taste, and frozen. Pack it in moisture-vaporproof, liquid-tight containers leaving ½ inch head space. Seal and freeze.

STRAWBERRIES

Select ripe-all-over, sound, firm berries with slightly tart flavor. Wash the berries, a few at a time, in ice water, drain them, and remove the hulls. Strawberries may be frozen whole in sugar syrup, or as a purée or juice, but for the fullest, finest flavor, strawberries should be sliced or crushed and mixed with dry sugar.

Sugar pack Slice the strawberries into a bowl and crush them lightly if desired. Sprinkle them with 1 cup sugar to 4 cups fruit and toss with a wooden spoon until the berries are coated with sugar.

Syrup pack Whole strawberries hold shape better if they are packed in **40 per cent sugar syrup,** as this method is less likely to bruise the delicate fruit. The flavor of whole strawberries packed in syrup is not so good, however, as the sliced sugar-packed berries. The syrup contains water which dilutes the strawberry flavor.

Pack berries in moisture-vaporproof, liquid-tight containers, leaving ½ inch head space in pint containers and 1 inch head space in quarts. Place a crumpled piece of freezer paper on top of the berries under the container lid to keep them immersed in the syrup. Seal and freeze.

WATERMELON

Any thoroughly ripened watermelon is excellent for freezing for fruit cups or fruit salads, but the red-ripe center of the watermelon is best. Prepare and freeze watermelon according to the directions for **cantaloupe.**

FRUIT JUICES

Most fruit juices, including cranberry, cherry, grape, raspberry and strawberry, apple, and citrus and tomato juice, make excellent frozen products and retain their fresh flavor from one season to another. They make refreshing drinks thawed and served cold, or they can be made into fruit sauces, ice creams, and sherbets, or boiled up with sugar and made into clear and sparkling jelly.

Orange and grapefruit need only be squeezed to extract the juice. The juice is then packed into liquid-tight containers and frozen. Select fully ripe fruit and chill it thoroughly in the refrigerator. Cut the fruit in half, ream out the juice, and strain it through a stainless-steel or plastic strainer or cheesecloth. Pour the juice into the containers, leaving 1 inch head space, and freeze immediately.

Apples as well as citrus fruits need no heat treatment. Extract the juice from sound winter apples, pour the juice into moisture-vaporproof, liquid-tight containers, allowing 1 inch head space, and freeze at once. The secret of really fresh-flavored golden apple juice is in the speed with which it is handled and put in the freezer. Fermentation starts almost immediately, and if the juice is allowed to remain at room temperature for even an hour, it begins to darken and develops a "cider" flavor.

Cherries, grapes, and berries must be heated to extract the juice. Select fully ripe, flavorful fruit. Wash, sort, and drain the fruit and put it in a stainless-steel or aluminum preserving kettle. Crush the fruit with a potato masher and heat it very gradually to between

160° and 170° F., stirring occasionally, to soften the fruit and release the juices. Strain the juice through a muslin jelly bag and cool by floating the saucepan containing it in ice water. Sweeten the juice with from ½ to 1 cup sugar per gallon of juice, or sweeten to taste. Pour the juice into moisture-vaporproof, liquid-tight containers, leaving 1 inch head space for expansion during freezing, and freeze immediately.

Apricots, peaches, and rhubarb must also be heated to extract the juice, and since these are drier fruits than cherries or berries, a little water should be added. Wash, sort, and drain the fruit. Put it in a stainless-steel or aluminum kettle and add about ½ cup water for each pound of fruit.

Bring the fruit to a simmer, mashing it occasionally with a potato masher, and simmer very gently for 10 minutes. Strain the juice while it is hot through a jelly bag and cool the juice by floating the saucepan containing it in ice water. Sweeten the juice to taste, pour it into moisture-vaporproof, liquid-tight containers, leaving 1 inch head space for expansion, and freeze immediately.

Tomatoes should be fully ripe and sound. Wash, core, and quarter, discarding any green portions. Heat the tomatoes slowly in a stainless-steel or aluminum kettle until the juice begins to boil and press juice and pulp through a fine sieve. Cool the juice over ice water and add 2 tablespoons salt to each gallon of juice, or salt to taste. Other seasonings such as pepper and celery salt, or herbs such as fresh marjoram, garlic, or thyme, may also be added to taste. Pour the seasoned juice into moisture-vaporproof, liquid-tight containers and freeze immediately.

FRUIT PURÉES

Fruit purées, or "sieved" fruit pulp, are destined to become one of the most popular and flavorful products you can store in your home freezer because they retain their quality for long periods of frozen storage and they can be used in so many glamorous ways: in ice creams, sherbets, and other frozen desserts; in puddings, cake frostings, pie and tart-shell fillings; in fillings for sweet rolls or breakfast rings; in whips, beverages, confections, and so on. A little purée may be cooked with sugar to make a small batch of fresh jam.

The purées are invaluable in dressing up any meal, as well as adding fruit to the daily diet. Berries, peaches, plums, apricots, cherries, and grapes are some of the best fruits for purées, and the making and freezing of them take little time.

Select fully ripe fruit of the finest flavor. Actually the fruit can be too mellow for canning and still produce the best flavor for a purée. It must, however, be perfectly good.

Wash and sort the fruit and trim away any blemishes or overripe spots. Mash the fruit pulp and deal with it in the same manner as if you were making **fruit juice,** except that instead of straining the juice through a sieve you must press both juice and pulp through a fine sieve, or put it through a food mill. Heat in a stainless-steel or aluminum kettle those fruits, such as cherries and plums and guavas, that need heating in order to start the juices flowing; soft fruits such as cantaloupe, papaya, persimmons, mangoes, and berries need nothing except mashing and being pressed through a sieve.

Mix the purée with a small amount of sugar to taste, cool over ice water, and package in moisture-vaporproof, liquid-tight containers, leaving ¼ inch head space. Freeze immediately.

Strawberries Select fully ripe strawberries of fine sweet flavor. Wash, drain, and stem them and press them through a fine sieve. Don't force through the very last of the pulp as this contains most of the seeds and is apt to give an off flavor to the purée. Five quarts of whole fresh fruit make about 6 cups of purée.

Other berries Wash and pick over the berries and press them through a fine sieve. Four quarts of whole fresh berries make about 6 cups of purée.

Cantaloupe Peel and slice fully ripe cantaloupe, discarding the seeds, and press the flesh through a fine sieve. Six pounds of whole melons make about 6 cups of purée. **Papayas, persimmons,** and ripe **mangoes** may be puréed in the same way.

Cranberries Wash and pick over the berries. Cook them in a little water in a tightly covered saucepan until the skins burst, and press both cranberries and the juice remaining in the pan through a fine sieve. Three quarts of whole fresh cranberries make about 6 cups of purée.

Concord grapes Wash and stem the grapes. Place them in a stainless-steel or aluminum kettle and crush them with a potato masher. Cover the kettle and bring the grapes to a simmer and heat until the juice begins to flow and the seeds are loosened from the pulp. Press through a fine sieve. Six pounds of fresh grapes make about 6 cups of purée. **Cherries, plums,** and **guavas** may be puréed in the same way.

Peaches, apricots, and nectarines   Select fully ripe, full-flavored fruit. Peel, trim away any bruised spots, quarter, and discard the pits. Drop the fruit into boiling syrup made by dissolving 1 cup sugar in 8 cups water and simmer for 3 minutes. Press the fruit through a fine sieve and cool the purée over ice water. Six pounds of whole fruit make about 6 cups of purée.

Rhubarb   Wash the rhubarb and cut the stalks into 1-inch pieces. Heat in a saucepan placed over boiling water until the rhubarb is soft and press through a fine sieve. Cool the purée over ice water. Four pounds of cut rhubarb make about 6 cups of purée.

Velva fruit   "Velva fruit" is the name given to a fruit purée, mixed with sugar to sweeten it and gelatin to make it smooth as velvet, by the Western Regional Laboratory of the Bureau of Agricultural and Industrial Chemistry, which was working with the original discoverers, the Bureau of Human Nutrition and Home Economics.

Velva fruit may be made and stored in your home freezer for a deliciously cool and flavorful dessert at any time, or it may be made from the frozen fruit purée.

To use the frozen purée, put the sealed container in cold or lukewarm water to speed the thawing. A quart of purée will thaw in about 2 hours. When the purée reaches room temperature, proceed as if you were using the freshly made fruit purée.

VELVA FRUIT RECIPE

6 cups fresh or frozen and defrosted fruit purée
1½ to 2 cups sugar, if fresh purée is used
2 tablespoons lemon juice, or to taste
½ teaspoon salt
2 tablespoons gelatin
½ cup water

Combine fresh fruit purée and sugar, lemon juice, and salt. Or combine frozen thawed fruit purée with only the lemon juice and salt. Soak the gelatin in the water for 5 minutes and dissolve it by heating it over hot water for 10 minutes. Add the flavored purée slowly to the gelatin, stirring continuously and vigorously. Freeze

315

the mixture in an ice cream freezer for the most enjoyable eating, or freeze it in the tray of your refrigerator. It will be good, but not as good as if it were made in the old-fashioned way.

TO FREEZE IN THE REFRIGERATOR: Place the fruit mixture in a deep refrigerator tray, turn the temperature control to the coldest point, and freeze until the fruit is firm. Turn it into a chilled bowl and beat it with a wooden spoon or an electric mixer until the mixture becomes smooth in texture and increases in volume. Return Velva fruit to the refrigerator tray and freeze for a few hours, or until it is firm again. Makes 1 gallon.

Serve for dinner, or pack in moisture-vaporproof cartons and store for not more than 2 weeks.

Freezing Vegetables

Vegetables that you enjoy raw and crisp, such as salad greens, radishes, celery, tomatoes, cucumbers, and onions, do not freeze satisfactorily.

Most of the rest that are normally cooked before they are served freeze well and retain much of their nutritive value, color, flavor, and fresh goodness if the rules for freezing them are strictly followed. But, like any processed food, frozen vegetables are never quite as good, nor should you expect them to be, as garden vegetables cooked in a small amount of water until barely tender and served, bathed in sweet butter, in a matter of minutes from the time they were picked from the vine or plucked from the earth.

SIX BASIC RULES FOR FREEZING VEGETABLES

1. Choose only well-ripened, tender, choice vegetables in quantities that you can handle with ease. Don't overestimate your energy or time.

2. Prepare vegetables as you would for the table, but sort them according to size.

3. Scald only 1 pound of vegetables at a time in 1 gallon of actively boiling water. Watch scalding time carefully.

4. Cool immediately in ice water.

5. Package in moisture-vaporproof materials only.

6. Freeze immediately, and not too many packages within a 24-hour period.

Vegetable purées When you are preparing vegetables for freezing you can, if you wish, cook some until tender and purée them for baby food or for cream soups.

Puréed squash, pumpkin, and sweet potato are all excellent for pies. Tomato purée can be used in many ways: in soups, tomato sauces, gravies, and casseroles.

Package purées in quantities to suit your various needs. Baby foods may be frozen in paper cups or ice-cube trays, then wrapped in moisture-waterproof paper, and stored. Small amounts of tomato purée may also be frozen in the same way.

COOKING FROZEN VEGETABLES

Whether fresh or frozen, vegetables are best when they are cooked quickly in a tightly covered container, with a small amount of water, until just barely tender. Since frozen vegetables have already been partially cooked, they need only about half the cooking time required for the fresh product. Care should be taken not to overcook them.

With the exception of corn on the cob and spinach and other similar greens, frozen vegetables do not need to be thawed before they are cooked. Simply break the frozen vegetables into several chunks and put the chunks in a saucepan with from ¼ to ½ cup boiling water and a little salt. Cook over a brisk fire until the chunks can be separated with a fork to allow the water and steam to circulate, reduce the heat, and simmer until tender.

If you cook more than one package of a frozen vegetable at a time, use a wide pan so that one package need not be placed upon another. A large skillet with a tight-fitting lid is a perfect cooking kettle and is superior to a deeper saucepan smaller in diameter.

Cook only the amount of vegetables to be eaten at one meal. Large packages may be cut in half with a sharp knife while still frozen and the unused portion wrapped and returned to the freezer.

Beets, squash, pumpkin, sweet potato, and vegetable purées that have been completely cooked before freezing should be heated to serving temperature in a saucepan placed over boiling water.

317

Partially thaw spinach and other greens. The water that clings to the leaves forms a solid block when frozen. The block should be thawed until it can be broken into chunks, otherwise the outer leaves will be cooked to a mush before the center is thawed.

Corn on the cob must be completely thawed before it is cooked. If frozen ears were dropped into boiling water, the kernels would be cooked before the cobs defrosted. Thaw the ears at room temperature in their wrappings.

Oven-cooked vegetables take longer, but this method is excellent if an oven meal is being prepared.

Break the frozen vegetables into chunks and place the chunks in a buttered casserole. Sprinkle with salt and pepper and dot with bits of butter. Cover the casserole tightly and cook in a moderate oven (350° F.) for 30 minutes. The vegetables are butter-steamed in their own juice.

ASPARAGUS

Harvest, prepare, and freeze within 2 hours. Avoid using iron utensils, as they discolor asparagus. Select young, tender asparagus with thick, compact tips. Wash thoroughly, discard the woody portion of the stalks, and sort into 3 groups according to the thickness of the stalks. The flavor of frozen asparagus is improved if the scales on the stalks are nipped off with a sharp knife, and any sand that lurks under these scales is also eliminated. Leave the stalks in lengths to fit the package, or cut them into 2-inch pieces. Scald in boiling water or steam with the tips up:

	BOILING WATER	STEAM
Small stalks	2 minutes	4 minutes
Medium stalks	3 minutes	5 minutes
Large stalks	4 minutes	6 minutes

Cool in ice water and drain. Pack into containers, alternating tip and stem ends. Seal and freeze.

BEANS, GREEN OR WAX

Avoid using iron utensils, as they discolor beans. Select only tender, crisp, stringless beans of bright color. Wash thoroughly; discard immature, bruised, or discolored beans, and sort for size. Cut off stem ends and tips. Leave whole, or cut into 1-inch pieces, or

318

slice lengthwise into thin strips for Frenched beans. Scald in boiling water or steam:

	BOILING WATER	STEAM
Whole beans	3 minutes	4 minutes
Cut beans	2 minutes	3 minutes
Frenched beans	1 minute	2 minutes

Cool promptly in ice water and drain. Pack into cartons or bags, leaving ½ inch head space. Seal and freeze.

BEANS, LIMA

Select young lima beans with plump pods. Shell the beans and sort them according to 3 sizes. Scald in boiling water or steam:

	BOILING WATER	STEAM
Baby beans	1 minute	2 minutes
Medium beans	1½ minutes	2½ minutes
Large beans	2 minutes	3 minutes

Discard any beans that turn white during the scalding, for this means that they are overmature and contain too much starch for a good frozen product. Cool in ice water and drain. Pack into pint cartons or bags, leaving ½ inch head space. Seal and freeze.

BEET GREENS. See GREENS

BEETS

Select deep red, young beets not larger than 3 inches in diameter. Wash the beets and sort them according to size. Trim the tops, leaving ½ inch of the stems. Cook in boiling water until tender:

Small beets	25 to 30 minutes
Medium beets	45 to 50 minutes

Cool in ice water and slip off the skins. Small beets not over 1½ inches in diameter may be frozen whole. Larger beets should be sliced or diced or quartered. Pack in cartons or bags, leaving ½ inch head space for cut beets. Whole beets need no head space.

319

BROCCOLI

Select compact, dark green heads with tender stalks. Soak broccoli for 30 minutes in a solution of 4 teaspoons salt dissolved in 1 gallon cold water to remove any insects. Wash in clear, cold water, discard the large leaves and any tough portion of the stalks, and split the stalks lengthwise, so that the heads are not more than 1½ inches wide. Scald in boiling water or steam:

BOILING WATER	STEAM
4 minutes	5 minutes

Cool in ice water and drain. Pack in cartons or bags, arranging the heads in opposite directions. No head space is necessary. Or wrap in moisture-vaporproof paper and protect the package with an outer wrap of locker tape. Seal and freeze.

BRUSSELS SPROUTS

Select firm, compact, bright green sprouts. Soak the sprouts for 30 minutes in a solution of 4 teaspoons salt dissolved in 1 gallon cold water to remove any insects. Remove the coarse outer leaves and discard any wilted or discolored sprouts. Wash the sprouts in clear, cold water and sort them into 3 sizes. Scald in boiling water:

Small heads	3 minutes
Medium heads	4 minutes
Large heads	5 minutes

Cool quickly in cold water and drain. Pack brussels sprouts in cartons or bags, allowing 5 to 6 heads per serving, depending on their size. No head space is necessary. Seal and freeze.

CABBAGE

Frozen cabbage is not suitable for use in coleslaw or salads. Select solid, green heads with crisp leaves. Discard the coarse outer leaves and cut the head into wedges, or shred rather coarsely. Scald in boiling water:

Wedges	3 minutes
Shredded cabbage	1½ minutes

Cool in ice water and drain. Pack cabbage into cartons, leaving ½ inch head space. Seal and freeze.

CARROTS

Select young, small or medium, bright orange carrots. Wash the carrots, scrape, and sort for size. Leave the small carrots whole. Cut the others into ¼-inch cubes, thin slices, or lengthwise strips. Scald in boiling water or steam:

	BOILING WATER	STEAM
Whole, small carrots	5 minutes	6 minutes
Lengthwise strips	3 minutes	4 minutes
Diced or sliced carrots	2 minutes	3 minutes

Cool in ice water and drain. Pack carrots into cartons or bags, leaving ½ inch head space for cut carrots. Alternate large and small ends of whole carrots compactly; for these no head space is necessary.

CAULIFLOWER

Select compact, snow-white heads. Cut the heads of cauliflower from their thick bases and surrounding leaves and break or cut them into flowerets about 1 inch across. Soak the pieces for 30 minutes in a solution of 4 teaspoons salt dissolved in 1 gallon cold water; wash in clear, cold water, and drain. Scald in boiling water or steam:

BOILING WATER	STEAM
3 minutes	5 minutes

Pack compactly into cartons or bags, leaving no head space. Seal and freeze.

CELERY

Select crisp, tender stalks.

Wash celery thoroughly, trim, and cut the stalks into 1-inch lengths. Scald in boiling water for 3 minutes. Cool in ice water and drain. Pack into cartons or bags, leaving ½ inch head space. Seal and freeze.

COLLARDS. See GREENS

CORN, WHOLE-KERNEL AND CREAM-STYLE

Select freshly picked sweet corn with full, regular kernels. The kernels should be golden and shiny and when one is ruptured with the thumbnail, the milk should spurt out. Husk the ears, remove the silk, and wash the corn. Scald the corn on the cob in boiling water for 4 to 5 minutes. Cool the corn in ice water and drain.

For **whole-kernel corn,** cut the kernels from the cob close to the cob. For **cream-style corn,** cut the corn from the cobs at about the center of the kernels. Scrape the cob with the back of the knife to remove the heart of the kernel and the corn juice. Package in cartons or bags, leaving ½ inch head space. Seal and freeze.

CORN ON THE COB

Select only the most tender, succulent ears. Husk the ears and remove the silk, wash the corn, and sort it according to sizes. Scald in boiling water:

Small ears 1¼ inches or less in diameter	6 minutes
Medium ears 1¼ to 1½ inches in diameter	8 minutes
Large ears over 1½ inches in diameter	10 minutes

Cool immediately and thoroughly in ice water and drain. Wrap each ear in moisture-vaporproof paper, seal, and freeze. When frozen, several ears may be tidily packed in a bag, a carton, or stockinette.

EGGPLANT

Select firm, ripe eggplant about 6 inches in diameter. Overmature eggplant is not good for freezing. Peel one eggplant at a time, cut it into slices ½ inch thick, and drop the slices into a solution of 3 teaspoons lemon juice and 1 quart water. Work quickly to prevent discoloration. Blanch the slices in boiling water or steam:

BOILING WATER	STEAM
4 minutes	5 minutes

Cool in 1 gallon ice water to which has been added the juice of 1 lemon. Rinse in ice water and drain. Reshape the eggplant, putting two pieces of freezer paper between the slices. Wrap the reshaped eggplant in moisture-vaporproof paper. Seal and freeze.

GREENS (Beet Greens, Collards, Kale, Mustard Greens, Spinach, Swiss Chard, Turnip Greens)

Select young, tender greens. Discard the bruised and imperfect leaves and cut off the tough stems before washing. Wash the greens thoroughly in several changes of cold water to remove all the sand. Scald only ½ pound at a time in 1 gallon boiling water. Twirl the container several times during the scalding to separate the leaves.

| Beet greens, kale, mustard greens, turnip greens, Swiss chard, spinach | 2 minutes |
| Collards | 3 minutes |

Cool immediately in ice water and drain. Pack greens into cartons or bags, leaving ½ inch head space. Do not press greens compactly into containers. Seal and freeze.

KALE. See GREENS

KOHLRABI

Select young, mild-flavored, small to medium-sized kohlrabi. Discard the tops and roots of kohlrabi. Wash and peel. The small roots may be left whole, or all may be cut into ½-inch cubes. Scald in boiling water or steam:

	BOILING WATER	STEAM
Whole kohlrabi	3 minutes	5 minutes
Cubes	2 minutes	3 minutes

Cool in ice water and drain. Pack whole kohlrabi into cartons or bags, or wrap in moisture-vaporproof paper. Pack cubes into cartons or bags, leaving ½ inch head space. Seal and freeze.

MUSHROOMS

Select fresh, white, cultivated mushrooms. Wash the mushrooms briefly. If they are white they will need little washing. Wiping with a damp cloth is sufficient. Discard the tough portion of the stems. Sort according to size. Leave whole the small button mushrooms not larger than 1 inch across. Slice the rest.

Sauté ½ pound mushrooms at a time in 4 tablespoons hot butter for 4 to 5 minutes, or until almost cooked. Turn them into a flat dish and cool them over cracked ice. Or soak the mushrooms for 5 minutes in a solution of 1 tablespoon lemon juice and 6 cups cold water. Steam:

Whole mushrooms not larger than 1 inch across	5 minutes
Tiny buttons, or quartered mushrooms	3 minutes
Sliced mushrooms	4 minutes

Cool promptly in ice water and drain. Pack in cartons or bags, leaving ½ inch head space in the packages containing the sliced mushrooms. Seal and freeze.

MUSTARD GREENS. See GREENS

OKRA

Select tender, young, green pods. Wash thoroughly, rinse, and sort for size. Cut off the stems without cutting into the seed cells, as this would let the juices leak out during the scalding. Scald in boiling water:

Small pods	3 minutes
Large pods	4 minutes

Cool in ice water and drain. Leave whole or sliced crosswise. Pack compactly in cartons or bags, alternating top and tip ends, leaving ½ inch head space. Seal and freeze.

PARSLEY

Not suitable for garnish, as frozen parsley becomes limp when it thaws. Select fresh, deep green curly or Italian parsley. Wash and discard the stems. Package small quantities of the clusters in tiny bags made by heat-sealing freezer paper on three sides. Pack several bags in one carton. Seal and freeze. To use, chop parsley while it is still frozen for use in stews, casseroles, croquettes, sauces, and other cooked dishes.

PARSNIPS

Select young, small to medium-sized parsnips with a small center core. Discard tops, wash, and peel. Cut lengthwise into ¼-inch-thick strips or cut into ½-inch cubes or slices. Scald in boiling water for 2 minutes. Cool in ice water and drain. Pack in cartons or bags, leaving ½ inch head space. Seal and freeze.

PEAS, GREEN

Harvest early in the morning and freeze within 1 hour from the vine. Select young, bright green, plump pods with sweet, tender peas. Shell the peas, discarding any overmature, immature, or wrinkled peas. Scald in boiling water or steam:

BOILING WATER	STEAM
1½ minutes	2 minutes

Cool promptly in ice water and drain. Package in cartons or bags, leaving ½ inch head space. Seal and freeze.

PEPPERS, SWEET

Select firm, crisp, brightly colored peppers with glossy skin and thick walls, uniformly deep green. Wash peppers thoroughly, cut out stems, and remove the seeds. Leave whole or cut into ½-inch strips or rings, or halve, or slice or dice according to use. Scald peppers in boiling water or steam:

	BOILING WATER	STEAM
Whole or halves	3 minutes	4 minutes
Slices or dice	2 minutes	3 minutes

Cool in ice water and drain. Pack in cartons or bags, leaving ½ inch head space, or pack small amounts in envelopes made by heat-sealing freezer paper on three sides, then package several envelopes in pint cartons or bags. Seal and freeze.

PIMENTOS

Select crisp, thick-walled, deep red pimentos. Roast the pimentos in a hot oven (400° F.) for 3 to 4 minutes and wash off the charred skins under cold running water.

Follow instructions given for **sweet peppers.** Pack pimentos into cartons or bags, leaving ½ inch head space. Seal and freeze. Thaw pimentos for use in salads and sandwich fillings, or as a garnish.

POTATOES, FRENCH FRIED

Do not store longer than 6 weeks. Select uniform potatoes. Peel, wash, and cut them lengthwise into ¼-inch-thick slices. Cut across the slices at ¼-inch intervals to make regular julienne strips. Soak the strips in cold water for 5 minutes, drain, and dry them on a towel. Fry the potato strips in hot deep fat (370° F.) until they are pale gold. Drain on absorbent paper. Spread the fried potatoes in a flat pan and chill them over cracked ice. Package compactly in cartons, leaving ½ inch head space. Cool and freeze.

PUMPKIN

Select full-colored mature pie pumpkins. Wash, cut into quarters, and discard the seeds and stringy fibers. Place the quarters in a low-sided baking pan containing ½ inch hot water and bake in a moderate oven (350° F.) for about 40 minutes, or until tender. Remove the pulp from the rind and mash or rub it through a sieve or food mill. Cool the pumpkin purée in a pan placed over cracked ice, stirring occasionally. Pack into cartons or bags, leaving ½ inch head space. Seal and freeze.

Pumpkin pie mix Pumpkin pie mix may be prepared according to your favorite recipe and frozen within a pie shell, or in a moisture-vaporproof, liquid-tight container. If the latter, save freezer space by leaving out the milk and cream from the recipe. This can easily be added when the mix is thawed.

RUTABAGAS

Select young, medium-sized rutabagas. Cut off the tops, wash, and peel. Cut into ½-inch cubes. Scald in boiling water for 2 minutes. Cool in ice water and drain. Or cook in boiling water until tender. Drain and mash, or rub through a sieve or food mill and cool by stirring the purée in a saucepan over ice water. Pack in cartons or bags, leaving ½ inch head space. Seal and freeze.

SOYBEANS

Select bright green, plump pods. Wash the pods and drain. Scald the beans in the pods in boiling water for 5 minutes. Cool in ice water and squeeze the soybeans out of their pods. Pack in cartons or bags, leaving ½ inch head space. Seal and freeze.

SPINACH. See GREENS

SQUASH, SUMMER

Select young squash with tender skin and small seeds. Wash the squash thoroughly and cut them into ½-inch-thick slices or cubes. Cook 1 pound squash in ½ cup water, without salt or seasonings, in a tightly covered saucepan for 5 minutes, or until tender. There should be little or no water left in the saucepan when the squash is cooked. Cool by placing the saucepan over cracked ice and stir frequently. The squash may be mashed if desired. Package in cartons or bags, leaving ½ inch head space. Seal and freeze. Or dip sliced squash or zucchini into lemon juice and roll in fine dry bread crumbs. Sauté the slices in hot melted butter until very pale gold and tender. Package the slices in layers in a carton, separating each layer with two layers of freezer paper. Seal and freeze.

SQUASH, WINTER

Select mature, hard-shelled varieties with firm flesh. Cut or break the squash into pieces and discard the seeds and stringy fibers. Place the pieces in a shallow-sided baking pan containing ½ inch hot water and bake in a moderate oven (350° F.) for about 40 minutes, or until tender. Or cook 1 pound squash in ½ cup water in a tightly covered container for 20 minutes, or until tender. Scrape the pulp from the rind and mash, or rub through a sieve or food mill. Cool the purée by placing it in a saucepan over cracked ice and stir frequently. Pack in cartons or bags, leaving ½ inch headspace. Seal and freeze.

SWEET POTATOES

Do not store over 3 months. Bake large sweet potatoes in a moderate oven (350° F.) for 1 to 1½ hours, or until tender. Cool the potatoes, peel them, and cut into halves or quarters, or slice them ½ inch thick. Dip the slices in lemon juice and roll them in brown sugar. Pack the potatoes flat, with a double layer of freezer paper between them. Or mash the potatoes and mix the purée with 2 tablespoons lemon juice or ¼ cup orange juice per pint. Package in moisture-vaporproof containers, leaving 1 inch head space. Seal and freeze.

SWISS CHARD. See GREENS

TOMATO JUICE. See FRUIT JUICES

TURNIPS

Select small or medium-sized firm, tender turnips with a mild flavor. Remove tops, wash the turnips, peel them, and cut into ½-inch cubes. Scald in boiling water or steam:

BOILING WATER	STEAM
2½ minutes	3½ minutes

Cool in ice water and drain. Pack in cartons or bags, leaving ½ inch head space. Seal and freeze.

TURNIP GREENS. See GREENS

Freezing Fish and Sea Foods

The ardent fisherman need no longer be forced to give away most of his proud catch to his friends. If he owns a home freezer he can enjoy the flavor of freshly caught fish long after his outing, by storing it at zero temperature.

As soon as the fish is landed it should be killed and either iced or refrigerated until it can be prepared for the freezer. Speed is essential, for fish is an extremely perishable food. It deteriorates rapidly from the moment it leaves the water and within a few hours bacteria from air and water begin their work of contamination. Packing fish in ice or refrigerating it merely retards the bacterial action, as the particular organisms that attack fish can survive at lower temperatures than those that attack meat.

The storage period for fish is relatively brief. One to 3 months is the maximum, and the more fatty a fish, the shorter the storage period. Fatty fish such as salmon, mackerel, and herring should not be stored more than 6 weeks. Fortunately there are more varieties of lean than fatty fish, and these retain their quality and flavor for as long as 3 months.

Some sections of the country have limits on the length of time fish can be stored, so consult your local game warden before packaging fish for your freezer.

Fatty fish include, among others: Barracuda, bonito, butterfish, eels, herring, kingfish, mackerel, millet, pilchard, pompano, rockfish, rosefish, salmon, shad, squid, catfish, tuna, whitefish.

Lean fish include, among others: Bass, blowfish, blue runner, bluefish, burbot, swordfish, cod, crevalle, croaker, flounder, fluke, gar, grouper, grunt, haddock, halibut, ling, cod, muskellunge, perch, pickerel, pike, pollock, porgy, red drum, red snapper, scrod, sea trout, sheepshead, smelt, snook, sunfish, sole, spot, trout, weakfish, whiting, wolf fish.

Fish should be prepared for the freezer as soon as reasonably possible and in exactly the same way as if they were going to be cooked immediately. Small fish may be left whole and pan-dressed —scales, entrails, and fins removed. The backbone may also be cut out and, to save freezer space, the head and tail are usually discarded. Large fish are generally fileted, or are cut crosswise into steaks an inch or more thick.

PACKAGING FISH FOR THE FREEZER

Before packaging, lean fish—whole, steaks, or filets—should be dipped for 20 seconds in cold salted water, made by dissolving 1 cup salt in 1 gallon ice water. Fatty fish should not be treated with a salt solution.

Whole fish Wrap whole fish individually in moisture-vaporproof paper. If whole fish are small, several or enough for one meal may be packaged together, individually wrapped, in a top-opening carton or bag. Seal and label.

Filets and steaks Pack filets and steaks in layers in top-opening cartons with two sheets of freezer paper between layers so they will separate easily when taken from the freezer. Close the carton, label, overwrap with moisture-vaporproof paper, and heat-seal all open edges with a warm hand iron, or seal with acetate tape.

Fish soups Use the fish heads, bones, and leftover scraps of flesh to make a good chowder or fish stew or a concentrated fish stock. Pour the soup, stew, or stock into leakproof cartons or glass jars, leaving 1 inch head space, seal, and freeze.

COOKING FROZEN FISH

Frozen fish is cooked just like fresh fish. It is best when cooked directly from the frozen state, but extra cooking time must be allowed. It may, however, be partially or completely thawed, depending on which method is more convenient.

To thaw, place the unopened package on the shelf in the refrig-

329

erator to defrost. A 1-pound package of frozen fish will thaw in 8 to 10 hours in the refrigerator. The same quantity will thaw in about 3 hours at room temperature, but there is less loss of juices and flavors if the fish is thawed slowly. Once thawed, cook it promptly, while it is still cold.

It is very difficult to give absolutely accurate cooking times for fish, since so much depends on the thickness, freshness, and texture of the particular fish. But the surest way is to cook the fish until the flesh flakes easily when tested with a toothpick or the prongs of a fork. Just be careful not to dry it out by overcooking.

LOBSTERS

Select only live lobsters. Small lobsters, 2 pounds or less, are the most delicate. Larger ones are apt to be tough. Plunge them into boiling salted water or **court bouillon** and simmer them from 10 to 20 minutes, depending on their size. Cool and split. Discard the intestinal vein and the sac behind the head and put two halves together again to form a whole lobster. Wrap in Saran, pliofilm, or aluminum foil, overwrap, and freeze to serve cold, when thawed, with mayonnaise or remoulade or ravigote sauce. Or remove the meat from the tail and claws, pack the meat in cellophane-lined cartons, leaving ½ inch head space, and freeze for use in lobster Newburg, or other cooked lobster dishes.

SHRIMP

Shrimp may be frozen cooked or uncooked. The uncooked retain their quality better, while the cooked are easier to use. All you have to do with the cooked frozen shrimp for use in cocktails and salads is to let them thaw.

Wash uncooked shrimp thoroughly in cold water. Remove the shells and the intestinal veins that run down the backs. Rinse and drain. Package in cartons with two layers of freezer paper between layers of shrimp. Wrap the carton in moisture-vaporproof paper, seal, and freeze.

To freeze cooked shrimp, simmer the shrimp in boiling salted water or **court bouillon** for 10 minutes. Cool them in the cooking liquor, shell them, and devein. Pack the cooked shrimp in cartons, leaving ½ inch head space. Overwrap, seal, and freeze promptly. Do not plan to store for more than 1 month. Freeze cooked shrimp only for convenience, as they tend to toughen during long storage at zero temperature.

SOFT-SHELLED CRABS

During the warmer months from May to October, crabs shed the hard shells that begin to pinch a little as the crustaceans grow one size larger. For 2 to 3 days the hard-shelled crab is a soft-shelled crab and, if caught at this particular time in its life, it is entirely tender and edible, including the new embryo shell.

Cut off the head, about ¼ inch behind the eyes. Squeeze gently to force out the green bubble behind the eyes which contains a bitter fluid. Lift the soft shell where it comes to a point at each side and cut off the white gills with kitchen scissors. Peel back the apron and cut it off. Dip the crabs in cold salted water and package them in cartons with two layers of freezer paper between layers of crab. Overwrap the carton with moisture-vaporproof paper, seal, and freeze.

Soft-shelled crabs may be partially thawed for 15 minutes in lightly salted milk and broiled under a moderate flame for about 15 minutes on one side and 10 on the other, basting them frequently with melted butter. Serve them sprinkled with lemon juice and parsley. Or they may be sautéed in butter directly from the frozen state for about 10 minutes on one side and 6 on the other, and served with lemon-butter sauce, with shredded almonds browned in butter, with finely chopped mixed herbs such as tarragon, chives, and parsley wilted in butter, or with *sauce diable*.

HARD-SHELLED CRABS

Wash hard-shelled crabs in cold water. Drop them into boiling water containing 1 teaspoon salt for every quart of water and simmer them for 15 minutes. Drain and cool thoroughly. Remove the edible meat from the body and claws and pack it into moisture-vaporproof cartons, leaving ½ inch head space. Seal and freeze.

Defrost the crab meat and serve it very cold as salad or cocktail with mayonnaise, or a more highly seasoned sauce such as remoulade, ravigote, or Russian dressing.

OYSTERS AND CLAMS

Oysters and clams must be handled very rapidly and carefully. Wash the shells in cold running water to remove any external sand. Shuck the bivalves, saving the liquor, and discarding any dead or injured ones. Wash them in a brine made of 2 tablespoons salt dissolved in 1 quart cold water, and drain. Package the oysters or clams in liquid-tight containers and fill the containers to within ¼ inch of the top with the liquor. Seal and freeze quickly.

Oysters and clams may be thawed and served cold with a cocktail sauce, or may be used in soups and chowders or baked seafood casseroles.

Freezing Poultry, Game Birds, and Small Game

Your home freezer can provide your table with a year-round supply of all kinds of poultry: chickens, turkeys, ducks, geese, guineas, quail, and pheasant. These great favorites may be preserved in any form—fryers, broilers, roasters, and so on. Frozen poultry is one of the most successful of all frozen foods, providing the birds are of high quality and well fed.

PACKAGING POULTRY

Effective packaging of poultry is necessary to keep the flesh from drying out, to prevent freezer burn, and to keep the meat from being contaminated with other flavors. Without proper moisture-vapor-proof wrappings, dehydration is bound to take place at the low storage temperature and the birds will be tough and dry when they are cooked.

Poultry should be packaged according to the type of bird, the method by which it is going to be cooked, and the number of servings for a meal.

To estimate the number of servings, weigh the bird after it has been killed, bled, and plucked. Allow 1 pound per serving of chickens, guineas, and capons, from ¾ to 1 pound for turkeys, and 1½ pounds for geese and ducks. This additional allowance for geese and ducks is necessary because the carcasses are bigger and there is more loss in weight when these birds are dressed and cooked.

Birds for roasting are best at a certain age:

Chickens	5 to 9 months
Capons	7 to 10 months
Turkeys	5 to 9 months
Guineas	5 to 10 months
Geese	5 to 11 months
Ducks	4 to 6 months

Cut-up poultry takes less freezer space than whole birds and if freezer space is limited, it is wise to freeze only the choice pieces of meat, such as the breast and thighs. The backbones, wing tips, necks, and legs can be made into concentrated soup stock, and the stock frozen, or the cooked meat from the wings and drumsticks may be made into croquettes or creamed and the prepared dishes frozen.

Whole poultry Once the bird is dressed it should be wrapped and frozen at once. If this is not possible, wrap the bird and place it in the refrigerator until it can be put in the freezer, but in any event no more than 1 hour should elapse from wrapping to freezing.

Wrap the giblets in moisture-vaporproof paper and place them in the cavity of the bird, tuck them under the wing, or freeze them in a separate package.

Trussing before freezing makes the carcass more compact, saves storage space, and glorifies the appearance of the cooked bird. Trussed birds are all ready to put in the oven or on the spit the moment they are taken from the freezer.

Fold the neck skin down over the back. Bend the wings around and lock them in back by twisting the wing tips over the forewings. Tie the center of a long piece of string around the leg joints, push the legs down, and tie them securely to the tail. Bring the ends of the string up the back of the bird, hitch them around the wings, and tie them over the neck skin in back.

Moisture-vaporproof Saran wrap, aluminum foil, laminated papers, pliofilm, and polyethylene are all excellent protectors. Wrap the bird carefully, forcing out any air pockets which might form during the wrapping. Fasten the paper with an acetate sealing tape, slip a stockinette over the bird if the wrapping needs this extra protection, and knot the ends close to the body of the bird. Slip a label between the paper and the stockinette for future identification.

Stuffed whole poultry Frozen poultry, stuffed and ready for the oven, is a great convenience at any time of the year when entertaining is expected to be heavy, but is especially useful for Thanksgiving, Christmas, and New Year's festivities. Fill the bird cavity loosely with dry bread crumbs, mixed with a little chopped celery and onion sautéed in butter and modestly seasoned with salt and pepper and thyme, sage, or savory. Do not overseason and *do not use pork-sausage meat, oysters, or nuts in the dressing.*

Stuffed poultry should not be stored longer than 3 months in the home freezer. Freeze birds only for the sake of convenience, for special occasions, not for long storage.

Wrap stuffed birds in the same manner as **whole poultry.** No overwrap is needed if a laminated paper is used, but aluminum foil or transparent papers such as pliofilm, polyethylene, and Saran have greater flexibility and can be smoothed to conform to the shape of the bird, eliminating air pockets. All these wrapping papers should be protected by a stockinette overwrap.

Broilers Turkeys, as well as chickens and guineas, halved or quartered and ready for broiling, make valuable additions to the food supply in your freezer. It isn't necessary to wait for a special event in order to enjoy the flavor of turkey. Turkey is frequently an excellent buy in the non-holiday season. A portion of turkey to suit your family requirements may often take the place of a Sunday roast.

Wrap and freeze the giblets separately. Place two pieces of freezer paper between the two halves of chickens or other small birds so that they can be separated while still frozen. Then wrap the two halves securely in a moisture-vaporproof bag or paper. If you wish to put more than one broiler in the same package, depending on the number of servings needed at one time, the halves may be nested with a double thickness of the paper between them. If the leg ends are sharp, wrap them so that they will not puncture the outerwrapping. Turkey halves may be packaged separately for broiling or roasting. Envelop them compactly in moisture-vaporproof paper, excluding as much air as possible.

Cut poultry Tender chickens, for frying or sautéeing; well-fattened birds past their prime for roasting, but suitable for braising or stewing; ducks and geese, and larger birds such as turkeys, can all be cut into serving pieces before they are frozen as an effective method of conserving space. Wrap each piece in a fold of freezer paper and pack tightly into a moistureproof carton that can be heat-sealed. Use small-, medium-, or large-sized packages to suit your family needs. If you are freezing a large quantity of disjointed fowl, you might lay aside and package certain pieces for special recipes.

PACKAGING GAME BIRDS AND SMALL GAME

Game birds, rabbits, and squirrels are packaged in the same manner as **poultry.** Some states do not permit game to be stored for more than 10 days, so it is wise to consult your state Conservation Department or your local game warden for details.

334

COOKING FROZEN POULTRY

Poultry may be cooked from the frozen state with excellent results. It requires longer cooking and should be cooked at moderate temperatures in order to let the heat penetrate and cook the bird uniformly. However, the quality of poultry is not affected if it is thawed, providing it is cooked soon after thawing. If you wish to stuff a bird that has been frozen unstuffed, it is necessary to thaw it completely before the stuffing can go in.

To roast unthawed birds, allow 30 minutes' longer cooking time for a 4- to 5-pound chicken or duck, 1 hour longer for a 6- to 8-pound capon or turkey, 1½ hours longer for a 10-pound goose or turkey, and 2 hours longer for a very large bird.

Thaw frozen poultry in the unopened package either in the refrigerator or at room temperature. A 3-pound bird will thaw in about 6 hours in the refrigerator and in about 3 hours at room temperature. A capon will thaw in about 24 hours in the refrigerator, or 12 hours at room temperature. A turkey needs 48 hours in the refrigerator, or 24 hours at room temperature, to defrost completely.

Freezing Meats

No other method of preservation retains the fresh taste and texture of meat and game as well as freezing. Whether you buy your meat or slaughter it yourself, whether you dress it yourself or have your butcher do it for you, you can enjoy better year-round eating and greater variety in your meals.

All meats, including specialties such as sweetbreads, heart, liver, and brains, freeze well. It is economical to buy a large portion of a carcass for use throughout the year, or to buy specially priced cuts to be enjoyed months later. Often the opportunity arises for the "city dweller" with limited freezer space to buy special meat or a specific cut of meat from the butcher at a real bargain. But any meat you buy for your freezer should be grade A quality, properly aged, cut, and boned, and packaged in the size most convenient for your family.

Some meats are slightly tenderer after freezing than when fresh. This does not mean that inferior grades of meat become choice after freezing. Freezing seals in the original quality and flavor, it does not improve it. If you fill your freezer with inferior, tough meat, it will still be tough and dry and of poor quality when taken out.

Selecting meat for your freezer   Whether you purchase retail cuts, or buy an animal or portion of a carcass to be dressed for you, or do your own slaughtering and dressing, choose prime meats, moderately fat and well finished.

A good animal is thickly fleshed in the ribs, loin, and hindquarters. An ample layer of fat not only protects the lean meat from drying out during the freezing period, but adds flavor when the meat is cooked. Too much fat, however, should be avoided, as fat oxidizes quickly and rancidity is likely to occur. Veal rarely has surplus fat and is an exception to the general rule. The less tender portions of an animal should be cut and packaged for braising or stewing, or ground for hamburgers and meat loaves.

Cutting and boning meat   Consider the size of your family and have the meat cut in family-sized portions. Give thought to your preference in cooking and have the less desirable cuts, such as brisket, plate, and shank, cubed for braising or ground for meat loaves or patties. Consider the number of guests you entertain in your home and you will want to have some attractive guest-sized cuts. Have your steaks cut good and thick. Thin steaks tend to dry out in several months' zero storage and also in cooking. Package roasts, chops, and steaks in meal-sized portions, planning some extra-thick, succulent steaks, some choice roasts, a few double lamb chops, and so on, for special occasions.

Boning meat has become popular during the past few years for several reasons. Boned and rolled meat requires less space in your freezer, generally saving 25 per cent space, and in the case of lamb, it saves as much as 50 per cent. Less dehydration and oxidation can take place because of the snug, compact wrapping possible around the smooth surface of the rolled meat, which has no protruding bones to rupture the wrapping. When a roast is boned and rolled and tied, it may be cut into family-sized portions, and when cooked it may be carved more easily than a roast containing the bones. The bones may be used to make soup stock, and the stock may be frozen in convenient-sized packages. The only disadvantage to boning meat is that it takes time and therefore increases the cost.

PACKAGING MEAT FOR THE FREEZER

Once meat has been cut, it should be packaged and frozen immediately. The meat should be shaped into its most compact form before it is wrapped, to avoid air pockets. Trim off the excess fat to conserve freezer space and wrap carefully and tightly in heavy moisture-vaporproof paper, pressing the paper firmly against the meat, again forcing out the air pockets. The **drugstore wrap** is most effective. As the fold is formed, the paper can be pulled tightly against the meat. As the ends are folded, the air pockets can be pressed out. Seal the ends with acetate tape and label with the kind of cut, number of pieces, and date of freezing. Once packaged, freeze immediately, or the meat will lose moisture and juice rapidly.

If meat is wrapped in a warm room, it should be chilled in the refrigerator before it is frozen. Freeze only as much at one time as can be solidly frozen within 24 hours.

Package the number of steaks, chops, or cutlets that you will need for one meal in each package with two pieces of freezer paper between them, so that they can be separated when you are ready to use them without first thawing the entire package. Keep the meat flat as you wrap it, packing the chops or steaks tightly together in neat, regular layers. Top-opening cartons stack well and conserve freezer space.

Ground meat should never be refrozen; therefore it should be packaged in the right amount for a specific recipe. Pack the amount of ground meat you will need for a casserole firmly in a top-opening carton, pressing out any air pockets. Make meat loaves all ready to pop in the oven, wrap in moisture-vaporproof paper, and seal completely. Form ground meat into patties and pack the patties in layers, separating the layers with two sheets of freezer paper. Or each patty may be wrapped separately and packed in a top-opening carton. Either way the patties may be easily separated for cooking directly from the frozen state, or a few may be cooked and the others returned to the freezer. Overwrap the cartons and heat-seal the edges and ends.

Variety meats such as liver, tongue, heart, and kidneys should be wrapped as soon as they are chilled. Liver may be cut into slices of the desired thickness, the slices separated with two sheets of freezer paper, and packaged flat. Hearts may also be sliced. Variety meats should not be stored longer than 4 to 6 months, with the exception of liver, which should be stored from 2 to 4 months only.

The keeping qualities of hams and bacon at zero temperature depend entirely on how well the meat was processed and the type of cure, but generally they should not be kept longer than a few months. It is especially important that these meats be wrapped tightly to prevent their drying out and to prohibit the transfer of flavor to other foods. Freeze bacon in 1- or 2-pound slabs rather than slices and slice it after it is thawed.

If hams and bacon are fully cured and hung in a cool, dry room, they will keep for as long as 6 months, so there is little reason to occupy freezer space with them. However, the flavor of hams and bacon that are only mildly cured is delicate and delicious, and a mild cure may be used if these products are to be frozen.

Spices and other seasonings such as black and red pepper, sage, and other herbs used to season sausage meat actually retard rancidity, but salt speeds up oxidation in any meat. Sausage meat may be completely seasoned, or the salt may be omitted and added before or during cooking. If salt is added, plan to use the sausage in a short time. Without salt, sausage meat may be safely stored in your freezer for as long as 6 months. Package in the same way as ground meat.

COOKING FROZEN MEAT

Frozen meat may be cooked when solidly frozen, when partially thawed, or when completely thawed.

When meat is thawed there is a considerable loss of juice and therefore flavor and for this reason the ideal method of roasting frozen meat is to place it in the oven immediately after it is removed from the freezer and unwrapped. An additional 15 to 20 minutes' cooking time per pound must be allowed, as the meat must defrost as it cooks. In order to have frozen meat cooked to perfection, insert a meat thermometer in the thickest part as soon as the meat is completely thawed, and continue to cook until the thermometer registers the degree of doneness you desire. This is the only accurate way to roast meat, whether it is cooked frozen or fresh.

Cooking time is certainly shortened if the meat is completely thawed or partially thawed, resulting of course in a saving of gas or electricity, a point in favor of this method of cooking frozen meat. In order to thaw meats, you must plan well in advance of your meal. A 5-pound roast will thaw completely in 24 hours at room temperature. In the food compartment of the refrigerator, it will need 36 to 48 hours. Defrost meats in their wrappers and cook them as soon as they are thawed, because all foods spoil rapidly after complete thawing.

Cooking partially thawed meats saves both thawing and cooking time. But here again, the use of a meat thermometer is necessary if you are going to have your meat cooked exactly the way you want it—rare, medium, or well done.

Steaks as well as roasts are superior in flavor and texture if they are broiled from the frozen state. The steaks will require an additional 20 to 30 minutes' broiling time, depending on the thickness.

Freezing Eggs and Dairy Products

EGGS

Eggs freeze perfectly—in fact you cannot tell frozen eggs from fresh after as long as 6 to 8 months' storage. Naturally we take for granted that they are strictly fresh before they are frozen, for, once again, the frozen product is only as good as the original.

Eggs are usually scarce from November through March. When they are plentiful and reasonable in price, however, they are most economical to store in your freezer.

Don't freeze large quantities of eggs in one container unless you know that the amount will be entirely used when it is removed from the freezer. Package eggs in amounts needed for specific recipes and cooking uses. You are well aware of your family's favorite dishes requiring eggs, so you will want to be prepared to take from your freezer just 3 whole eggs for that special chocolate cake, 5 egg yolks for a custard or spongecake, 8 egg whites for an angel food. If you are fond of cream puffs, you will want several packages containing 4 whole eggs, and so on.

Eggs cannot be frozen in their shells, as the expansion during freezing would crack them. After being removed from the shells, they may be frozen whole or separated into yolks and whites.

Whole eggs and egg yolks must be lightly beaten and mixed with a small amount of salt or sugar. The amount needed is so small that it is not noticeable in the cooked product. Still, you may wish to designate the sweetened eggs for use in baked products and the salted ones for omelettes, mayonnaise, et cetera. But the amount of salt added would be imperceptible in any dish and most baked products and sweet dishes of all kinds are improved by the touch of salt. Should a recipe call for a pinch of salt, you may simply eliminate it from the ingredients when using frozen salted eggs.

339

Whole eggs   Wash the eggshells and break each egg into a cup before combining in a bowl, so it can be discarded if it is not strictly fresh. Beat the eggs with a fork or a rotary beater just long enough to combine thoroughly the yolks and the whites, but without beating air into them. Stir in 1 teaspoon salt or 1 tablespoon sugar or corn syrup for each 2 cups of mixed whole eggs. It will take about 5 whole eggs to make 1 cup.

Separated eggs   Wash the eggshells, break each egg carefully, and separate the yolks from the whites. Remember that even a speck of the fat egg yolk left in the whites will prevent them from being beaten into a thick, stable foam. Should a speck of yolk fall into the whites, lift it out with the sharp edge of a broken eggshell.

Beat the egg yolks lightly with a fork or rotary beater until they are thoroughly mixed, but be careful not to beat air into them. Stir in 1 teaspoon salt or 1 tablespoon sugar or corn syrup to each cup of yolks. It will take about 14 yolks to make 1 cup. Strain the egg yolks through a fine sieve and skim off any air bubbles from the surface before freezing to prevent a crust from forming.

Egg whites do not coagulate when they are frozen and they need no mixing or any addition of salt or sugar. Simply pour them into a container, label, and freeze. It will take about 8 egg whites to make 1 cup. When they are thawed, they beat to a volume equal to that of the fresh product.

Packaging eggs for the freezer   Eggs may be frozen in small cellophane bags, each bag containing the number of eggs for a specific use, and several bags may be packed into a carton. Or the eggs may be frozen in leakproof wax-lined cartons, leaving ½ inch head space for expansion. But the neatest trick of the year, and I don't know who dreamed it up or I would give credit here, is to freeze eggs in plastic ice-cube trays. One whole egg, mixed white and yolk, or 2 egg whites, or 2 or 3 mixed egg yolks, can be frozen in each cube. Once frozen, they can be taken from the tray and packaged in a long, thin bag of heat-sealing moisture-vaporproof material. Use a lukewarm curling iron and seal directly across the bag, separating each frozen egg cube. Packaged this way, a cube or two, depending on how much you need, may be snipped off with a pair of scissors and the bag returned to the freezer.

Label each package of eggs with the amount, whether mixed with salt or sugar, the date, and proposed use: "Egg Whites, 1 cup for angel food"; "4 egg yolks with sugar for custard," et cetera.

Using frozen eggs Let the eggs thaw in the unopened package in the refrigerator or at room temperature. Small amounts of eggs packaged for specific cooking purposes will thaw in 30 minutes at room temperature. In an emergency, eggs packed in watertight packages may be defrosted quickly in a bowl of lukewarm water.

Use defrosted whole mixed eggs and yolks promptly. Egg whites will remain fresh in the refrigerator for several days. Use whole eggs in omelettes, scrambled eggs, custards, ice cream, cakes, breads, pancakes, fritters, waffles, croquettes, and cream puffs. Use egg yolks in spongecakes, custards, sauces, and mayonnaise. Use egg whites in meringues, icings, angel food and other white cakes, candies, cookies, sherbets, and desserts.

AMOUNTS EQUIVALENT TO 1 FRESH EGG

2½ tablespoons mixed whites and yolks
1½ tablespoons whites
1 tablespoon yolks

BUTTER

Butter will keep fresh and sweet for many months in your freezer providing it is made from freshly pasteurized sweet cream. Butter made from unpasteurized sweet cream does not retain its quality as long and that made from unpasteurized sour cream may become rancid in a few weeks. Sweet butter will keep for a year. Salted butter should not be stored for longer than 6 months, since the salt speeds up the development of rancidity in any fat.

Cream may be pasteurized by heating it to 145° F. and holding it there for 30 minutes. Cool the cream quickly to 50° F. and let it stand for 3 hours before churning. After churning, work it well to remove the buttermilk.

Pack butter in heavily waxed cartons or wrap it in moisture-vaporproof paper. Commercial butter should be left in its original carton and overwrapped with moisture-vaporproof paper.

CHEESE

Cheeses of all kinds, with the one exception of cream cheese, freeze well, and may be kept from 4 to 6 months in the freezer. The quality of soft cheeses that are purchased at the exact degree of ripeness to suit your palate will retain this perfect stage and the flavor and texture are not affected. Blue cheese or Roquefort that have been frozen are apt to be more crumbly than fresh.

Cut cheese into family-sized portions and wrap in moisture-vaporproof paper so that the cheese will not dry out or transfer its flavor to other foods.

Cottage cheese Cottage cheese, uncreamed and of good quality, will keep well in the freezer for 3 to 4 months. Package it firmly in moisture-vaporproof cartons, pressing out as much air as possible and leaving ½ inch head space for expansion. Thaw in the refrigerator and add cream, if desired, at the time of serving.

CREAM

Cream separates during freezing and is not suitable for table use, nor does frozen cream whip as well as fresh. There seems little reason for the city dweller to freeze cream, as heavy cream is readily available and, if left in its sterile container, will keep fresh in the average refrigerator for at least a week. Those who live on farms may have good reason to freeze their surplus.

Cream to be frozen should contain from 40 to 60 per cent butterfat and the more butterfat it contains the better it will freeze. After separating, cream should be pasteurized within an hour at 145° F. for 30 minutes. It should be cooled quickly to 50° F. or lower, packed in liquid-tight, moisture-vaporproof containers—allowing 1 inch head space for expansion during freezing—and frozen promptly. Cream should not be stored longer than 4 months and is best used in pastry creams and custards. Frozen cream should be defrosted slowly in the refrigerator, in its original container.

ICE CREAM

Both homemade and commercially made ice cream and sherbet can be stored in the home freezer for several months to make quick and nourishing desserts. High-quality ice creams made from pasteurized cream and milk retain their flavor for 2 months. Those made from high-fat-content cream remain smooth in texture longer than those made from light cream or milk.

Commercially made ice cream and sherbet can be stored in the original container and overwrapped with moisture-vaporproof paper, or may be purchased in bulk and repacked in smaller moisture-vaporproof containers.

Homemade ice cream is a better way to use up surplus cream, than freezing the cream itself. Use a recipe calling for a large percentage of heavy cream and a stabilizer such as egg yolks or gelatin. Make it in a hand or electrically turned ice cream freezer so that it will not become grainy during storage.

Freezing Bakery Products, Sandwiches, and Canapés

Since the discovery that frozen bread is as fresh as freshly baked bread, that frozen pie dough is flakier than unfrozen, and that cakes and cookies remain fresh and retain their homemade quality for months, the freezing of a wide variety of home-baked products has rapidly become one of the most popular and efficient ways to use the home freezer.

It is practical to make a sizeable batch of bread dough for loaves and rolls, instead of a small quantity. It's economical to make 2 or 3 cakes, or 3 or 4 pies, while the oven is hot. Double or triple the quantity of any pastry or cake recipe can be made as quickly as the single recipe, and no more utensils need be washed!

Time is saved, your baking chores for a week or more are finished in a single afternoon, and your family will enjoy the flavor and the goodness of home-baked products.

BREAD AND ROLLS

Baked yeast breads   Yeast bread and rolls, baked before freezing, will remain fresh in your freezer for 6 months. Cool breads to room temperature after baking them, then wrap and seal in moisture-vaporproof material and freeze. Frozen loaves may be sliced while they are still frozen, or the amount needed for a meal can be cut from the loaf and the rest returned to the freezer.

Cool baked rolls to room temperature and package them in amounts sufficient for one meal.

A good-sized batch of sweet yeast dough can be made into a wide selection of breakfast breads, tea rolls, buns, and sweet yeast cakes. They can be easily and quickly thawed by heating them in the oven, and served hot. Before they are packaged for the freezer they must all be cooled to room temperature.

Baked breads thaw quickly at room temperature, because of their low moisture content. But the best way to serve them is hot. Heat them in a moderate oven (350° F.) for 10 to 20 minutes, depending on the size. Sliced frozen bread may be toasted without thawing.

343

Partially baked yeast breads Yeast bread and rolls that are baked just long enough to destroy the action of the yeast and set the dough may be stored in your freezer for 3 months. Cool the partially baked breads, wrap them or package them in the same manner as the fully baked product, and freeze. Bake them, unthawed, in a moderate oven (350° F.) for about 30 minutes, or until they are golden brown. They will taste exactly like freshly baked bread.

Unbaked yeast breads Unbaked bread and rolls are less satisfactory for freezing than the partially or fully baked products and should not be stored longer than 3 weeks. Make your favorite recipe, let the dough rise until it is double in bulk, and punch it down. Shape the dough into loaves, rolls, or coffee rings. Brush the surface with olive oil or melted sweet butter to prevent the dough from drying out, and freeze. Remove them from the freezer as soon as they are frozen and package. Wrap loaves and coffee rings in moisture-vapor-proof paper and seal. Package frozen rolls close together in shallow cartons with freezer paper between them.

The activity of the yeast is slowly destroyed in frozen unbaked yeast breads, so plan to use them in a short time. Even less storage time than a 3-week period results in fluffier, lighter breads.

To use, unwrap the frozen breads and let them rise, covered lightly, in a warm place away from drafts for 2 to 3 hours, or until light. Bake in the usual way.

Baking powder breads Nut breads, fruit loaves, steamed brown bread, gingerbread, corn breads, baking powder biscuits, muffins, and other quick breads may be frozen before or after baking, but as in the case of yeast bread, they will hold for much longer periods if they are baked first. The unbaked products should not be stored for longer than 3 weeks. The baked will retain their freshness and flavor for as long as 6 months.

Nut and fruit breads and steamed brown bread should be thawed in their original wrappings at room temperature for 1 hour. Then, if you wish to serve them hot, place in a 350° F. oven for 15 to 20 minutes. Muffins, corn bread, and baking powder biscuits do not need to be thawed, but may be heated in a moderate oven directly from the freezer. Frozen waffles may be thawed and heated in a toaster.

SANDWICHES

Often it is advantageous to make sandwiches ahead of time for sandwich lunches, lunch boxes, teas, and evening snacks, and this can be accomplished with a home freezer.

Not all sandwich fillings freeze successfully. Lettuce, celery, cucumbers, fresh tomato slices, and other foods that should be served crisp should not be used, for they lose their crispness on freezing. Jam and jelly filling are not good either, for the jelly soaks in the bread. Hard-cooked eggs are a poor choice, for the whites become tough and leathery.

Good sandwich fillings for frozen sandwiches are cheese and cheese spreads; sliced, cooked meats; poultry; sea food; and ham or liver spreads.

Cut bread very thinly and remove the crusts if you wish. Butter the bread to prevent fillings such as tuna fish or crab meat salad, deviled ham, or peanut butter from soaking into the bread. Wrap each sandwich separately and freeze. The sandwiches may be husky ones destined for the lunch box or dainty teatime ones in a variety of shapes—rolled, open face, ribbon, or checkerboard. Sandwiches packed in the lunch box directly from the freezer will be completely thawed and ready to be enjoyed by noon.

Sandwiches may be stored in the freezer for 1 month.

CANAPES

Not all canapés freeze well, but those that do are delicious and great last-minute timesavers. They can be made at your leisure weeks in advance of a party. Toasted canapés are particularly good in both texture and flavor. They remain much crisper than untoasted bread canapés and stay crisp for a couple of hours after they are thawed.

Butter thin slices of bread and cut them into strips, rounds, or triangles. Place the cutouts on a buttered baking sheet and toast them in a moderate oven (350° F.) until they are golden. Place the filling on the toast and freeze the canapés on the baking sheet. As soon as they are frozen, pack an assortment in a carton, 1 or 2 dozen per carton, separating the layers with two sheets of freezer paper. Seal the cartons, label, and store in your freezer.

When you wish to serve canapés, remove them from the freezer 30 minutes before they will be needed. Place them on a serving tray, garnish them attractively, and let them thaw at room temperature.

Bread canapés such as tiny cheese rolls may be toasted in a moderate oven (350° F.) directly from the freezer and served hot.

Canapés may be stored in your freezer for 1 month.

CAKES

Cakes, baked and frosted or not as preferred, are frozen most satisfactorily. Angel food and butter cakes of all kinds freeze beautifully, although the texture of butter cakes may become finer and firmer during frozen storage. Fruitcakes actually improve with freezing. The flavors of the fruits and spices become blended; the cakes remain moist and do not crumble when sliced after they are thawed. Filled cakes are not recommended for freezing, as the filling is apt to soak into the cake and cause sogginess. Baked cakes may be cut into family-sized portions before freezing.

Frosted cakes Uncooked butter frostings made with confectioners' sugar are the best to use on cakes that are to be frozen. Boiled frostings crumble when cut after 2 to 3 weeks' storage and egg-white icings become frothy. Cool the cake thoroughly before icing or decorating. Place it on a sturdy cardboard base and put it in the freezer until the icing is solid. Remove and overwrap cardboard base and cake in moisture-vaporproof paper and return to the freezer.

Iced cakes must be unwrapped immediately after they are removed from the freezer to prevent the frosting from sticking to the wrappings. Let the cake thaw at room temperature for 30 to 40 minutes. Iced cakes should not be stored longer than 4 months.

Unfrosted cakes Cool the cakes before wrapping them in moisture-vaporproof paper. Since cakes do not freeze solidly, some outer protection is needed to prevent them from being crushed during storage. Metal containers are best, but heavy cardboard cartons may be used. Wrap layers of cake separately and then wrap two or three together, depending on their ultimate use.

Fruitcakes do not need support. Wrap them in cellophane, pliofilm, or Saran and overwrap with freezer paper or aluminum foil.

Cakes will thaw at room temperature in 30 to 40 minutes. Keep uniced cakes in their original wrappings to prevent moisture from condensing on the surface. Frozen cakes may be unwrapped and filled and frosted directly from the freezer.

Unfrosted angel food, spongecakes, and butter cakes keep well for 6 to 8 months. Fruitcakes will keep a full year or longer.

Cake batters   While cake batters may be frozen, it is much better to freeze the baked cake. In an emergency, however, pour the batter into the utensil in which it is to be baked. Freeze the batter in the pan, then package pan and batter in moisture-vaporproof paper. Cupcakes may be frozen in paper baking cups in pans, removed from the pan when frozen, and packaged. Thaw batter for a large cake for about 1 hour at room temperature, then bake as usual. Batter frozen in 8-inch layer-cake pans may be baked without thawing at 375° F. for 35 to 40 minutes. Cupcakes need no thawing. Bake them directly from the freezer at 375° F. for 15 minutes. Reduce the oven temperature to 350° F. and continue to bake for 15 minutes longer. Do not store cake batters longer than 2 months.

COOKIES

Baked cookies or the cooky dough may be frozen, but there is little logic in occupying freezer space with the baked ones. Most baked cookies stay fresh in cooky jars for many days, longer at least than they can be preserved from a hungry household. I've never known cookies to go stale in my house. It's simply a question of finding enough time to keep a supply on hand. Freezing cooky dough is the answer. Making the dough takes very little time and most recipes can be doubled, tripled, or quadrupled without ill effects. It is cutting and baking the cookies that is the time-consuming part. So make a large batch of dough, bake a jarful, and freeze the rest of the dough to cut or roll out and bake as needed.

Baked cookies   Baked cookies will keep in your freezer for 8 months. Pack them in cartons, separating the layers with two sheets of freezer paper, overwrap, seal, label, and freeze. To use, simply thaw the cookies at room temperature.

Rolled cooky dough   Roll out the dough and cut it into various shapes. Stock the cutout dough in cartons with two pieces of freezer paper between layers, overwrap, label, and freeze. They may be baked without thawing and will keep in your freezer for 6 months.

Unrolled cooky dough   Form the dough into long rolls or bricks, wrap, and freeze. Slice the dough while it is still frozen, place the slices on buttered baking sheets, and bake immediately. They will keep well for 6 months.

Drop cooky dough   Drop the dough on a baking sheet by the teaspoon ¼ inch apart in exactly the same manner as if you were going to bake the cookies. Place them in the freezer until they are frozen. Remove the frozen drops of dough from the freezer and pack them by layers in cartons, with two sheets of freezer paper between layers. To bake, remove them from the carton without thawing, place them on a buttered baking sheet, and bake like the freshly made dough.

PIES

In general, pies that are frozen unbaked have flakier, tenderer crusts and fresher flavor than those baked before freezing, and the very best are double-crust pies such as fruit, berry, or mince. But baked pie shells filled with chiffon mixtures and creams are also delicious. Meringue toppings toughen and separate during frozen storage, so save the topping to put on and brown in the oven before serving. Baked custard pies are not satisfactory frozen, as the custard separates during storage.

Unbaked pies Make pies in the usual way in metal, glass, or special metal-rimmed paper baking plates. They may be packaged and frozen in the pie plate or they may be frozen first, removed from the pie plate, and then wrapped. Package them in moisture-vaporproof wrappings and protect them from damage by inserting them in a carton. Unbaked frozen pies need no thawing. Bake them in a preheated oven (425° F.) for 15 to 20 minutes, reduce the heat to 375° F., and bake them for 30 minutes longer, or until the crust is golden. Don't store unbaked pies longer than 2 months.

Baked pies Bake the pies and let them cool. Package them in the pie plate in moisture-vaporproof wrapping and freeze. Let them thaw for 30 to 45 minutes at room temperature, or thaw them in a slow oven (250° to 300° F.) for 30 minutes and serve them warm. Baked pies will keep for 6 months.

Filled pie shells Baked pie shells filled with chiffon or cream mixtures should be frozen before they are wrapped. They must also be protected from damage by inserting the wrapped pie in a sturdy box or carton. Let them thaw at room temperature for 30 to 45 minutes. They may be garnished with whipped cream before they are frozen, or they may be topped with meringue after they are thawed and baked in the oven until the meringue is browned. They will keep well in your freezer for as long as 6 months.

Freezing Ready-cooked Foods and Leftovers

Once a busy housewife discovers that the real joy of a home freezer is in being able to store ready-cooked foods and entire meals and then merely heat and serve them, a home freezer becomes no longer a luxury or convenience but an essential adjunct to modern living.

Much of the food for special occasions, holiday meals, and dinner and luncheon parties may be prepared, cooked, and frozen weeks in advance, so that last-minute confusion and clutter in the kitchen are eliminated and you can present your relaxed, unruffled self to your guests—really glad to see them! For the first time in your life, *you* can actually enjoy your own parties.

Don't be afraid to experiment. Practically every cooked food in the average housewife's repertoire can be frozen and you will certainly want to freeze your family's favorite dishes made from your pet recipes. You will discover that some freeze better than others. Maybe you will decide that the dish would be better had you left out a certain vegetable or spice, adding this particular ingredient to complete the recipe while the dish is being thawed and heated. Maybe it will be perfect as it is, providing you do not store it too long.

Some dishes keep their flavor and quality for many months; others for a few weeks only. So don't try to see how *long* you can store them. Leave the experiments in storage-life tests to recognized authorities in the freezing field. Store your ready-cooked foods for convenience and not for the dim future. As a general rule, don't plan to store them longer than 1 month for highest quality of flavor, texture, and eye appeal.

Right here it might be wise to remind you of the very few foods that have not yet been frozen and thawed satisfactorily. If you will stay away from these danger foods and remember the basic principles of packaging, you have little to worry about.

1. Cooked starch products such as potatoes, rice, and macaroni become soggy if frozen in a stew, soup, or sauce, though potato croquettes, Spanish rice, and macaroni and cheese all freeze well. It is only when the cooked starch product is immersed in a large quantity of liquid that it is unsatisfactory.

2. Salad vegetables that you wish to eat crisp cannot be frozen, as they lose their crispness.

3. Custards and some cream puddings or cake fillings are apt to curdle.

4. Gelatin salads and gelatin desserts do not hold up in frozen storage.

5. Mayonnaise will curdle.

6. Hard-cooked egg whites become tough and leathery.

SOUPS AND SOUP STOCKS

Once a month, or once every two months, enough rich, fragrant stock can be made to satisfy the soup and sauce needs of your family. Make chicken or beef stock according to your favorite recipe. Strain the broth through a fine sieve lined with cheesecloth. Cool, remove the fat, and package the broth in moisture-vaporproof, liquid-tight containers, leaving 1 inch head space. Seal, label, and freeze.

To thaw broths Remove the broth from the package and heat it in a covered saucepan over a low flame for 45 minutes.

In warm weather the broth may be thawed overnight in the refrigerator and served as a refreshing jellied consommé, topped with finely chopped parsley mixed with minced onion and lemon juice.

Concentrated broths Concentrated broths save freezer space. Make your stock, season lightly with salt and pepper, and strain. Return the strained broth to the stove and simmer it gently until it is reduced to half, one third, or one quarter its original quantity. Package it in moisture-vaporproof, liquid-tight containers and be sure you label each container with the type of stock and the amount of concentration. You will need to know that you must add 1 cup water for every cup of 50 per cent concentrated stock, 2 cups water for every cup of 33⅓ per cent concentrate, and 3 cups water for every 75 per cent concentrate to make a consommé.

Concentrated stock may be frozen in ice cube trays and packaged in little blocks in the manner recommended for **eggs.** Many times you will want just that much concentrated stock to enrich a sauce or gravy, or to add to a chicken sauté.

Hearty soups Many hearty soups make nourishing meals in themselves, accompanied by hot French bread, baking powder biscuits, or corn bread. Make your favorite vegetable soup, your best minestrone, but leave out the macaroni, rice, or potatoes. These ingredients should be cooked later and added to the soup when it is reheated.

Keep on hand several containers of fish and sea-food chowders. Chowders that use milk or cream do not freeze too well. Leave out the milk or cream and add it when the soup is thawed. Remember to add this valuable bit of information to the label, or you may forget that an ingredient must be added to complete the chowder. Navy bean, black bean, and lentil soups also freeze beautifully.

Package soups in pint or quart containers, leaving ½ inch head space in pints and 1 inch in quarts. Glass containers are good, but any container for soup must be not only moisture-vaporproof but liquid-tight as well. Seal, label intelligently, and freeze.

Thaw heavy soups in a covered saucepan over a gentle flame for 1 hour.

READY-COOKED VEGETABLES

Not many ready-cooked vegetables freeze well, but fortunately the ones that do are those long-cooking vegetables such as yams, pumpkins, squash, whole beets, and beans, which take time and fuel to prepare for a meal. Vegetable purées also freeze well, and for these you should refer to the **vegetable** section in this chapter.

The average vegetable, whether fresh or frozen, takes only a matter of minutes to ready for the table and presents little problem to the busy housewife. So when you do have time, prepare a large quantity of the longer-cooking, time-consuming vegetables that you want to store in your freezer to add variety and color to your daily meals. Most of these take 30 minutes to thaw and reheat in a moderate oven, so, to save fuel, plan to serve them when the oven is already busy cooking a roast or heating a casserole.

Baked beans Baked beans will keep well in your freezer for as long as 1 year. Bake the beans New England style, or according to your favorite recipe. Cool the beans and package them in pint or quart cartons or bags. The containers must be moisture-vaporproof. Seal and freeze.

To cook, remove the beans from the container and put them in a baking dish. Cover the dish and bake the beans in a moderate oven (325° F.) for 1½ hours.

Peppers In the fall, when peppers are at their peak, in the stores or on the vine, they may be stuffed with rice, cottage cheese, shrimp, combinations of rice and sea food, or almost any leftover and stored

351

in your freezer for as long as 4 months to make economical and appetizing luncheon dishes.

Potatoes Cooked potatoes, both white and sweet, can be successfully stored in your freezer. Keep on hand a few packages of **French fried potatoes** and **sweet potatoes** for quick meals.

Freshly mashed potatoes, whipped until light with milk or cream and butter, may be frozen in pint or quart containers ready to thaw and heat over boiling water, or they may be formed into potato croquettes or patties and packaged in layers with two sheets of freezer paper between layers for easy separation before they are thawed. They need no thawing before heating, but may be browned slowly on both sides in butter in a skillet or in the oven, directly from the frozen state. Sweet potatoes may be treated in the same way.

Baked white or sweet potatoes may also be frozen. Bake yams or sweet potatoes, halve them, and cool. Re-form each potato with two layers of freezer paper between the halves and wrap each re-formed potato individually. White potatoes may be baked and stuffed. Cut the baked potatoes in half and scoop out the pulp. Mash the pulp with cream, butter, and seasonings and refill the halves, piling the potato purée high in the center. Freeze and when frozen wrap each filled potato half in moisture-vaporproof freezer paper and store in freezer. Thaw baked white or sweet potatoes in a moderate oven (325° F.) for 30 minutes.

Potato chips or French fried potatoes should not be stored for longer than 6 weeks. Other cooked potatoes may be kept from 4 to 6 months.

Squash and pumpkin All varieties of winter squash and pumpkin can be cooked, puréed, and frozen for use as a vegetable, in pies, or in puddings (**see "How to Freeze Vegetables"** section in this chapter). Baked acorn squash is a nice "variety" vegetable to store in your freezer and will keep well for 4 to 6 months. Bake the halved squash according to your favorite recipe, until barely tender. Cool, package each half individually in moisture-vaporproof paper, and freeze. Thaw in a moderate oven (325° F.) in a baking dish containing 1 inch of hot water for 30 minutes.

COOKED FISH AND SEA FOOD

Creamed fish, lobster and shrimp Newburg, lobster Thermidor, cooked lobster tails, and shrimp may all be prepared and stored in your freezer for 2 to 4 weeks. But since most fish dishes can be

352

quickly prepared from either the fresh or frozen raw fish, little seems to be gained by freezing the prepared dish.

There may be a time when a cooked fish dish such as *coquille Saint-Jacques* or a deviled crab seems to be just right to complete an otherwise perfect menu and if you wish to prepare it in advance your home freezer is at your service.

Fish or sea food baked in individual shells or ramekins and stored in your freezer can add variety to many a menu. They may be served as a first course to a dinner or as a luncheon dish. Freeze the sea food, then wrap each shell or ramekin individually in moisture-vaporproof paper and return to your freezer. To serve, unwrap the shells and bake them in a moderate oven (350° F.) for 30 minutes.

READY-COOKED POULTRY

Turkeys, geese, chickens, ducks, and poultry of all kinds may be cooked completely, plain or stuffed, and stored in your freezer ready for warming up in a moderate oven. Your Christmas or New Year's turkey may be stuffed with your favorite dressing and roasted to golden perfection as long as a month before the holiday.

Stuffed roast poultry Stuff, truss, and roast the bird. As soon as it is cooked, discard the trussings, carefully remove all the stuffing, and put it in a casserole or baking dish. This *must* be done in order to prevent the possible spoilage of the dressing deep in the center of the bird, where it would take hours to cool were it not removed. Cool the bird and the stuffing partially, then put them in the refrigerator for 2 to 3 hours to chill thoroughly.

Pour off half the drippings from the roasting pan into a small, moisture-proof, liquid-tight container to freeze as soon as it is cool, for later use in basting the bird when it is reheated. Use the rest of the drippings in the pan to make a pan gravy. Cool the gravy, package, label, and freeze.

Wrap the bird tightly and carefully in moisture-vaporproof paper and freeze. Wrap the dressing, baking dish and all, in similar paper, label, and freeze.

To reheat the bird and stuffing, allow 5 hours per pound thawing time, in the refrigerator, to thaw the bird completely. In the case of a turkey, it may be necessary to remove it from the freezer a good 2 days before you want to serve it. Return the thawed cooked bird to the roasting pan, add the drippings, and brush the bird generously with softened butter. Cook it in a moderate oven (325° F.) for 1 hour, basting frequently with the drippings.

The stuffing needs no preliminary thawing. Remove it from the freezer, cover the baking dish, and put it in the oven with the bird to thaw and heat.

Chicken or **turkey pies,** family size or individual, cooked and then frozen, are convenient to have on hand for emergency meals. They may be stored for as long as 6 months and in just about 1 hour can be served hot and succulent directly from your freezer. The topping of the pie may be made of pie dough, baking powder biscuit dough, or fluffy mashed potatoes. The pies may be frozen in a glass baking dish or in crockery casseroles and reheated in the same casseroles without any preliminary thawing.

Cool the pies and chill thoroughly. Wrap in moisture-vaporproof paper, label, and freeze. To serve, remove a pie from the freezer and place it directly in a moderate oven (325° F.) for 1 hour.

Creamed chicken or **turkey** is another appetizing dish that can be ready to serve in an hour or less and that retains its quality in frozen storage for 6 to 8 months.

Cool the creamed chicken or turkey and chill it thoroughly in the refrigerator. Package it in moisture-vaporproof, liquid-tight containers, seal, label, and freeze. To serve, turn the creamed chicken or turkey from the container into a saucepan and cook it, covered, for 1 hour over simmering water, stirring occasionally. Serve in patty shells; on toast, hot biscuits, squares of corn bread, or English muffins; in a noodle ring; rolled in thin pancakes, or with hot rice.

READY-COOKED MEATS

Almost any kind of cooked meats may be frozen satisfactorily. The only ones to avoid are fried steaks and chops which, while edible after a month in frozen storage, will have lost some of their original flavor and crispness.

The storage time for various kinds of cooked meats varies from 2 weeks to 6 months. Chile con carne, for example, will retain its original flavor and texture for as long as 6 months. Hashes, made from corned beef or other cooked meats, and baked ham may be stored for 4 months, while sliced cooked meats, packaged plain or covered with gravy, meat loaves, and meat balls, sauced or plain, should be used within 2 weeks, or 4 at the very longest.

Many meat dishes, such as broiled chops, sautéed lamb kidneys,

354

veal scaloppine, shish kebab, and so on take only moments to prepare and little would be gained by cooking and freezing them. It would actually take longer to thaw and reheat them than to cook them when needed. It is wiser by far to concentrate on those meat dishes that require long cooking.

Fortunately braised meats, pot roasts, and stews that require many hours of slow cooking over gentle heat will keep in frozen storage for 6 months. The time it takes to ready them for the table is so much less than the actual cooking time that you will save many hours of keeping a wary eye on the kettle, as well as a substantial amount of electricity or gas. Many of these dishes make attractive casseroles for entertaining and buffet suppers, so it is most practical and timesaving to make a large quantity of any of these long-cooked braised meats and freeze for future use the portion not eaten for dinner that night.

Remember to omit potatoes, rice, noodles, spaghetti, or macaroni from meat stews to be frozen. Any of these ingredients can be cooked and added to the dish while the frozen product is being heated. No time is lost and the starchy foods will be fresh and not sodden with juice.

In addition to meat dishes that require long cooking, you will undoubtedly want to prepare in advance many of your favorites to have on hand for quick emergency meals. Veal birds, Swedish meat balls, and curry of lamb freeze well.

All meat dishes must be cooled and thoroughly chilled before they are packaged and frozen. Stew may be frozen right in the casserole in which it was made. Once solidly frozen, it may be removed from the casserole to save freezer space, wrapped, and stored. Or stew, chili con carne, chop suey, and so on may be packed in either pint or quart containers that are moisture-vaporproof and liquid-tight. Use the size best suited to your family's needs. Baked ham and meat loaves should be carefully wrapped in Saran, pliofilm, or cellophane and overwrapped with stockinette, but if a laminated freezer paper is used, no overwrap is necessary.

To serve stew, remove as many packages as needed and turn the stew into a casserole or baking dish. Heat in a moderate oven (325° F.) for 1 hour, or turn into a saucepan, cover, and heat over a low flame for 1 hour. Baked ham requires 15 minutes per pound in a 350° F. oven to thaw and reheat. Meat loaves may be thawed, sliced, and served cold, or they may be put directly into a 350° F. oven and reheated for 1 hour.

OTHER COOKED FOODS

Gravies, barbecue sauces, and spaghetti sauces may all be prepared according to your favorite recipe, cooled, and frozen for 1 to 2 months. Spaghetti, rice, and macaroni may be cooked, rinsed in cold water, drained well, and stored for 6 months in your freezer. If these starch foods are combined with vegetables or sauce, they should not be stored for longer than 2 to 4 weeks.

LEFTOVERS

With a home freezer, the stigma can be forever erased from the word "leftover." Much as you may relish a turkey, ham, or a roast of beef, no one wants to eat the leftovers from a roast several more times that same week. Your freezer is the perfect solution to mealtime monotony, for leftovers of all kinds may be frugally frozen and served as long as 2 weeks later, when they seem to be entirely new and not pallid reminders of yesterday's dinner.

Slice leftover roasts and wrap the slices compactly in moisture-vaporproof paper, or, if you have time, make the meat or poultry into ready-to-serve dishes, creamed dishes, casseroles, croquettes, et cetera. The details for wrapping and freezing and the maximum storage times for these prepared dishes have already been given.

Plastic refrigerator dishes are ideal for storing leftover soups, stews, and gravies. They can be washed and used over and over again. With tight-fitting lids, they may be simply filled and the lid fitted down securely in place. Without lids, smooth aluminum foil down firmly over the top of the dish. Or wrap the entire dish in Saran wrap. Even the Saran wrap may be used again.

FROZEN FOOD MEALS

Entire meals—for emergencies, for everyday use, for special holiday dinners, or for parties—may be prepared in advance and stored in your home freezer. Whether you prepare and freeze every dish for the menu or whether you buy commercially frozen products to store in your freezer, you may like the idea of packaging all the items for one meal together in a large bag and labeling the contents. Perhaps you will want to include on the label the menu and simple heating directions, or you might like simply to number the bag and keep on hand a little log book that lists not only the menu by number and the steps for preparing it, but any foods that you should have on hand to complete the meal, such as butter, cream, milk, salad greens, condiments, and coffee.

Index